"NO-NONSENSE ADVICE ABOUT LAW BOARDS, GRADES, INTERVIEWS, APPLICATIONS, RECOMMEN-DATIONS, AND FINANCIAL AID."
—*National Law Journal*

Catalogs are great for reading course descriptions and learning about application deadlines. But you need much more information than that before you can make an informed decision about law schools. This invaluable guide describes career placement services, educational environment, campus life, and social atmosphere, along with the latest tuition/financial aid/enrollment/requirements data. Over one hundred law schools coast to coast are reviewed by the students and recent graduates who have lived and worked there. So get the firsthand, "we were there" story straight from the only guide that tells you what living and learning will be like at the law school of your choice.

INSIDE THE
LAW SCHOOLS

S. F. GOLDFARB, a graduate of Yale Law School, is a lawyer in New York City.

INSIDE THE LAW SCHOOLS

A GUIDE FOR STUDENTS BY STUDENTS

Sixth Edition, Revised and Updated

S. F. GOLDFARB

A PLUME BOOK

PLUME
Published by the Penguin Group
Penguin Books USA Inc., 375 Hudson Street,
New York, New York 10014, U.S.A.
Penguin Books Ltd, 27 Wrights Lane,
London W8 5TZ, England
Penguin Books Australia Ltd, Ringwood,
Victoria, Australia
Penguin Books Canada Ltd, 10 Alcorn Avenue,
Toronto, Ontario, Canada M4V 3B2
Penguin Books (N.Z.) Ltd, 182-190 Wairau Road,
Auckland 10, New Zealand

Penguin Books Ltd, Registered Offices:
Harmondsworth, Middlesex, England

Published by Plume, an imprint of Dutton Signet,
a division of Penguin Books USA Inc. Previously published in a Dutton paperback
edition.

First Plume Printing, July, 1991
10 9 8 7 6 5 4 3 2 1

 REGISTERED TRADEMARK—MARCA REGISTRADA

Library of Congress Cataloging-in-Publication Data

Goldfarb, Sally F.
  Inside the law schools : a guide by students for students / S.F.
Goldfarb.—6th ed., rev. and updated.
    p.   cm.
  ISBN 0-452-27014-6
  1. Law schools—United States—Directories. I. Title.
KF266.G64   1993
430'.071'173—dc20   93-4041
                                                          CIP

Printed in the United States of America
Set in Baskerville
Designed by Leonard Telesca

To Joe
and
Michael

Contents

Why
You
Need
This
Book

If you're thinking about going to law school, you need all the help you can get. Consider these facts:

• Getting into law school has never been harder. Every year, there are a total of 44,000 places in the entering classes of all the ABA-accredited law schools in the country. Every year, more than 90,000 people apply for those 44,000 places.
• Attending law school has never been more expensive. Tuition alone can easily cost you $50,000, not to mention three years of living expenses.
• Finding a job after law school is tougher than ever. At some schools, as many as 20 or 30 percent of recent graduates remain unemployed months after getting their diplomas.

Clearly, before making such a huge investment of time and money, you need to gather as much information as possible. The questions you are asking should run the full gamut. Do you really want to go to law school? If so, how will you choose where to apply? What characteristics are important in selecting a law school? How can you maximize your admission chances? Will you be able to afford to go? These fundamental questions are the subject of the introductory chapters of this book.

Once you've explored those issues, it's time for the toughest question of all: which school? This book contains descriptions of more than a hundred law schools all over the country. What's special about these descriptions is that in addition to statistical data on everything from median LSAT scores to job placement, they contain a frank assessment of each school based on the insights and observations of currently enrolled students and recent graduates. After attending a school for a few years, there is very little—good or bad—that a student doesn't know about it. Unfortunately, few law school applicants are lucky enough to know someone enrolled at every law school that interests them. That's where this book comes in. In these pages, you'll find an "inside view" of American law schools, full of firsthand information from people who have lived and studied there.

This book is certainly not the only place to look for information about law schools. There are other, more "official" law school guides; there are school catalogs; there is word of mouth; there are prelaw advisers. The problem is that all of these other sources, though useful, will leave major gaps in your knowledge—gaps that this book is designed to fill.

There are plenty of law school guides on the market, but most of them print only what each school's administration tells them. You'll discover that there are exactly 192,536 bound volumes in a law school's library, but not that the school's reputation extends for all of three city blocks.

School catalogs have the same problem: they tell you only what the school wants you to hear. Catalogs are great for finding out about application deadlines, course offerings, and the date the school was founded. But there's a lot more to a law school than some breezy facts and figures, and a few photographs of students smiling at benevolent-looking professors aren't going to give you much of a feeling for the nitty-gritty reality of life at the school.

Grapevine reports about a law school can be misleading. Law schools are not immune to change, and by the time a truism about any school becomes public knowledge, it's probably outdated—if it was ever accurate in the first place. What makes things even more complicated is that the popular conception of a law school is often all mixed up with that of its affiliated university, even though the two may have entirely different personalities.

A college career counseling office is as good a place to start as any. However, you'll probably find that the counselors are too busy to sit down and help you thrash out your individual questions. Even if you succeed in finding a prelaw adviser willing to try to help you, how likely is it that he or she will have the inside scoop on every law school that you might want to consider?

In short, the only people who can give you the straight story on any law school are the people who have been there. Are you prepared to fly around the country to dozens of law schools and meet for several hours on each campus with a group of students willing to tell you the truth about the strengths and weaknesses of their school? If not, you need this book.

For this edition, the statistical information that leads each school's entry has been newly updated. Current students and recent graduates have been consulted about the school descriptions and, where appropriate, the text has been revised.

I extend my gratitude to the law school correspondents listed on the following pages, as well as to the many others who preferred to remain anonymous. Without their cooperation, this book could never have been written. Of course, the researchers are not responsible for the contents of the book; the author accepts full responsibility.

We who have worked on *Inside the Law Schools: A Guide by Students for Students* have tried to create the kind of book that we felt a need for when *we* were applying to law schools. We hope you find it useful.

Your comments and opinions on the book are welcome. Please send them to: S. F. Goldfarb, *Inside the Law Schools,* NAL/Dutton, 375 Hudson Street, New York, NY 10014.

S. F. Goldfarb
Yale Law School, Class of '82

Researchers

Alisha Amburgey
Nicole René Atchison
Tom Baker
David Ball
Brigida Benitez
Victoria Bennett
Arthur B. Berger
Danton Asher Berube
Richard Bierman
Barry R. Blankfield
Cindy Boersma
Thomas K. Bond
R. Stephen Burke
Malcolm Burt
Marc Callahan
Joe Callow
Leslie Carlough
G. Marcus Cole
David Cox
Jay M. Dade
Deirdre Davis
Donn M. Davis
Marc Dinardo

Elizabeth L. Earle
Nancy L. Erwin
Eric Falkenstein
Amy L. Freeman
Judy Goldfarb
Lori Grange
Cynthia Green
Bonnie Greene
M. Brent Hall
John T. Hammarlund
Will Harrell
Mary K. Hartigan
Timothy T. Hui
Michael L. Humiston
Lee F. Jantzen
Janis C. Jerman
Margaret Johnson
Paul Kaufman
Sheila A. Kelley
Ernest W. Kohnke
Deborah Kravitz
Brad Kukuk
Evan M. Kushner

Viviana Langou
Ilyse Levine
Ken Levit
Sarah T. Luthens
Doretta Massardo McGinnis
Mark D. McMillan
Greg Magarian
Margaret Marrin
Kyriakos Marudas
Lisa Morowitz
Jeffrey Naness
Barry Negrin
Doreen Paluch
Scott Price
Michael M. Raeber
John E. Randolph, Jr.
Heather Reichert
Beth Rinaldo
Richard A. Ruffer, Jr.
Kali Sabnis
Harry Schessel

John Scorza
Lindal L. Scott
David M. Shearer
John M. Sigman
Diann L. Smith
Felice A. Sontupe
Bert Spence
Sharon M. Statz
Frederick W. Stein
David Steinberg
Beth Stekler
Matthew J. Sullivan
Kathleen Sweet
Jay G. Volk
William M. Welch
Jennifer Welsh
Carolynne White
Stephen P. Wink
Phillip Kevin Woods
Jennifer Wurzbacher

INSIDE THE LAW SCHOOLS

A
GUIDE
FOR
STUDENTS
BY
STUDENTS

1

Do You Want to Go to Law School?

Question: Why have applications to law schools soared in recent years?

Answer: (a) Because widely publicized Wall Street layoffs have made MBA programs less attractive.
(b) Because jitters about AIDS and high malpractice insurance rates have scared people away from medical school.
(c) Because of the popularity of *L.A. Law.*
(d) All of the above.

If you guessed (d), you're right. And the experts tell us that factors like these will probably continue to drive thousands of people to enter law school every year.

People have always gone to law school for strange reasons—or for no reason at all. Ask a group of current law students how they made their career choice, and they'll say things like, "What else could I do with a liberal arts degree?," "My father's a lawyer and I always assumed I would be too," "I want to change the world," and "I want to make big money and never have to worry about losing my job." All of these reasons are suspect, and if they strike a chord of recognition deep in your soul, it's time to explore your interest in law school a bit more closely.

Don't misunderstand—law is a perfectly nice, respectable career, and many people who have drifted into it are pleased with what they're doing. Unfortunately, many others aren't, and even those who feel lucky that they fell into law by chance would doubtless have benefited from a clearer sense of purpose.

So, if you're tempted to go to law school, take a few minutes to figure out why. You might find that your reasons are more substantial than you'd thought—or you might wind up throwing your LSAT booklet in the garbage.

What Else Is There?

First of all, let's face the fact that one cause of law school's appeal for so many people is that it's a structured education that feeds directly into a structured profession. It's intimidating to try to define a job for yourself. Going into a ready-made profession is much easier.

If you're in college, and especially if you followed the "Go Directly to College, Do Not Pass Go, Do Not Collect $200" route, it can be hard to think of any career opportunities outside of a few visible, clearly delineated possibilities. After all, you're not having much contact with working people, except for professors and the dining hall staff. Your summer jobs most likely bear no resemblance to the kind of thing you want to do for the rest of your life. If you're like most people, you're at a loss.

Well, don't panic. Your first job doesn't have to be any more permanent than your first relationship. Once you get out in the working world, you'll probably discover jobs that interest you that you'd never even known existed. Don't believe the myth that says you have to go into a "profession" to have a satisfying career.

Similarly, if you're already in the working world and your current job is going nowhere fast, you probably know better than to assume that having a professional degree is going to be the answer to all of your job-related prayers.

Nevertheless, some people want and need the structure of a traditional profession. That's perfectly legitimate. However, this desire doesn't get you very far toward choosing *which* profession.

Jobs, Money, and Status

Which brings us back to the question, "Why law school?" One frequently heard answer is, "Because I'll be able to get a job when

I get out." And that answer's close relative: "Because I'll be able to get a *well-paying* job when I get out."

The truth of both of those generalizations is questionable. As almost everybody knows by now, there is already a profusion of lawyers in this country—about three quarters of a million of them. And the law schools are churning out more all the time—more than 35,000 annually. Americans may be a litigious people, but even so, that's a lot of lawyers, and the traditional work force can't absorb all of them.

Roughly 14 percent of accredited law schools' grads are unemployed six months after graduation, according to a survey of 1991 graduates by the National Association for Law Placement. Others hang out a shingle and attempt to eke out the living of a solo practitioner, often without much success. Still others settle for jobs they don't really want, in fields that don't particularly interest them, in geographical areas that are their third or fourth choice.

But before you get discouraged, it's important to note that difficulty in landing employment is not distributed evenly across the law-school-graduate board. If you can get into a law school with a strong reputation, or if you get outstanding grades and/or get on the law review at almost any law school, you'll have a considerably improved crack at the jobs—because there *are* jobs for lawyers.

Very often when you hear about a law school grad who "couldn't" find a job, it means a law school grad who had *trouble* finding a job. Even Harvard students get rejection letters. At many law schools, employers come to recruit infrequently or not at all, meaning that the students have to send out résumés and pound the pavement. Also, it's only fair to say that age, sex, race, ethnic group, and disability discrimination remain strong among many legal employers. Effort and flexibility are the key. Almost everybody finds *something* eventually, but it can take a long time.

Even those who land the highly-sought-after positions at prestigious firms have no guarantee of still being on the payroll a few years later. Many become disillusioned and quit because of brutal hours and repetitive work; others are politely told that they are not partnership material and are asked to leave; still others are laid off when bad business conditions cause a law firm to shrink or even (yes, it has happened) go out of business.

In sum, the employment picture in law is good compared to

that in many other fields, but it's not good enough to be a reason in itself for going to law school—especially not for going to a so-so law school where you'll have to struggle to make yourself marketable.

What about salary? The U.S. Department of Labor says law is one of the twenty best-paying occupations in the country. The "going rate" for beginning associates at major New York City firms has passed the $85,000 mark. A lawyer who is made a partner (usually after several years working at the same firm) takes a percentage of the firm's profits, which can amount to a tidy sum; partners in some large firms earn over half a million dollars annually.

Note, though: these salaries are paid by private firms. A large chunk of the lawyer population is self-employed or works for the government, corporations, academia—not to mention legal aid and public-interest organizations. Their pay is often considerably lower. Other factors that affect the paycheck are the size of the firm (the smaller, the cheaper), the type of practice (not many criminal lawyers can command a corporate lawyer's fees), and the location (Duluth doesn't pay like Dallas or D.C.).

According to the National Association for Law Placement, 1991 law school graduates throughout the country had the following starting salaries:

Job Type	Median	Mean
Law firm	$51,000	$51,000
Business	$43,500	$46,300
Academic	$38,000	$41,800
Judicial clerkship	$31,000	$29,600
Government	$30,000	$31,800
Public interest	$25,000	$26,500
Total	$40,000	$44,300

If you want big money, you're going to be competing for relatively few legal jobs. If you want *really* big money, become a plastic surgeon in Hollywood, launch a wildly successful business venture, or win the lottery.

Some people will tell you that lawyers are all sitting in palatial offices and pulling in six-figure incomes. Others will say that law school graduates are standing on breadlines. The truth lies somewhere between the two.

The law school grad who spends a year searching for a job, the ground-level associate in a small, low-paying firm, and the impoverished public defender all benefit from a less tangible form of compensation: status. Law is the kind of profession that makes your relatives brag about you. Lawyers don't get their fingernails dirty, there's no heavy lifting, and after all, they run the country, don't they?

But before you conclude that being a lawyer means never having to say you're sorry, be aware that for every person who admires lawyers, there are three or four others who blame them for all that's wrong with America.

It's incontrovertible that the national bar is very powerful, and for many people, that's enough in itself to inspire undying awe. The way the profession has used that power, however, hasn't always inspired public confidence. Lawyers are often viewed as a conservative or even reactionary group with a strong stake in the inequalities of the status quo and an overwhelming concern for their own pocketbooks. After all, look at the profession's unwillingness to discipline its own members and to require lawyers to provide free legal services to the poor. And look at the professional background of lots of white-collar criminals who have been in the headlines lately.

Obviously, many lawyers are committed, progressive, far-sighted, and moral. But if you're attracted to law because you think the popular stereotype impresses people, you may be barking up the wrong tree. When you announce at a cocktail party that you're a lawyer, you'll encounter admiration for making it through law school and envy for your (supposedly) hefty income. You'll also get flak for defending criminals and/or corporations, perpetuating a problem-riddled judicial process, hindering the work of the police, aiding and abetting the work of the police, charging (supposedly) exorbitant fees, etc., etc. Even if you don't do any of these things, you'll be taken to task for your colleagues who do.

Without even tackling the issue of whether guaranteed employment, high salaries, and social status constitute a valid basis for choosing a career, it's clear that law is no sure bet on any of those three counts.

The Altruism Aspect

So far, we've been dealing with the issue of how a law career will or will not help *you*; how about helping other people? A widely cited reason for going to law school is that a law degree gives you a unique position to be of service to individuals and to effect social change. A lawyer's opportunity to help underprivileged people is real, and those for whom that is the main incentive for entering the profession deserve applause. There should be more like them. But it's the people who *act* on this principle after they get out of law school who really merit praise, because they're fewer yet.

You don't have to be cynical, just realistic, to recognize that many of the same people who wrote application essays about their futures as legal aid attorneys—and meant it—have gone on to represent bank presidents, multinational corporations, insurance companies—in short, everybody but those who need assistance most. Why (aside from the obvious fact that legal aid attorneys don't make $85,000 a year) does this happen?

Defending ghetto residents in daily disputes with their land-lords can be frustrating, dull, and repetitive. In comparison, a complex corporate case can seem more conceptually challenging. On the other hand, employers outside the profit-making sector are almost always understaffed, which can spell more responsibility for the young lawyer who, in a large corporate firm, might be consigned to carrying the senior partner's briefcase.

We have to look beyond the jobs themselves to understand why so few law school graduates go into public-interest law. The most likely answer is that virtually all law schools—and to a large degree the profession itself—are oriented toward the attorney who prac-tices with a private firm. When interviewers come to law schools to recruit, they're just about always representing private employers. Public-interest organizations (and most government agencies) can't afford to jet around the country scouting talent—nor are they able to anticipate in the fall what their staff needs and budget resources are going to be a year later. Even at the law schools where highly qualified third-year students can sit back and wait for the corporate law firm offers to pour in, it takes effort to line up a public-interest job. This is especially true when massive budget cuts have reduced the number of nonconventional legal jobs available.

At most law schools, if you're looking for work with anything but a private law firm, you're fighting against a tide of peer pressure and practical convenience. (An important note: many for-profit firms will let you donate a portion of your time to charitable, *pro bono publico* work.)

By no means is this intended to deter you from entering law for altruistic reasons. It *is* intended to make you realize that social service isn't handed to you on a silver platter along with your law degree. A good start is to find a law school guided by principles that accord with yours. Politically progressive law schools with an "alternative" focus do exist, as do conventional law schools with large groups of progressive students.

The opportunity to help oppressed people as a lawyer is just that—an opportunity. Like anyone else, a lawyer has to decide what his or her moral commitments are and work to maintain them. A legal career is no easy route to a clear social conscience—but then, what is?

It's the Law

Strangely, most of the reasons people name for choosing a legal career could serve just as well as reasons for entering other professions, because they don't address the one thing that sets the law apart—namely, the law, in its various and sundry forms.

It can be hard to tell whether you're going to find a lawyer's work interesting. (If you're already working and have contact with lawyers, you have a head start.) Lawyers work in many different areas, and little of what they do finds its way into the public eye. However, it's a good bet that if a newspaper article on the latest Supreme Court ruling makes you yawn and turn to the sports page, you'll be better off in another field. When people discuss the progress of a newsworthy suit, are you intrigued? In your history courses, have you found the legal aspect of things thought-provoking? Even if your answers are yes, you may not be enraptured with the life of a lawyer (you won't be spending your days arguing *Brown* v. *Board of Education*), but it's a start.

Some other traits that come in useful for a lawyer include a zest for problem solving. Most lawyers' work has to be approached like a puzzle. You should have some tolerance for structure, because even if your immediate work environment is freewheeling (which is rare in legal jobs), you'll have to deal with the legal system, one of the most highly structured cultural artifacts you could ever hope to come across. You should be willing to reason logically and analytically. Also, it helps to enjoy—and to be good at—verbal skills such as reading, writing, and public speaking, since laws, and all the arguments that go on about them, are words. An interest in contemporary society and its problems goes a long way in a legal career. A strong ethical sense is not only good for the profession and the country in general but keeps you from running afoul of your state bar association disciplinary committee.

Possessing these attributes doesn't guarantee you'll be a good lawyer. Even if you meet these general criteria, they're probably insufficient in themselves to make up your mind. If you're serious about finding out whether law is for you, you'll have to look further.

Testing the Waters

Before you write a report or a term paper, you do research, right? It stands to reason that you should do the same when you're making a decision as important as your career choice.

A good place to find out more about law is the library. Read anything in sight by lawyers, about lawyers, about the legal system, and about legal education.

Classes are also a good way to familiarize yourself with the subject. Many colleges have undergrad courses in the American legal system, constitutional history, contemporary juvenile justice problems, and the like. If you're fairly sure you want to go to law school, you might want to use your precious undergraduate years to take liberal arts courses instead of learning subjects you'll get again in law school. But if law school is a big question mark in your mind, you need all the information you can get. (Be aware, though, that college courses in legal issues are usually taught from a social-science perspective that has little in common with law school or with the workaday world of a lawyer.)

If your college has an affiliated law school, or if you're out of college and your town or city has one, get hold of its catalog. Ask some of the professors if you can sit in on their classes. Attend the conferences, lectures, and symposia that the law school sponsors. And—this can be hard—try to talk to people. Law school administrators, faculty, and students all have insights to share—if they have time for you.

Legal folks love to talk, so once you get them cornered and have led off with a general question, like "What do you *do*, anyway?" you shouldn't have much trouble. If your next-door neighbor's son is a lawyer, if your third cousin is at law school, or if you currently have a career that entails contact with lawyers, find a chance to pump them for inside information.

One reason for speaking to many people is that the profession and the people in it are so diverse. After hearing a few contradictory answers to the same questions, you'll realize that generalizations about all law schools or all lawyers are of limited use—and you'll be better able to decide what type of law school or legal career (if any) is for you.

Time Out!

When it comes to finding out about the day-to-day work of a lawyer, there isn't a next best thing to being there. If you have a lawyer in the immediate family, you've probably heard about his or her legal adventures over the years. Maybe you've even dropped in at the office from time to time. (If you haven't, try to do so now.)

For most of us, though, the only way to have more than a fleeting glimpse of the legal world is to get a job in it. Working for a legal employer is an excellent way to help you make up your mind.

Many law firms, especially large ones, and especially in large cities, hire paralegals. In many cases, an intelligent college graduate can acquire on-the-job training and doesn't have to go through a formal paralegal course.

Paralegal jobs vary widely—from shuffling documents and making coffee to sitting at your employer's side through a big trial. The largest firms often have separate paralegal departments, where dozens of staffers are assigned paperwork on the same case for months at a time and never stray from their desks. If you decide to go the paralegal route, try for a situation where you're in contact with lawyers instead of just with other paralegals, and where you'll be working on a variety of projects. The tasks you perform may not be intrinsically interesting, but you're bound to learn from the exposure to legal vocabulary, methods, and principles.

To find out about paralegal jobs, check the want ads in bar association newsletters and local or regional legal newspapers and magazines. See if your college career-placement office has any openings listed. If it doesn't, it (or any library) will have a copy of the *Martindale-Hubbell Law Directory*, which lists virtually all the lawyers in the country. Fire off cover letters and résumés to the firms in the geographical area where you want to work. Concentrate on the ones with lawyers who graduated from your college; you might as well play up the old school ties. And keep your ears open for any other leads.

The pool of applicants for paralegal jobs is growing. Landing one of these jobs can be tough. A potential paralegal can't be too particular about the type of firm he or she wants to work for, because as a rule it's the corporate ones that have the money to hire extra help. There are many different kinds of corporate work, though, from securities to litigation, so there's some choice available. If you're willing to forgo pay, your options become wider. Many government, public-interest, and legal aid groups are eager for volunteer interns.

For one reason or another, you may be unable to get a paralegal job for the summer or part time during the school year, or you may feel that's not enough time to get a feel for the profession. Should you take time off after college before you go to law school?

If you have serious doubts about whether law school is for you, or if you're sick and tired of school—and most people are at least one of those upon graduating from college—then the answer is a resounding *yes*. Taking time off not only can help you define your goals but—if you learn a lot from it and milk a good essay and strong recommendations out of the experience—you can significantly improve your law school admissions chances. (For a discussion of the pros and cons of deferring admission, see Chapter 3.) Try to get as much out of the time off as possible; otherwise it's a waste and the law schools will see through your indifference.

The consensus among people who've worked as paralegals is that a year or so is optimal before moving on to better things. At the end of a year, you've seen about as much as you're going to on that level, and after that you're marking time.

Another alternative is to take time off in order to pursue some non-law-related interest. But although taking this approach may tell you whether you have a future as a concert pianist or flower arranger, it won't go very far toward clarifying your future as a lawyer. The process of elimination isn't the best way to make a career decision. Still, there's a lot to be said for any change of pace.

If you've been out of school for a while and have pursued another career, this doesn't mean it's too late for you to become a lawyer. It does mean that you'll want to examine your interest in law and make sure that it goes beyond your dissatisfaction with your present job.

The average age of entering law students is rising all the time. There's nothing that says you have to go straight from college. In many cases—depending upon how you use the between-time—you're better off not doing it that way.

Straddling the Fence

If you've reached a point where you're fairly sure you want a legal career, but you still want to keep one foot in a nonlegal job (or family life or whatever), an excellent option is provided by the many law schools that offer part-time programs. You don't always have to sacrifice quality for the flexibility of a part-time education. Many good schools have evening sections or grant permission for students to take less than a full course load in the regular day section. Generally, part-timers take four years instead of the normal three to graduate.

There are some important questions you should ask to help you determine the quality of a part-time law program. Is it taught by the school's regular, full-time faculty? Are admissions standards different for part-time students—and if so, in what way? Will you have access to administrative services (like the financial aid and career counseling offices) and meetings of student organizations during the hours when you'll be at the school? Ask to see job placement statistics specifically for the part-time program.

Of course, law school is tough, and combining it with other obligations is tougher still. The distractions you'll face from outside sources may keep you from concentrating on your studies as much as you'd like—and vice versa.

Also, a part-time student sacrifices much of the informal contact with professors and fellow students, which can be a valuable part of law school. It helps if the part-time group makes up a significant percentage of the law school population; then there's less chance of being treated like a second-class citizen.

If you decide to go to law school part time, you may come to feel that you're part of the school—but it definitely takes more effort than it would for a full-timer.

It's Up to You

If you can't seem to make a clear-cut decision as to whether you want a legal career, that's a healthy sign. There are few born lawyers—or born anythings, for that matter. People who keep their minds and eyes open realize that they could be happy in a number of different jobs. Not *perfectly* happy; no job is going to offer all pluses and no minuses. It's a question of figuring out the merits of each, weighing them, and deciding on the basis of the trade-offs involved.

There's nothing wrong with choosing to become a lawyer on measured, pragmatic grounds. In fact, if you wait for a light from heaven to tell you that law is your calling, you'll probably wait a long time. It *is* unfortunate to make your decision from a solely negative or resigned point of view—the "Why not?" approach—because you'll always be nagged by doubts. Get the doubts in the open now, and if you can't eliminate them, at least deal with them rationally.

If you're still wavering, think about this: the variety within the legal profession is greater than in almost any other field. Lawyers put their backgrounds to effective use as politicians, writers, academics, business executives—you name it. Even practicing attorneys come in myriad types and serve myriad clients. You can go to law school and still leave open the question of exactly what to do with that degree.

But once having decided on a legal career, you unfortunately have little choice about whether to go to law school. "Unfortunately," because who wants to go through three more years of formal education, and difficult years at that? Most people don't find law school inherently rewarding. Unlike college, where most of us take whatever courses catch our fancy, law school is primarily designed to prepare people for a profession.

It's easier to get enthusiastic about being a lawyer than about being a law student. Don't be surprised if you come to see law school as a means to an end; so do most people. As long as the "end" is well chosen, and you make a sincere effort to get as much out of law school as you can, there's nothing hypocritical about it.

But law schools do differ, and there's no doubt that some are better suited to you than others. To maximize your satisfaction with those fateful few years, it pays to choose carefully—but that's the subject of another chapter.

2

Choosing the Right Law School

When you were choosing a college, it was fairly easy to narrow down your list of possibilities. It's a long way from a frat-oriented midwestern megauniversity to an artsy college tucked away in the hills of Vermont. MIT is not UCLA—not only because their moods are different but because they teach different things. Chances are that if you were interested in one, you weren't interested in the other. The choice of a law school can seem next to impossible, because they all look so much alike. They all teach the law, and most of them teach the law the same way. If you could ask first-year students at a hundred law schools to describe their experiences, you'd hear the same things over and over.

A typical response would go something like this. The first-year courses, which are all required, include torts, contracts, civil procedure, legal research and writing, property, criminal law, and perhaps constitutional law. The professors are tough. Most of them rely on the Socratic method, where instead of *answering* questions, they call on the students at random and *ask* questions, in a way that's supposedly intended to challenge students into a rigorously logical analysis of the subject matter. The classes are large. The work load is grueling, and it's impossible to do at all well without attending class regularly and studying consistently. The books are big and expensive and consist of a string of judicial opinions in specific cases, from which you're supposed to extrapolate the general principles of a given area of law (this is called the *case method*).

The final exams are pressure cookers, especially because they are the first time that students receive any formal feedback in most courses. The student body is highly motivated. The main topics of conversation are classes, the law, and jobs. Competition is a way of life.

So how do you make up your mind?

Well, to begin with, if you look hard enough, you can find schools that deviate from the norm in almost every respect. "Alternative" law schools, although greatly outnumbered by the more traditional type, do exist. But even within the ranks of standard law schools, there are differences.

For instance, the first-year curriculum may be prescribed, but do you have your pick of electives after that? If a school relies on the Socratic method in introductory courses, does that go for the upper-level courses too, or are lecture-and-discussion classes and seminars available? If the classes are large, does that mean 70 or 170? Does student competition take the form of working hard to get good jobs, or is it grade-grubbing, or is it stealing books from the library? Is everyone nervous because large numbers of students flunk out, or do people feel reasonably secure that they'll make it through to graduation? These may only be differences of degree, but they can have a huge impact on shaping a school's personality.

You'll find some of the same courses in almost every law school catalog. But others, such as Mental Hospital Legal Services or Delimitation of Maritime Boundaries, are rarer. If you know that you're interested in a specialty like entertainment law or environmental law, by all means look for a school that offers courses in that area.

Even if a school has a page-long list of international law electives, are they sufficiently well taught to be worthwhile? Of two schools that offer exactly the same curriculum, one might be better for tax, the other for criminal law, depending on the strengths and weaknesses of the professors. So check out the faculty's backgrounds, qualifications, lists of publications, and professional activities. Incidentally, when assessing the faculty, the student-teacher ratio is an important consideration, but the professors' attitude toward and accessibility to the students is even more important.

If you're interested in pursuing a joint degree (a joint J.D./M.B.A. is a popular choice), that will help you narrow down your selection. Even if you don't go that route, you might be interested in finding out how flexible different schools are about awarding course credit for non-law-school courses.

In response to student pressures, and in answer to complaints from the judiciary that recent law graduates are unprepared for actual practice, almost every law school now boasts some kind of clinical program—that is, an opportunity to gain practical experience doing a lawyer's work. But there's a difference between a school that provides actual legal aid internships on the premises and considers them an important part of the curriculum, and one that offers a single "simulated" trial practice class as an afterthought. Clinical programs are expensive to run, and at many schools they are threatened by the faculty's attitude that they're "unintellectual." A good way to gauge a school's commitment to clinical training is to find out how much of it is required for graduation, how much course credit it carries, whether a variety of classes and internships are available, how many students participate, whether students handle real cases for real clients, and whether you have to meet special qualifications or spend years on a waiting list in order to take part.

Similarly, you'll find the same student organizations listed in most catalogs, so it's important to know which ones are active and which ones exist only on paper. Is the campus mood dominated by the beer blasts of the legal fraternity, by the annual moot court competition (where students argue a hypothetical appellate case, often to qualify for regional and national competition), by the meetings of the National Lawyers Guild (a politically progressive organization with chapters at many law schools), or by activities of the Federalist Society (a conservative group with ties to prominent Republicans)? Is the Student Bar Association—the student government at most schools—a mere figurehead and a haven for self-serving politicos, or is it a visible force in the school's social and political life?

In general, large schools can offer more courses and more activities to choose from than small schools. However, you may feel that an institution with 2,000 students (which is about as big as law schools get) will leave you overwhelmed. Keep in mind that a small school may combine students into large classes, and a large school may divide students into small classes (for example, by teaching first-year courses in multiple "sections").

A diverse student body is regarded by many people as a crucial component of a stimulating educational atmosphere. You may want to seek out a school where students represent a variety of ethnic and racial groups, ages, geographic backgrounds, experiences, and so on. On the other hand, you may prefer to go to a school where other people's backgrounds and interests remind you of your own, or you may choose to go to a state school that is required by law to enroll virtually all in-state residents.

In any event, a school may say it has a commitment to affirmative action, but do the numbers of minority group members and women in the student body and faculty show it? Even more important, do women students and minority group members feel fully accepted? Are the Women's Caucus, the Black Law Students Association, and the Latin American, Native American, and Asian-American groups on campus organized, effective, and heeded by the faculty and administrators?

Any law school worth its salt has a law review. Is everyone fighting tooth and nail to get on it? Does it choose its members solely on the basis of grades, or is there a chance to make it by way of a writing competition? Are law review members the only students who succeed in finding jobs? Is there more than one law review, to cater to students with different interests?

Are the facilities comfortable and adequate to their purposes, or dilapidated and overcrowded? Is the library (where *all* law students spend a lot of time) equipped with the books you'll need, are there enough terminals for computerized legal research, and will you be able to find a quiet, comfortable place to study?

Is the school's placement office a recently launched, half-baked affair, or a well-established and well-run operation with a successful track record? Is it staffed by glorified clerical workers whose skills are limited to shelving publications in alphabetical order, or by knowledgeable counselors who can help you define and reach your individual goals? The ideal placement staff will line up hundreds of varied employers to come to campus to recruit students for job openings. Failing that (and few schools can match that standard), does the placement office have a lengthy list of employers who have written to the school inviting direct applications; does it arrange for students to attend off-campus recruitment conferences; does it run seminars and panel discussions on job-hunting and career options; or does it just provide a standard law firm directory and leave you to your own initiative?

Look at the hard numbers on how many graduates are employed by the time they graduate, how many are employed six months later, what kinds of jobs they take, and in what areas of the country. That kind of information will be far more revealing than the typical vague and cheery statements in law school catalogs, like "XYZ Law School has a superb career planning center that helps every student find satisfying employment."

Cost is something most prospective law students look at carefully. But don't make the mistake of thinking that tuition is the determining factor in choosing a law school. For one thing, high tuition may be offset by a low cost of living in a certain region, and vice versa. What's more, financial aid can make an expensive law school free, whereas a law school with a more moderate but still substantial price tag might offer you no financial aid at all. Chapter 4 of this book will tell you more about getting financial help to pay for law school. By the way, if the fees to apply to law school are more than you can handle, don't hesitate to ask any law school admission office to waive its own application fee as well as the fee for taking the LSAT.

The list of variables could go on and on. And we haven't even mentioned the obvious ones like urban, suburban, or rural; North, South, East, West, or in-between; church-sponsored or nonsectarian; university-affiliated or independent; and publicly supported or private.

Clearly, there are many factors to investigate when choosing a law school—and the more you investigate them, the more you'll discover that you *do* have a choice. Many people hesitate to go to law school because they think there's no way around reliving *The Paper Chase*. No law school—not even the one *The Paper Chase* was based on—is really like that, and some bear less resemblance to the stereotype than others.

The Prestige Puzzle

"Why should I care about all these incidentals," you may be wondering, "when what really matters is getting into the best law school?" When people say "the best law school," they rarely realize that they should be saying "the best law school *for me*."

A lot of time is spent polling lawyers and law school administrators, trying to figure out just which are the top ten or twenty law schools, and in what order. That kind of enterprise is automatically suspect. Who is really equipped to say whether a given school is number 9 or number 10? Furthermore, these polls are a self-fulfilling prophecy: the same school names crop up again and again, because the people who are surveyed are inevitably influenced by all the other rankings they have read.

Looking for a high-status school may seem like a shortcut to finding a place where you'll get a marketable degree among bright professors and capable students. This is not necessarily a reliable way of making your choice. The criteria used by people who rank law schools may not include many factors important to you.

Reputation is important, insofar as it indicates prestige among employers. Law school is there to prepare you for a profession, and you shouldn't be ashamed of wanting to maximize your chances of employment once you get out. An elite school can also be a way to keep your options open for a while longer. It may be easier to use your degree in another field—business, government, or journalism, for instance—if it comes from a "top" school.

But law school is also three years of your life, and you ought to think long and hard before you decide to mortgage that time solely for the elusive goal of a hundred job offers. If you head for a totally uncongenial law school and make yourself miserable for three years, your grades will probably show it, and you haven't done yourself any favors.

What's more, you want to find a law school that has a strong reputation *among those employers you're interested in working for.*

For starters, law schools can be divided into two categories: those with national reputations and those with local reputations. The national ones give you more flexibility when seeking employment. But if you already know where you're going to settle, you might fare just as well—if not better—with a degree from a local school that's popular in the area than with a sheepskin from an Ivy League institution 2,000 miles away. Many permanent jobs grow out of part-time internships; if you're going to law school in Oregon, how can you compete with the people who are on the spot in Boston?

The law schools with the top national names attract interviewers from all over the country, but more come from their own region than from farther away. It's easier for a San Francisco firm to hire from Stanford than from Columbia. This is a self-perpetuating process, because when lawyers reach the position of having some say in the hiring process, they tend to favor their alma mater. A Georgetown grad can certainly find a job in Milwaukee, but it may require some extra effort.

In addition to considering location, think about what kind of work you want to do. Most of the prestigious schools are well regarded throughout the profession, but look for where the emphasis is. Who's doing the recruiting and hiring? Is it the big Wall Street firms? That's terrific, if Wall Street's your goal; those jobs are hard to come by. On the other hand, if you want to open your own practice, you may be better off at a less prestigious school that's particularly strong on teaching the nuts-and-bolts basics.

If you're thinking of entering public-interest law, look for a school with programs geared toward people like you. Some schools require volunteer legal service to the underprivileged as a prerequisite for graduation; some have special career counselors dedicated to public-interest work; some provide grants for summer internships in public-interest settings; and a few even have programs to postpone or forgive loan repayment obligations for graduates who take low-paying public-interest jobs.

If you're interested in any kind of career other than that of a practicing attorney, it's especially crucial that you scrutinize every aspect of a law school to make sure you can fit in, because in most cases it will be an uphill battle. Are there courses that approach law from a theoretical point of view and cover topics like civil rights issues and the sociology of law, or is every course geared toward passing the bar exam? You're bound to be in the minority, but are there a good number of students whose goals are similar to yours? A person who wants to be a law professor or run for political office won't be very happy at a school where everybody else is headed straight for clients and courtrooms.

One more word about reputation. Some law schools haven't been around long enough to acquire one. They can be among the most exciting, creative, innovative places to get your legal education, and they can spare you the nonsense of stuffiness and tradition. Unfortunately, you'll have only a tiny pool of alumni waiting to pull strings for you when you get out, and nonalumni won't even have heard of the place. That can decide whether or not you get an initial job interview. You shouldn't reject a law school out of hand just because it was accredited last week, but if you go there, be prepared to work at finding a job.

Prestige is not a worthless commodity. It can mean jobs—but it might not mean the kind you want, so examine the situation carefully.

"But Can I Get In?"

There was a time when just about everybody who applied to law school got in. There was a time when just about everybody who applied to *Harvard* Law School got in—and then a third of the class would flunk out by the end of the first year. Whether today's highly competitive law school admissions process is more or less humane than the old way is open to question, but it's clear that getting into the law school of your choice is no longer an easy matter.

The root of the problem is numbers. The total enrollment of students in ABA-approved law schools in 1963 was 49,552. Today, that number has climbed to 135,157. Part of this growth is attributable to the influx of women and minority group members into a profession that was virtually closed to them until recently. Mostly, though, the increase is due to the fact that law school has caught on as a good place to go when you're not quite sure what you want to do—and there are many college graduates who fall into that category.

Not only are people competing to get into the well-known law schools, but schools you've never heard of are receiving so many applications that they can accept only 30 or 40 percent of them. The students at ABA-approved law schools across the country are a handpicked bunch: the total number of people applying for admission to accredited law schools each year is roughly double the number of available first-year slots.

As you look into law schools, one of the features you will of course investigate is admissions standards. If a school's median LSAT is miles above yours, and the median GPA leaves yours in the dust, you might not stand much of a chance there. But many different factors can affect your candidacy—including how you go about applying. These factors are discussed in the next chapter. There are equal numbers of students above and below the median (sometimes far below it). You might very well be one of the ones in the "below" half.

Even if a careful evaluation of your candidacy shows that you have a slim chance of getting into a given school, you might still want to apply. If you're particularly attracted to the school, give it a try. The law school admissions procedure can be very unpredictable. Just be sure to apply to some other places where the odds are more in your favor—and to one or two "safety schools" where you're virtually a sure bet.

The Quest for the Perfect School

It's not uncommon for people to apply to as many as fifteen or twenty law schools. (Five is closer to average.) The applications are no picnic, and the application fees can really add up, but if your qualifications put you on the borderline for most of the schools you're interested in, it pays to give yourself as many chances as possible.

There's probably no one perfect law school for you. When you're deciding where to apply, try to find a range of schools where you could be happy—happier at some than at others, perhaps, but reasonably satisfied at any.

A good place to start is with the law school descriptions in this book. But don't stop there. Send away for a catalog from any school you're even remotely interested in; it's free. If a law school representative pays a visit to your college, or if you can conveniently get to a law school forum (gatherings of law school representatives held in many major cities), drop by to learn more. Talk to any law students or alumni (preferably recent) whom you're lucky enough to know. Speak to lawyers about the schools' reputations among employers. Visit the schools if you can—sit in on classes, check out the library and job placement office, gauge the mood in the corridors, and ask everyone questions. In short, think of yourself as a comparison shopper about to make one of the most significant purchases of your life.

The next step is getting in.

3
Getting
In

In most cases, you'll find the law school admissions procedure much simpler than what you went through to get into college. A typical folder in the admissions office of a selective college bulges with information about Joe or Susie Applicant—four or five recommendations, a complex application form, an essay question like "Which six historical figures would you most like to invite to dinner?," reports from an admissions staff interviewer and an alumni interviewer, and a stack of finger paintings to demonstrate artistic aptitude. By the time you apply to law school, you'll discover that the admissions people won't ask you about every aspect of your multifaceted personality. They want you to keep it short and sweet.

The matter-of-factness of the law school admissions process may seem like a blessing. Who wouldn't prefer a two-page application form to a ten-page one? The problem is that two pages give you very little to work with. In order to make the law school admissions procedure work for you, recognize what flexibility you have and use it for all it's worth.

The Sooner the Better

If you can put time on your side, you've already cleared the first hurdle. Even the schools that don't advertise a rolling admissions procedure tend to evaluate applications as they're received; there are too many to leave them all for the end. By the time applications trickle through in mid-February, there may be fewer seats left in the entering class. Admissions committees are only human, and the five hundredth National Merit Scholar who captained the college soccer team inevitably looks less impressive than the first.

Getting an application in even a little late in the game can work against you; getting it in after the published deadline is really pushing your luck. Aside from all the general reasons why earlier is better, another factor comes into play: law schools like people who can read directions and follow them. If you're late, you haven't demonstrated your talents in that area. The admissions people will assume you're not too interested in the school, and they'll be pretty sure they're not too interested in you.

To get an application in early, it's necessary to start looking into law schools earlier still. Choosing schools, sending away for catalogs, taking the LSAT and having the scores reported, lining up recommendations—all those preliminaries take longer than you might think.

Even after you think you've finished the application process, don't take anything for granted. Keep a copy of everything you send. Then, double-check later to be sure that the schools have received every piece of paper they should have received. (Some schools will send a postcard to each applicant for this purpose.) A missing letter of recommendation or a lost transcript can hold up the school's consideration of your application for months.

The LSAT: Can It Make or Break You?

Before law school applications proliferated out of control, admissions committees had more leisure to lavish personal attention on everyone. Now that the schools are snowed under with thousands of applications every year, they tend to rely heavily on numbers that can be compared quickly and easily. One of those numbers is the Law School Admission Test (LSAT) score.

Law school admissions officers are usually concerned less with what kind of lawyer you'll be than with what kind of law student you'll be. They like the LSAT because surveys seem to show that it's a fairly accurate predictor of law school grades. It's similar to the reason that undergrad schools are fond of the SAT—only more so.

The LSAT consists of five thirty-five-minute-long sections of multiple-choice questions designed to test logical reasoning, analytical reasoning, and reading comprehension. There is also a thirty-minute writing sample (based on an essay question for which there is no right or wrong answer), which gets sent directly to the law schools, ungraded.

Since June 1991, the test has been scored on a scale of 120 to 180. Previously, the scores ranged from 10 to 48.

To get free information on the LSAT, including forms to register for taking the test, write to Law School Admission Services, Box 2000, Newtown, PA 18940.

The LSAT doesn't assume any prior knowledge of law. Being able to define a writ of certiorari is for *after* you get to law school. The test examines some basic intellectual skills that come in handy for law students.

As with the other standardized exams you've taken over the years, it won't help to cram the night before the LSAT, or to gnaw all your No. 2 pencils to a pulp in anticipation. If you got a 200 on the SAT, don't try to reeducate yourself from start to finish for the LSAT. Panic can only work against you.

One of the few tools at your disposal to exercise any control over your LSAT score is *familiarity*. It may or may not breed contempt, but it will certainly help you feel more comfortable when faced with that computerized answer sheet. At least half the battle with these standardized tests is finding out what the examiners are looking for, so try to get to the point where you can think on their wavelength. Start familiarizing yourself with the test's format early—and then, when it's time for the real thing, relax.

The easiest and cheapest way to prepare for the exam is by studying the free LSAT information booklet provided by Law School Admission Services. Be sure to take the complete sample test included in the booklet. For further practice, which is definitely desirable, you can order actual past versions of the exam and other study aids from LSAS. There are also commercially marketed books that contain made-up practice tests, but they may be less reliable than the official versions available through LSAS.

As you rehearse for your performance, try to duplicate the conditions of the real exam. Observe the time limits for each section of the test. Many people are taken by surprise when they find they have to rush through the LSAT in order to finish.

The various LSAT review courses offered by eager entrepreneurs across the country are a mixed blessing. If you don't have the self-discipline to work through a regimen of sample tests, you might benefit from having a teacher dish out regular assignments. But these courses are very expensive, and again, only the people who put the test together can provide you with consistently dependable practice questions.

Don't wait to take the LSAT until the last test administration date permitted by the schools to which you're applying. You might wake up that day with a 104° temperature. Also, if you take the test early enough, you'll have time to consider retaking it if you really do miserably; if the second score is dramatically higher, it can improve your admission chances. Disabled students should leave plenty of extra time to make special test-taking arrangements with LSAS. In any event, the sooner you know your score, the sooner you can plan your application strategy. Many college students find it advantageous to take the LSAT during the summer after junior year, when they're rested and away from the competitive pressures of school.

Here are a few more useful tips for taking the LSAT: Study the instructions for each type of question in advance, so you don't have to waste time deciphering instructions during the exam. Don't worry if more than one answer to a question seems correct; this is absolutely standard for the LSAT. The trick is to choose the *best* of the answers offered. If you have trouble with a question, don't be afraid to guess; you gain points for every correct guess, and you don't lose any points for an incorrect answer. Time yourself as you go, pacing your progress so that you get through all the questions. Of course, if you have time left over, use it to check your answers. And don't forget the three cardinal rules for any machine-scored test: make sure the number of the question you are answering matches the number you are filling in on the answer sheet; be sure to fill in the little circles on the answer sheet completely; and bring plenty of extra pencils.

About six weeks after you sit through the law boards, you'll get an envelope in the mail from LSAS. Do the numbers inside determine your law school fate? Not by themselves. Board scores are much less important at some schools than at others, and even the number-conscious schools look at several other factors when evaluating an application. Many schools that have been LSAT-oriented for years are starting to reexamine their policies in the face of accusations that the test is monopolistic, biased toward a white middle-class norm, invalid for small differences in scores, and vulnerable to coaching.

So if your score was less than prodigious, don't get discouraged; just try to get as much out of the rest of your credentials as you can. And if you did well, don't count on coasting from here; people with perfect scores do get rejections. It all depends on how the rest of your application shapes up.

The GPA

Many law schools arrive at an "admission index" score for each candidate by combining the LSAT with the undergraduate grade point average (GPA). It's often on the basis of that score that the first cuts are made. Like the LSAT, your performance in the undergraduate classroom is considered a helpful clue to your performance in the law school classroom. (If you've taken many of your courses pass/fail, that may lead admission officials to an increased reliance on your LSAT score.)

Because of grade inflation at colleges, many law school applicants sport GPAs somewhere in the B+ range. In order to draw distinctions among them—and, sometimes, in recognition of the fact that grades can be highly arbitrary—the law schools have to look beyond the bare four-year average.

One of the most important variables governing how your GPA will be regarded is the undergraduate school you're coming from. Most law schools use something called the Law School Data Assembly Service (LSDAS). You can register with LSDAS at the same time as you register for the LSAT. (They're run by the same people.) LSDAS takes your undergraduate transcript, compensates for the quirks of your college grading system, and ends up with a profile of your undergraduate performance that can be compared easily to those of students from other schools. You then tell the LSDAS people to send the report to the law schools where you're applying.

The LSDAS organization claims that it only irons out differences in grading scales and course credit systems from college to college. The rumor that they use a *weighting factor*—a different number for each college, reflecting its relative difficulty, by which they multiply the GPA of everyone from that school—is completely unsubstantiated. In any event, it's clear that law schools don't regard a 4.0 from High Competition University the same way as one from Podunk Community College. When you compare your grades to the median, take into account your college's reputation for tough or easy grading standards.

Law school admissions committees are rarely so narrow-minded that they don't recognize that we all go through academic slumps. If you had one or two abysmal semesters but performed well the rest of the time, they'll probably make allowances. Similarly, if you got straight As in your major but picked up a C in the Introductory Buddhist Musicology course you tried out, don't lose sleep over it.

As for majors, as long as you don't spend four years concentrating on automotive mechanics or physical education, it doesn't really matter what you choose. If it's something that you are genuinely interested in, that should help. There's a good chance that your interest will be demonstrated by high grades and strong recommendations. Sure, a lot of law students majored in history or political science, but a lot of *everybody* majored in history or political science, and a degree in one of those fields isn't a sine qua non for law school admission. If anything, law schools like diversity—but that's no reason to avoid popular majors either.

If your major doesn't provide much in the way of reading, writing, logical reasoning, and critical analysis, you should take other courses to hone those talents. Whatever you major in, try to expose yourself to a variety of disciplines and types of thought. The day of the prelaw major is over; the day of the well-rounded, liberally educated lawyer is here.

Studying and getting good grades are highly recommended activities for the future law student. But too much worrying about your GPA can be counterproductive. For one thing, some college professors (although not all, by any means) can tell the difference between a grade-grubber and someone who's really interested, and they may grade accordingly—or at least mention it in the recommendation. For another thing, law school admissions staffers have a remarkable ability to sniff out gut courses a mile away, and they're not too impressed by a transcript that's padded with them.

In short, college is for learning what you want to learn, challenging yourself, and doing as well as you can. There's a wide range within which the law schools don't much care about exactly what courses you selected.

If you've gone to graduate school, the law schools will want to see your graduate school transcript, but they generally will not include your graduate school grades when computing your GPA.

Your GPA is one of the most important ingredients in the admissions recipe, but again, it's not all-important. By the time you're reading this, there may not be much you can do about your college grades. So focus on the things you *can* do something about.

The Application

Application forms are self-explanatory, and there's no opportunity for filling them out "better" or "worse," right? Wrong.

In conversations with law school admissions officers, it is amazing how many times they complain about applications filled out with great haste and greater indifference. Applications that are written in pencil, illegible, misspelled, covered with coffee stains and cross-outs—they get plenty like that every year. Just make sure yours isn't one of them.

Another truth we hold to be self-evident but which many applicants ignore: It's crucial to read the directions and follow them. All else being equal, law schools tend to be partial to people who provide the information that's asked for, where it's asked for, how it's asked for.

If you turn in a neat, correctly completed application that looks as if it's been filled in with care, you're ahead of thousands of your fellow applicants. And it's not half as hard as getting good grades.

The Essay

An essay is rarely strong enough to make up for an otherwise hopeless record or weak enough to get a genius the thumbs-down, but if you're in the middle group—and most people are—a good essay can help tip the balance in your favor.

A lawyer needs to have an adequate command of the English

language. Judges don't respond very well to "Well, like, you know, like my client's not guilty, you know?" One of the purposes of the admissions essay is to prove you're literate. Before you consign your essay to the mailbox, show it to some people whom you admire for their command of grammar, style, syntax, punctuation, and the like. Your essay doesn't have to be publishable, but it shouldn't be incomprehensible.

Similarly, use the essay to show that your mind works clearly and methodically. Whatever you're saying, you should have a central theme or organizing principle, your reasoning should be easy to follow, and each point should proceed logically from the one before. (This goes for the writing sample on the LSAT, too.)

So much for form. How about content? Most law schools have an essay question that's vague and open-ended, such as "Tell us anything you think we should know about you." Think of this personal statement as one of your few chances to present yourself as a human being instead of as a bundle of scores and grades. It's the perfect opportunity to distinguish yours from the thousands of other applications on the admissions director's desk. If the personal statement is optional, by all means submit one. Write about any topic at all—as long as you use that topic to convey your personality and your strengths.

Put yourself in the admissions officers' place. They have read lifeless essays about "How I Plan to Help Poor People" and "Why I've Been Interested in Constitutional Law Since Age Three" until they're bleary-eyed. What's pathetic is that three quarters of the people writing those essays did so because they thought that's what the admissions people want. What they really want is an essay that looks at something—*anything*—in a fresh light.

There is no secret formula for writing the perfect application essay. Think about a subject you're interested in, a major accomplishment, a significant experience, or an activity you enjoy, and tell about it—sincerely, concisely, and straightforwardly. If you want to use humor, fine; just make sure it's infallible. In short—and this is difficult—do what comes naturally, and chances are that it will work.

You'd be surprised at the subjects successful candidates write about. Their love of gourmet cooking. ("My wife got an excellent recipe for duck flambé that way," reported the dean of admissions at Yale.) Why they majored in bioethics. What they learned from a summer in Eastern Europe, or ten years as a nurse.

There's no need to be apologetic, but if your candidacy has a weak point that you think could be put into perspective by further elaboration, go ahead. Bad college grades could appear in a new light to an admissions officer who's read an essay about the student's Appalachian childhood or a death in the family during sophomore year. The director of admissions at one large state school recalls that the best essay he's ever seen was an explanation of the applicant's arrest record, which stemmed from politically inspired civil disobedience.

If you have pressing personal reasons for wanting to become a lawyer, tell them, but be aware that you're treading on ground where clichés lie hidden like land mines. And admissions officers approach lofty plans, as outlined in application essays, with considerable skepticism. Experience has shown them that the noblest intention has a tendency to fall by the wayside when it comes time to find a job.

Unfortunately, the same essay might not do for every application. Some schools ask specific questions, and substituting a preformulated answer (the way some politicians do) doesn't go over very well. If there's a space limitation, stick with it. They might not care if you're five words over the maximum, but an additional two pages is out of bounds.

The Recommendations

Letters of recommendation are another way for you to add a dimension to your flat numerical qualifications. The right ones can substantially improve your admissions chances.

Who should write your recommendations? Many schools make it clear that they want professors and only professors, unless you've been out of school for a long time. In that case, think of the teachers who are most familiar with you and your work. Good recommendations, from the admissions committee's point of view, are specific. They talk about the student's strengths, accomplishments, and individual projects; they compare the student to his or her classmates; and they give an insight into the student's choice of major and courses. It helps if the law school knows the professors and their "recommendation history." It really helps if the professors know the law school enough to outline exactly why you'd be a good student there—and how you compare to other students who've gone there from your college in the past.

In cases where you're given more flexibility as to who can write the recommendations, follow your imagination. But don't lose sight of the fact that probable academic performance in law school is the crux of most admissions decisions. If you ask an employer to write for you, he or she should stress that you're a quick learner and function well under pressure, not that you're terrific with the switchboard.

If someone seems reluctant to agree to write a recommendation for you, by all means take the hint. If you press the point, you will probably end up with a letter that is at best unenthusiastic and at worst downright negative.

And always remember that someone who doesn't know you well isn't going to be able to write the kind of recommendation that can really help. The municipal judge who happens to be your father's golf buddy, the boss at your summer job who never saw your work, the famous lecturer to whom you were a name on a class list—all of them are better left alone when it comes time to line up a recommendation. If you're required to get a recommendation from a dean who's never seen your face, make an appointment to talk to the person—and bring along a list of your activities and achievements.

When a school specifies that a maximum of two recommendations is preferred and there's nothing extraordinary about your circumstances, send only two. You may be lucky enough to have more than two good possibilities. If so, pick the two best people, or have your prelaw adviser or college dean select the two best recommendations after you've arranged to have several letters placed in your official undergraduate file. (Law schools prefer that you not see the recommendations after they've been written.) Law school admission decisions are not made on the basis of the sheer volume of your application materials, and where instructions are explicit and unambiguous, it pays to follow them.

Interviews

Remember all those hours you spent in college admissions offices trying to make your summer job behind the deep fryer at Burger King sound meaningful? You probably don't have to go through that again. Most law schools don't require interviews, and most won't even give you one if you ask for it.

That's a relief, but it's also scary. It implies that the law schools are interested only in whether or not you can cut the academic mustard, not the kind of person you are. That's true of some. Others simply don't have the time or personnel to speak to thousands of applicants.

The well-known law schools do reject a number of *summa cum laude* types on the grounds of blah and/or abrasive personalities. They form that impression from the essay and recommendations, not from an interview.

If *you* have questions you want to ask, many schools will arrange for you to speak to someone, often a student representative. The discussion will hardly ever have any bearing on your admissions chances—although openly derogatory comments about the school are usually not wise.

Extracurriculars and Employment

Law school applications typically ask about your nonacademic activities and your employment history. An impressive roster of extracurriculars or a strong work record can work in your favor, especially if you're on the borderline for admission.

Extracurriculars or community activities are particularly likely to carry positive weight if you have excelled at them and/or held a leadership position. The mere fact that you belonged to a club or organization doesn't tell a law school much about your commitment, energy, or capabilities, so take advantage of this opportunity to summarize the exact nature and extent of your out-of-the-classroom accomplishments.

Similarly, if you've had a job that has been particularly challenging, taught you a lot, consumed much of your time during college, occupied you since your college graduation, or had any other notable aspects, don't leave the admissions people guessing; tell them.

Usually, the application form invites you to attach additional pages if necessary. You may want to do so to explain your extracurricular or work background fully—or you may decide to save those details for your personal statement.

Other Factors: Diversity

Most law schools receive applications from so many clearly qualified students that they can afford to be choosy, not only about which are the best qualified (in the limited sense of grades and scores), but also about which would make the school a more stimulating place. To an extent that varies widely from school to school, the admissions people try to assemble a group that's diverse in background, interests, and experience. If you're lucky, your application may gain a bit of strength just because you're different from most other candidates (all the more reason not to package yourself as the typical law school applicant you might think they want). Of course, being unusual is never enough in itself to get you in.

Some of the criteria for evaluating diversity bear further examination.

Women

In 1963, less than 4 percent of the students in ABA-approved law schools were women. Today, that proportion has risen to 43 percent. Things have come a long way, and applications from women will probably continue to climb.

Some law schools are still actively seeking to increase their female enrollments. They recruit women applicants (by sending representatives to women's colleges, for example) and try to talk those they accept into matriculating.

But fewer and fewer schools are giving special consideration to women in the admissions process. In part, this is because women are close to half of the applicant pool anyway; in part, it is due to the fact that as women's undergraduate and work experiences become more similar to men's, it becomes easier to evaluate their candidacy according to traditional standards.

If a school welcomes an older woman who has interrupted her education to raise a family and excel at volunteer work, you can bet it is rewarding something other than her gender. If anything, traditionally female pursuits tend to be undervalued by most admissions committees. So if people tell you, "How nice that you got into Harvard Law School, but of course it's so easy for a woman," they are off-base.

Racial and Ethnic Minorities

As recently as 1979, members of minority groups constituted just 8 percent of students at ABA-approved schools. But with rapid gains in the late 1980s, minority group students now make up 15 percent of the law school population.

Since the Supreme Court's decision in the *Bakke* case, admissions programs in public institutions that set aside a definite number of places for nonwhite students have been ruled unconstitutional. However, the *Bakke* decision did *not* dictate that race can't be taken into account in the admissions process.

Many schools are taking affirmative action measures within the context of a standard two-step admissions process. At these schools, most minority students—like most applicants in general—fall into the category of those who are neither clear "accepts" nor clear "rejects." Their applications are held in a pool for further consideration of all aspects of their candidacy. One of those aspects is the opportunity they offer the school and the profession for racial and ethnic diversity.

Some schools have separate special admissions programs, open to disadvantaged students and/or those who will add diversity to the student body. Still other schools admit, say, half of the class solely on the basis of grades and board scores, and the other half on the basis of a host of factors ranging from extracurricular accomplishments to work experience to race and ethnic group.

Amid the confusion, one thing is clear: most law schools are willing to look beyond LSATs and GPAs, especially when judging students who have lacked the privileges that come with being white and upper middle class. (This makes perfect sense, since a strictly number-based approach is probably unfair to *any* group of applicants, but particularly to those who many believe are systematically disadvantaged by biases in standardized testing.)

So if you've had to overcome significant obstacles in your life—

including but not restricted to those arising from your racial or ethnic background—it's likely that the law school admissions committees will evaluate your credentials accordingly. They *will* evaluate your credentials, though. No one who's considered unable to do the work is going to be accepted by a law school, no matter what his or her background is.

Disabled Students

Federal law dictates that no law school may discriminate on the basis of handicap. This does not mean, however, that law schools have to engage in affirmative action to boost their enrollment of disabled students, although some of them seem to be doing so.

Almost every school seeking diversity gives special consideration to applicants who show evidence of having overcome significant disadvantages, and if you're disabled, you can certainly fall into that category. The important word is *overcome;* since few schools will welcome you on the basis of your disability itself, you want to portray yourself as a highly motivated person who has (to some degree) triumphed over adversity. Use the essay to present yourself in a positive light. Of course, if your disability has caused significant weaknesses in your record, you might want to discuss them.

Your biggest obstacle to admission will probably be paternalistic admissions officers who are concerned that you won't be able to handle the work and the environment. Let these people know that you've been functioning successfully in other contexts, including (most importantly) other academic contexts. Some people might tell you that paternalism is so rampant that you shouldn't even mention your disability if it won't appear from other elements of your application, and you may wish to follow that advice. But there's no question that presented properly—and given a reasonably enlightened admissions committee—your disability can be regarded favorably.

Some disabilities may prevent you from complying with the standard admissions requirements. If that's the case, contact the school and describe your situation. Many schools are willing to be flexible. Special versions of the LSAT are available for students with certain disabilities; contact LSAS directly to make arrangements. The scores on these tests may not be readily comparable to regular scores, and some students may not be able to take the LSAT at all, so by all means ask the schools to which you're applying whether they'll waive the LSAT requirement.

Use the information in this book and from other sources to apply to schools that are reasonably receptive to students with your disability. As you apply, keep in mind what's approaching down the road. If you're accepted to more than one school, you should ask each one for the addresses or phone numbers of recent students with the same disability as yours, contact the on-campus disabled students' organization if there is one, and definitely try to check out the administrators and facilities in person—all with the aim of choosing the school that's best equipped for your needs and/or that has the administration most willing to make any adaptations you need. Once you're admitted, it's time to tone down the message of how capable and adaptable you are and focus on anything the school has to provide to make your life there livable.

After you've chosen a school, present the administrators with a *specific* list of necessary structural modifications and support services in plenty of time so everything will be in place when you arrive. If you've carefully chosen a school that's responsive to you, you should fully expect them to build ramps, alter the locations of classes and other programs, help you arrange for readers, note-takers, or interpreters, or whatever.

Diversity of Undergraduate Schools

Law school administrators are fond of boasting that students from hundreds of different colleges attend their schools. Such a claim suggests that a law school is in great demand, and promises an interesting atmosphere. A degree from an unusual college can be a small plus—in some cases.

Unfortunately, if you're coming from a college with a weak reputation or none at all, that can work against you. You're going to be an unknown factor in comparison to applicants from highly regarded colleges that have been feeding into that law school for years. A valedictorian from Nowhere U often has a harder time getting into Somewhere Law than does a so-so Ivy Leaguer.

If you're applying to the law school affiliated with your undergraduate school, you might find things harder yet. Many private law schools are besieged by applications from their own campuses, and in order to avoid a totally inbred student body they have to reject much of the homegrown product. Even so, you'll find huge numbers of Yalies at Yale Law, Harvard grads at Harvard, Stanford alums at Stanford, etc.

Geographic Diversity

Most private law schools like to enroll students from as many different places as possible. If you're from a remote locale like South Dakota or Wyoming, you'll add variety to an East Coast law school, and that might help your admissions chances a bit.

On the other hand, most state-supported schools are required by their friendly state legislators to give a substantial preference to state residents. Some of these places—like Berkeley, Michigan, and Virginia—are among the most sought-after law schools in the country. If you're a resident of the state, your application will get a big boost (and you'll qualify for lower tuition, too). If you're an out-of-stater, you'll have to compete with everyone else in your category for as few as 10 to 20 percent of the seats. State schools usually have a double admissions standard, pure and simple.

Does It Help to Take Time Off?

Another kind of diversity that law schools look for is what's known in the jargon as life experience. Having pharmacists, home-makers, airplane pilots, and psychiatrists in the classroom, in addition to just-out-of-college types, makes it more interesting for everybody. The law schools find that older students are often better motivated and have a healthy sense of perspective about the educational process. More than a third of law school applicants are over 25. So don't be intimidated about competing with applicants several (or many) years your junior.

Don't make the mistake of thinking that taking time off automatically improves your admissions chances, though. It all depends on what you have done with that time and how well, and on what you and others have to say about it when you're applying. Admissions committees know that older does not necessarily mean wiser.

There's a difference between someone who's drifting from

graduate school to law school for lack of anything better to do and someone who wrote a brilliant sociology master's thesis and is now looking for a more pragmatic approach to social problems. Similarly, someone who took a paralegal job because it seemed like what the law schools look for is in a different category from someone who pursued a genuine interest in the workings of a certain branch of the law. Make sure that your essay and recommendations let the law schools know which category you fall into— the latter, one hopes.

If you've already been out of college for a while, take stock of all your activities—graduate school, jobs, family life, hobbies—and try to tie as many of them as possible to your interest in law. However, if you can't think of any connection whatsoever, don't force it; law schools know that many adults want to enter the profession for money, upward mobility, or a change of pace, and they won't be fooled by a preposterous essay. In that case, just use your postcollege activities to show how directed, persevering, bright, responsible, and interesting you are.

If you're in college now and decide to take time off before law school, should you apply beforehand and defer admission, or should you wait until you're ready to go? In general, it's better to get the agony of the application procedure over as soon as possible. If you get into a school where you think you'll be happy, you can usually have them hold your place for a year or two (although holding places in more than one school is verboten), and then you can relax with the sense of a job well done. If you don't get in where you'd hoped, you can almost always reapply without prejudice, and in the meantime, you've gained a realistic sense of what you're up against.

One of the best reasons for applying while you're a senior in college is that the professors you need to write recommendations for you are on the spot—and they still remember you. So if you decide for whatever reason to delay applying, at the very least ask some of your teachers to write recommendations now and put them in your permanent file.

A stint in the "real world" can give you a competitive edge on getting into the law school of your choice. Whether or not you need that edge will become clear if you apply while you're still in college.

Family Ties

Some law schools give a slight edge to applicants whose relatives attended (or are attending) the same school or university. If there's a line on the application form for this information, and you have a family connection, be sure to fill it in—but connections alone aren't going to get you admitted anywhere.

A Question of Balance

In thinking about the individual elements that make up your admissions profile, don't forget that you'll be judged on the basis of the whole picture. Several strong factors can outweigh one or two weak ones.

Figure out what your prime assets are, and emphasize them as much as possible. If your grades were iffy because you were always at sports practice, write an essay about your extracurriculars. If you were a star in only one course, have that teacher write one of your recommendations even if the subject seems totally irrelevant to your major and to law.

Above all, don't waste too much time worrying about a liability that's a fait accompli. Just do the best you can with the raw material at hand.

Prevarication, Dissimulation, and Mendacity

Doing the best with the raw material does *not* mean substituting other raw material.

Strangely enough, considering that we're talking about a profession dedicated to upholding the law, many law school hopefuls lie on their applications. They try to get "ringers" to take the LSAT for them, they misrepresent their awards and activities, they forge recommendations, and they stretch the truth in any other way that occurs to them.

One word about cheating: don't. You think these admissions people have been in the business for years but don't know when an application's not kosher? If you're caught—and you probably will be—you'll become an untouchable. No law school will ever give you the time of day. It's not worth it.

The Wait

As winter pushes on toward spring, the sun begins to get brighter, the birds migrate northward—and law school applicants start visiting their mailboxes ten times a day.

If you're tearing your hair out wondering why it's taking the admissions committees four months to decide whether they want you, look at it this way: no news is good news. If you were a definite "no way," they would have let you know much sooner.

When the letters start arriving, law school applicants engage in a solemn tribal ritual of feeling each envelope carefully before opening it. Thin usually means thumbs down, thick usually means thumbs up.

If yours is a thin one, remind yourself of how many well-qualified people were competing to get into that place. Whether you get into a given law school often has little to do with whether you can, or will, get a good legal education and become a good lawyer. Worse things can happen than going to your "safety school," which is probably a perfectly good school in its own right. And if worse things do happen, and your safety wasn't enough of a safety, there's always a chance to plan your applications better next year—or reconsider the whole law school issue.

If a thick envelope turns up in your mailbox, congratulations! If you get more than one thick one, however, you have a problem—not the kind of problem you'll get much sympathy for, but a problem all the same. You'll have to rehash your entire research process, trying to remember why you were attracted to these schools in the first place. If you didn't have the time or money before, definitely try to visit the schools now. Then weigh the advantages and disadvantages of each (remembering that academics and job placement will probably be the most crucial factors once you get there), and choose the school with the most pros and the fewest cons.

If you get on the waiting list, you're in a tough position. You may not find out until late summer—or early September—whether there's going to be room for you. Sometimes a phone call to the school will give you a clearer idea of your chances. Indeed, though this is risky, a series of persistent but *extremely polite* letters and phone calls about your desire to attend the school can sometimes succeed in getting you in, particularly if you can point out some new honors or accomplishments you've achieved since the application was filed. But rather than counting unhatched chickens, it's shrewd to make contingency plans and pay your deposit somewhere else.

Transferring

There's a chance that this isn't your first law school application season but your second. If you're trying to transfer, you're in a distinctly unenviable position. Most law schools have little room for transfer students; the ones that have more, due to a high attrition rate, probably aren't the kinds of places where you'd want to go. And even if you manage to get admitted somewhere as a transfer, you might encounter difficulties when you try to transfer course credits or get admitted to the law review.

If you're married to someone at a law school 3,000 miles from yours, you stand a good chance of getting in as a transfer. And if you have a sterling first-year law school record, you may be able to make a move up the ladder of law school prestige. But only masochists would want to put themselves through the admissions wringer more than once. The first time around, try to find someplace where you'll be able to stick it out for the full three years.

4
Paying for It

Unless you have a sizable trust fund, a spouse who's an oil mag-
nate, or very understanding parents, you're probably going to have
some trouble paying for law school. Some schools are cheaper
than others, and residents' tuition at state schools is often the
cheapest of all. But no matter where you go, chances are you
won't be able to get through three or four years without help—
especially since annual tuition hikes are virtually guaranteed.

Scholarships and Grants

Most law schools don't have money to throw around. The cost
of providing a legal education is rising all the time, especially with
the growing emphasis on clinical programs. Economic troubles
have caused many schools' endowments to shrink even as op-
erating costs rise. There isn't much left over to hand out to
students.

It can't hurt to ask, though. Applying for financial aid will
almost never affect your admission chances.

Some law schools are relatively generous with financial aid. If
your academic and personal credentials are particularly impressive,
there are some schools that will shower you with money to entice
you to come, without regard to the size of your bank account.
And if you really need assistance in order to be able to attend,
just about any school will make it its business to help you out.

But in all likelihood, only a fraction of your expenses (at the most) will be covered by scholarships and grants. "Gift aid" is the hardest kind of financial aid to get. To meet the bulk of your costs, you'll probably have to rely on jobs and loans.

Work

Most students work for pay during all or part of their law school years. During the full-time academic term, law school officials discourage first-years from working at all and frown on upper-level students working more than twenty hours a week. But part-time jobs remain a common feature of the full-time law school experience. Some schools have formal work-study programs, and others provide a few research posts, teaching assistantships, or jobs in the school offices and library to help students make ends meet. Second- and third-year students often find off-campus clerkships that are profitable financially as well as providing experience and future employment connections.

How about summer employment? At most schools, students have some trouble finding law-related jobs for the summer after their first year. The story for the second summer is different; that's the time when many employers are eager to give law students a "trial run" to see whether they deserve a permanent job offer. "Summer associates" are often paid at the going rate for beginning lawyers, which at some firms is high indeed.

Still, working a few afternoons a week or during the summer probably isn't going to pay all the bills, particularly at a private school with high tuition. Working is the hardest way of financing your education, and if you do too much of it, your course work (and your sanity) may suffer.

Another possibility is to reverse the usual full-time school, part-time work formula. As discussed in Chapter 1, being an evening student brings with it a host of challenges, not the least of which is finding the energy to concentrate on courses at the end of the day.

Loans

Loans are a lot easier than working. Unfortunately, they have an annoying tendency of having to be repaid. Some people will tell you not to worry about that, because you're sure to make a fortune as soon as you graduate. But if your dream is to open a bilingual legal clinic in the barrio or launch your own practice from scratch, being $60,000 in debt could put a damper on your plans.

Many law schools have loan money of their own available, often at very attractive interest rates. But these funds are limited, with many students competing for the same pot of gold. It's rare for a law school to be able to meet all of a student's borrowing needs out of its own funds.

The federal government provides some of the most advantageous and readily accessible loans you are likely to find. There are several different federal loan programs. Perkins loans are administered by school financial aid offices, have a very favorable interest rate, and are limited to people found to be exceptionally needy. Stafford loans are also need-based but available to a broader range of applicants than Perkins loans and have a higher interest rate. The Supplemental Loans for Students (SLS) program awards loans regardless of need. However, unlike the other two federal programs, interest on SLS loans starts to accrue while you're still in school (although some lenders will allow you to wait until graduation to pay the accrued interest), and the interest rate is higher. Parents of dependent students are eligible for PLUS loans, on essentially the same terms as SLS loans.

To find out more about the Stafford, SLS, and PLUS programs, go to any bank, savings and loan, or credit union and ask. Many of them act as lenders. The law schools themselves generally don't grant these types of loans, but they will probably be willing to refer you to a lender that does.

Government loan policies are subject to change, so be sure to get up-to-date information. Information is available from the Federal Student Aid Information Center, P.O. Box 84, Washington, DC 20044, and at many schools and public libraries.

Some states have established their own financial aid programs that are open to law students. Ask about these, too.

An alternative route to loan dollars is through the Law School Admission Services folks, who have established a program called Law Access to channel loans to law students. You can get details from LSAS at Box 2500, Newtown, PA 18940.

Commercial education loans, not guaranteed by the government, are offered by many private lenders. Check all the terms carefully; they can vary widely and are usually far less desirable than those the government offers.

The Financial Aid Process: How It Works

The best place to start your quest for financial support is at the financial aid offices of the schools where you're applying. The people there are in the business of distributing money, and it's their job to help you.

Many law school financial aid programs require you to fill out a standardized "need analysis" form, such as the Graduate and Professional School Financial Aid Service (GAPSFAS) form, the Financial Aid Form (FAF), or the Family Financial Statement (FFS). For additional information about these forms, you can write to: GAPSFAS, P.O. Box 23900, Oakland, CA 94623; FAF, College Scholarship Service, P.O. Box 6300, Princeton, NJ 08541; and FFS, American College Testing Program, 2201 North Dodge Street, P.O. Box 168, Iowa City, IA 52243. These forms require you to provide extensive financial information about yourself, your spouse, and your parents. The need analysis company then runs the form through a computer and comes up with a standardized financial profile that can be compared easily to that of any other applicant. After the analysis is sent to the individual law school, it's up to the school to decide whether to offer you aid, and if so, what kind and how much.

Typically, once it has received your completed application for financial aid, the school will calculate your cost of attending the school (including tuition, fees, books, transportation, and living expenses). It will also determine your expected family contribution—that is, the amount that you (and your spouse and/or parents, if applicable) will be expected to contribute to your own education. The family contribution figure takes into account such factors as income, assets, debts and other financial obligations, number of family members, and unusual medical or dental expenses. The school then computes your level of financial need by subtracting the family contribution amount from your cost of attending the school. (By the way, the need-based federal loan programs use a similar formula, and you will probably have to fill out a separate application form if you want to receive any federal loans.)

Finally, if you're lucky, the school will offer you a financial aid "package," consisting of some combination of loans, work-study funds, and/or scholarships or grants. The terms of the package are *not* written in stone. If you feel that you have special circumstances that weren't properly recognized, you can ask the school to reconsider its financial aid offer.

Other Places to Look

Many law school applicants don't realize that they might be eligible for specialized scholarship and loan programs that are administered by various private groups throughout the country. Although the applications for these programs are often time-consuming, and there may be many applicants and relatively few awards to go around, you just might be the one to win the jackpot. Possible sources to explore include state, county and local bar associations; fraternities and sororities; clubs, community organizations, and civic groups; foundations and charitable organizations; religious and ethnic societies; and employers, trade associations, and labor unions. Directories of these types of programs are available at public libraries and career counseling offices.

Disadvantaged and minority students have access to a variety of funding sources. One of the best-known programs is the Council on Legal Education Opportunity, 1800 M Street, NW, Suite 160, South Lobby, Washington, DC 20036. Scholarships are also available from the Earl Warren Legal Training Program, c/o NAACP Legal Defense and Educational Fund, 99 Hudson Street, Suite 1600, New York, NY 10013; Puerto Rican Legal Defense Fund, 99 Hudson Street, 14th floor, New York, NY 10013; Mexican American Legal Defense and Educational Fund, 634 South Spring Street, 11th floor, Los Angeles, CA 90014; and the Indian Fellowship Program, U.S. Department of Education, 400 Maryland Avenue, SW, Room 2177, Mail Stop 6335, Washington, DC 20202.

Veterans benefits are also worth looking into, if you're eligible.

Declarations of Independence

As you go about trying to prove how impoverished you are to the law schools, the government, a private scholarship foundation, or whatever, you probably won't want to count in your spouse's or parents' income and assets. That isn't as easy as it seems.

For need-based federal loans, your spouse will automatically be included in the calculation of your expected family contribution. So will your parents, unless you're classified as "independent." You will be considered independent if you are 24 or older by December 31 of the academic year in which you'll be receiving aid; you are a military veteran or a ward of the court; or you have legal dependents other than a spouse. You can also qualify as independent if you are not claimed as an exemption on either parent's income tax return for the year during which you apply for aid. Many law school financial aid offices use a similar definition of "independence." In unusual circumstances, you might be able to argue successfully for independent status even if you don't meet these criteria.

It can be very frustrating to discover that you are not considered independent when you fully intend to pay for law school yourself. (Even if you are found to be independent, some schools will expect your parents to kick in a certain amount—although they will usually let you borrow additional money to cover the parental portion.) If your parents want to see you get your diploma, they may have no choice but to ante up in accordance with the judgment of potential financial aid providers.

The Early Bird

Given that there's a limited amount of money around for people in your position, it pays to apply early for whatever financial aid options you're considering.

Financial aid applications take a long time to fill out and a long time to be processed. Start gathering information well in advance from a career counseling office and/or law school financial aid offices.

Many law schools have special deadlines for financial aid applications. Even if they don't, it helps to get your bid in as soon as possible. Waiting until the last minute is easier, but isn't the chance for even a little extra cash worth the trouble?

5

How to Use This Book

A Word About the Schools in This Book

Only schools that have received American Bar Association accreditation are included in this book. The ABA seal of approval guarantees that the facilities, course offerings, and faculty meet certain minimal standards.

Even more important, going to an ABA-accredited school is usually the only way to become a lawyer. In the overwhelming majority of circumstances, you're not qualified to practice law just because you've got a law degree. Rules for admission to the bar differ considerably from state to state, but almost everywhere, you have to pass the state's bar exam, give character references, and present evidence of graduation from an ABA-approved school. Although there are exceptions to the ABA requirement (for example, the state of California allows graduates of some non-ABA schools to become lawyers), you're limiting your future options if you go to a law school that doesn't have the ABA sanction.

There's one other important form of national accreditation: membership in the Association of American Law Schools. All AALS schools are ABA-approved, but not all ABA-approved schools are AALS members. AALS membership is primarily important because member schools often refuse to recognize work done at non-AALS institutions when they're evaluating applications from transfer applicants or from candidates for graduate law degrees.

This book covers 112 of the 176 ABA-accredited law schools in the country. Criteria for a school's appearance in these pages include its size, the extent to which it seeks a national student body, and the availability of information about it. Neither the inclusion nor the exclusion of a school constitutes a judgment on its quality.

Interpreting the Statistics

At the beginning of each school description, you'll find a list of statistical information. You can acquire useful information from these facts and figures. Just remember to look to other sources—such as the text of the school description—to flesh out the statistical skeleton.

In most cases, the statistics were provided by the schools' administrations and were compiled during the 1992–1993 school year. In some instances where it was not possible to obtain current statistics, figures from a previous academic year were used. Many of the data provided will change annually; contact the schools directly for the most recent and complete information.

Throughout the statistics, the abbreviation *NA* indicates that information was not available.

Address: The mailing address provided is the one to use for requesting admissions materials. A simple postcard is the best way to request a catalog, application, and financial aid information.

Phone: The phone number of the admissions office can be useful for specific, important questions. Don't use it if you can possibly write instead.

Degrees: Many law schools offer more than one degree. The J.D. (juris doctor) is the basic professional degree, typically earned after three years of full-time or four years of part-time study. The LL.M. is a master's degree in law, awarded to people who already have a J.D. and popular for professional specialization or preparation for law teaching. LL.M. programs in specialized fields are indicated as such. The J.S.D. (or S.J.D.) is an advanced research degree, similar to a Ph.D. The M.C.L., a master's degree in comparative law, is usually geared toward graduates of foreign law schools, as is also true of some LL.M. programs. Joint degree programs, which usually award two degrees in less time than it would take to pursue both individually, are offered by many law schools in conjunction with other graduate and professional schools. Among the most common are J.D./M.B.A. (master's in business administration) and J.D./M.P.A. (master's in public administration). Many schools will allow you to devise your own joint degree; ask to be sure. (Degrees other than the ones discussed above are explained where they appear.)

Median LSAT: These figures, computed on the basis of the scores of the entering class, will give you some idea of how you measure up to a school's admission standards. But other factors in your application may substantially affect your candidacy, and keep in mind that there are always as many people below the median (sometimes far below) as above it.

Some schools have provided scores based on the old 10–48 scoring system; others have provided scores based on the current scale of 120–180; and some have provided both. For a useful perspective on a given school's LSAT standards, find the school's median score on the following charts, which show the approximate percentage of all test-takers falling below each score:

LSAT Scores: old scale

Score	Percentile	Score	Percentile
48	99.5	28	32.9
46	98.3	26	24.9
44	96.1	24	18.6
42	92.3	22	13.7
40	86.5	20	9.7
38	79.6	18	6.7
36	70.0	16	4.4
34	61.2	14	2.9
32	51.3	12	1.8
30	41.8	10	0.0

LSAT Scores: new scale

Score	Percentile	Score	Percentile
180	99.9	148	41.0
178	99.8	146	32.3
176	99.5	144	26.2
174	99.1	142	20.0
172	98.4	140	15.1
170	97.6	138	10.9
168	96.0	136	7.5
166	93.9	134	4.7
164	90.9	132	3.3
162	87.7	130	2.1
160	82.9	128	1.2
158	77.8	126	0.7
156	70.7	124	0.4
154	64.2	122	0.2
152	55.7	120	0.0
150	47.7		

Median GPA: As with the median LSAT, remember that there are always plenty of people admitted who fall below the median. The figure given here is the median for all students in the entering class, calculated on a 4.0 scale.

Applicants accepted: This figure represents the percentage of applicants who were offered a spot in the entering class. Not all of them enrolled.

Transfer students: Often an average or a representative range. Annual transfer acceptances are shown first. The number of transfer applicants, where available, is shown after a diagonal slash.

Law enrollment: The total of all students—full- and part-time—pursuing any legal degree. The J.D. enrollment, which includes those getting joint degrees, is shown separately, where available, for schools that offer more than one legal degree.

Campus enrollment: This is the sum of all full- and part-time, undergraduate, graduate, and professional students, in all the divisions and schools at this campus. Many campuses are very diffuse, and what is in principle a unified institution may be in fact an aggregate of semiautonomous parts. The contact between law students and others is usually slight but can vary significantly from school to school.

Part time: The percentage of J.D. students who attend the school less than full time—for example, in a four-year evening session. Part-time programs often have different admissions criteria, application deadlines, tuition and financial aid policies, course requirements, etc.—get full details from the schools.

Women: The percentage of all J.D. candidates who are female. Compare with the national average: 43%.

Minorities: The percentage who are minority group members. The national average for comparison is 15%.

Dorm residents: This figure indicates the portion of the law student population living in any type of university-sponsored housing, on or off campus, including traditional dormitories, university-owned apartments, and married students' housing.

Library: This statistic is given to provide you with a rough idea of the research facilities. The number given includes bound volumes as well as "microform volume equivalents," which is a standardized method of counting publications on microfilm and microfiche. Increased reliance on computerized legal research services like LEXIS and WESTLAW means that the library resources may actually be better than they appear from this statistic.

Student-faculty ratio: This figure includes only full-time faculty. Keep in mind that some schools also have a large number of part-time adjunct instructors.

Tuition: The tuition and required fees are for a full-time J.D. student. Where costs differ for in-state residents and out-of-state students, both are given.

Financial aid: This statistic shows what percentage of the student body receives any type of financial aid administered by the school, from a full school-supported scholarship to a government loan that the school helped arrange. A separate figure for the percentage of the student body receiving "gift aid" (scholarship or grant) is given where available.

Apply by: You make things very hard for yourself if you get your application in after the deadline. Chances are that many people just as good as you will get theirs in on time. If the school uses *rolling admissions,* it evaluates applications as soon as they are received; it pays to get yours in early. Earlier deadlines for financial aid applications are provided where available.

Disabled students: Schools were asked to rate the law school's accessibility: fully accessible (all facilities and programs accessible); moderate/full accessibility (not all facilities accessible, but all requested courses, activities, meetings, etc., made accessible by scheduling in accessible locations); moderately accessible (some but not all facilities and programs accessible); or minimally accessible. They were also asked for numbers of students enrolled in a one-year or five-year period who were blind (or visually impaired), deaf (or hearing impaired), wheelchair users, or had other mobility problems (such as crutches).

Placement: This information is provided to give you a general idea of the employment patterns of law students and new graduates from each school. The types of statistics provided differ from school to school.

Compare the percentage of graduates having jobs six months after graduation with the national average of about 86%. (Each school's figure is based on responses to a questionnaire that may not have been answered by many of the graduates.)

Among the other figures provided are the percentage of students in each class with noncredit legal jobs during the academic year, and the percentage of students in each class who have lined up a summer job (for first- and second-year students) or permanent job by the time school ends in the spring.

The number of employers sending one or more recruiters to campus in a given year is an excellent indication of how easily job leads will come to you, but at some schools employers are allowed to prescreen and interview only the top students. The distribution of the recruiting employers according to geography and type of enterprise is given where available. Bear in mind that many schools provide some access to employers through means other than on-campus interviews, like regional recruitment conferences and letters from employers inviting direct applications.

The geographical distribution of the graduating class's first jobs is a clue to where a certain school's degree is most marketable. The geographical categories most often used in this book are as follows: New England (Connecticut, Maine, Massachusetts, New Hampshire, Rhode Island, and Vermont); Middle Atlantic (New Jersey, New York, and Pennsylvania); East North Central (Illinois, Indiana, Michigan, Ohio, and Wisconsin); West North Central (Iowa, Kansas, Minnesota, Missouri, Nebraska, North Dakota, and South Dakota); South Atlantic (Delaware, District of Columbia, Florida, Georgia, Maryland, North Carolina, South Carolina, Virginia, and West Virginia); East South Central (Alabama, Kentucky, Mississippi, and Tennessee); West South Central (Arkansas, Louisiana, Oklahoma, and Texas); Mountain (Arizona, Colorado, Idaho, Montana, Nevada, New Mexico, Utah, and Wyoming); Pacific (Alaska, California, Hawaii, Oregon, and Washington); and Foreign.

To figure out a school's career focus, compare the distribution of jobs taken by the most recent graduating class with the national averages, as computed by the National Association for Law Placement: 60.8% private practice (including firms and solo practice); 12.5% judicial clerkships (one- or two-year apprenticeships with a judge); 11.9% government (federal, state, and local, including prosecutors and public defenders); 7.4% business and industry (including both legal counsel and straight business jobs in corporations, accounting firms, and banks); 2.0% public interest (including federal legal services programs and private nonprofit public interest groups); 1.5% military (usually positions with the Judge Advocate General's Corps, the legal branch of the military); and 1.0% academic employment (some schools also include further academic study under this category). For a given school, job distribution figures may not add up to 100 percent because of rounding, or because of students who didn't fit in any category or didn't report the information.

The data on salaries are for the graduating class's first jobs. Nationwide, the mean salary for 1991 law graduates six months after graduation was $44,300 and the median was $40,000. Some schools have provided salary ranges, reflecting either the range of salaries earned by individual graduates or the range of average salaries for different types of jobs held by graduates.

As another measure of professional preparation, success

rates among new graduates taking the bar exam for the first time are given where available. The statewide average pass rates, shown for the sake of comparison, may differ among schools in the same state, depending on the year for which the school provided its own figures. (By the way, bar exams usually consist of a set of essay questions drawn up by the state's bar admission officials, plus a standardized multiple-choice test known as the multistate exam; many states also require a standardized multiple-choice professional responsibility exam.)

Placement information of a general, nonstatistical nature—such as the characteristics of the school's reputation—is provided in the body of the school description.

The Law Schools: An Inside View

University of Akron School of Law

Address: **Akron, OH 44325**
Phone: **(216) 972-7331**
Degrees: **J.D., J.D./M.B.A.,
J.D./M.P.A., J.D./M. Tax,
J.D./M.U.P. (urban
planning)**
Median LSAT: **34**
Median GPA: **3.1**
Applicants accepted: **26%**
Transfers: **2**
Law enrollment: **605**
Campus enrollment: **30,000**

Part time: **37%**
Women: **39%**
Minorities: **11%**
Dorm residents: **NA**
Library: **210,200**
Student-faculty ratio: **17:1**
Tuition: **$3912 (in-state),
$6872 (out-of-state)**
Financial aid: **66%**
Apply by: **rolling admissions,
April 1 recommended (aid)**

Disabled students: **Moderate/full accessibility.**
Placement: **Approximately 91% employed six to nine months after graduation. Graduates took jobs in East North Central (85%), South Atlantic (4%), Middle Atlantic (4%), West North Central (2%), Mountain (2%), Pacific (1%), East South Central (1%), Foreign (1%). Graduates entered private practice (48%), business (17%), judicial clerkships (15%), government (11%), academic (4%), military (2%), public interest (1%).**

Until 1966 the University of Akron School of Law was a night school. Roughly two thirds of the students are now full-time day students, but the school is still working to improve its reputation and facilities.

When your thoughts turn to America's garden spots, downtown Akron, Ohio, isn't the first thing that comes to mind. At least the law school, which is on the outskirts of the university campus, is close to the downtown office buildings and municipal, county, and federal courts.

Many of the students are already residents of Akron or its environs when they start here. Those who aren't are faced with the ordeal of locating housing, since there is very little university housing for law students. The university is quite helpful, though, and after perusing the law school bulletin board and the local newspaper, most students find an apartment or house nearby or within close commuting distance.

The school is easily accessible by car. The winter weather does present a challenge, but it's rarely insurmountable.

First year consists of required classes, most of them a bit overwhelming in the beginning. The work load is heavy, and students find little time for anything but schoolwork. By the end of the first year, however, most of the pressure has disappeared and a definite student camaraderie has developed.

During second year, there are yet more required core courses, but you can begin to choose from a smattering of electives. The third-year student might have one elective that has only 3 or 4 students in the class, and another course that has 60. Moot court and law review are also sources of course credit.

The Student Bar Association is rated "active" and provides parties throughout the year. It also runs a critique of professors and courses. The other student organizations run the usual gamut, including two law fraternities that conduct programs in legal areas not covered by the curriculum.

Although you'd have a hard time confusing it with Chicago or Boston, the social scene in Akron isn't really bleak. In addition to many theaters and restaurants, the city is home to the Blossom Music Center, which has excellent programs in the summer. Nearby is the Coliseum, for sports events and concerts. The university provides movies, and the performing arts hall, across the street from the law school, sponsors events ranging from Broadway plays to the Ohio Ballet to the Akron Symphony.

The law students can be counted on to provide their own entertainment. Student parties are common. Married and single students intermingle; there is no noticeable distinction between the two groups, just as there is no distinction between younger and older students. There *is* a noticeable difference between the day and night students; different hours of attendance preclude much association between the two.

For second- and third-year students, lawyers put notices on the bulletin board advertising clerkship openings, and the various courts in the city offer numerous employment opportunities. Students often work as research assistants for professors or as student assistants in some of the first-year classes. There are a few clinical programs.

The permanent job situation isn't nearly as promising. One student writes, "The placement office has in the past provided minimal assistance to graduates, but new procedures are being implemented and it appears that the office will be more effective in the near future." The school focuses on preparing people to become practicing attorneys.

The University of Akron is improving with each passing year. In the meantime, it offers a diverse curriculum, a personalized atmosphere, and a convenient choice for area residents planning an Ohio practice.

University of Alabama School of Law

Address: **Box 870382,**
   Tuscaloosa, AL 35487
Phone: **(205) 348-5440**
Degrees: **J.D., LL.M. (tax),**
   M.C.L., J.D./M.B.A.
Median LSAT: **37**
Median GPA: **3.4**
Applicants accepted: **31%**
Transfers: **2**
Law enrollment: **564 (549 J.D.)**

Campus enrollment: **15,000**
Part time: **0**
Women: **36%**
Minorities: **8%**
Dorm residents: **NA**
Library: **302,700**
Student-faculty ratio: **22:1**
Tuition: **$2644 (in-state),**
   $5508 (out-of-state)
Financial aid: **61%**
Apply by: **March 1**

Disabled students: **Fully accessible.**

Placement: **Approximately 65% placed by graduation. Graduates took jobs in East South Central (67%), South Atlantic (6%), West South Central (2%), Middle Atlantic (2%), East North Central (1%), Mountain (1%), Pacific (1%), Foreign (3%), location not known (19%). Graduates entered private practice (51%), judicial clerkships (17%), academic (4%), business (3%), government (3%), military (1%), category not known (21%). Average salary: $36,781.**

For some people, the word *Alabama* calls to mind the Ku Klux Klan, George Wallace standing in the schoolhouse door, and beer-guzzling rednecks. Many of the problems those images suggest are still in need of solution, and U of A Law School is trying to do its part—for instance, by making some effort to increase its enrollment of black students and women. The school also recognizes its responsibility to teach legal theory and produce lawyers who will fill the state's leadership positions. Yet, on a day-to-day level, the school's main goal is to teach the nuts and bolts for the average practitioner, and most of the students are satisfied with the emphasis.

Students here proudly report that the Law Center building, which opened in 1978, is one of the best law school facilities in the nation. The classrooms and study areas are well suited to student needs. The law library has a great layout that makes access to information simple and fast.

The admissions committee is described as "conventional," which means that LSAT and GPA are the all-important letters in the alphabet. Most of the students are Alabamans who intend to practice in Alabama; almost half also did their undergrad work at U of A. Because U of A is not as selective as many other schools, it gets its share of those who are trying law school to see if they like it. An 8 percent attrition rate is not unusual.

Tuscaloosa is strictly a small university town. What cultural and social stimulus the university doesn't provide doesn't exist. Student social life consists largely of intramural sports, present in a wide variety. There's also drinking at bars, drinking at private parties, drinking at law school keg parties and frat parties, and drinking at major events like Homecoming or the Barristers' Ball.

Movie theaters in the area are above average, and the university has a good film society. Musical and dramatic offerings are collegiate-grade, so the connoisseur may be dissatisfied.

Tuscaloosa is well supplied with inexpensive apartments, some within two or three miles of the law school, others less conveniently located. Although Tuscaloosa has a population of only about 75,000, it has the traffic problems of a much larger city. Because the Law Center is located near both the stadium and the coliseum, the school is almost inaccessible during those hours when sports fans (and there are *many* sports fans here) are leaving the games.

The spirit of competition at the law school never overshadows a basic mood of amiable cooperation. Most students are friendly and helpful, and the same goes for the professors. Students say that faculty members range from terrifying to soporific. The Socratic method (a bit watered down) is the method of choice in first-year classes; straightforward lectures predominate in upper-level courses.

Students may gain practical experience in the usual ways. Many are able to find part-time law clerk jobs with Tuscaloosa firms. Some do research for faculty members. Others participate in the law school's clinical programs, which include opportunities to work for the Tuscaloosa County Public Defender and the U.S. attorney in Birmingham, which is about fifty miles away. Judicial clerkships are another possibility.

Instruction in law unique to Alabama is available, but rarely required. Exceptions are evidence and civil procedure courses, where Alabama rules are normally taught alongside prevailing federal guidelines.

The school publishes specialized journals on law and psychology, the legal profession, and taxation, but all three are firmly in the shadow of the *Alabama Law Review*. The moot court program historically has done very well in regional competition.

Students in the top 10 percent of the class and/or on law review can find jobs at some of the nation's most prestigious firms. But the remaining 90 percent of the class does not have an easy time of it. The lower the class rank, the more likely the graduate will be restricted to an Alabama firm, and a smaller firm at that.

Even so, U of A is a solid school in many ways, with expanding opportunities for its graduates. The relatively low tuition makes Alabama a good choice for applicants who know that their future lies in the South—and who can tolerate a university campus oriented toward football and fraternities.

Albany Law School, Union University

Address: **80 New Scotland Ave., Albany, NY 12208**
Phone: **(518) 445-2326**
Degrees: **J.D., J.D./M.B.A., J.D./M.P.A.**
Median LSAT: **157**
Median GPA: **3.27**
Applicants accepted: **40%**
Transfers: **11/26**
Law enrollment: **785**

Campus enrollment: **785**
Part time: **3%**
Women: **45%**
Minorities: **11%**
Dorm residents: **11%**
Library: **406,400**
Student-faculty ratio: **18:1**
Tuition: **$15,595**
Financial aid: **75% (44% gift)**
Apply by: **March 15**

Disabled students: **Moderate/full accessibility. In a five-year period, four blind students and two wheelchair users.**

Placement: **90% employed six months after graduation.**
Approximately 150 employers on campus in one recent year; 80% private firms, 10% government, 5% business, 5% public interest. Graduates took jobs in Middle Atlantic (82%), South Atlantic (9%), New England (7%), Pacific (1%), Foreign (1%), Mountain (.5%). Graduates entered private practice (61%), government (15%), business (8%), judicial clerkships (7%), public interest

(4%), military (2%), academia (.5%). Salary range:
$16,000–$87,000. Median salary: $32,000. Mean salary: $38,789.
New York bar pass rate in a recent year: approximately 85%
(statewide average: 72%).

Albany Law is a sound school in most respects, but it definitely helps if you're a once-and-future New Yorker.

The great majority of Albany's students are from New York State, largely from the counties north of Westchester. In addition, most of the student population attended New York colleges. The curriculum emphasizes New York law.

The good side of all this New Yorkiness is a good pass rate on the fairly difficult New York bar exam. Law firms in Albany and elsewhere in upstate New York love to hire the results of the practical type of education given at Albany Law. So does the state government (the legislature is located two minutes from the school), and part-time jobs and internships during the year are plentiful. The school's Government Law Center should continue to expand opportunities for students interested in government.

Many students remain in Albany, and others secure good positions in Rochester and Syracuse. Prospects for jobs in New York City as well as out of state are a source of concern, but things are improving. In recent years, the placement office has arranged several days of interviews with New York City firms in a Big Apple hotel early in the fall. The Career Center was expanded in the late 1980s, and students describe it as helpful and supportive.

Upstate New York is not known for its lovely climate, but students are quick to point out that Albany Law, located in a suburban setting, is a livable place. Albany State University (around 10,000 students) is close by, making for a good social mix in the city. The Albany College of Pharmacy and the Albany Medical Center and College are also in the neighborhood; although they and Albany Law are affiliated with Union University, the link is in name only since the Union College campus is a half hour away. The law students have no contact with the college whatsoever.

There are a number of drinking establishments that law students frequent and a number that they don't—in case you get tired of the same faces. The law school itself throws parties every couple of weeks, which are all-you-can-drink affairs. In addition, there are the usual lectures, movies, and social events, most of them run by the active Student Bar Association. The SBA has also secured student representation on faculty committees.

Albany Law is a virtual mecca for the athletically minded of both sexes. Men's sports include rugby (bring the first-aid kit), hockey, basketball, and soccer. The women are active in basketball, softball, and coed volleyball. Activities center on the full-size gym located in the heart of the law school. Two recent classes earmarked their class gift for renovations to the structure.

Most of the law students live in apartments within a twenty-minute walk of the school. Clean, inexpensive places to live are fairly easy to come by. An eight-story dorm, which houses over 160 law and medical students in single rooms, is cheap and conveniently located down the block from the law school. Living in Albany is most satisfying if you have a car, but a well-run bus line connects the school with downtown. The food in the cafeteria (which is where everyone relaxes between classes) is decent and inexpensive.

There is a wide range of personalities among Albany students, but a fairly common characteristic is an easygoing attitude about grades. Most students do their work, but if there is a party on the agenda, the books get left behind in the dust. Brownnosing is rare, and throat-cutting unheard of. The school welcomes "nontraditional" students who have worked before going to law school, and there is reportedly a big push to increase the number of minority group students.

There is little division in the student body. Most upperclass students are very willing to help first-years with used books, advice, and outlines.

Typically, freshmen are by far the hardest workers, partly because they're not yet involved in outside activities, but mostly out of fear. (The fear disappears in the upper years, except during job-hunting season.) First-year students usually do thirty to fifty hours of studying a week in addition to their fifteen class hours. Legal research and writing and one other freshman course are taught in small sections, while the rest are taught in three groups of approximately 100 students each.

Albany offers an unusually large number of opportunities for oral advocacy practice. The school conducts a moot court competition open to all second-years and a third-year trial competition that is very popular. Teams are selected for a host of intramural competitions in such categories as international law moot court, constitutional law moot court, and trial skills.

The quality of the professors runs the gamut from good to terrible. There are only two or three stars, but with a little juggling you can manage to avoid the clinkers and still take the courses you want. The curriculum is said to be strong in procedure and tax; students point to environmental law as a weak point.

The student body is generally bright, but the admissions standards are not frighteningly competitive. Word has it that Albany seems especially willing to admit someone with high boards and low grades or vice versa.

Albany Law is one of the oldest schools in the nation, with many prominent alumni. The school is now enjoying a rebirth, thanks to some well-chosen curriculum changes. Employers who hire Albany grads for the first time are often surprised to find them as competent as graduates of "national" schools. As the word gets around, the big firms in New York City and Washington should open their doors to even more Albany students.

Meanwhile, if practicing in New York State appeals to you, Albany is one place where you can still live like a human being while obtaining your legal education.

American University, Washington College of Law

Address: **4400 Massachusetts Ave., NW, Washington, DC 20016**

Phone: **(202) 885-2606**

Degrees: **J.D., LL.M. (international law), J.D./M.B.A., J.D./M.S. (justice), J.D./M.A. (international affairs)**

Median LSAT: **160**

Median GPA: **3.3**

Applicants accepted: **24%**

Transfers: **15/140**

Law enrollment: **1232 (1063 J.D.)**

Campus enrollment: **10,500**

Part time: **25%**

Women: **48%**

Minorities: **21%**

Dorm residents: **4%**

Library: **318,300**

Student-faculty ratio: **28:1**

Tuition: **$16,990**

Financial aid: **70% (35% gift)**

Apply by: **March 1, February 15 (aid)**

Disabled students: **Fully accessible. In a five-year period, one blind student, two wheelchair users, and one with other mobility problems.**

Placement: **50% of second-years and 65% of third-years employed in legal jobs during the academic year. 50% placed by graduation; 88% employed six months after graduation. 100 employers on campus in one year; 80% private firms, 20% government or public interest. Graduates took jobs in South Atlantic (65%), Middle Atlantic (19%), Pacific (5%), New England (4%), East North Central (2%), West South Central (2%), Mountain (1%), Foreign (1%). Graduates entered private practice (37%), judicial clerkships (25%), government (21%), business (4%), public interest (3%), academic (.5%), unknown (10%). Salary range: $18,000–$97,000. Median salary: $38,000.**

The most important feature of American University's Washington College of Law (WCL) is the fact that it is in Washington, DC. According to T-shirt lore, Virginia is for lovers, Maryland for crabs, and Washington for lawyers. The location is the reason a lot of people come to WCL—that, and the fact that they didn't get into Georgetown or George Washington.

But don't worry about developing a permanent inferiority complex if you enroll here. Although comparisons to other area schools, especially Georgetown, are frequent and not always favorable, WCL students seem happy where they are. Some Georgetown students have been known to advise younger siblings that WCL is a more pleasant place to spend three years.

The popular image of back-stabbing law students is worse than actual conditions anywhere, but probably no place belies it as much as WCL. It is a common practice in the placement office for the first student who meets a job interviewer to give a "scouting report" that tells subsequent interviewees what to expect. The WCL students' approach is to help each other succeed as a group.

It's a small group, which is why that type of approach works. Each of the three first-year daytime sections has about 85 students, as does the one part-time evening section. The professors know their students and are, almost without exception, available after class, during office hours, and sometimes even at social events.

One disadvantage of the intimate class size (aside from the fact that you can't slip in and out of class unnoticed by the professor) is the Peyton Place aura that develops by the end of the first year.

WCL is proud of its feminist roots. The school was founded in 1896 by two women and has been coed from the start. Minority recruiting has increased in recent years. The school's long-standing commitment to social change and liberal activism remains strong, but students with conservative views are also represented, leading to an interesting give-and-take during classroom discussions of policy issues.

Also, the hundred foreign students in the International Studies Program lend the school an international air. They receive LL.M. degrees but often take courses with J.D. students.

The WCL social life is dominated by the Student Bar Association. Each fall, the SBA hosts its annual first-year picnic on the quad, a wide, grassy area surrounded by large oak trees. Recently, the group has been holding fall cookouts on the Virginia estate of a WCL graduate. The SBA also works as an effective liaison between the administration and the student body. Student governance is taken seriously here.

The SBA's social events are supplemented by over twenty specialized student groups catering to every conceivable constituency, including the International Law Society, National Lawyers Guild, Federalist Society, Women's Law Association, Lambda Law Students Association, Christian Legal Fellowship, and the Black Law Students Association.

Although the law school is on the American University campus, there tends to be little interaction between law students and the rest of the student body. As some do attempt to bridge this gap, it may be helpful to note that AU undergrad has a reputation as a haven for pampered Long Island types. The undergraduate population also has an unusually high number of foreign students.

The student center and Boyden Pavilion are the limited options for on-campus dining (the latter is popular for its thick-crust pizza). The pavilion also offers a basketball court, pool, and weight rooms. After morning classes or in the late afternoon, law students reportedly outnumber undergraduates in the recreational facilities.

The university bursar takes your money—lots of it—but the remainder of the law school's administrative work is handled separately from the rest of the university, which is a good thing. Generally, the law administration appears to be sensitive and responsive to student concerns. The law school registrar's office gets particularly high marks from students for its helpfulness and efficiency.

One notable area of contact between the law school and the rest of AU is the joint degree program. The law and international studies combination is particularly strong. In fact, with or without the joint degree, you can get a good education in international law at WCL.

The curriculum is not geared to the law of any particular state and will suffice for any. Pretty much anything one would want or need for a basic legal career is offered at one time or another during one's two years of elective courses (first year consists of the usual required subjects). The school draws on talented local lawyers to teach a host of sophisticated seminars.

WCL has an unusually strong and varied moot court program. The clinical program is excellent. Blessed with three jurisdictions (Maryland, Virginia, and DC) in which students can work, and with traditionally generous allocations of school funds, the clinics turn out litigators who are much better prepared than most new attorneys. Clinical courses include public interest law, women and the law, appellate advocacy, criminal justice, tax, and international human rights. Be forewarned, however, that competition to get into the clinical program is fierce.

WCL is near the northwestern edge of Washington. That means that the campus is beautifully green but is still near the Kennedy Arts Center, national monuments and parks, restaurants, theaters, discos, and the inimitable bars of the Georgetown area. Even more important, it's near government agencies, the Library of Congress, the Supreme Court, and legions of law firms. In recent years, WCL has placed an extraordinarily high percentage of grads in Uncle Sam's employ. The school has been particularly good at taking advantage of the plentiful part-time jobs available nearby.

For years, the price that WCL paid for its excellent location was extremely overcrowded facilities. Fortunately, in the early 1990s the administration gave the official go-ahead for a move to a new building.

The placement office tries hard and with many alums working in DC, lots of job tips roll in. Numerous firms that until recently wouldn't give the time of day to a non-Ivy school are now interviewing and hiring on campus. Although finding work isn't effortless, most students find a good job soon after graduating. The placement office is responding to demands for more assistance to public-interest job-seekers. A fledgling loan repayment assistance program is helping WCL grads who take low-paying public-interest jobs.

While Washington is fascinating, it is also expensive. Housing can be a major source of aggravation, since Washington has been hit by the condominium craze; small apartments are decreasing in number and increasing in price. The best deal is usually a group house; quite a few are usually put up for rent. Prices go down when you venture into Maryland and (especially) Virginia. But public transportation, very good within DC, may be inadequate when you cross the district line, making a car a necessity. Parking on campus is neither cheap nor plentiful, and D.C. traffic is no joy either.

Overall, however, there are fewer and fewer things to complain about at WCL. Its friendly students, small classes, and accessible faculty make it more humane than many schools. And DC is a great town. If it weren't almost a contradiction in terms, one might call WCL a fun law school.

University of Arizona College of Law

Address: **Tucson, AZ 85721**
Phone: **(602) 621-3477**
Degrees: **J.D., J.D./M.B.A.,**
J.D./M.P.A., J.D./Ph.D.
(philosophy, psychology,
economics), J.D./M.A.
(economics)
Median LSAT: **160**
Median GPA: **3.41**
Applicants accepted: **20%**
Transfers: **3–5/30**
Law enrollment: **470**

Campus enrollment: **35,000**
Part time: **0**
Women: **46%**
Minorities: **24%**
Dorm residents: **NA**
Library: **325,000**
Student-faculty ratio: **16:1**
Tuition: **$1590 (in-state),**
$6996 (out-of-state)
Financial aid: **80% (30% gift)**
Apply by: **March 1**

Disabled students: **Fully accessible. In five-year period, two blind students, two deaf, ten wheelchair users, two with other mobility problems.**

Placement: **88% employed six months after graduation. 33% of second-years and 33% of third-years employed in legal jobs during academic year. 50% of first-years, 75% of second-years, and 50% of third-years placed by end of spring term. 50 employers on campus in one year; 60% from Arizona, 10% California, 10% New Mexico, 10% Nevada, 4% Washington, DC, 2% Texas, 2% Utah; 84% private firms, 12% government, 4% legal services. Graduates took jobs in Arizona (70%), California (12%), Nevada (9%), Washington, DC (2%), other (6%). Graduates entered private practice (59%), government (21%), judicial clerkships (16%), business (2%), legal services (2%). Salary range: $22,000–$60,000. Mean salary: $35,968. Arizona bar pass rate: 87% (statewide average: 75%).**

Picture a strong academic community located on a sunny, palm-tree-lined campus in the midst of breathtaking desert and surrounded by four mountain ranges. That's the University of Arizona. Now picture a spacious multimillion-dollar building, opened in 1979, with classrooms surrounding an outdoor brick patio. That's the law school.

The U of A College of Law's setting is a great asset. Many students take advantage of Arizona's varied natural wonders to go hiking, running, biking, skiing, and fishing. Perhaps the greatest advantage of the southwestern surroundings is that everyone—students and locals alike—is very open and friendly. The atmosphere on the university campus, and even in the law offices of downtown Tucson, is casual.

Students report that the academic environment is rigorous, yet collegial. Admission is competitive, but the classroom atmosphere is described as "cooperative and friendly."

The curriculum at U of A is very strong in corporate law, tax law, antitrust, trial practice, torts, remedies, American Indian law, and constitutional law. Environmental, international, employment, and public-interest law are represented in the course offerings.

Class sizes vary from a high of 100 students to 10 students in some upper-level courses. After the first year, all but two classes (Ethics and Evidence) are elective, and every student must take a seminar requiring a substantial paper.

The professors all have scheduled office hours and generally make themselves available to discuss academic and personal matters with students. Student-faculty relations are said to be cordial, open, and relaxed. The focus of the curriculum is national rather than limited to Arizona, and many of the faculty are nationally known.

Students who have completed the prerequisites can get course credit for supervised practice in the offices of public defenders, prosecutors, legal aid and public-interest organizations, and state and federal judges and legislators.

In addition to the established J.D./Ph.D. programs, you can work out a special interdisciplinary graduate program, but be prepared to deal with some red tape. Those not pursuing a joint degree can earn up to six credits toward their law diploma by taking graduate courses elsewhere in the university.

Student groups cover a wide variety of special interests. Recent surges in interest in international and environmental law have resulted in student-sponsored activities in those two fields. Other organized groups include the Minority Law Students Association, Law Women's Association, National Lawyers Guild, the *Arizona Advocate* (the student newspaper), Native American Law Students Association, Black Law Students Association, Lesbian and Gay Rights Activists, Jewish Law Students Association, two legal fraternities, moot court, and law review.

The Student Bar Association is a visible presence. It selects student members for faculty-student committees (which govern many aspects of the school), allocates student organization funds, and negotiates student issues. The SBA also keeps busy sponsoring programs for first-year students and school-wide social events.

The College of Law has an active affirmative action policy and has strong minority enrollment and support. A number of students are married, and a fifth to a quarter of recent entering classes were 30 or older.

Entering classes are generally limited to a maximum of 150 students. Of this number, non-Arizona residents are limited to 25 to 30 percent. Even after admission, residency status has its advantages: annual out-of-state tuition is several times that for in-state residents. Many out-of-state students succeed in establishing residency for their second and third years.

Virtually all law students live off campus in apartment complexes, duplexes, and small adobe houses in the residential communities that surround the U of A. Good housing can be found within biking distance of the law school. (Bikes are extremely popular.) There is a married students' complex about five miles away.

The job placement process is a combination of students' individual efforts, notices posted by the placement office, and on-campus interviews. The statistics show that the typical graduate goes to a private Arizona or West Coast law firm. If your goals fit this pattern, you could have a very satisfying stay at the U of A.

University of Arkansas at Little Rock School of Law

Address: **1201 McAlmont,
  Little Rock, AR 72202**
Phone: **(501) 324-9439**
Degrees: **J.D., J.D./M.B.A.**
Median LSAT: **155**
Median GPA: **3.15**
Applicants accepted: **34%**
Transfers: **2–4/3–5**
Law enrollment: **386**
Campus enrollment: **386**

Part time: **30%**
Women: **50%**
Minorities: **18%**
Dorm residents: **0**
Library: **215,000**
Student-faculty ratio: **14:1**
Tuition: **$2400 (in-state),
  $5088 (out-of-state)**
Financial aid: **30%**
Apply by: **April 1**

Disabled students: **Fully accessible. In one year, one disabled student.**

Placement: **Approximately 30% placed by graduation; approximately 90% employed six to nine months after graduation. Nine employers on campus in one year. 95% of graduates remained in Arkansas. Graduates entered private practice (53%), government (18%), judicial clerkships (18%), business (5%), unknown (6%). Salary range: $22,500–$47,000. Arkansas bar pass rate: 91% (statewide average: 86%).**

Arkansas has changed quite a bit between the days of Orval Faubus and the days of Bill Clinton. Meanwhile, UALR School of Law has been going through some changes of its own.

As of 1975, the principal attraction of the school was convenience—it was located in Little Rock, the center of Arkansas commerce and politics, and it had a night program. But by the early 1980s, it had acquired a full-time day program, new blood in the administration, several top-quality professors, ABA and AALS accreditation, and a much-needed boost in its prestige.

It also acquired a rehabilitated nineteenth-century building complete with high ceilings and oak-paneled walls. But despite its beauty, the old building had a somewhat erratic air-conditioning system, and frozen pipes sometimes caused sudden wintertime showers *indoors*. So in the early 1990s, the school built and moved into an entirely new building.

Because the law school is a few miles from the main university campus, there's little contact between the two—a situation law students say is to their advantage. They can use the university libraries and athletic facilities and attend campus cultural events, but the law school has separate admissions and registration, a local bookstore, and autonomous dean and faculty. In short, the relationship is ideal.

One major advantage of the location is that the courts (including the Arkansas Supreme Court), various state offices and commissions, the State Capitol, and most of the law firms in Little Rock are easily accessible.

There are over twenty lakes, several thousand acres of forest, parks, trails, and rivers, all within a couple of hours' drive from Little Rock. Whatever you think of Arkansas's political environment, its physical environment is very beautiful.

With a small student population, UALR is the kind of place where students become close friends. Social activities are varied and numerous. There are no dorms, so most students live in houses or apartments in the area, and many make their humble abodes available for parties. Single students, married students, and faculty all mingle at social functions.

The UALR law journal takes most of its members based on grades, but there are several "write-on" competitions each year that allow students with lower GPAs to become members. In addition, professors may recommend the publication of exceptional material written by nonmember students.

Classes are conducted by modified Socratic method, with a minimum of lecturing except in the statutory courses. The core curriculum is more than adequate preparation for the bar exam and, supplemented by the trial advocacy and clinical courses, it enables a graduate to enter solo practice with sufficient general skills. The clinical programs have been expanded beyond their origins as a criminal law internship program.

The curriculum is somewhat limited, in that most areas of specialization begin and end with introductory courses. The exceptions are tax and estate planning, criminal law, and medicine-related law.

UALR's proximity to legal employers is a boon when it comes to finding term-time jobs, which often go hand in hand with graduation-time jobs. Thanks to an excellent relationship with the local and state bar, UALR grads are becoming a more common sight in Little Rock area firms and in Arkansas judicial clerkships—not to mention in state government and business.

UALR has come a long way in a short time. With a creditable performance on the part of the recent graduates, the school can expect its prestige to extend beyond the Arkansas borders in the near future. For the time being, though, there's an important fact you should remember about UALR: its reputation for job placement is still limited to the area within a few hundred miles of the school.

Baylor University School of Law

Address: **P.O. Box 97288, Waco, TX 76798**
Phone: **(817) 755-1911**
Degrees: **J.D.**
Median LSAT: **159**
Median GPA: **3.63**
Applicants accepted: **22%**
Transfers: **2–7/10–20**
Law enrollment: **422**
Campus enrollment: **10,500**
Part time: **0**

Women: **38%**
Minorities: **13%**
Dorm residents: **NA**
Library: **154,000**
Student-faculty ratio: **22:1**
Tuition: **$6947**
Financial aid: **77% (58% gift)**
Apply by: **February 15 (fall), November 1 (spring), January 15 (summer)**

Disabled students: **Fully accessible. In five years, two wheelchair users.**
Placement: **93% employed six months after graduation. 34% of second-years and 60% of third-years placed by end of spring term. 100 employers on campus in one year; 99% from Texas; 91% private firms, 9% government. 99% of graduates stayed in**

Texas. Graduates entered law firms (82%), judicial clerkships (10%), government (2%), corporations (2%), other (4%). Salary range: $27,000–$72,000. Texas bar pass rate: 97.1% (statewide average: 79%).

Deep in the heart of Texas—in Waco, to be exact—lies Baylor Law School. Despite its population of 100,000, Waco offers an atmosphere that could best be described as small-town. If you decide to study law here, you won't have to cope with a lot of distractions.

On the other hand, the forbidden fruits of the big city are available at the end of an hour and a half's drive to Dallas–Fort Worth or Austin. If you're willing to drive a little longer, you can visit Houston or San Antonio. Waco itself offers lakes, parks, and a warm, dry climate for outdoor activities.

Most law students at Baylor are Texans who intend to remain in Texas, but there are a number of out-of-staters to keep things from becoming too parochial. Speaking of parochial, Baylor has the distinction of being the world's largest Baptist university. Southern Baptists are known for their conservative political and moral views, and the university administration is no exception. The "Baylor Bubble" is often said to surround this campus and protect its students from the outside world and liberalizing influences. The law school, however, exhibits more open-mindedness and political and religious variety than the rest of the university.

The curriculum at Baylor is narrower than at some larger law schools. Opportunities for specialization are not abundant, but there is a sufficient number of electives to make for a diversified course of study. The faculty boasts recognized authorities in a number of areas, including procedure, evidence, property law, and antitrust.

As evidenced by awards from the American College of Trial Lawyers and the National Mock Trial Competition, Baylor turns out crack trial lawyers. Students give most of the credit to the practice court program, a six-month course required of every senior law student. The course offers intensive study of trial procedure as well as simulated trial experience.

The semiannual moot court competition is one of the most popular extracurricular activities on campus, with about 60 percent of the students participating. Clinical programs include Legal Aid and cooperative programs with the offices of the county district attorney, the U.S. attorney, and the federal district and bankruptcy courts.

Students concur that the best thing about Baylor is the small student enrollment, which makes for class sizes ranging from 65 in first-year courses to 15 in some upper-level courses, with an average of between 30 and 40 students per class. First-year courses are typically conducted along modified Socratic lines, with considerable class recitation required to enforce daily preparation. Upper-level courses employ more lecturing, but class discussion is encouraged, and the atmosphere in the classroom is relaxed and personal. It's easy to develop friendships with professors as well as with students in all three classes.

In addition to the university-wide concerts and speakers, the law school offers its own round of social activities. Students at Baylor Law work hard, and many play hard whenever the opportunity arises. The Student Bar Association and the legal fraternities offer a variety of social diversions.

Baylor runs on a quarter-system calendar, with four three-month quarters each year. The course of study takes at least nine quarters if you go straight through, but you can take any quarter off after your first year to get some work experience (and most students do). About 65 percent of Baylor's students attend the summer quarter. The quarter system allows concentrated study of three or four courses at a time instead of four or five, but a drawback is the feeling that you're almost always studying for finals—without any reading period. The pace can get hectic.

Students are admitted in three groups, in August, February, and May. This arrangement is a definite plus for people who graduate from college in midyear and don't want to wait until fall to begin law school. Baylor also admits a few students after only three years of college; they get their B.A. after their first year of law study.

The biggest factors in determining admission are the usual: grades and law board scores. Standards for transfer students are tough, since only a handful are accepted each year. Baylor does encourage students from other schools to attend Baylor's summer quarter, though.

A Baylor education emphasizes the practical aspects of a civil trial practice in the Texas or federal courts. Nuts-and-bolts required courses occupy about two thirds of the total credit hours needed for graduation.

The placement office is extremely active. Baylor's reputation attracts a healthy number of prospective employers who interview students for both quarterly clerkships and permanent jobs. But despite the fact that out-of-state law firms seeking Baylor applicants are increasing each year, most of the recruiters are based in Texas. If you decide to come to Baylor, you'd better like living in Texas, because the odds are in favor of your staying there.

Boston College Law School

Address: **885 Centre St., Newton, MA 02159**
Phone: **(617) 552-4350**
Degrees: **J.D., J.D./M.B.A., J.D./M.S.W. (social work), other joint degrees**
Median LSAT: **41**
Median GPA: **3.41**
Applicants accepted: **15%**
Transfers: **5**
Law enrollment: **847**

Campus enrollment: **847**
Part time: **0**
Women: **47%**
Minorities: **17%**
Dorm residents: **NA**
Library: **298,600**
Student-faculty ratio: **20:1**
Tuition: **$15,570**
Financial aid: **75%**
Apply by: **March 1**

Disabled students: **Fully accessible. In one year, three disabled students.**

Placement: **96% employed six months after graduation. 315 employers from 35 states on campus in one year; 71% private firms, 13% government, 13% public interest, 3% business. Graduates took jobs in New England (57%), Middle Atlantic (26%), Southwest/West (7%), Midwest (4%), Southeast (3%), Foreign (3%). Graduates entered private practice (73%), judicial clerkships (13%), government (8%), public interest (2%), business (2%), academic (2%). Salary range: $22,000–$85,000. Mean salary: $54,900.**

Aside from its good reputation, there are two things for which Boston College is noted by many prospective students: its pleasant suburban location and its mercifully short application form. Both of these characteristics offer some clues to the school's strengths and weaknesses.

BC Law School is set on a green campus in the Boston suburb of Newton, a short hop by the Massachusetts Turnpike or public transportation to the center of Boston. The grass, trees, squirrels, and gently contoured lawns make a relaxed setting for what will never be an entirely pleasant experience. The atmosphere is informal. Teachers commonly address students by their first names and welcome student contact. The classic Socratic grilling is encountered, but infrequently after first year.

The Newton location is more than a mile from the main campus of Boston College, which is actually a sizable university. The central administration is reportedly reluctant to adjust to the special needs of the law school outpost. Fortunately, the law school has its own financial aid office.

The short application form reflects a trim bureaucracy that is too busy to waste your time. Administrative doors are open, but the burden is on the student to find the right door, enter it, and ask the appropriate question.

The entering class is divided into two sections, and students tend to make friends within their section. First-years are more diligent than upper-level students, but almost everyone works hard during the week.

BC has a strong faculty, with a few weak links. Except for the first year, when faculty are assigned by section and can't be avoided, students can fairly easily steer clear of the weaker teachers—although that may entail slighting a few subjects. Some topnotch faculty grace the school's successful clinical programs, which range from the Legal Assistance Bureau in Waltham to the Urban Legal Laboratory, which places students in law offices. In addition, many of the visiting professors are excellent and add variety to the curriculum.

A universal failing of law students is their tendency to get absorbed in courses and publications at the expense of all else, and the temptation is particularly strong at BC, where there are publications to suit every conceivable interest. In addition to the law review, which offers membership according to class rank or a writing competition, there are journals on environmental affairs, international and comparative law, the Uniform Commercial Code, and Third World legal issues—as well as a school yearbook and a newspaper. The school also has competitions for moot court and mock trial.

For those who want to get away from legal matters, the Boston area offers an infinite number of distractions. The area abounds in students, the institutions that spawn them, and the institutions that cater to them: museums, theaters, movie houses, tourist attractions, and watering holes. Boston's high concentration of under-twenty-five culture can get fairly overwhelming, however, and leads some BC students to stay put in the suburbs.

Back on campus, active extracurricular student groups are numerous, and the minority and women's groups seem to function effectively.

The job hunt for those coming out of Boston College generally compares with that at most of America's other "better" law schools. The placement office does a great deal to set the stage, but the script rests squarely in the students' hands. Those with distinguished school careers may find themselves being courted; the rest will find satisfactory legal employment, although perhaps with fewer options to choose from.

Boston University School of Law

Address: **765 Commonwealth Ave., Boston, MA 02215**
Phone: **(617) 353-3100**
Degrees: **J.D., LL.M. (tax, banking, international banking), J.D./M.B.A., J.D./M.A. (preservation studies, international relations), J.D./M.S. (mass communication), J.D./M.P.H. (public health)**
Median LSAT: **162**
Median GPA: **3.3**
Applicants accepted: **29%**

Transfers: **5–15/50–100**
Law enrollment: **1495 (1244 J.D.)**
Campus enrollment: **25,800**
Part time: **0**
Women: **45%**
Minorities: **20%**
Dorm residents: **20%**
Library: **454,100**
Student-faculty ratio: **21:1**
Tuition: **$16,800**
Financial aid: **85% (35% gift)**
Apply by: **March 1**

Disabled students: **Fully accessible. Within five years, one blind student, four deaf, two wheelchair users, two with other mobility problems.**

Placement: **43% placed by graduation; approximately 86% employed six months after graduation. 242 employers on campus in one year; 44% from New England, 43% Middle Atlantic, 8% Midwest, 7% West, 2% South, 1% Southwest; 85% private firms, 8% government, 5% corporations, 2% public interest. Graduates took jobs in Middle Atlantic (41%), New England (35%), West (8%), Midwest (7%), South (4%), Southwest (2%), Foreign (1%), unknown (3%), Graduates entered private practice (77%), government (9%), judicial clerkships (6%), public interest (4%), unknown (3%), business (1%). Salary range: $15,000–$86,000. Mean salary: $55,533. Massachusetts bar pass rate: 83.4% (statewide average: 78%). New York bar pass rate: 84.8% (statewide average: 73%). New Jersey bar pass rate: 84% (statewide average: 65%).**

BU looks different to its different types of students. There are those who regard the school as a life-or-death race for grades and law review. Others are here for lack of anything better to do for three years. Most, however, are at BU to learn a marketable skill, and there's no question that the school provides a solid, traditional legal education.

The admissions office here seems to like variety. Although high numbers go a long way, other factors are genuinely considered. Many of the students have spent at least a year or two out of school, and an advanced degree appears to give a BU applicant a competitive edge. The school seems to have made an honest commitment to accept disabled students.

The diversity of the student body is limited in that most students come from eastern homes and/or private eastern universities; many of them are New Yorkers. Also, some students wish there were more racial diversity. The administration claims that qualified minority students are recruited by other schools that can offer more financial aid and a bigger name. Students feel that BU's recruitment procedures might be more to blame. Some students have also objected to the paucity of women and minority group men on the faculty.

BU's clinical programs are well organized and thorough, and students who participate usually get extremely involved in them. However, long waiting lists attest to the inability of many interested students to get slots in the clinical courses of their choice.

BU provides excellent opportunities for publication experience. Aside from the law review, journals cover international law, law and medicine, banking law, tax, probate, and public-interest law.

First-year students attend classes in sections of 100. The rigorous first-year writing program is excellent and is well known for producing students who actually know how to write like lawyers.

Most faculty members are easily approachable, and a smaller number will initiate individual contact. Generally, the faculty is of high caliber, well prepared, interested, and good at teaching. A few are terrible, and a couple are superb. Unfortunately, first-years can't choose their professors in the required courses and may find themselves stuck with one or more unimaginative adherents to the tired old Socratic approach. Second semester, the first-year students have one elective—a privilege not offered at some other schools.

The second and third years are entirely elective, with the exception of constitutional law and professional responsibility. Courses run the spectrum from small seminars to huge classes crowded into a large room. BU offers an admirable array of specialized seminars. The school does a good job attracting an interesting mix of visiting professors who are well versed in their fields.

While the curriculum is broad enough to permit specialization in any number of areas, the strongest subjects are tax, corporate law, real estate, and litigation (thanks in part to a superb trial advocacy course).

Students can take courses for credit in BU's other graduate schools, including the business school. The J.D./M.P.H. joint degree program is well regarded, and J.D./M.B.A. graduates are virtually guaranteed their pick of jobs.

BU's large law library generally serves its students well. Unlike some other schools, BU virtually never sees shortages of popular reference books or computer research terminals. However, there are complaints that excessive noise and erratic temperatures sometimes make the library a less-than-ideal study environment.

Students here are competitive, intelligent, and hardworking.

Most are interested primarily in their GPAs and getting a job. The results: little or no campus activism; widespread apathy about politics and national affairs; and a low level of involvement in student organizations.

Some university housing is available, but most students choose to live off campus and take advantage of this most student-oriented of cities. A trolley and several buses stop in front of the school, so you can reach BU from many parts of Boston. Most students stick fairly close to campus in Allston, Brighton, or Brookline.

Social activities are less dependent on the university than they would be in a rural location. Most students spend leisure hours in the city, not on campus. The law school is close to the rest of BU, but contact between the two is minimal. One of the main gathering spots is the law library—especially for first-year students, who develop anxiety attacks if they get too far away from their books.

While first-year students are worried about studying, the greatest concern of second- and third-years is job placement. The placement office is great at arranging on-campus interviews with big firms, which are primarily interested in the top 10 to 25 percent of the class and/or journal participants. Although BU's burgeoning reputation means that job opportunities are improving for everybody, the fact remains that public-interest-oriented students and those with lower class ranks must definitely make an extra effort to identify and pursue job openings. The student-run Public Interest Law Project raises and distributes money to fund a limited number of students for summer internships with public-interest groups. Unfortunately, BU does not yet offer a loan-forgiveness program for graduates in public-interest jobs.

Word has it that financial aid is a problem. Tuition is high, and the average grant award barely makes a dent in the staggering bill. Most students take out hefty loans.

BU's problems are less the fault of the law school than of a tightfisted university administration. A perfect example is the fact that funds never seem to be available for desperately needed repairs to the law school's building.

BU is a high-quality school in a great town for students. Though many students initially apply to BU as a backup, they find when they arrive that it's a stimulating and challenging place with a growing national reputation.

Brigham Young University, J. Reuben Clark Law School

Address: **Provo, UT 84602**
Phone: **(801) 378-4277**
Degrees: **J.D., M.C.L., J.D./M.B.A., J.D./M.P.A., J.D./M.O.B. (organizational behavior), J.D./M.Acc. (accounting), J.D./M.Ed. or Ed.D. (education)**
Median LSAT: **162**
Median GPA: **3.52**
Applicants accepted: **35%**
Transfers: **2/35**
Law enrollment: **475 (469 J.D.)**

Campus enrollment: **27,000**
Part time: **0**
Women: **27%**
Minorities: **11%**
Dorm residents: **NA**
Library: **335,000**
Student-faculty ratio: **21:1**
Tuition: **$4020 (Mormons), $6030 (non-Mormons)**
Financial aid: **80% (35% gift)**
Apply by: **February 15**

Disabled students: **Moderate/full accessibility. In five years, one blind student, three deaf, two wheelchair users, three with other mobility problems.**

Placement: **92% employed six months after graduation. 45% of first-years, 61% of second-years, and 86% of third-years placed by end of spring term. 92 employers on campus in one year; 80% from Mountain or Pacific; 90% private firms, 7% government, 3% corporations. Graduates took jobs in California (27%), Utah (25%), other Mountain (24%), South Atlantic (8%), West South Central (5%), other Pacific (4%), Middle Atlantic (3%), West North Central (3%), East North Central (1%), New England (1%). Graduates entered private practice (61%), government (13%), judicial clerkships (13%), business (7%), public interest (2%), academic (1%). Salary range: $29,250–$83,000. Median salary: $44,000. Mean salary: $44,300. Utah bar pass rate: 93% (statewide average: 90%). California bar pass rate: 78% (statewide average: 55%).**

"Law students uphold high moral and ethical standards in a clean, wholesome atmosphere. Alcohol, drugs and other harmful substances have no place at the J. Reuben Clark Law School. Students dress and groom themselves in a manner which reflects their future professionalism. The school's honor code, to which students voluntarily subscribe, sets standards of conduct which contribute to the school's clean-cut and professional reputation."

So reads one student's description of this school. Brigham Young University is privately sponsored by the Church of Jesus Christ of Latter-day Saints, otherwise known as the Mormons. Applicants must have a Mormon bishop, a clergy member, or a judge vouch that they will abide by the school's code of conduct.

The atmosphere among students is described as harmonious and friendly. The students represent a wide variety of undergraduate schools, but the large majority are from western states. Close to half hail from Utah.

The law school is separated from the rest of the university by "the street." Across "the street" are the cafeteria, recreation facilities, bookstore, undergraduates, and other necessities of life. The BYU campus is very modern, with outstanding facilities for sports, outdoor recreation, crafts, hobbies, music, drama, and of course, courting, marriage, and families. Traditional fraternities and sororities have been replaced by clubs and service organizations at BYU. "BYU students also partake of social activity programs in their church congregations," one student reports.

The law school has its own beautiful building (circa 1975). Each student is assigned an individual study carrel that can be locked to keep everyone except the library staff out of one's books, notes, briefs, etc. The law building also has well-appointed classrooms, the latest technology for class instruction, and one of the most extensive law libraries in the West, as well as a small lunchroom and a student lounge with TV and Ping-Pong.

In a recent magazine survey, the Provo-Orem area was voted the most livable city in America. The community of approximately 160,000 is situated at the foot of the Wasatch Mountains, which rise from an elevation of just over 4,000 feet virtually straight up to about 11,000 feet. This location gives students the opportunity to enjoy golf and tennis one day and ski Utah's famous powder snow the next. There are seven major ski resorts within an hour of the campus, the closest being Robert Redford's Sundance Resort a scant eight miles up Provo Canyon from town. (Of course, these activities are generally limited to undergraduates who have nothing better to do.)

Housing for singles is abundant and inexpensive. Housing for married students is tougher to find. Since the majority of students at the law school are married, they enjoy a strong support network and many social activities. Single students have activities available to them as well; however, graduate student men far outnumber graduate student women, and nightlife in Provo is subdued, to say the least. On the other hand, Salt Like City and its broader range of amenities are just 45 minutes away around the point of the mountain.

The Student Bar Association is generously funded and very active. The Law Student Division of the ABA functions, for better or for worse, as an arm of the SBA. The usual legal fraternities, women's caucus, and other clubs are also present.

Academic activities outside the classroom include the law review, *Journal of Public Law, Journal of Law and Education*, and the Environmental Law Forum. The school boasts an outstanding moot court program and an up-and-coming trial advocacy program.

The school also can lay claim to the nation's first chapter of Inns of Court. Modeled after their English predecessors, the Inns are small groups of law students, attorneys, professors and judges who gather on a regular basis to mingle, discuss legal developments, and sharpen their advocacy skills. There are now Inns in many cities nationwide.

Relations among students, faculty, and administrators are very cordial, thanks to activities like the annual law school picnic, spring formal, and Rex Lee Run for Cancer Research (named for the Solicitor General in the Reagan administration, now BYU's president). Most of the professors are young, competent, caring— and Mormon. Classes are usually small, except for the standard first-year courses. Instruction is by modified Socratic coupled with lecture, or by informal seminar discussion.

Brigham Young grads have a strong reputation in the West for energy, ambition, and clean-cut appearance. Naturally, the school's name is biggest in Utah, followed by nearby states like California, Colorado, Arizona, Idaho, New Mexico, and Nevada. Students venturing out of the West have also been successful in landing jobs with some major firms.

There's a very good legal education to be had at BYU. Postgraduate placement is surprisingly high for a young school. The BYU standards of dress and conduct would no doubt create an uncomfortable environment for some, but from an academic point of view, the school is worth investigating.

Brooklyn Law School

Address: **250 Joralemon St., Brooklyn, NY 11201**

Phone: **(718) 780-7906**

Degrees: **J.D., J.D./M.B.A., J.D./M.P.A., J.D./M.A. (political science), J.D./M.U.P. (urban planning), J.D./M.S. (planning, library science)**

Median LSAT: **160 (full time), 157 (part time)**

Median GPA: **3.25 (full time), 3.21 (part time)**

Applicants accepted: **29%**

Transfers: **5–10/30–40**

Law enrollment: **1439**

Campus enrollment: **1458**

Part time: **27%**

Women: **41%**

Minorities: **14%**

Dorm residents: **approx. 5%**

Library: **399,600**

Student-faculty ratio: **20:1**

Tuition: **$15,725**

Financial aid: **40%**

Apply by: **rolling admissions, February 1 recommended**

Disabled students: **Fully accessible. In one year, three blind students, three deaf, one wheelchair user.**

Placement: **91% employed eleven months after graduation. Graduates took jobs in Middle Atlantic (97%), Pacific (2%), South Atlantic (.5%), New England (.5%). Graduates entered private practice (58%), government (13%), business (8%), nonlegal jobs (7%), judicial clerkships (6%), public interest (5%), advanced degree (2%), military (1%). Salary range: $15,000–$106,000. Average salary: $43,100.**

No, Brooklyn Law isn't part of public Brooklyn College. And no, it's not an impersonal subway school.

Brooklyn Law *is* an independent private law school that traditionally has trained the first-generation professional from New York City. Although Brooklyn Law continues to fulfill that role, the admissions committee also tries to gather a student body that's diverse in geographical background, race, work experience, age, and other characteristics. After admitting a student, Brooklyn Law makes a sincere effort to help him or her succeed.

Among its advantages, Brooklyn Law can boast a full evening division. This enables the presently employed to make a career change. It also allows the full-time day student the flexibility of evening classes, and the security of knowing that a transfer to the evening session is possible should a job become necessary and/or full-time school become unbearable. A large number of the students are returning to school after pursuing other professions.

Students at Brooklyn Law speak of a sense of community. The guiding forces are cooperation and supportiveness, rather than competition and grade-grubbing. Spontaneously formed study groups make first year livable. In August, all first-years are assigned an upperclass student counselor who will attempt to answer all the pressing questions on an incoming student's mind (like "Should I use a spiral-bound notebook or a looseleaf?").

The entering class is divided into small seminar sections for legal writing and one other class. Students' remaining classes are taught in larger sections, each of which combines several small seminar groups. The first-year student gets to know and work with some hundred students who take the majority of first-year courses together.

Second- and third-year students choose their courses and professors. Seminars and esoteric courses are smaller, while the bread-and-butter bar courses may continue to be large. The Student Bar Association publishes an annual student survey of professors and courses, a boon for the student consumer.

The faculty is a diverse group (including many minority and women professors), many of them preeminent in their fields. As a nice complement to their reputations, the faculty members—with a few exceptions—can actually teach. "Full-time faculty are enthusiastic, encouraging, and accessible," reports one student. Students are encouraged to raise issues of concern with the administration, but do not always get their way. Attempts to change the academic calendar—which has first-semester exams in January and the second semester beginning one week later—have so far been unsuccessful.

Participation in student government is limited to a small but active group. A few people put in the time to run the book exchange, housing clearinghouse, speakers' programs, and parties. Intramural sports and happy hours at nearby bars contribute to the relaxed atmosphere (or as relaxed as a law school can be).

Other student organizations are the Jewish, Black, Hispanic,

Asian-American, and Italian-American Law Students associations, the Legal Association of Women, the National Lawyers Guild, the International Law Society, Phi Delta Phi, and the school newspaper, among other groups. The *Brooklyn Law Review* and the *Brooklyn Journal of International Law* are possibilities for students who pass a writing competition.

The moot court program guides first-year students through a required brief-writing and oral argument course. If selected to join the Moot Court Honor Society, a second-year student has the opportunity to compete in intramural contests. Over the last several years, Brooklyn's teams have walked away with top prizes from various national moot court competitions; in the process, they've become a source of great school pride.

Thanks to its location, Brooklyn Law is able to offer joint degree programs with other area schools.

Contrary to some people's mental image of Brooklyn, Brooklyn Law is adjacent to some of the loveliest residential areas in New York City. Brooklyn Heights is a landmark district known for its nineteenth-century brownstones, tree-lined streets, and the Promenade—the walkway along the river that offers the most beautiful view anywhere of the Manhattan skyline. To the south and west, the neighborhoods of Cobble Hill and Boerum Hill are similarly charming, but less expensive and still in the process of brownstone renovation.

In 1992, the school broke ground on a multistory addition and undertook renovations of the original building. Students graduating in the late 1990s and beyond will benefit fully from the $28 million construction project, which features an extensive library, large student lounge and cafeteria, and modern classrooms.

The school is situated at the hub of one of the most active court and government agency systems in the country. Within several blocks are a host of federal and state courts and numerous government offices. It's a convenient subway ride or walk across the Brooklyn Bridge to downtown Manhattan and other courts and administrative agencies.

The law school takes advantage of its location by offering a wide range of clinical programs. The most prestigious clinic is the judicial clerkship, reportedly largest in the nation in its number and range of placement positions. Students can work with the U.S. attorney, legal aid, the district attorney, and the SEC, to name just a few. BLS also hosts its own "in-house" clinics where students get excellent practical experience under faculty supervision, handling cases in the fields of civil litigation, criminal prosecution and defense, and elderly law. Whether your interests are in landlord-tenant, consumer, welfare rights, environmental, community development, or family law, you'll be able to get credit for real jobs that bring your law school courses to life.

The placement office gets high marks for effort. It offers career information programs, counseling sessions, public-interest information, and an always-current job source file, in addition to inviting potential employers to interview at the school.

Those students who are at the top of their class or have law review or law journal experience are recruited by many of New York City's top firms and government agencies. Other students must rely on contacts or their clinical experiences to land jobs in the glutted legal market of New York. Fortunately, Brooklyn Law School has a secret weapon: an active network of thousands of alumni in the New York area, many of them in very high places, who are willing to give a recent graduate a helping hand.

University of California—Berkeley, Boalt Hall School of Law

Address: **220 Boalt Hall, Berkeley, CA 94720**
Phone: **(510) 642-2274**
Degrees: **J.D., LL.M., J.S.D., J.D./M.B.A., J.D./M.A.L.D. (law and diplomacy), J.D./M.P.P. (public policy), J.D./M.A. (Asian studies, city planning, economics, journalism, library science, public policy, social welfare, jurisprudence & social policy), J.D./Ph.D. (legal history; jurisprudence & social policy), other joint degrees**
Median LSAT: **44/166**

Median GPA: **3.7**
Applicants accepted: **14%**
Transfers: **25–30/150–175**
Law enrollment: **830 (786 J.D.)**
Campus enrollment: **31,000**
Part time: **0**
Women: **42%**
Minorities: **33%**
Dorm residents: **approx. 25%**
Library: **833,000**
Student-faculty ratio: **10:1**
Tuition: **$3688 (in-state), $11,387 (out-of-state)**
Financial aid: **89%**
Apply by: **February 1**

Disabled students: **Fully accessible. In five years, three blind students, six wheelchair users.**

Placement: **97% employed six months after graduation. Approximately 400 employers on campus in one year; 58% from California, 5% other West, 9% Washington, DC, 8% New York, 6% Midwest, 6% Northwest, 4% Southwest, 3% East, 1% South; 95% private firms. Graduates took jobs in California (75%), Pacific Northwest (10%), South/Southwest (10%), East (8%). Graduates entered private practice (84%), judicial clerkships (9%), government (4%), public interest (1%), business (1%). Salary range: $25,000–$83,000. Median salary: $66,000. California bar pass rate: 90% (statewide average: 55%).**

One of the first things one notices about Boalt Hall is its student body, a remarkably diverse crew in age, experience, class, and ethnic background. A special admissions program that helped assure a significant minority population had to be revamped after George Bush's Education Department found it to be discriminatory, but Boalt has promised to continue seeking a broad mix of students.

In reputation, Boalt is undeniably a national school—well within the top fifteen, in most people's estimation—but don't forget that it's a state institution. Three quarters of the seats are reserved for Californians, who pay greatly reduced tuition. Over half the students attended in-state undergraduate schools. Still, people flock to Boalt from over a hundred colleges nationwide, with those most represented in a typical year including Harvard and Yale, as well as Berkeley, Stanford, UCLA, and Santa Cruz. You'll find lots of former political science, economics, and English majors, and many people with advanced degrees.

Statistics are the easiest way to describe Boalt. The rest of the story is what you make it. Considering the school's prestige, the atmosphere is quite relaxed. Many students look at their three years as a process of experimenting or merely "credentialing"; they're as concerned with outside work, home, or the pursuit of pleasure as they are with what goes on in the classroom. Nevertheless, a growing number of Boalt students work constantly and competitively.

In class, the atmosphere is equally varied. Some courses are rigid, and many of the faculty persist in teaching (often disastrously) according to the Socratic method. Others are remarkably relaxed and feel free to lecture and call students by their first names. Some professors are approachable, although in such a large school, the first move is up to you.

Classes range in size from seminars of 5 to lectures of 150 or more. Good, offbeat electives are available for those who are willing to experiment. Among the offerings in recent years were Media Law, Modern Chinese Law, and Biomedical Ethics.

Academic requirements are few and easily met. An orientation program of lectures and discussion groups is designed to introduce entering students to "thinking like a lawyer." Legal research and writing, moot court, and six basic courses are mandatory in the first year; bar-exam-related courses and work-study often take up the rest of the time.

One of Boalt's strong points is a clinical externship program that enables students to work in public-interest firms, government agencies, judicial chambers, and other legal jobs virtually anywhere in the country, for credit and occasionally for pay. Recently, the administration has tightened up requirements for the program and has encouraged students to work in the Bay Area with more traditional firms or in judicial clerkships. But those who are determined can still pursue more exotic options. Boalt also encourages students to take occasional leaves of absence, often a wise move for those who need to figure out where they're heading.

As everywhere, many students aspire to the law review, which has adopted a write-on policy for membership. But Boalt's other journals, including the *Ecology Law Quarterly,* the *Berkeley Women's Law Journal,* the *Industrial Relations Law Journal,* and the *Asian Law Journal,* are strong alternatives. Another venture gaining in popularity is the Berkeley Law Foundation, one of the first of the growing number of law school organizations that use student and alumni donations to support public-interest projects.

Boalt's student body, one of the most radical in the early 1970s, is now solidly mainstream liberal. Radicals can still be found, and the number of conservative voices is increasing. The Women's Association is actively feminist. A lesbian and gay caucus makes its presence felt. The minority law students' associations have always been strong. The local National Lawyers Guild chapter is sporadically energetic and has organized an alternative orientation session for entering students.

Student government is ignored, but in the recent past, Boalt students haven't been afraid to confront the administration on such issues as affirmative action in faculty hiring and minority student input to the admissions process.

Jobs are increasingly a source of student tension. Boalt's prestige among local employers is high, but so is the level of competition for San Francisco jobs. The placement office wisely counsels students to widen their job horizons beyond the Bay Area. The placement people do an admirable job of minimizing pressure and providing all kinds of help, from first-year counseling through postgraduate references. Most students who go through traditional placement channels end up in private firms; if you seek a less traditional spot, you may be left to your own devices to find it, although the Berkeley Law Foundation has worked with the placement office to expand the public-interest information available.

UC—Berkeley has come a long way from the days when Dustin Hoffman sought out Katharine Ross here in *The Graduate,* but it's still a unique institution. The town's reputation as "an open ward" is well deserved. Rents are high, especially in the beautiful hills, and housing is very hard to get; one should begin looking for an apartment in early August at the latest. Many students head for nearby Albany or Oakland to find more space and more moderate rents, and others go across the bay to San Francisco. If a student atmosphere is what you're looking for, Berkeley is the better bet.

With a minimum of effort, you'll find plenty of those all-too-necessary diversions in the Bay Area. Close at hand are movie houses, bookstores, coffeehouses, and running trails. Twenty minutes away by car, and a manageable commute, is San Francisco, with its good cheap restaurants and plentiful entertainment. The northern coast, Tahoe, and Yosemite are a bit farther away, but accessible for weekend trips.

While the southern Californians at Berkeley complain about the cold, the easterners smile all winter long. And both groups agree that they're getting a first-rate legal education in a relatively laid-back setting.

University of California—Davis School of Law

Address: **King Hall, Davis, CA 95616**
Phone: **(916) 752-6477**
Degrees: **J.D., J.D./M.B.A., joint degrees**
Median LSAT: **162**
Median GPA: **3.4**
Applicants accepted: **18%**
Transfers: **4–7/70**
Law enrollment: **481**
Campus enrollment: **22,870**

Part time: **0**
Women: **47%**
Minorities: **27%**
Dorm residents: **NA**
Library: **335,600**
Student-faculty ratio: **17:1**
Tuition: **$3650 (in-state), $11,349 (out-of-state)**
Financial aid: **69%**
Apply by: **February 1**

Disabled students: **Fully accessible. Within five years, one blind student, one deaf, one wheelchair user, three with other mobility problems, five with dyslexia, two with other learning disabilities.**
Placement: **67% of first-years, 86% of second-years, and 50% of third-years placed by end of spring term. 88% employed six months after graduation. 135 employers on campus in one year; 95% from West; approximately 87% private firms, 12% government or public interest, 2% corporations. Graduates took jobs in California (81%), Alaska/Hawaii (7%), Southwest (5%), Northwest (2%), Northeast (1%), Southeast (1%), unknown (4%). Graduates entered private practice (70%), government (18%), judicial clerkships (11%), public interest (1%). Salary range: $23,000–$75,000. Mean salary: $35,650. California bar pass rate: 90.8% (statewide average: 55%).**

The youngest of California's four state law schools is the one at Davis, popularly known as King Hall (its building is named after Martin Luther King, Jr.). Its national reputation is overshadowed by those of its sister campuses, especially UC—Berkeley's Boalt Hall. But King Hall's in-state recognition is good, and wider renown seems not too far off, especially in the fields of agricultural, environmental, energy, and water law.

King Hall is also the smallest of the state law schools, which guarantees lots of individual attention from faculty. The largest classroom in the building seats only 110 students, and the average class has 40 students. Each entering student attends one of the first-year courses in a "small section" of 25 to 30, taught by a professor, not a teaching assistant. Most of the faculty are young, accessible, and receptive. Many have practiced in the areas they now teach (which is rare elsewhere), and many are on a first-name basis with students (which is even rarer).

Because of the school's size, students sometimes discover that a course they want to take isn't being offered during the current year. Fortunately, the administration is sensitive to this problem and will often revise the course catalog to meet student demand. In addition, the school encourages independent and group study. The curriculum boasts many imaginative electives, but there's also a strong emphasis on courses to prepare for the California bar exam.

King Hall's opportunities for practical training are unusually good. Thanks to a growing number of enthusiastic faculty, students can enroll in a variety of skills-training courses covering all aspects of lawyering, from counseling to negotiations to trial and appellate litigation. Students may also choose from a number of for-credit clinical programs or design their own. The school encourages participation in interscholastic skills competitions and often rewards it with academic credit.

Competition within King Hall is minimal. Most students freely exchange notes, outlines, and friendly advice. Each year, second- and third-year students volunteer to serve as "Big Sibs" to entering first-years. Even the Moot Court Competition rules foster cooperation among the contestants.

Grade-consciousness is also at a low ebb, except for the minority looking for employment with large, blue-chip firms. While first-year professors are officially encouraged to conform to certain grade distribution guidelines, adherence is reportedly spotty. In any event, there are generally few As, but also very few Ds and almost no Fs. Exams are graded anonymously (each student uses an identifying number, and the professor doesn't know which number is for which student). Best of all, law review membership is conferred not according to GPA, but on the basis of submission of a completed article showing superior legal research and analysis.

Because of the school's size, students get to know each other well. Parties are usually informal and open to everybody. Many King Hall students are married and have children, so social and extracurricular activities are structured with families in mind. (The law building houses an infant-care co-op.)

Despite a three quarters or larger California contingent, the student body contains a lot of variety. The admissions process is complicated. Scores and grades are the points of departure, but this is one school that carefully considers essays, extra letters of recommendation, and former experience—for everyone, not just for borderline cases. For those who remember Davis as the home of the *Bakke* case, it should be noted that admissions of women and minorities are strong and improving, largely due to an energetic and vocal alliance of Third World and women's groups.

Politically, most King Hall students classify themselves as liberal to leftist. It is not uncommon for professors to stress social responsibility. The school has a strong group of students interested in public-interest law and local chapters of the American Civil Liberties Union and the National Lawyers Guild. The King Hall Legal Foundation funds many student public-interest projects.

Both the Environmental Law Society and Student Lawyers for the Arts have large and enthusiastic followings. There is also a small International Law Society. The law school newspaper, printed monthly, has consistently won national honors. Students have a strong say on faculty committees (including admissions) and in general school affairs. The Law Student Association has proven a valuable instrument for reform.

The law building is modern, air-conditioned, and well suited to its purposes. The library gets high ratings. Each student gets a key to the building to ensure twenty-four-hour accessibility.

Davis is very much a college town. The community prides itself on environmental awareness, and outdoor recreation is something of a religion. Bicycles are the most common means of transportation. Automobile parking is scarce and expensive, and some streets are closed to cars. Unfortunately, a car is practically indispensable to get out of Davis to do clinical work or to visit San Francisco or nearby Sacramento. Big-city entertainment is conspicuously absent in Davis, which offers only two movie theaters and the events on campus.

Most King Hall students live in apartments, but quite a few share houses on a cooperative basis. Rents are rising but are cheap compared to San Francisco. The university has a very helpful off-campus-housing office. The limited campus housing has a long waiting list. In general, students should start looking for housing early in the summer.

Student evaluations of the placement office are mixed. Unlike many law schools, King Hall doesn't prescreen applicants for the convenience of employers, but rather views itself as a clearinghouse for information of interest to students.

Most of King Hall's students are glad they came here. Those disillusioned by law school feel it would have been worse at a larger, more conservative school. People accustomed to an urban life-style usually find it difficult to adjust to Davis's slower pace, but even they agree that it's a pleasant place to study law while keeping your sanity.

University of California, Hastings College of the Law

Address: **200 McAllister St., San Francisco, CA 94115**
Phone: **(415) 565-4623**
Degrees: **J.D., J.D./M.B.A., other joint degrees**
Median LSAT: **42**
Median GPA: **3.31**
Applicants accepted: **28%**
Transfers: **0–10/20–50**
Law enrollment: **1270**
Campus enrollment: **1270**

Part time: **0**
Women: **48%**
Minorities: **25%**
Dorm residents: **NA**
Library: **502,000**
Student-faculty ratio: **21:1**
Tuition: **$3161 (in-state), $10,860 (out-of-state)**
Financial aid: **70%**
Apply by: **February 1**

Disabled students: **Moderate/full accessibility. In five years, three partially sighted students, two deaf, four wheelchair users, seven with back problems.**

Placement: **Approximately 82% placed by graduation. Graduates took jobs in Pacific (91%), Mountain (3%), Middle Atlantic (2%), East North Central (2%), South Atlantic (2%), New England (1%), West South Central (.5%). Graduates entered private practice (82%), government (8%), judicial clerkships (7%), business (2%), public interest (2%). Salary range: $10,000–$61,000.**

Hastings offers an attractive combination of a traditional law school education and a politically aware student body.

The curriculum here follows the typical pattern. First-year sections of 80 to 100 students are given year-long courses in contracts, civil procedure, and torts, as well as semester-long classes in property and criminal law. Professors almost universally employ the case method, and almost as many continue to use the Socratic method. One-Ls also take a full-year legal research and writing class with approximately 20 students. Although the research and writing grade is not included in a student's GPA, one student reports that One-Ls are more competitive about their writing assignment than about any other course because it is the only faculty feedback they get before grades are posted at the end of the term.

Very few students receive As, reports one student, while 35 to 50 percent of each class will score Cs. Grade inflation—so prevalent at other schools—apparently remains unknown at Hastings. (The board on which grades are posted is known as the wailing wall.) Fortunately, voluntary discussion groups led by successful upperclass students help the first-years master their courses and learn the fine art of taking exams.

No discussion of academics at Hastings would be complete without a mention of the famous "65-Club." Hastings is unique for its policy of hiring the big names in law when they've retired elsewhere, which has its pros and cons. Long years of experience are valuable, but the policy means that the faculty is heavy on older, white, conservative males.

On the other hand, the student body at Hastings—which is one of the largest law schools in the nation—is diverse and tends toward liberal politics and social views. (The same can be said of some of the younger faculty.) Women and minority group students participate in a full range of student organizations geared to their interests, and a sizable number of older students serves to reduce the competitive pressures present at all law schools. Sign language translators are a familiar sight at lectures.

How about the finer things in life? San Francisco is a center of ethnic and cultural diversity. Theaters—there are big ones, small experimental ones, and everything in between. Clubs—choose from jazz, bluegrass, salsa, and Irish. The symphony, ballet, and opera are world class. And for those seeking the ideal jogging terrain, there's always Golden Gate Park.

Within a few blocks of Hastings are the Civic Center (with its park, modern art museum, opera house, symphony hall, and library), as well as government offices and an impressive array of state and federal courts.

Hastings' urban location is not without its drawbacks. The school consists of two modern buildings situated on a street corner, with a thirty-story dorm at the end of the block. The school is on the edge of a less-than-scenic area called the Tenderloin. The Tenderloin provides a valuable daily reminder of the needs of the impoverished members of our society. Although the area has seen some improvement in recent years, the school provides an escort service for those who feel uncomfortable walking alone at night.

San Francisco can be hard on a student's budget. Living alone—even in a rent-controlled studio apartment—is very expensive. Moving in with a group or a roommate makes city living more affordable. Those attracted to quieter suburban or semirural surroundings may live in El Cerrito, Daly City, or Marin County (approximately an hour commute), while those looking for a college community can live in Berkeley. The school is easily reachable via bus, BART (when it's running), trolley, or cable car.

Comparatively speaking, Hastings has a good number of extracurricular activities, even beyond the five journals and the moot court board. The more than thirty student groups on campus offer many opportunities to get involved in forums, speaker programs, films, peer counseling, and tutoring. Many of the campus organizations offer legal services to the community.

Hastings students recognize the need to work together on issues like preserving the special admissions program, recruiting minority students and faculty, and expanding the public-interest curriculum. They don't hesitate to come in conflict with the administration in pursuit of these goals. Conservative students tend to remain quiet.

Many Hastings students aspire to move on to the law offices in the San Francisco Bay Area. Hastings is often counted as one of the twenty top law schools in the country, and there are jobs out there for its graduates—but the quality and quantity of your employment opportunities will have a definite correlation to how well you do academically.

Getting into the tight San Francisco legal community isn't easy. If you're willing to work hard enough to get good grades, a Hastings degree can provide the entrée you need.

University of California—Los Angeles School of Law

Address: **405 Hilgard Ave.,
Los Angeles, CA 90024**
Phone: (213) 825-2080
Degrees: **J.D., LL.M.,
. J.D./M.B.A., J.D./M.A.
(architecture and urban
planning), other joint
degrees**
Median LSAT: **44**
Median GPA: **3.68**
Applicants accepted: **14%**
Transfers: **22**
Law enrollment: **941 (932
J.D.)**

Campus enrollment: **35,000**
Part time: **0**
Women: **39%**
Minorities: **37%**
Dorm residents: **NA**
Library: **454,700**
Student-faculty ratio: **13:1**
Tuition: **$3323 (in-state),
$11,022 (out-of-state)**
Financial aid: **75%**
Apply by: **February 1**

Disabled students: **Fully accessible. In one year, six disabled
students.**

Placement: **Approximately 88% placed by graduation; approximately
95% employed six to nine months after graduation. Graduates
employed in Pacific (84%), South Atlantic (4%), Middle Atlantic
(4%), East North Central (3%), Mountain (2%), Foreign (1%),
New England (.5%). Graduates entered private practice (65%),
government (9%), judicial clerkships (6%), business (2%), public
interest (2%), unknown (17%). Salary range: $20,000–$83,000.**

Ten minutes from the beach, twenty from downtown, UCLA Law
is located on the university's campus in Westwood, on the west side
of Los Angeles. Westwood has dozens of first-run movie theaters,
restaurants, and stores (bring your credit cards; everyone else
does). The university itself offers terrific films, concerts, art, swimming pools, tennis courts, and video games. The campus is so
lovely that it's a shame more law students don't see it, although
some have been spotted studying torts in the quiet splendor of
the sculpture garden.

UCLA law students are a highly motivated group. A substantial
portion of each class is admitted strictly on the basis of LSAT and
undergraduate GPA, and the competition is stiff. The remainder
are selected according to a combination of factors, including

grades and economic, ethnic, and career background. A good percentage of each incoming class is older than the early-twenties majority. UCLA has a well-developed diversity program to attract and keep students whose backgrounds lend variety to the school's atmosphere.

As elsewhere, first year is a tense period, as students who've always done well start to feel average. Nevertheless, most students are not unduly competitive. Everyone shares notes, and professors encourage students to see them to discuss concerns. Professors also often give practice exams to alleviate the fear of the unknown.

Fall of second year is trying too, because it's the interview season for summer clerk jobs. One student reports, "The mental health counseling is excellent and often frequented by stressed-out law students."

But the last three semesters are a much more relaxed time, when most UCLA law students regain their membership in the human race and a few even get a tan. And there are second-year "mentors," faculty advisers, and a survival guide to help the first-years—and frequent barbecues, beer busts, and parties for everyone—so don't worry too much about being worked to death.

The courses here are good enough to warrant the time they demand. During the first year, a student has two classes each semester with 25 to 30 students and two or three classes enrolling 75. Enrollment in upper-division courses averages about 45, but popular standbys can attract 100 students or more. The pressure to perform brilliantly in class is reduced by the fact that exams are graded anonymously, and class participation is rarely included in final grades.

While the curriculum is essentially geared toward producing mainstream corporate lawyers, many courses are more theoretical than practical, and most of the professors are fairly liberal politically. The curriculum ranges beyond the standard meat and potatoes and includes strong business-related courses as well as copyright and entertainment law (remember, this is Los Angeles). Recent offerings have included Law and Literature, Sports Law, and Women and the Law.

In addition to a highly developed clinical program, UCLA has the distinction of offering an unusually flexible externship program that permits students to spend a full semester working in

LA or anywhere in the country. About a third of the students take advantage of this option and work in such diverse settings as a judge's chambers, the Securities and Exchange Commission, the National Labor Relations Board, the ACLU, or the Actors or Directors Guild.

The law library is reportedly a weak point. Resource materials sometimes have to be sought out in the University Research Library.

Law review membership is based not on grades but on either winning a writing competition or producing a publishable comment (student article) acceptable to the board of editors. Six alternative journals cover environmental law, international law, communications law, and issues pertaining to women, blacks, and Chicanos.

There are numerous student organizations that are active, including the student government. The minority student associations work hard at recruiting minority applicants and sponsor speakers and events. The Public Interest Law Foundation, supported by alums and students, makes grants for public-interest summer jobs and also sponsors speakers and events throughout the school year. The annual variety show, the Law Revue, gives everyone an opportunity to indulge in low humor.

Living space in Los Angeles is somewhat expensive and difficult to find, but on-campus housing is even more elusive. The law school has a housing board, and there is a campus housing office. Despite the difficulties, no one yet has had to sleep in the student lounge in order to attend the school.

UCLA has a national name, and campus recruiting is quite strong. Students have to go through a computerized lottery system to land interviews. The placement office is understaffed, so it mainly provides resources and workshops to help students run their own job search. Information on public-interest opportunities is expanding. Second-year summer jobs (which often lead to offers for after graduation) are based heavily on grades, so one student advises tersely, "Do well first year."

UCLA is often inaccurately portrayed as a laid-back, palm-tree haven of a law school. In fact, the school's southern California location does not preclude a large amount of hard-core intellectual activity. If you come here, you'll find time to go to the beach—but usually with a book in hand.

California Western School of Law

Address: **350 Cedar St., San Diego, CA 92101**
Phone: **(619) 239-0391**
Degrees: **J.D., M.C.L.**
Median LSAT: **156**
Median GPA: **3.07**
Applicants accepted: **34%**
Transfers: **15/30**
Law enrollment: **774 (769 J.D.)**
Campus enrollment: **774**

Part time: **0**
Women: **41%**
Minorities: **16%**
Dorm residents: **0**
Library: **198,000**
Student-faculty ratio: **16:1**
Tuition: **$14,400**
Financial aid: **95% (17% gift)**
Apply by: **May 1 (for fall), November 1 (for spring), March 30 (aid)**

Disabled students: **Moderately accessible. In five years, one deaf student, one wheelchair user.**

Placement: **88% employed six months after graduation. 50 employers on campus in one year; 50% from San Diego, 32% other California, 7% Nevada, 7% Washington, DC, 4% Hawaii; 64% private firms, 29% public service, 7% other. Graduates took jobs in Pacific (69%), Mountain (13%), Middle Atlantic (6%), South Atlantic (4%), New England (3%), West South Central (2%), East North Central (2%), Foreign (2%). Graduates entered private practice (65%), government (20%), business (9%), public interest (2%), academic (1%). Salary range: $12,000–$95,000. Mean salary: $40,000. California bar pass rate: 71.7%.**

Cal Western is situated in sunny, salubrious, and scenic San Diego. Popular images of southern California notwithstanding, one can go through an entire three years here without once hearing "surf's up" in the hallways.

Students report rising admissions standards, but in the meantime, this is one place where a comparative low-scorer can get a crack at a legal education. Many feel this is one of Cal Western's strongest points: the gamble the school is willing to take with the people it admits. The gamble doesn't always pay off. Happy admittees may find themselves back on the streets as unhappy first-year flunk-outs.

Student life here is greatly affected by the locale. San Diego is one of the best places to be when winter rolls around. If you've gone to college in the northern reaches, imagine a place where down jackets are seen only in meat lockers. Attracted by the beneficent clime, students, married and single—and faculty—come from places like New York, New Jersey, Hawaii, Alaska, and Nevada, in addition to the substantial contingent from California.

A professional attitude, not throat-cutting, prevails. As one student puts it, "Everyone knows this isn't Harvard, so why try to fool yourself, let alone anyone else?" As everywhere, there are a few overachievers (usually known by less polite terms), but the dominant attitude is "Work, pass the bar, and buy your first Mercedes." A more competitive approach wouldn't fit the relaxed life-style of southern California. (This doesn't apply to LA, but everyone in San Diego blissfully ignores the metropolis up north.)

Cal Western itself is located a few blocks from the heart of San Diego. It's an easy commute to the courts, government offices, and tattoo parlors, the last of which are world-renowned.

The role of the student government has grown in the past few years from that of gadfly to almost-equal in school policymaking. According to students, some of the professors seem to feel it's a case of the inmates running the asylum. Relations between the Student Bar Association and the administration have been amicable lately, but this followed a couple of years of intense "conversation."

Since Cal Western broke away from United States International University, it has been independent and unaffiliated with any other university or the state system. So, fortunately, there's no out-of-touch bureaucracy to deal with. Unfortunately, there are also none of the facilities and resources that go along with a diversity of student interests and activities. San Diego has a lot to offer, though.

The school's academic diet adheres to the standard ABA menu. The required core courses encompass the basic areas of law as covered on the California bar exam. The school offers a generally solid background; strengths and weaknesses in individual areas vary greatly, as at most schools, depending on the interests (or lack of same) of the professors.

Teaching ranges from stimulating to stultifying. On the whole, the faculty is young and not afraid to try such new things as videotape, in extensive use here. Any practice court class or appearance can be taped and played back to teach the art of better oral argument.

California allows certified students to appear in court under the supervision of an attorney. Recognizing the importance of practical skills, Cal Western offers one of the most extensive clinical programs in the state, including both full- and part-time internships during the school year and the summer. If none of the school's existing programs suits your fancy, you can create your own. Most of the programs are tremendous learning laboratories.

The school is willing to be innovative, which is a major plus in the tradition-laden world of legal academia. Cal Western allows students to start in September or January, which can be attractive to students graduating from college in the middle of the year. It also allows students to take the option of graduating in two or two and a half calendar years, instead of the normal three. Other examples of the school's willingness to be imaginative are the optional concentrations in international law and sports and entertainment law.

Jobs are no problem for the Cal Western grad whose father is a senior partner of the firm. For everybody else, it comes down to knocking on doors. A large number of students clerk after their first year, but the ratio of work to wages approximates that of slave labor. San Diego is a buyer's market for legal clerks. From all reports, the placement service is running smoothly and providing strong leads.

At Cal Western, you can slide by, do the minimum, and get a great tan, or you can work day and night and live like a monk. Most people fall somewhere in between the extremes. The Cal Western advantage is that you can choose the style that suits you best.

Benjamin N. Cardozo School of Law, Yeshiva University

Address: **55 Fifth Ave., Room 1047, New York, NY 10003**
Phone: **(212) 790-0274**
Degrees: **J.D.**
Median LSAT: **39**

Median GPA: **3.18**
Applicants accepted: **36%**
Transfers: **5–10/45–50**
Law enrollment: **960**
Campus enrollment: **960**

Part time: **0**

Women: **43%**

Minorities: **8%**

Dorm residents: **0**

Library: **326,100**

Student-faculty ratio: **18:1**

Tuition: **$14,520**

Financial aid: **NA**

Apply by: **April 1 (for fall),**

December 1 (for spring)

Disabled students: **Moderate/full accessibility. In a recent year, two wheelchair users and two with other mobility problems.**

Placement: **Approximately 85% employed six to nine months after graduation. Graduates entered private practice (65%), government (19%), business (7%), judicial clerkships (5%), public interest (2%), academic (1%), unknown (2%).**

As one of the newer law schools in the country—it graduated its first class in June 1979—Cardozo is still getting its act together. It has gained overnight recognition by assembling a quality faculty and solid student body. Concentrating on these key areas meant that initially other needs went unmet, but clinical education programs, internship opportunities, and the school record in intermural moot court have all improved steadily.

The student Arts and Entertainment Society has been active almost since the school's inception; 1982 saw the inaugural issue of the *Art and Entertainment Law Journal.* The *Cardozo Law Review* grants membership on the basis of first-year class rank and/or a writing competition.

The hardest task for any new school is to build up dependable contacts for job placement. Cardozo has done surprisingly well, considering its youth. However, the placement effort remains hampered by a wait-and-see attitude toward the school on the part of some employers (though the number of New York firms interviewing on campus is growing). While law review members have generally been successful in finding permanent positions, many others have found the job search to be an exercise in frustration, particularly for first-years, who do not have transcripts to show employers until well into June. Still, the school's extensive summer internship program, judicial internships, and criminal law clinical opportunities help students gain experience and make contacts.

The faculty combines professors who have achieved distinction at other law schools with younger professors who have less teaching experience but offer practical expertise in diverse legal fields.

Adjunct professors taking time out from private practice in specialized areas add spice to the usual selection of course offerings.

As at other "national" law schools, casebooks are the basic texts for most courses. The Socratic technique dominates the classrooms. To some professors, this means an opportunity to sharpen their talent for witty repartee; others see it as a duel that the student must never win.

Most faculty members are easily approachable during their relatively infrequent office hours. Appointments are generally a good idea, but catching a professor in the hallway is not deemed a breach of etiquette. Class sizes vary from 20 to 150; seminars are smaller. Few courses are devoted exclusively to New York law.

The diversity of Cardozo's student body can only be compared to the diversity of New York itself. The most immediately apparent variety is among age groups: in addition to the majority of under-twenty-five-year-olds, many of Cardozo's students are starting second (or third) careers. Women have always been present in large numbers. Ethnic and religious diversity can also be found, despite the Yeshiva University affiliation and a preponderance of Jewish students. Above all, the impression is one of diversity of life-style. Classroom attire ranges from T-shirts and jeans to silk and cashmere. New Jersey carpools are as popular as Greenwich Village walk-up apartments.

Due to its Yeshiva affiliation, the law school observes all the Jewish holidays. Students have a great deal of time off in the fall. Spring break is scheduled to coincide with Passover. Every week the doors are locked from sundown on Friday until Sunday morning, in observance of the Sabbath. The lack of access to the library during this time has produced controversy, but the administration has made arrangements for another law school to open its Saturday library hours to Cardozo students.

Although a very serious work ethic prevails at 55 Fifth Avenue, students still seem to find the time to be social. Cardozo is located on the northern fringe of Greenwich Village, one of the most attractive parts of Manhattan. You'll find plenty of music, theater, coffeehouses, local color—everything but inexpensive housing— right nearby. Cardozo has no campus or residential facilities. Many students double or triple up in nearby apartments that rent for princely sums. Others commute; the school is easy to reach by public transportation.

Cardozo has come a long way in a short time. *U.S. News &
World Report* has named it one of the country's "up-and-coming"
law schools. The school even produced a U.S. Supreme Court
clerk in the first graduating class. Still, the school has a way to go
before its reputation among employers can be taken for granted.

Case Western Reserve University School of Law

Address: **11075 East Blvd.,
Cleveland, OH 44106**
Phone: **(216) 368-3600**
Degrees: **J.D., J.D./M.B.A.,
J.D./M.S.S.A. (social work),
J.D./M.A. (legal history),
J.D./M.N.O. (nonprofit
management), other joint
degrees**
Median LSAT: **39**
Median GPA: **3.4**
Applicants accepted: **29%**

Transfers: **5–15/5–15**
Law enrollment: **698**
Campus enrollment: **8000**
Part time: **2%**
Women: **44%**
Minorities: **9%**
Dorm residents: **9%**
Library: **291,800**
Student-faculty ratio: **18:1**
Tuition: **$14,880**
Financial aid: **79%**
Apply by: **April 1**

Disabled students: **Fully accessible. Within five years, two wheelchair
users and two students with other mobility problems.**
Placement: **Approximately 57% placed by graduation; approximately
85% employed six to nine months after graduation. Graduates
took jobs in East North Central (69%), Middle Atlantic (17%),
South Atlantic (9%), New England (2%), Mountain (2%), East
South Central (1%), Foreign (1%). Graduates entered private
practice (66%), government (13%), judicial clerkships (10%),
business (6%), self-employed (2%), military (1%), public interest
(1%), advanced degree (1%), nonlegal (1%). Salary range:
$21,000–$83,000.**

Case Western Reserve has long been in the middle ranks of law
schools, but campus morale is high and students hope the school
may soon be inching its way into the big time.

The school's facilities are one source of pride. The building is
modern, well designed, and attractive. Ground breaking for a new
addition took place in 1992.

For an urban campus, Case Western Reserve University is very
pretty. The surrounding University Circle area is one of the nicest

parts of Cleveland. The area includes four museums and lots of greenery. Unfortunately, the neighborhood borders on a high-crime area, so it leaves something to be desired in the way of safety at night.

The dorms are as unpleasant as dorm living usually is. There is plenty of good (but not necessarily inexpensive) housing nearby, in old apartment houses with big rooms and high ceilings.

Despite the school's efforts to get a geographical mix, close to half of each year's students are from the Midwest, especially Ohio, and the rest are largely from the East Coast. As financial aid money dries up, Case has done a good job helping students in need to find alternative sources of funding.

"The faculty is absolutely top-notch, which gives me great confidence in the future of the school," writes one student. There are several big names, but still it's easy to talk to most of the professors without feeling intimidated. Grade inflation never took hold at Case, so sliding by with no work really isn't a possibility.

The curriculum is diverse and includes opportunities to study international law and problems relating to law and medicine. All course work first year is required, and after that everything except professional responsibility is elective.

The Moot Court Board is first rate and has done well in national competitions. The law review has a good reputation, as do the *Journal of International Law* and *Health Matrix: The Journal of Law-Medicine*. Other organizations include the usual caucuses for women and black students and the Student Bar Association.

Placement is a serious worry for at least half the class. The student perception is that Case grads don't find jobs as easily as their peers at some comparable schools. This is one of the places where distinguishing yourself academically can be the key to your future. Graduates seem most welcome in Cleveland and surrounding cities (Akron, Toledo, Columbus), or elsewhere in the Midwest or East. Receptivity toward Case grads has increased among Chicago firms lately. Obviously, however, a Case degree is not an easy ticket to big-city, big-money practice.

More than one Case graduate is perfectly content with the idea of staying in Cleveland. In fact, some of them turned down law schools in other cities precisely to take advantage of Cleveland's lower cost of living and less competitive job market. Cleveland offers excellent cultural and social resources, most of which are accessible from the law school by foot or public transportation. So before you write off Case, keep in mind that there are reasons why the current students think so highly of the place.

University of Chicago Law School

Address: **1111 East 60th St., Chicago, IL 60637**
Phone: **(312) 702-9484**
Degrees: **J.D., LL.M., J.S.D., M.C.L., D.C.L., J.D./M.B.A., J.D./M.A. or Ph.D. (economics, history), J.D./M.A. (public policy, international relations), other joint degrees**
Median LSAT: **46**
Median GPA: **3.64**
Applicants accepted: **NA**
Transfers: **NA**

Law enrollment: **579 (546 J.D.)**
Campus enrollment: **9000**
Part time: **0**
Women: **38%**
Minorities: **15%**
Dorm residents: **NA**
Library: **541,500**
Student-faculty ratio: **14:1**
Tuition: **$17,247**
Financial aid: **75%**
Apply by: **rolling admissions, January 15 recommended**

Disabled students: **In one year, one disabled student.**
Placement: **88% of first-years, 99% of second-years, and 98% of third-years placed by end of spring term. 480 employers on campus in one year; 37% from Northeast, 30% Midwest, 25% West, 8% South. Graduates employed in Midwest (40%), East (34%), West (15%), South (8%). Graduates entered private practice (71%), judicial clerkships (23%), business (2%), government (2%), public interest (2%).**

Given its awesome reputation, you would expect the University of Chicago to have an outstanding law school, and it does. Despite the ungodly Chicago winters, a devoted law faculty and hard-working student body engage in an educational interchange that consistently breeds top-notch lawyers and legal scholars.

Chicago's dedication to the fundamentals is evidenced by the rigorous research and writing tutorial that supplements the basic first-year courses. The program is supervised by graduate fellows (not third-year students as at some other schools), runs for the entire year, and demands about fifteen to twenty hours of work per week. The dozen or so required legal memoranda and briefs are the bane of every first-year student's existence, demanding many hours for little credit. But the payoff is that it works: Chicago students agree that they get a superb education right from the start.

One of the law school's primary attractions is its small size. Located across the "Midway" from the main university campus, the law school is a close-knit community where everyone (well, almost everyone) knows everyone else, students and professors alike. Professors are *very* accessible—they virtually live at the law school. While this creates an atmosphere of involvement and academic intensity, some students feel claustrophobic, especially when they bump into a professor after they've just cut his class. (Yes, students do, on occasion, cut class, particularly during the baseball season.)

Classes tend to be smaller here than at many schools. Most important, oversubscribed courses that wreak havoc on student schedules simply don't exist at Chicago.

Unlike an increasing number of other law schools, Chicago does not encourage its students to substitute practical experience for classroom learning. Although the school operates an excellent legal aid clinic in which students obtain law school credits by working on real cases, the clinical program is open to only a small group. Every year students place their names in a lottery from which only about sixty are chosen and thirty actually choose to participate. Chicago does not give credit for any other types of law-related work experience.

Students here prepare well for class, but more for the sake of pride than anything else. Contrary to what you may have heard, students neither stand up when called upon nor are put down for giving the wrong answer (or for not answering at all). The students support each other's efforts and generally respect each other's views.

Chicago has its share of overly competitive students. But the competition is not engendered by professors' attitudes and is ignored by the majority of students. Classroom "grandstanding" or "flaming" is not particularly appreciated. Neither is it necessary; few if any students fail. Chicago's blind-grading system, where every student is given a confidential test number for identifying exams, makes class performance scholastically irrelevant. Grades are never posted.

One thing about Chicago that *is* highly competitive is the admissions process. Your college grades, LSAT scores, and recommendations had better be outstanding if you want to come here. Lest you get too discouraged, however, it should be noted that the admissions committee seeks a diverse student body; an interesting personality or unique background goes a long way to compensate for numerical deficiencies. This is one of the few law schools where interviews play a role in the selection process. Many students have pursued other professions or engaged in various interesting activities before entering law school.

The school does not pursue diversity with respect to the racial and ethnic makeup of its student body as actively as many students would like. The number of black students is on the low side for schools of this caliber. (A further indication of Chicago's anti-affirmative-action stance is the traditional underrepresentation of blacks and women on the faculty.)

Once you've been accepted, Easy Street (if that's what you choose) is just a few years away. As befits a "Top Five" law school, U of C has an extraordinary placement record. Each year, private-firm recruiters flock to Chicago from all parts of the country. Students interested in public-interest groups are rare and, though usually successful in finding jobs, they are generally left to their own devices. The placement office is not insensitive to this problem but hasn't yet cured it.

First-year students also reap the benefits of Chicago's placement record. Over the past few years, firms have come in increasing numbers to interview students who have yet to finish their contracts course. The negative aspect of this is that the pressure to find a job mounts almost as soon as classes begin.

Most of U of C students, like their professors, live in Hyde Park, close to the law school. (There is one law school dorm, but many students avoid it to escape the pressure-cooker environment.) Hyde Park, while pleasant, is very quiet, intensely intellectual, and a bit boring. It is a predominantly middle-class townhouse community and virtually the only truly integrated neighborhood in the city. Hyde Park is safe, if you're careful,

112 | **University of Cincinnati College of Law**

but it's surrounded by districts that might euphemistically be called "marginal." Good restaurants and bars are not Hyde Park's biggest attraction. What with these drawbacks, more and more students, particularly after the first year, commute from Chicago's North Side, where there is considerably more activity after dark.

Chicago's popular image exaggerates two aspects of the school—aspects that should be kept in perspective. First, despite its reputation, the law school is not overly conservative. (Milton Friedman is an economist, not a law professor.) The faculty is perhaps less liberal than at some other schools, but there is a healthy diversity of political views among both students and professors. "Traditional" is a better description.

Second, although "economic analysis of the law" is a specialty that Chicago pioneered and of which it is deservedly proud, it is not a pervasive influence at the school. There is no single school of thought to which all Chicago professors subscribe.

A good example of Chicago's approach to legal education is an annual meeting for first-year students to talk about exams. Topics covered include what professors are looking for in an answer, and how to deliver it. Old exams and sample answers are kept on file in the library.

Every Thursday night, Chicago students trek up to the North Side for "Bar Review," a weekly drinking mecca exploring Chicago's many pubs and clubs. And every Friday afternoon, Chicago students gather for a friendly wine mess. It's amazing how different a professor looks after several gin and tonics all around. There's music, an annual contest for the most job rejections, and everyone has a good time. Wine mess ensures that no work will be done on Friday night and, in many cases, on Saturday as well. But come Monday, Chicago students are back at work. They know how to relax, but they're here to take advantage of a superb legal education, and they don't forget it.

University of Cincinnati College of Law

Address: **Mail Location 40, Cincinnati, OH 45221**
Phone: **(513) 556-6805**

Degrees: **J.D., J.D./M.B.A., J.D./M.C.P. (community planning)**

Median LSAT: **161**

Median GPA: **3.35**

Applicants accepted: **24%**

Transfers: **5–10/10–20**

Law enrollment: **400**

Campus enrollment: **35,000**

Part time: **0**

Women: **51%**

Minorities: **22%**

Dorm residents: **NA**

Library: **279,600**

Student-faculty ratio: **15:1**

Tuition: **$5241 (in-state),**
$10,227 (out-of-state)

Financial aid: **75% (50% gift)**

Apply by: **April 1, March 1**
(aid)

Disabled students: **Fully accessible.**

Placement: **91% employed six months after graduation. 70% of second-years and 60% of third-years employed in legal jobs during academic year. 50% of first-years, 80% of second-years, and 55% of third-years placed by end of spring term. 66 employers on campus in one year; 48% from Cincinnati, 39% other Ohio, 9% Kentucky, 2% Florida, 2% West Virginia, 2% Pennsylvania, 2% Indiana; 65% private firms, 18% government or public interest, 14% corporations, 3% other. Graduates took jobs in Ohio, California, Kentucky, Illinois, West Virginia, Nevada, Pennsylvania, other. Graduates entered private practice (60%), judicial clerkships (12%), business (10%), government (8%), nonlegal (8%). Salary range: $15,000–$58,500. Mean salary: $39,576. Ohio bar pass rate: 91% (statewide average: 83%).**

The University of Cincinnati stands atop one of the seven hills of Cincinnati, which is widely thought of as a conservative, staid city. Both the university and the city are growing and changing, however, and they offer modern-day law students more than you might think.

The city's vibrant downtown is home to two of the nation's 250 largest law firms, as well as consumer products giant Procter & Gamble. Cincinnati is also the site of the U.S. Court of Appeals for the Sixth Court, the U.S. District Court for Southern Ohio, several Ohio state courts, and an abundance of state and federal agencies. All this commercial and legal activity generates clerkships for law students and permanent jobs for graduates.

On the UC campus, old facilities have been renovated, and the law school enjoys a new structure of its own. "A law student couldn't hope for more," one student says of the building. In addition to excellent classrooms and special activity facilities, there's a superb law library.

In the classroom, first-year students face an exhausting schedule of required courses. There is no choice of professor, and class size varies from 25 to 75. Advanced courses are largely elective. In practice, many students make their selections according to which subjects are tested on the various bar exams.

Second- and third-year clerkships are common and help provide the practical experience lacking in the theoretical classroom approach. Upperclass students may also gain experience through an extern program and trial practice course. (First-years are discouraged from working until the summer and can seldom find jobs until then anyway.)

Professors serve as student advisers. The arrogant and apathetic are in the minority, and most are well respected by students. Students evaluate professors at the end of each semester and even participate in the selection of new faculty. Favoritism is prevented by an anonymous grading system (in which students are assigned numbers). Grade posting is also by number.

Outside the classroom, student organizations include the Student Bar Association, Phi Alpha Delta, a student newspaper, organizations for black students and women, and many other groups. Students who participate in the Voluntary Income Tax Assistance program complete tax returns for low-income and elderly people. The Urban Morgan Institute for Human Rights awards fellowships to students, does research on human rights, and edits the *Human Rights Quarterly.*

Although it could never be mistaken for Chicago or New York, Cincinnati has strong traditions in music, the arts, and sports. In addition to the internationally recognized Cincinnati Symphony and May Festival, there are outstanding programs offered by UC's Conservatory of Music. Professional, college, and high school athletics are extremely popular in Cincinnati. Parks, golf courses, the Ohio River, and nearby lakes are all possible choices of recreation.

Clifton, the neighborhood that surrounds the university, is primarily residential, but it offers small shops, taverns, and nightclubs with a variety of atmospheres. The adjacent areas are equally promising. Bus transportation to all parts of the city is usually available, but students are advised to have their own transportation as well.

One word of caution, however: parking near UC is often impossible.

The cost of living in Cincinnati is much lower than in most large cities. Tuition at this state-supported school, though rising annually, remains reasonable. The cost of housing is less so. Because campus housing for law students is scarce, students are forced to rent near campus, where prices are often steep. Wise students will shop early.

Although placement in other cities is not unusual, UC's strong reputation is largely limited to its hometown. If you plan on settling in Cincinnati (as most UC grads do), you might do very well after three years at UC.

Columbia University School of Law

Address: **435 West 116th St., New York, NY 10027**
Phone: **(212) 854-2670**
Degrees: **J.D., LL.M., J.S.D., J.D./M.B.A., J.D./M.P.A., other joint degrees**
Median LSAT: **168**
Median GPA: **3.6**
Applicants accepted: **16%**
Transfers: **20–25/90–100**
Law enrollment: **1109 (999 J.D.)**

Campus enrollment: **19,500**
Part time: **0**
Women: **38%**
Minorities: **26%**
Dorm residents: **75%**
Library: **1,196,000**
Student-faculty ratio: **19:1**
Tuition: **$18,924**
Financial aid: **70% (30% gift)**
Apply by: **February 15**

Disabled students: **Fully accessible. In five years, three blind students, three deaf, two wheelchair users.**

Placement: **91% of first-years, 96% of second-years, and 96% of third-years placed by end of spring term. Approximately 98% employed three months after graduation. 450 employers on campus in one year; 31% from New York, 18% California, 17% Washington, DC, 4% Massachusetts, 3% each Texas, Connecticut, Illinois, Pennsylvania, and New Jersey, remainder from 19 other states; 93% private firms, 5% government, 1% public interest, 1% business. Graduates took jobs in New York (60%), California (8%), Washington, DC (7%), Texas (3%), 23 other states. Graduates entered private practice (75%), judicial clerkships**

(12%), government (3%), public interest (2%), advanced degree
(2%), business (1%), other (1%). Salary range: $24,000–$86,000.
Mean salary: $65,400. Mean salary for graduates entering private
New York City firms: $82,420.

Perhaps no other law school can equal Columbia's close ties to
Wall Street. A huge number of Columbia students remain in New
York City after graduation, and most of them are working for the
cream of corporate law firms. A recent wave of student activism—
focused primarily on adding women and minorities to the faculty—is noteworthy mainly because it takes place against the
backdrop of wave upon wave of Wall Streeters-in-training.

The faculty is a mixed bag of traditionalists who know Socrates
and his method on a first-name basis, and recent lateral hires
from other law schools who take a more humane approach to
instruction.

In light of that division, it is somewhat amazing that the faculty
instituted in 1989 what may be the newest trend in legal instruction. The first year saw a decrease in hours devoted to basics like
contracts and civil procedure, and the institution of three novel
subjects. Several weeks of Law and Economics, which applies economic theory to legal cases, was added to the Legal Method class
during the first semester. Perspectives on Modern Legal Thought,
which surveys contemporary jurisprudence ranging from libertari-
anism to critical legal studies to feminist jurisprudence, was added
to the spring term. Also in the spring, Foundations of the Regulatory State teaches students about the importance of legislative history and governmental agencies.

The changes initially occasioned a lot of grumbling among the
faculty and students, who suddenly had two and a half more semester hours during the first year. By now, the new curriculum is well
entrenched and widely accepted.

In the upper years, when almost all courses are electives, students typically enroll in corporations, federal income tax, evidence, debtor/creditor law, and trusts and estates. The school's
constitutional, corporate, and international areas are often considered to be among the finest in the country.

Most first-year classes are in sections of 110, although some
courses provide smaller sections. In the second and third years,

classes range from three students to 150 for the most popular subjects. In addition to lecture courses, there are numerous seminars. Clinical courses are offered in such areas as community development, immigration law, law and the arts, child advocacy, and race and poverty law. Additionally, several dozen clerkship opportunities are available in the federal courts during term time. A unique summer human rights internship program places students in public-interest work in the United States and foreign countries.

The work load at Columbia is heavy but manageable. During the first year, exclusive of class hours, students can expect to spend six hours daily, Monday through Thursday, slightly less on Friday, and more on weekends absorbing the assigned work.

Cross-registration in other Columbia grad schools is encouraged, and many students pursue joint degrees to take advantage of Columbia's top-notch schools of business, journalism, and international affairs. Some get joint degrees with Princeton's Woodrow Wilson School of Public and International Affairs.

Columbia demands some sort of legal writing from its students in five of the six terms. Upperclass students have a variety of ways of satisfying this requirement, including participation in moot court, independent research under a faculty member, writing in conjunction with a regular course or seminar, or journal work. Columbia students publish eight legal journals. In addition to the *Columbia Law Review,* there are specialized publications on human rights law, environmental law, law and social problems, transnational law, Chinese law, gender and the law, and law and the arts. Selection for the *Columbia Law Review* (the most prestigious of the group) is based on a combination of grades and performance in a writing competition.

First-year students satisfy the writing requirement with assigned memoranda in the fall (totaling thirty-five to forty pages) and moot court in the spring. Known for long hours and burdensome revisions and rewrites, the Columbia moot court program is an especially fine opportunity to learn the art of brief-writing. Second-year moot court is optional and more rigorous. It climaxes with arguments by the four top participants before three actual judges, one of whom is almost always a member of the Supreme Court of the United States.

Extracurricular activities are abundant at Columbia. Students elected to the student government, the Senate, work on student-faculty committees ranging from curriculum to faculty appointments to placement. The faculty listens to student senators' ideas but sometimes seems reluctant to act on the issues that concern students. The Senate has greater effect running various social events.

Additionally, Asian-Americans, African-Americans, and Latin Americans maintain active ethnic associations. There is a women's group (open to male members) and a Society of International Law, which sponsors frequent lectures and an annual conference. Among other groups, students may also join the Public Interest Law Foundation, the A.C.L.U., and the National Lawyers Guild.

The law school building, across the street from the university's main campus, is a major focus of student dissatisfaction. Dubbed "The Toaster" because of its modernistic design, it is cold in winter and stifling in summer. Although some piecemeal improvements have been made in recent years, a long-awaited addition was put on hold in 1990 when the university's Board of Trustees floated its own plan that might include tearing down the present structure. With time allotted for fund-raising and construction, change may not come until the next century.

As for Columbia's environment, New York offers the best and the worst of everything. A cutural, financial, and (especially) legal mecca, it is also noisy, dirty, slushy in the winter, and hot and humid in the summer. Morningside Heights (Columbia's neighborhood) is not terribly unsafe by New York standards, but it's no Sausalito or Marblehead either. The nearby restaurants and stores are almost uniformly mediocre, and barhopping requires a large hop to another part of town. The low quality of the watering holes in the college area is surpassed only by their infrequency.

Much of the law school social activity centers on the Rites of Spring, a week-long affair featuring an extremely enjoyable student musical and a faculty show, among other events. The student government and a law school social club organize weekly pubs and happy hours. There are even joint student-faculty social events.

As you've no doubt heard by now, finding housing in New York is extremely difficult. Columbia is reputed to be the second-largest landlord in the city (after the city itself), and the university-owned apartments are generally attractive and relatively inexpensive. Another possibility: dorm living. Most of those requesting dorm space get it; the rooms are small but livable. Columbia also maintains an office to lend a hand finding non-university-owned apartments.

Finally, a word about life after law school. Though jobs have definitely become scarcer with the glut of new lawyers on the market, the pace of recruiting and hiring here would still leave students from most other schools breathless. The preponderance of that activity is among private firms, but the few students headed for a public-interest practice benefit from visiting speakers and a loan-forgiveness program. Although Columbia can't eliminate all the difficulties of your transition *into* law school, your transition *out of* law school will be relatively painless.

University of Connecticut School of Law

Address: **55 Elizabeth St., Hartford, CT 06105**
Phone: **(203) 241-4697**
Degrees: **J.D., J.D./M.B.A., J.D./M.P.A., J.D./M.S.W. (social work), J.D./M.L.S. (library science), J.D./M.A. (public policy)**
Median LSAT: **160 (day), 158 (evening)**
Median GPA: **3.32 (day), 3.17 (evening)**
Applicants accepted: **22%**
Transfers: **0–5/50–60**

Law enrollment: **658**
Campus enrollment: **658**
Part time: **34%**
Women: **51%**
Minorities: **15%**
Dorm residents: **0**
Library: **360,800**
Student-faculty ratio: **17:1**
Tuition: **$7774 (in-state), $11,660 (MA, NH, RI, VT residents), $16,396 (others)**
Financial aid: **55%**
Apply by: **March 1**

Disabled students: **Moderate/full accessibility. Within five years, one deaf student, one wheelchair user, two with other mobility problems.**
Placement: **85% employed nine months after graduation. Graduates took jobs in Northeast (84%), Middle Atlantic (9%), North Central (2%), Southwest (1%), South Central (1%), Foreign (1%). Graduates entered private practice (56%), judicial clerkships (14%), business (13%), government (9%), academic (4%), public interest (2%), military (1%). Salary range: $20,000–$88,000. Connecticut bar pass rate: 79% (statewide average: 77%).**

Are you looking for a solid and inexpensive legal education? If you want to practice in New England, consider applying to the University of Connecticut.

U Conn (pronounced like Yukon) is proud of its low student-faculty ratio. The largest first-year class doesn't exceed 75 students, and each entering student is assigned to a small section of about 25 students for one of the required courses. Because of the small student body in both the day and evening divisions, it's easy to get to know the faculty, most of whom are young, dedicated, and very good at what they do.

The early 1980s saw the law school move from a state building that looked like a junior high to a spacious campus on the former site of the Hartford Seminary. The campus extends over twenty acres and includes five Gothic-style buildings. The law school is geographically separate from U Conn's main campus in Storrs, a rural community thirty miles away.

The state university affiliation is not easily forgotten, however. About three quarters of the students are Connecticut residents. Many attended college outside the state and are returning to practice law in Connecticut. Because the school mainly attracts students who have already decided to settle in New England, the network of U Conn alumni on hiring committees elsewhere is limited. Still, the curriculum doesn't particularly emphasize Connecticut law, and a growing number of students are moving outside the Northeast to practice.

The admissions committee strives for a diverse student body. A limited special admissions program is in effect. In the past, it has brought physically disabled, educationally disadvantaged, and minority students to the school.

The evening division students tend to be older than their daytime colleagues, and many are working full time. The evening students have been heard to complain that services like placement and financial aid counseling are primarily scheduled for the convenience of the day division students and the staff, although all maintain some evening hours. The same predominantly full-time faculty teaches both divisions.

Scheduling is unusually flexible at U Conn. Part-time enrollment is permitted in the day as well as the evening division. Commuters from towns throughout Connecticut and Massachusetts can sometimes schedule classes over a two- to four-day week. Upperclass students may take courses in either the day or evening, and many students take advantage of the numerous opportunities to work for law firms.

The school's Hartford location has permitted the development of a truly comprehensive clinical program. Students represent indigent clients in both civil and criminal matters. The Criminal Clinic's assistance is routinely solicited for some of the biggest and most publicized criminal cases in the state, and students may even argue criminal appeals before the Connecticut Supreme Court. Academic credit can also be earned by working for a state administrative agency, clerking for a state or federal judge, drafting and analyzing legislation for state lawmakers, assisting patients in state mental health institutions, and doing labor relations work. This is one school where legal studies are not carried on in a theoretical vacuum.

Of course, the theoretical side is not ignored. As at most schools, the core curriculum is taught through casebooks. There are "big names" teaching corporations, tax, and international law. The mandatory courses are standard: civil procedure, constitutional law, contracts, criminal law, property, torts, legal method, and professional responsibility. An upperclass writing project is also required for graduation.

In conjunction with certain University of Connecticut graduate schools, Southern Connecticut State University, and Hartford's private Trinity College, students may pursue several dual degrees. Students may also get credit for courses at other U Conn schools and at other accredited institutions, often without paying additional fees. Interested faculty from Trinity College and the university's Storrs campus sometimes teach courses at the law school.

Among a good-size group of student organizations, the "big three" are law review, the moot court board, and the Student Bar Association. Membership in the *Connecticut Law Review* and the *Journal of International Law* is determined by class standing and a writing competition. The moot court board picks its members from several annual intramural competitions, and moot court teams go on to compete in about ten national and international competitions yearly. The SBA organizes social functions, invites speakers, selects students to serve on faculty committees, and is generally active on student issues.

U Conn's students are a loyal group. Most of them like and

are proud of the school. Given the moderate tuition (especially for residents of Connecticut and of other New England states without public law schools) and the first-rate clinical opportunities, you may want to join them.

Cornell Law School

Address: **Myron Taylor Hall, Ithaca, NY 14853**
Phone: **(607) 255-5141**
Degrees: **J.D., LL.M., J.S.D., J.D./M.B.A., J.D./M.R.P. (regional planning), J.D./M.I.L.R. (industrial and labor relations), J.D./M.A. or Ph.D. (various)**
Median LSAT: **165**
Median GPA: **3.55**
Applicants accepted: **19%**

Transfers: **5–10/50–75**
Law enrollment: **570 (550 J.D.)**
Campus enrollment: **19,000**
Part time: **0**
Women: **40%**
Minorities: **22%**
Dorm residents: **approx. 20%**
Library: **740,000**
Student-faculty ratio: **15:1**
Tuition: **$18,100**
Financial aid: **70% (45% gift)**
Apply by: **February 1**

Disabled students: **Moderate/full accessibility. In a recent year, one blind student, one deaf, two with mobility problems.**
Placement: **95% employed six months after graduation. 90% of second-years and 90% of third-years placed by end of spring term. 450 employers on campus in one year; from New York, California, Washington, DC, Pennsylvania. Graduates took jobs in Middle Atlantic (37%), Pacific (22%), New England (13%), South Atlantic (13%), East North Central (9%), East South Central (3%), Mountain (1%), West North Central (1%), West South Central (1%), Foreign (1%). Graduates entered private practice (60%), judicial clerkships (20%), government (10%), public interest (5%), other (5%).**

High above Cayuga's waters, at the gateway to the Ivy League's largest university, lies Cornell Law. Cornell's reputation as a first-rate law school is well established and well deserved. For students attracted to the idea of a small law school in a uniquely picturesque college town, Cornell's program is unsurpassed.

Admissions at Cornell become more selective all the time, and the result is a serious, bright, accomplished student body. What sets Cornell apart from many of the other so-called top schools is its size: each entering class has only about 180 students. The small student body eases access to faculty and administration and promotes involvement in programs and activities outside the classroom. As for the faculty, it is small in number but large in stature.

Both Cornell and the rest of Ithaca are second to none in architectural and natural beauty. Ithaca is located at the southern end of Lake Cayuga, within a fifteen-minute drive of Taughannock Falls, the highest straight-drop waterfall east of the Rockies. The price of the upstate New York location: a very cold and very white winter that lasts from late November until the end of March, and sometimes beyond.

Ithaca's cultural offerings, while extraordinary for a town of its population, cannot match those of any large city. But as the rigors of law school rarely allow for extensive forays beyond the realm of study, all but the most confirmed urbanites find Ithaca's charming beauty and mellow, late-1960s atmosphere both entertaining and relaxing.

First year is a grueling experience anywhere. Since the entering class at Cornell is small, and most frosh don't have the foresight or resources to avoid the law dorm, it's hard to escape the feeling that others know your every move before you do. Classes range in size from 25 to 100 people; professors swear by the Socratic method. Add a long winter, and the result is pressure. The pressure, however, does not lead to cutthroat competition. Rather, students tend to develop camaraderie, often studying for exams in groups. Another tension-reliever is the school's squash court, which is located (literally) in the library. Students play among themselves, and with the faculty.

The initial pressure tends to dissipate after the first year. Second- and third-year students generally move off campus, although there are some open spaces in the law dorm and a few resident adviser positions available throughout the university. Housing becomes cheaper and more spacious the farther one is willing to venture away from the college-town area, with a few particularly nice places for rent (or for sale) along the lake and back in the hills.

The administration emphasizes that after a traditional first-year curriculum, students are largely free to follow their own interests in selection of courses. It is true that there are classes offered in a variety of legal areas. For example, the legal aid clinical program is superb, especially considering the size of the school and its location. International law courses are numerous. (A strong international studies program brings in an impressive array of outside speakers. Foreign LL.M. students also add an international flavor.) Nevertheless, many of the most heavily subscribed upperclass courses are corporate-oriented. The result isn't surprising; as at most elite law schools, the emphasis on corporate practice throughout the school is strong.

Cornell participates in semester externship programs at the National Wildlife Federation, the Sierra Club Legal Defense Fund, and the National Women's Law Center. Although student interest in these programs is growing, few choose to study away from Cornell.

The power at Cornell, according to students, resides in the faculty. The deans have little unilateral authority. Policy decisions are made by various faculty committees, with token student representation. These representatives are appointed by the popularly elected Cornell Law Student Association. CLSA dispenses a meager student activities budget and organizes social events, which are increasingly held in conjunction with other graduate schools at Cornell. (By the way, there is little law school romance, and what there is, you hear about the next day.)

The Public Interest Law Union, Black Law Students Association, Women's Law Coalition, Environmental Law Society, International Law Society, and other groups all do their best, but for most students, studies come first.

Cornell recently completed an award-winning addition to and renovation of the law school. The project added considerably to the library stack space, as well as increasing study areas.

The law review and moot court board are separately and generously funded. Admission to the law review is granted either for first- or second-year grades or for victory in an exhausting writing competition at the start of the second year. Students also edit journals on international law and law and public policy. The moot court program is very active and very good.

Whatever faults Cornell might have, the recruiting situation isn't one of them. Cornell grads are sought by as good a representation of New York firms as those of any school in the nation. Aided by the prestige of the Cornell name, grads get jobs all over the country, sometimes in offbeat places like Honolulu or the Virgin Islands. The placement office is reportedly slanted toward big-city private firms; nevertheless, the school has launched a loan-forgiveness program for graduates in low-paying public-interest jobs.

Cornell offers a distinctive alternative among the nation's top law schools because of its size and its setting. The mood is intimate and friendly, if perhaps a bit monastic. But the fact remains that as at most law schools, pressure is a way of life, and avoiding it, while possible, is difficult.

Creighton University School of Law

Address: **2133 California St., Omaha, NE 68178**
Phone: **(402) 280-2872**
Degrees: **J.D., J.D./M.B.A.**
Median LSAT: **155**
Median GPA: **3.22**
Applicants accepted: **31%**
Transfers: **2/6**
Law enrollment: **592**
Campus enrollment: **6225**

Part time: **3%**
Women: **41%**
Minorities: **6%**
Dorm residents: **NA**
Library: **158,000**
Student-faculty ratio: **23:1**
Tuition: **$11,157**
Financial aid: **75% (24% gift)**
Apply by: **May 1, April 1 (aid)**

Disabled students: **Moderate/full accessibility. One wheelchair user in one year.**
Placement: **87% employed six months after graduation. Graduates in a recent year took jobs in West North Central (66%), Pacific (8%), Mountain (7%), East North Central (5%), South Atlantic (5%), New England (3%), Middle Atlantic (3%), West South Central (2%). Graduates entered private practice (47%), government (23%), judicial clerkships (13%), business (6%), military (3%), public interest (3%). Salary range: $20,000–$50,000. Nebraska bar pass rate: 96%. Iowa bar pass rate: 87%.**

Creighton University is located in downtown Omaha, Nebraska, the largest city in the state. Right across the Missouri River is Council Bluffs, Iowa. The two cities and surrounding metropolitan regions have a combined population approaching 600,000, but it would be hard to consider the area cosmopolitan.

Creighton is a private Jesuit institution with the predictable Jesuit emphasis on hard work and a liberal education. The law students come from diverse religious, social, and geographical backgrounds. Religion seems to play no part in the selection process or most school activities.

The work load, at least for the first two years, is grueling. Creighton is not the place for those who wish to continue an undergraduate major in social activities. The adage here is that the first year, students are scared to death, the second year they're worked to death, and the third year they're bored to death. (The third-year phenomenon is probably the result of a voluntary strategy of avoiding challenging classes.)

A first-year student takes a completely required curriculum as a member of one of two sections, each with about 100 students. (Legal writing and research is taught in smaller groups.) Business courses such as federal income tax, sales, and corporations are heavily emphasized. Other strong areas are estate planning and criminal representation. The number of credit hours required for the degree is higher than at many schools.

Competition for grades is fierce. Many students who were formerly at the top of their class are disappointed by their new GPA (although a class rank higher than one's grades would suggest provides some solace). The trend here is toward grade deflation. To compensate, many students vie for other résumé builders, like law review (an invitation to which is extended based on a combination of GPA and a writing competition), the moot court competition, clerking jobs in the local community, or an officership in one of the campus legal organizations.

There are a few diversions in the community, including the Orpheum Theatre for plays, operas, and symphonies, a civic auditorium for rock concerts and Creighton Blue Jay basketball games, the Joslyn Art Museum, numerous movie theaters (including an on-campus series), the Omaha Royals baseball team, and, of course, the local pubs. A few of the more adventuresome go west for camping and fishing, but there is usually little time for such extracurriculars.

Most of the student entertainment centers on private parties or gatherings sponsored by the Student Bar Association, which occasionally include a mixer with Creighton's medical, dental, and nursing schools. There is a permissive attitude toward drinking, and many "keggers" and wine and cheese receptions are held at the law school.

Each fall, Phi Alpha Delta legal fraternity kicks off the new school year with a bacchanalian pig roast, and each spring the seniors remind everyone that they have no fear by hosting the annual Spoof Day skits, whose primary objective is to parody the faculty and administration. The professors generally attend, and some even stay until it's over.

Creighton would like to become a nationally respected university. Its newly hired professors tend to have Ivy League or other big-name degrees. Local politics is dominated by former Creighton grads. The school commands great respect locally, which basically means an area bounded by Chicago, Kansas City, and Denver.

The school has some graduate student housing, and finding housing in the surrounding area is no problem. Most students commute to campus. Omaha is small enough that students rarely live more than about twenty minutes away. The undergraduate food service and snack bar are available to all, as is the modern physical fitness center. The law school has its own coffee break area whose machine-supplied food belies its old-fashioned name (the Malt Shoppe).

Students have criticized the placement office for not getting more potential employers to interview on campus. The school is doing its best to respond, and everyone hopes for improvement. In the meantime, Creighton students have to work hard in class and out, in order to gain the distinctions that improve one's crack at a job.

University of Denver College of Law

Address: **7039 East 18th Ave., Denver, CO 80220**
Phone: **(303) 871-6135**
Degrees: **J.D., LL.M. (tax), M.S.L.A. (legal administration),**
J.D./M.B.A., J.D./M.S.W. (social work), J.D./M.A. or Ph.D. (international studies), other joint degrees
Median LSAT: **157**

Median GPA: **3.2**

Applicants accepted: **33%**

Transfers: **15/30**

Law enrollment: **1094 (1027 J.D.)**

Campus enrollment: **1094**

Part time: **33%**

Women: **44%**

Minorities: **14%**

Dorm residents: **15%**

Library: **259,200**

Student-faculty ratio: **23:1**

Tuition: **$14,384**

Financial aid: **75% (30% gift)**

Apply by: **March 1, February 15 (aid)**

Disabled students: **Moderate/full accessibility. In five years, two blind students, three wheelchair users.**

Placement: **Approximately 70–80% employed six months after graduation. About 80% of second-years and 90% of third-years employed in legal jobs during academic year. Approximately 15% of first-years, 85% of second-years, and 50% of third-years placed by end of spring term. 50 employers on campus in one year; 98% from Colorado; 98% private firms. About 85% of graduates remained in Colorado. Graduates entered private firms (50%), business (12%), government (12%), judicial clerkships (7%), other (19%). Salary range: $18,000–$75,000. Average salary: $37,739. Colorado bar pass rate: 82% (statewide average: 84%).**

Perhaps the best way to get at the essence of DU College of Law is to examine the type of student most likely to succeed here. He or she (the number of women is high) is white, middle class, and interested in a relaxed, basic education to prepare for a life as a practicing attorney.

DU's tuition is comparable to, if not greater than, that of any equivalent private school. But, as one student reports, "Unless you're extremely resourceful, you're likely to have difficulty getting substantial financial aid." The result is that many day students, even those on scholarship and even during the first year, work twenty or more hours a week while carrying a full load of courses.

Another good reason DU attracts the middle class is that going without your own set of wheels in Denver is particularly disconcerting. How else are you ever going to get to those beautiful mountains on the weekends to go skiing or hiking? Or, if you must remain in the city, how will you propel yourself to places of entertainment?

Aside from the above-mentioned class characteristics, there is considerable variety in the student body. Out-of-staters from all over the country are present in healthy numbers; there are a few students from foreign countries; there's an evening as well as a day division; and students' ages range from twenty to the upper fifties, with many of the older students holding graduate degrees.

Despite a broad range of electives and particularly impressive offerings in international and natural resources law, the DU curriculum remains firmly centered on the basic skills needed by the future practicing attorney.

The clinical program is strong, and programs in litigation, oral advocacy, and legal research and writing skills are treated as major components of the regular curriculum. Denver offers lots of employment opportunities, enabling students to earn credits while working in the community. The friendly and competent people in the placement office see to it that there's little difficulty in finding clerking positions.

There are six law journals available for the honing of scholarship skills. In keeping with the general excellence of the international law program (which includes a joint degree in law and international relations), the international law journal is one of the few of its caliber in the country.

DU boasts a relatively relaxed classroom atmosphere in which humor is welcomed by most teachers. The professors demand class participation, but they manage to do it in a friendly and sympathetic way. Some full-time profs have limited private practices, but most are devoted to teaching and are easily accessible.

In 1984, the law school moved from its downtown location to a spacious thirty-three-acre campus in northeast Denver, formerly the home of Colorado Women's College. The move, along with associated construction and renovation projects, represents an ambitious step toward the future. The new campus is entirely self-contained; law students rarely set foot on DU's main campus.

Students serve on faculty committees. There's an honor board, composed of and elected by students, that administers the student-drafted honor code. Specialized organizations like the National Lawyers Guild and Women's Law Caucus are active. Particularly vigorous groups include the International Law Society and the newly formed Public Interest Law Group.

Still, most people's interests don't extend to extracurricular or political activities. The average student is far more attuned to the latest job opportunities on Denver's Seventeenth Street than to the most recent civil disobedience at the Rocky Flats Nuclear Power Plant. Speaking of job opportunities, DU has a strong reputation in Colorado and neighboring states. Elsewhere, it's less well known.

Most DU students are reasonably satisfied to be here. Their primary goal is to get an education, not to have a good time. With some extra effort, it's possible to do both.

University of Detroit—Mercy School of Law

Address: **651 East Jefferson Ave., Detroit, MI 48226**
Phone: **(313) 596-0200**
Degrees: **J.D., J.D./M.B.A.**
Median LSAT: **34 (full time), 31 (part time)**
Median GPA: **3.13 (full time), 3.0 (part time)**
Applicants accepted: **42%**
Transfers: **2**
Law enrollment: **821**

Campus enrollment: **821**
Part time: **27%**
Women: **43%**
Minorities: **9%**
Dorm residents: **NA**
Library: **222,800**
Student-faculty ratio: **29:1**
Tuition: **$10,500**
Financial aid: **50%**
Apply by: **April 15**

Disabled students: **Fully accessible.**
Placement: **Approximately 65% placed by graduation; approximately 90% employed six to nine months after graduation. Graduates took jobs in East North Central (99%), Middle Atlantic (1%). Graduates entered private practice (82%), judicial clerkships (2%), military (2%), business (1%), government (1%), academic (1%), unknown (11%). Salary range: $19,000–$65,000.**

Students say the U of D's location is one of its strongest attractions. Given that it's in Detroit, the law school is situated in a convenient and desirable area adjoining the business district and the Renaissance Center. This area, once a haven for winos, now sports trendy dining and shopping spots and new office buildings—many of which house successful law firms. The downtown firms and federal and state courts are all within safe (always a consideration in Detroit) walking distance. All this legal activity makes it easy for students to work full- or part-time as messengers or research clerks during law school. (As for Detroit itself, it's becoming a reputable cultural center—theaters and museums are proliferating.)

Another attraction is the modern Kresge Law Library. Its furnishings are comfortable, the shelves are organized efficiently, and computer research training is available. The library collection is less complete than that of U of D's main competitor, Wayne State, but it's adequate for most purposes except arcane research projects.

The school's Dowling Hall is a pleasant, well-kept building dating from the nineteenth century. Most large classes (especially first-year ones) meet in one of two large lecture halls, the bigger of which seats about 125 people. Other classrooms vary in size, and should you get bored with the subject at hand, several have excellent views of the Detroit River and its international shipping traffic.

Mandatory classwork consists of the predictable first-year basics plus tax, constitutional law, evidence, professional responsibility, and a seminar. The school catalog lists a variety of electives, some of which, according to one correspondent, are hardly ever offered. Other classes, including some on subjects covered on the Michigan bar exam, are offered only once a year. This leads to some difficulty when a class is taken out of the usual sequence.

The school offers a good number of courses in business, commercial, and tax law. In general, there is a pervasive business orientation, though most courses offer a blend of the theoretical with the practical.

"The faculty deserves a rating of adequate," says one student. Like most schools, U of D has its stars and its dimwits. Unlike most, the tenure committee is willing to act on student criticism of the dimwits. U of D often hires talented local practitioners to serve as adjunct professors.

Grading is tough.

Extracurriculars adhere to the typical law school mold and suffer from limited student participation. Most students are too busy with classes and jobs to get excited about student organizations, though those who take part often find them worthwhile.

The law review is improving all the time and remains a big

draw for those who qualify. The rigorous multistage selection process weeds out all but a select few. The rewards are commensurate with the labor involved; law review members land the plum jobs and judicial clerkships. Michigan State Bar Association journals on taxation and corporate law are also written and edited by students.

The admissions policy seems receptive to older students. A "special admission" program consists in part of a mandatory summer course, after which full admission is available only to students earning adequate grades.

"U of D is a thoroughly middle-level school in quality and prestige," one student complains. "The majority of the students are destined to practice in Detroit-area law firms of average quality paying an average salary." Yet the school has an excellent relationship with its alumni, who comprise a large share of the city's legal community. If you're interested in working in one of those offices surrounding the school, U of D can be a good place to start.

Dickinson School of Law

Address: **150 South College St., Carlisle, PA 17013**
Phone: **(717) 240-5207**
Degrees: **J.D., LL.M. (commerce or comparative law), M.C.L.**
Median LSAT: **156**
Median GPA: **3.4**
Applicants accepted: **28%**
Transfers: **3/25**
Law enrollment: **519 (509 J.D.)**

Campus enrollment: **519**
Part time: **2%**
Women: **48%**
Minorities: **6%**
Dorm residents: **13%**
Library: **407,300**
Student-faculty ratio: **18:1**
Tuition: **$11,400**
Financial aid: **75% (20% gift)**
Apply by: **February 15**

Disabled students: **Fully accessible. Within a five-year period, two blind students, two deaf, three wheelchair users, two with other mobility problems.**
Placement: **87% employed six months after graduation. Approximately 33% of second-years and 54% of third-years employed in legal jobs during academic year. 68% of first-years, 96% of second-years, and 84% of third-years placed by end of spring term. 64 employers on campus in one year; 84% from**

Pennsylvania, 8% Delaware, 5% Maryland, 2% New Jersey, 2% Texas; 83% private firms, 13% government, 5% business. Graduates employed in Pennsylvania (73%), New Jersey (10%), Delaware (3%), Washington, DC (3%), Maryland (3%), New York (3%), Virginia (2%), California (1%), Georgia (1%), Maine (1%), New Hampshire (1%), Wisconsin (1%). Graduates entered private practice (52%), judicial clerkships (25%), government (14%), business (6%), academic (4%). Salary range: $18,300–$70,000. Median salary: $29,950. Mean salary: $33,188. Pennsylvania bar pass rate: 93% (statewide average: 81%).

Dickinson Law is a small school in a small town at the western edge of the Harrisburg, Pennsylvania, metropolitan area. The atmosphere is challenging but not cutthroat. While it may lack some of the amenities of a large university in a major city, Dickinson has great advantages for students who value a personal approach to learning the law.

When asked what they thought was Dickinson's outstanding attribute, most students agreed: it's the openness and accessibility of the faculty members. The aloof professor is just about nonexistent at Dickinson, and the same holds true for the administrators. The school once went to the trouble of holding a "meet the deans night" early in the second semester, but by that time it was almost superfluous.

For its size, Dickinson's faculty is quite varied, perhaps more so than the student body. The professors range from the inevitable *éminence grise* to several bright young iconoclasts, both men and women. The full-time core faculty is complemented by a number of adjunct professors who are practicing attorneys and judges.

The majority of the student body is from Pennsylvania, but the number of out-of-state students is increasing, due in part to a considerable effort by the school to attract a more diverse group of students. Many students have worked for several years or done some graduate study before coming to Dickinson, so members of the over-twenty-five set need not worry about feeling out of place.

In addition to the small Master of Laws and Master of Comparative Law programs, there are international and comparative law summer programs in Florence, Vienna, and Strasbourg, taught by Dickinson faculty and European professors and lawyers.

Required classes for first-year students (called juniors) are taught in multiple sections. Many small electives, seminars, and clinics are available to second- and third-year students. A legal assistance program provides free legal advice weekly to over one thousand prison inmates. Third-years may also serve in the disability law and family law clinics, or work with lawyers in state, local, or federal administrative agencies, legal services offices, public defender programs, or public prosecutors' offices. There's even a clinic in art, sports, and entertainment law.

While no single teaching method prevails, classroom participation is encouraged, and in many courses total preparation and frequent participation are a must. The work load first year is enormous but manageable.

The library is a first-rate facility. It is equipped with both LEXIS and WESTLAW computerized legal research systems and a personal computer lab. There are also excellent audiovisual facilities for moot court and trial training. The library staff (which includes a number of moonlighting students) is casual and very helpful, especially to bewildered juniors.

The dormitory is a recently renovated colonial-style red brick building with a central courtyard. Conveniently located next door to the law school, the dorm is a popular choice for first-year students. Upperclass students generally rent apartments or houses with friends.

There are few excitements in this part of the world to divert attention from the books. Carlisle is long on historic flavor but short on hustle and bustle. Much of the downtown consists of nineteenth-century brick townhouses carefully maintained by proud owners. Locals will point out where a Rebel cannonball nicked one of the courthouse pillars when the Confederates were in town during the battle of Gettysburg. The former Carlisle Indian School was where Pop Warner coached Jim Thorpe. There are eight movie theaters in Carlisle and many fine restaurants are nearby. There are also several watering holes, enticing law students to drink until the small hours—making it even more of a challenge to face Contracts at 8:30 the next morning.

The area also offers many outdoor amenities. There are a few public golf courses, and nearby state parks, the Appalachian Trail, and Conodoquinet Creek provide excellent camping, hunting, hiking, and fishing. Other local attractions in the Harrisburg area include minor-league baseball, football, and hockey, museums, and the symphony. In addition, Hershey, Pennsylvania, just thirty minutes away, offers a great amusement park and beautiful gardens. Excellent skiing is not far away.

Dickinson College—no relation to the law school—is right next door and offers a wide variety of entertainment, much of it excellent. Philadelphia, Baltimore, and Washington are within two and a half hours' driving time. New York and Pittsburgh are within four hours. The law school features a Student Bar Association-sponsored keg each Friday afternoon after classes, as well as a number of other social functions and athletic programs throughout the year.

For the more serious sort, there are a number of law-related activities, provided, of course, that you have the time, which first-year students do not. There are two law reviews and ten different moot court teams, which participate in national competitions. In addition, there are organizations ranging from the International Law Society to the Women's Law Caucus, all offering excellent programs. It can be frustrating when two or three of the best events are scheduled for the same evening.

The law school heartily discourages first-year students from holding jobs. After the shakedown cruise of the first year, however, you will find the school well situated for summer and term-time employment. Many legal internships with state government involve part-time work in Harrisburg during the second and third years, which gives anyone attending Dickinson an obvious advantage in the employment market. Students find jobs, too, with local governments and with private firms in Harrisburg and other neighboring cities.

After graduation, many students stay with their state jobs. One-year clerkships with judges are a popular first job both for their learning potential and for their nine-to-five hours.

Dickinson graduates are in practice all over the country, but most do not go far afield. Dickinson does not emphasize training for big-city practice, nor does it teach strictly Pennsylvania law, so students are well equipped to practice in diverse situations. In or out of the Keystone State, Dickinson has a good reputation.

If you are looking for a solid law school in peaceful surroundings, Dickinson could be a good choice.

Drake University Law School

Address: **2507 University Ave., Des Moines, IA 50311**
Phone: **(515) 271-2782**
Degrees: **J.D., J.D./M.B.A., J.D./M.P.A., J.D./M.A. (mass communication, political science), J.D./M.S. (agricultural economics), J.D./B.S. (pharmacy)**
Median LSAT: **155**
Median GPA: **3.2**
Applicants accepted: **36%**
Transfers: **3–5/5–10**

Law enrollment: **525**
Campus enrollment: **8000**
Part time: **5%**
Women: **42%**
Minorities: **10%**
Dorm residents: **NA**
Library: **230,000**
Student-faculty ratio: **23:1**
Tuition: **$12,700**
Financial aid: **80% (40% gift)**
Apply by: **March 1, February 15 (aid)**

Disabled students: **Fully accessible. In five years, one blind student, two deaf.**

Placement: **80% employed six months after graduation. 60 employers on campus in one year; 100% from Midwest; 80% private firms, 10% corporations, 10% government. Graduates took jobs in West North Central (75%), East North Central (12%), South Atlantic (9%), East South Central (1%), West South Central (1%), Mountain (1%), Pacific (1%). Graduates entered private practice (39%), judicial clerkships (22%), government (11%), business (5%), public interest (1%), other (7%). Salary range: $20,000–$110,000. Median salary: $35,000. Mean salary: $37,800. Iowa bar pass rate: 88%.**

Drake is located in Des Moines, which, although the capital and largest city in Iowa, has never been accused of being cosmopolitan. Still, Des Moines has air you can breathe and enough to do for the typical law student in search of diversion. The modern Civic Center attracts an assortment of concerts and plays, and there are some good casual bars and restaurants.

Des Moines has long been a center for the insurance trade, and more recently it has diversified into other white-collar industries. Clerking opportunities are plentiful, and practically all second- and third-year Drake students have jobs ranging from private practice to state government. Although the faculty might prefer total dedication to schoolwork, students find the mixture of theory and practice more rewarding both academically and financially (tuition is not cheap).

Drake was founded at its present site in 1881. The campus is rather attractive, but the surrounding neighborhood has declined over the years, and consequently housing is a problem. On-campus housing is scarce for law students because most of the dorms are populated by undergrads. The close-to-campus housing tends to be run-down and expensive, and walking around in the area late at night can be dangerous. There is no problem getting off-campus housing, but if you're picky about where you live, you'll need a car or a bike for transportation. Public transport is best to the downtown area, which is helpful for commuting to jobs.

Drake's greatest curricular strengths are its clinical and internship programs. There are internship programs in administrative law with city, state, and federal agencies, not to mention judicial and legislative internships. Those interested in trial work can benefit from a country prosecutor internship, which gives the student second-chair experience in criminal cases and pays a salary as well. In the one-semester legal clinic, students get to handle their own cases (under faculty supervision) from the initial interview through the trial.

With all this emphasis on litigation, the most prestigious and sought-after extracurricular at Drake is moot court (unlike many schools, where law review is the be-all and end-all). On the other hand, there are offerings for those who aren't headed for the courtroom. The curriculum in tax and other business-related areas is strong, and the school is attempting to cover the expanding subject of agribusiness.

The faculty usually knows two groups of students automatically: the top 10 percent and the bottom 10 percent. It's not too difficult for others to get to know individual professors, and, on the whole, it's worth the effort. Many of the professors remain active in private practice, so their classroom approach is tinged with practicality. The teaching style is the Socratic method during the first three semesters. After that, it varies from Socratic to straight lecture, depending on the professor.

The students come from all over, but a majority are midwesterners, with a large number from Iowa and Illinois. Drake's reputation is highest in Iowa. Law firms and businesses in other midwestern cities, like Kansas City and Chicago, welcome Drake grads, and placement outside the Midwest is by no means unknown, but the effort the student must put forth increases geometrically with the distance of his or her destination from Iowa.

The active student organizations include the Student Bar Association, Phi Alpha Delta law fraternity, and caucuses for women, black, and Hispanic students. Drake's future litigators gather in a student division of the Association of Trial Lawyers of Iowa. The *Drake Law Review* publishes four times a year; the fourth issue is the *Drake Insurance Law Annual,* which is well regarded as a reference work in insurance circles.

The premier annual event is the moot court competition, held before the Iowa Supreme Court, which is followed by a dinner and guest speaker. There's also the Fall Ball, an opportunity for students to lampoon professors with impunity.

Drake offers a legal education that's heavy on the practical. A good way to decide about this school is to figure out whether you're going to take full advantage of the clinical programs—and whether you want to spend three years (including three midwestern winters) in Des Moines.

Duke University School of Law

Address: **University Tower, 3101 Petty Rd., Suite 207, Durham, NC 27707**
Phone: **(919) 489-0556**
Degrees: **J.D., LL.M., LL.B., S.J.D., M.L.S. (legal studies), J.D./M.B.A., J.D./M.D., J.D./M.H.A. (health administration), J.D./M.A. (economics, history, philosophy, English, humanities, public policy studies), other joint degrees**
Median LSAT: **44**

Median GPA: **3.7**
Applicants accepted: **19%**
Transfers: **10/34**
Law enrollment: **641 (594 J.D.)**
Campus enrollment: **10,700**
Part time: **0**
Women: **40%**
Minorities: **12%**
Dorm residents: **NA**
Library: **414,400**
Student-faculty ratio: **20:1**
Tuition: **$16,753**
Financial aid: **73% (47% gift)**
Apply by: **January 15**

Disabled students: **Fully accessible. In one recent year, two students with learning disabilities, one wheelchair user, one with other mobility problems.**

Placement: **91% employed three months after graduation. Approximately 500 employers on campus in one year. Graduates took jobs in South Atlantic (38%), Middle Atlantic (14%), Pacific (7%), East North Central (7%), New England (6%), West South Central (5%), West North Central (4%), East South Central (2%), Mountain (2%). Graduates entered private practice (70%), judicial clerkships (20%), advanced degree (4%), government (3%), military (2%), business (1%). Salary range: $25,000–$87,000.**

Duke's most notable features are its small size, its reputation for high-quality legal education, and its rural/small-town setting. These factors combine to produce a top-ranked national law school with a refreshingly low-key atmosphere.

Duke is in Durham, a small city (population approximately 135,000) whose principal industries are tobacco and education. Durham is nobody's idea of exciting; liquor-by-the-drink was legalized for the first time in 1979, and there is little nighttime entertainment off campus. (Many Duke law students take advantage of the fine restaurants, numerous bars, and exciting cultural events at Chapel Hill, six miles down the road.) If you want three years of law school amid the sights and sounds of the big city, go to Columbia, Georgetown, or Chicago, not Duke. But if you want to take life at a slower pace, enjoy a mild climate, and go to school in the middle of a forest on one of the most beautiful campuses you'll ever see, then Duke is a perfect choice.

Because Duke is smaller than most of the other reputed top ten or fifteen law schools in the country, its students can take advantage of some unusual opportunities. As one of his or her six courses, each first-year student is assigned to a small section of about 25 students. In addition to teaching the standard course material, the small-section professor (who's as often as not one of the best in the school) conducts a legal research and writing program related to the course. The small sections enable students to establish close ties with each other and the professor. The work load in these courses is tough (seventy to a hundred pages of writing during the year), but it's worth it.

The small number of students also enables the faculty to maintain an open-door policy. Professors are almost always available to students throughout the day.

The library, though small in comparison to some other schools', is adequate for the needs of Duke students. In fact, it frequently serves students from the nearby law schools at the University of North Carolina at Chapel Hill and North Carolina Central University. The library's collection is sure to grow as a result of its designation as an official federal depository library. Duke students enjoy the privilege of having keys to the library for use after closing time. This practice not only enables students to set their own work schedules for writing assignments but also promotes a spirit of camaraderie through the trials and tribulations of first year.

Many of Duke's graduates join large corporate law firms, and not surprisingly, course offerings in tax, corporate finance, and securities abound. Still, the highlight of the curriculum is the clinical program. The advanced clinical classes allow third-year students to work with local attorneys and make real courtroom appearances.

The Duke Bar Association has grown from a social organization into a political one. The DBA analyzes curriculum problems and admissions requirements and makes sincere recommendations and proposals. Besides the law journal and moot court, the law school is fortunate in having an active and effective Women Law Students Association, Black Law Students Association, and Federalist Society. The International Law Society enjoys a large membership and sponsors speakers and programs about global concerns. The Duke Law Forum invites notables from the legal world for formal and informal speeches, often in conjunction with the undergraduate forum.

Also worthy of mention is *Law and Contemporary Problems,* a prestigious interdisciplinary journal edited by faculty and students. The school also produces the *Alaska Law Review,* for a state with no law schools.

Law students are free to take courses in other divisions of the university for law school credit, but only if they convince the administration that the course is law-related and academically rigorous. Fortunately, these standards do not restrict law students to economics, business administration, and public policy, and an interesting liberal arts course with some redeeming intellectual value will usually be approved.

The growth of the faculty has highlighted the school's major fault, which is a shortage of space. Fortunately, the law school has embarked on a major series of building renovations. Another problem is the lack of a law school cafeteria, but law students are free to use any of the university's cafeterias, which are only a short walk away. The magnificent Bryan University Center is an awesome complex with theaters, study areas, food services, a co-op, a Rathskeller, and much more.

Law students have full use of the ample university athletic facilities. In this sports-conscious community, law students take part in, and often dominate, intramural competition. Evening law classes are sometimes rescheduled to accommodate intercollegiate basketball games, and every first-year student is well advised to buy a precious home game season ticket for incomparable ACC basketball excitement.

Durham is ideally situated for the outdoorsperson. Four hours to the west lie splendid mountains with surprisingly good skiing; four hours east and you can frolic on the beaches. Both are popular weekend retreats for those times when reading one more case will drive you to committing unnatural acts with your hornbooks.

The housing situation is one of Durham's strong points. Several apartment complexes are within reasonable walking, biking, or short driving distance. Most of these complexes have swimming pools, dishwashers, garbage disposals, and air-conditioning, and rents are low. One who perseveres can locate a house for a reasonable rent within a five-mile radius. On-campus housing for law students is sparse, but a number choose to live in the Duke Central Campus Apartments, which are attractive on the outside and have the advantage of being furnished.

Although the students at the top of the class and on the law journals get the most employment choices, the high ratio of recruiting employers to students ensures that those with less prodigious records also fare nicely in the job market. What's more, the placement office does not prescreen students as some other schools do, so all students have an equal chance to meet with a particular employer. Faced with charges that it was ignoring the student not interested in a large urban corporate practice, the placement office has begun providing more information about alternatives. Still, big-name, big-city firms are large draws for Duke students. As the placement director frequently mentions, a Duke grad can even become president of the United States, as did the school's most famous alumnus (a claim of dubious distinction): Richard Nixon, class of 1937.

Thanks to gorgeous surroundings and tight camaraderie, Duke is one of the most livable law schools you'll ever come across.

Emory University School of Law

Address: **Atlanta, GA 30322**

Phone: **(404) 727-6801**

Degrees: **J.D., LL.M. (tax), J.D./M.B.A., J.D./M.Div. (divinity), J.D./M.T.S. (theological studies)**

Median LSAT: **162**

Median GPA: **3.4**

Applicants accepted: **26%**

Transfers: **approx. 10/25–30**

Law enrollment: **700 (683 J.D.)**

Campus enrollment: **10,000**

Part time: **0**

Women: **42%**

Minorities: **14%**

Dorm residents: **approx. 40%**

Library: **260,000**

Student-faculty ratio: **18:1**

Tuition: **$16,420**

Financial aid: **75% (35% gift)**

Apply by: **March 1**

Disabled students: **Fully accessible. In five years, one visually impaired and one deaf student.**

Placement: **92% employed six months after graduation. Approximately 55% of first-years, 75% of second-years, and 68% of third-years placed by end of spring term. About 150 employers recruiting on campus and at off-campus job fairs in one year; 27% from Georgia, 39% other Southeast, 25% Northeast, 6% Midwest, 2% West; 81% law firms, 11% government, 5% corporations, 3% public interest. Graduates employed in Georgia (45%), other Southeast (19%), Northeast (26%), Midwest (5%), West (5%). Graduates entered private practice (63%), judicial clerkships (19%), government (9%), public interest (5%), business (3%), academic (2%). Salary range: $20,000–$83,000. Median salary: $38,000. Mean salary: $43,553. Georgia bar pass rate: 90% (statewide average: 65%).**

Emory is expensive and southern. Although the attitude and dress may be casual, with a hint of country-club atmosphere, the students are serious about their education.

Limited financial aid has proven to be an obstacle to attracting a socioeconomically diverse student body, but many top students are offered scholarships. On the other hand, geographical variety is good, with roughly 20 percent of the students from Georgia and an equal number from the New York/New Jersey area. Every type of college and undergraduate major is represented, and once here everyone finds a niche.

First-year courses range in size from 30 to 100 students. The first-years take the usual assortment of beginning courses, plus a required term of Business Associations (symbolic of Emory's emphasis on teaching corporate law). Sections of 10 students in the legal writing and advocacy program are taught by local attorneys or judicial clerks, who add a "real world" outlook.

The first-year work load is burdensome. Thorough preparation is always required but rarely possible. Fortunately, professors are pretty good about breaking the students in slowly and offering how-to advice. Orientation programs and a series of survival skills workshops offered by the women's law group help alleviate fears. Faculty advisers arrange small dinners and practice exams.

At the end of first year, the *Emory Law Journal* opens its arms to a group of students with the highest GPAs and to a group selected from a combination of grades and a writing competition open to all first-year students. For a neurotic few, this emphasis on grades promotes keen competition; the rest either are quietly confident or know they'll never make it.

For those who make the cut, the next year will be grueling. A less rigorous way to get publication experience is by joining either the international or bankruptcy law journals. They are open to the top 10 percent of the class, and also allow students to "write on" through a competition at the end of the year.

Registering for upper-level courses is the focus of much frustration. Students feel they have little voice in who teaches what and when. To avoid inequities when demand exceeds supply, each student is allowed thirty points to "bid" for admission to classes. Some popular seminars have closed out at thirty points—and not everyone who bid thirty got in. Third-year students have no priority, and have been known to get closed out of even large lecture classes. Be prepared to become a gambling expert.

Why are people so intent on getting into particular courses?

Some classes are offered once every two years, so it's now or never. Others are one-shot deals—visiting professors or special topics. Finally, differences among faculty members are pronounced. Almost all are readily accessible to students, however.

The second-year requirements include a term of evidence and a course in professional ethics—with some of the students taught by former President Jimmy Carter in recent years.

After the close of the second semester, all second-year students must complete an intensive two-week litigation program. This training program in trial techniques draws more than 100 visiting faculty members from around the country. Many are judges, district attorneys, or trial lawyers themselves. Speech and drama teachers coach students on presentations to juries, and the results can be reviewed on videotape.

Trial advocacy, client counseling, and appellate advocacy skills can be further developed in intramural, regional, and national competitions. Two groups that put students face to face with real people and real problems are Student Legal Services, which gives legal advice to members of the university community, and the Center for Women's Interest Law, which offers legal assistance to Atlanta women. For more hands-on experience, the clinical program offers opportunities to work with law firms, the juvenile courts, the U.S. attorney's office, the public defender, government agencies, and corporations.

Grade-consciousness does not end with first year. There are numerical grades, and although exams are marked on a curve, paper courses are not. A tenth of a point difference in a GPA can have a big impact on numerical class rank, which influences job prospects. People are competitive (although not cutthroat).

Gambrell Hall, the law school's home base, is modern but suffers somewhat from an inefficient use of space. The student lounge areas have the ambience of a bus station, but except for a few short months, students can escape to the outdoors.

Because Emory University has no big-time spectator sports and undergrad life is centered around the Greeks, law students are left to make their own fun. The SBA-run snack bar offers coffee, conversation, video games, and the latest episode of your favorite soap opera. The SBA also sponsors events like the Harvest Moon Ball, a spring picnic, and beer blasts.

There are active intramural leagues every season, and students can use a modern sports complex donated by Coca-Cola, one of Atlanta's largest companies. Outdoor enthusiasts can find enjoyment on the lawn of the law school, at the pool, in the mountains of North Georgia, on the waters of Lake Lanier, or rafting on nearby rivers. Those who just want to watch sports will be glad to know Atlanta has pro teams in all three major sports.

Atlanta has ample entertainment for the law student who should be studying but isn't: good bars with good bands, concerts for most tastes, old and new movies for which discount tickets are available through Emory, and more. Entertainment options are limited for those without cars.

The same is true for housing options. Some married-student housing is available on campus, and a few university-owned apartments adjacent to the law school are available at low prices, but most people live off campus. Renovated apartments and houses of varying desirability are available in the older sections of town. Countless apartment complexes, ranging from student slums to tennis-court-and-pool developments, are nearby. Roommates can live well at reasonable prices.

Students who come to Emory with no intention of settling in Atlanta find the living is easy and would like to stay. Not all can. Although part-time work during the school year is not hard to find, the market in Atlanta for summer and full-time employment is very tight. Atlanta firms recruit nationally and are very choosy. Top Emory students capture their share of the Atlanta jobs, as well as postings in other major eastern cities. While placement outside the Southeast is growing, students who want to venture into other regions must be prepared to confront people who have only recently heard of Emory.

The placement office does a good job organizing mass mailings of résumés and attracting firms to interview—but most of them want to speak to the same top students. Job fairs in Washington, DC, and New York, as well as a job fair for minority students, have helped many students.

Despite its southern setting, Emory is not a place for sipping mint juleps on the veranda. With plenty of hard work, an Emory degree can be an entrée to legal practice in Atlanta, one of America's most livable cities.

University of Florida College of Law

Address: **Holland Hall, Gainesville, FL 32611**
Phone: **(904) 392-2087**
Degrees: **J.D., LL.M. (tax), J.D./M.B.A., J.D./Ph.D. (history), J.D./M.A. (accounting, communications, urban and regional planning, political science and public administration, sociology)**
Median LSAT: **41**
Median GPA: **3.5**
Applicants accepted: **34%**
Transfers: **18**

Law enrollment: **1170 (1059 J.D.)**
Campus enrollment: **35,000**
Part time: **0**
Women: **42%**
Minorities: **12%**
Dorm residents: **NA**
Library: **497,800**
Student-faculty ratio: **17:1**
Tuition: **$2895 (in-state), $9220 (out-of-state)**
Financial aid: **85%**
Apply by: **February 1 (fall), May 15 (spring)**

Disabled students: **Fully accessible. In five years, one blind student, one deaf, six to eight wheelchair users.**

Placement: **Approximately 70% placed by graduation; approximately 93% employed six to nine months after graduation. Graduates took jobs in South Atlantic (93%), Middle Atlantic (3%), East South Central (1%), West South Central (1%), other (2%). Graduates entered private practice (72%), government (16%), judicial clerkships (6%), military (2%), business (1%), public interest (1%), academic (1%), unknown (1%). Salary range: $30,000–$50,000.**

The University of Florida law school is nestled among pine and oak trees surrounded by green open spaces. Lake Alice, located three hundred yards from campus, is a favorite of students and faculty for picnic lunches. Ichetucknee Springs, Ginny Springs, White Springs, Crescent Beach, Cedar Key, and Payne's Prairie are all great getaways for weekend breaks. The university owns recreational facilities on nearby Lake Wauberg, where students can canoe, fish, windsurf, and sail free of charge.

But don't be deceived by the students in shorts and T-shirts enjoying the Florida sunshine. The University of Florida is considered the top law school in the state and one of the best state law schools in the Sunbelt. In spite of the relaxed atmosphere, the competition here can be intense.

Approximately 50 percent of each class is accepted solely on the basis of having college grades and LSAT scores above prescribed levels. The remainder are selected on the basis of quantitative and qualitative factors, including a combination of grades, scores, graduate degrees, leadership positions, and other relevant activities. The law school actively solicits African-American and Hispanic applicants. Out-of-state applicants face somewhat higher admissions standards.

The law school admits two entering classes, one in the fall and the other in the spring. The spring class tends to have a higher number of second-career students. Students in their early twenties study and socialize with students in their thirties and forties. Camaraderie that develops among first-year classmates generally lasts throughout the remaining two years.

Many law students who attended UF as undergrads have their own social circles. However, to some degree, everyone's social life revolves around the law school. Each semester, special events help students relax and get better acquainted. The Student Bar Association sponsors regular activities and occasional keg parties, with or without live music. Also, class sections and the law fraternities hold schoolwide parties through the school year. The most formal event of the year is the Barrister's Ball held each February.

As at any law school, the only way to be really successful at the University of Florida is through hard work. This hard work is made easier by the excellent facilities and faculty. The law school library, the largest in Florida, contains hundreds of videotaped lectures as well as videocassette players. Computers and computer-aided legal research are also available to the students. UF is reputed to be one of the country's top law schools for expenditures on faculty and facilities.

UF provides many opportunities for the law student who wants to get involved in extracurricular activities. Second- and third-year students may compete to participate in the *Florida Law Review,* moot court, trial team, the *Florida International Law Journal,* and the *Journal of Law and Public Policy.* There are also many other student organizations, including the American Civil Liberties Union, Black Law Students Association, Christian Legal Society,

Environmental Law Society, International Law Society, Jewish Law Students Association, Law Association for Women, and Spanish American Law Students Association.

UF's law school includes the Center of Governmental Responsibility, a law and policy research institute focusing on international and national studies, state and local government, social policy, and the environment. Students may become involved in primary research on these issues as research assistants to the Center's professional staff or as Public Interest Law Fellows sponsored by the Florida Bar Association.

The University of Florida sees legal education as more than a glorified bar exam course. For example, Florida is one of the few law schools in the country to require a course in jurisprudence in the first year. Seminars offer in-depth examination of evolving legal topics, supplementing a strong curriculum in the legal fundamentals.

First-year classes are divided into two sections of about 100 students each, and upper-level courses range from 10 to 60 students. Encouraging students to "discover" the law through Socratic questioning is the most common teaching style. After the first year, students and professors are more likely to engage in discussions rather than Socratic dialogue. Perhaps the nicest thing about the school is the way professors and students mingle, whether in a professor's office over a cup of tea, in the cafeteria, or after jogging a few miles.

Most law students find their summer and permanent jobs through the career planning office. Many are openly heading for high-paying jobs at in-state corporate law firms. The mood among some students here combines conservatism with a spirit of in-state elitism. But then, with the attractions of UF's law school, Floridians have something to be chauvinistic about.

Fordham University School of Law

Address: **140 West 62nd St., New York, NY 10023**
Phone: **(212) 636-6810**
Degrees: **J.D., LL.M. (international business;** banking, corporate and finance), **J.D./M.B.A.**
Median LSAT: **41 (full time), 40 (part time)**

Median GPA: **3.3 (full time)**, **3.2 (part time)**

Women: **43%**

Applicants accepted: **21%**

Minorities: **16%**

Transfers: **3**

Dorm residents: **NA**

Law enrollment: **1390 (1346 J.D.)**

Library: **408,600**

Student-faculty ratio: **28:1**

Campus enrollment: **NA**

Tuition: **$15,100**

Part time: **26%**

Financial aid: **66%**

Apply by: **March 1**

Disabled students: **Fully accessible. Fourteen disabled students in one year.**

Placement: **Approximately 85% placed by graduation; approximately 94% employed six to nine months after graduation. Graduates took jobs in Middle Atlantic (92%), New England (5%), South Atlantic (2%), Pacific (1%). Graduates entered private practice (51%), government (9%), judicial clerkships (8%), business (5%), public interest (1%), unknown (26%). Salary range: $20,000–$175,000.**

Fordham Law, long a preeminent regional law school, is now trying to go national.

The school is well respected within the New York legal community; many partners of major Big Apple firms are Fordham graduates. The school's dean was even appointed head of the city bar association in 1992. There is good reason to believe that the rest of the nation will hold Fordham in equally high regard if and when more grads disperse themselves geographically.

The faculty is generally of high quality and includes a number of eminent, nationally known authorities. Because of its access to the New York legal community, Fordham has made excellent use of adjunct professorships and forums featuring outside speakers.

When students seek a faculty member outside the classroom, they are frequently surprised to find that the professor is quite affable and willing to discuss law, professional goals, or the previous night's Yankee game. Students complain that the faculty council wields the real power, while the Student Bar Association is relegated to running orientation programs and providing parties, but there is hope that even this problem can be alleviated.

Located in midtown Manhattan directly across the street from Lincoln Center, the school is accessible by all forms of transportation and is within walking distance of every sort of amenity. As one student put it, "Fordham is probably closer than any law school in the world to stores, restaurants, theaters, clubs, bars, museums, sporting events, etc." Central Park is two blocks away.

Fordham law students are very involved in clinical externship programs that place them throughout New York City with federal and state judges, U.S. Attorney and district attorney offices, government agencies, and so on. The New York location gives second- and third-year students many firms to choose from for part-time jobs.

There is the usual assortment of law school activities. The *Fordham Law Review* is a prestigious journal, and positions are coveted. The selection process involves both grades and a writing competition.

The *Fordham Urban Law Journal, International Law Journal, Environmental Law Report,* and *Entertainment, Media & Intellectual Property Forum* hold writing competitions each year that are open to all students regardless of grade-point average. Another area in which Fordham excels is moot court competition. There is a mandatory first-year competition and numerous additional contests for interested students.

Although the university was established in the Jesuit tradition, there is no religious cast to the education, and you'll find followers of all religions in attendance. Thanks to the efforts of minority student organizations, minority enrollment has grown somewhat. More than half the students come from the New York metropolitan area, and a full 75 percent are from New York State.

A beautiful, brand-new dorm with extensive facilities, located next door to the law school, was completed in 1992. Apartments in the Lincoln Center area are hard to come by and very expensive when found.

Spirit among the student body is strong. The prevailing attitude is friendly and helpful. Although a decade ago very few students pursued a legal education for a purpose other than practicing law, today there are students whose career objectives include teaching, consulting, business administration, politics, and journalism.

An added plus is the excellent four-year evening program. It offers a double advantage: It allows the recent college graduate to work through law school and gain law firm experience along the way, and it permits those already established in the working world to get a legal education without interrupting their careers.

New construction and renovations have recently given the school a boost. If the trend continues, and there is no reason to think it won't, Fordham Law will be an exciting place to be over the next several years.

Georgetown University Law Center

Address: **600 New Jersey Ave., NW, Washington, DC 20001**

Phone: **(202) 662-9010**

Degrees: **J.D., LL.M. (general, tax, international and comparative, labor, securities, common law, advocacy), J.D./M.B.A., J.D./M.S.F.S. (foreign service), J.D./M.P.H. (public health)**

Median LSAT: **43/166**

Median GPA: **3.54**

Applicants accepted: **22%**

Transfers: **0–5/60–75**

Law enrollment: **2657 (2057 J.D.)**

Campus enrollment: **2657**

Part time: **20%**

Women: **50%**

Minorities: **29%**

Dorm residents: **NA**

Library: **697,200**

Student-faculty ratio: **24:1**

Tuition: **$17,800**

Financial aid: **60% (29% gift)**

Apply by: **February 1**

Disabled students: **Moderate/full accessibility. In five years, three blind students, two deaf, two wheelchair users, five with other mobility problems.**

Placement: **79% placed by graduation; 84% employed six months after graduation. 43% of first-years, 70% of second-years, and 73% of third-years employed during academic year. 545 employers on campus in one year; 66% from Northeast, 14% Midwest, 12% West, 7% Southeast; 89% private firms, 5% government, 2% corporations, 2% public interest, 2% other. Graduates employed in Northeast (72%), West (14%), Midwest (6%), Southeast (5%), Southwest (3%), Foreign (.5%). Graduates entered private practice (74%), judicial clerkships (11%), government (8%), business (2%), public interest (1%), military (1%), nonlegal (2%). Salary range: $20,000–$88,000. Median salary: $64,000.**

Washington is probably the best place to study law in the country, and Georgetown is probably the best place to study law in Washington.

Note the use of "probably" in both cases. To get the most out of Washington, it helps if you're interested in government, and to get the most out of Georgetown, it helps if you have a tolerance for large amounts of course work and competition.

Georgetown is located on Capitol Hill, where you can practically smell the power in the air. Congress and the Supreme Court are next door, and students may slip away from classes to attend committee hearings or sittings of the Court. If you get bitten by the trial bug, Judiciary Square is only a few blocks away.

What's more, Washington has an immense legal community, which translates into lots of employment opportunities. Many second- and third-years work twenty hours a week during the term. These jobs develop into excellent connections for permanent employment.

Washington has a cultural life that's nothing to be ashamed of. First-rate museums, galleries, theaters, restaurants, parks, concerts, bars, clubs—they're all here. There are several interesting neighborhoods in which to jog, sightsee, and/or have a drink. Right near the law school is newly refurbished Union Station, which offers chic shopping, movies (with student discounts), and lots of eating opportunities. And the National Zoo gets better all the time.

One thing Washington—at least the Capitol Hill area—doesn't have is affordable, safe housing. Students breathed sighs of relief when the Georgetown administration announced its plans to complete a dormitory across the street from the law school by late 1993. A dorm gives students another option besides group houses on the Hill and commuting from the Virginia suburbs.

It's very easy to get around within the city (thanks mainly to the Metro and inexpensive taxis). However, if you plan to drive to school, be sure to arrive by 8:15 A.M. or else the parking lot will be full, leaving you to fight for the scarce and expensive parking spaces elsewhere.

So much for Washington. What about Georgetown? Almost everyone agrees that it is one of the fifteen top law schools in the country; the exact rank is the source of a certain amount of bickering here. One of the country's largest law schools, Georgetown offers a rare combination of varied and challenging upper-level courses, seven law journals, moot court competitions, and legal service opportunities. Clinical programs permit students to do everything from teaching law to prisoners, to defending accused criminals in court, to writing proposed legislation for public-interest groups.

International law is very strong, thanks largely to a joint degree program with Georgetown's outstanding School of Foreign Service. Corporate, tax, constitutional, and administrative law are also taught well.

Entering students may apply to be Public Interest Scholars. Those who are selected take expanded professional responsibility courses and receive funding from the school to enable them to do public-interest work during the summer. Georgetown also has a loan forgiveness program for students who take full-time public-interest jobs after graduation. However, most agree that the loan forgiveness program could stand some improvement.

The professors are mostly superb teachers and remarkable people. Because of its location, Georgetown is able to attract judges and private practitioners to its part-time faculty. These adjunct professors are a great source of war stories and practical experience.

First-year classes are the Socratic mob scenes you've been warned about. In each of the sections, there are over 100 students who have all of their classes together, except for one small class of approximately 30 students, and legal research and writing, which is taught by upperclass students to groups of about 12. Students can expect to get to know practically everyone in their first-year section. Journal membership, clinic participation, and club activities provide other opportunities to overcome the large class size and develop friendships.

The students here are much smarter than average. The school is very selective and the students represent a wide variety of colleges, regions, age levels, and ethnic and racial groups. Most were strong on undergraduate extracurriculars and leadership. Georgetown students work very hard. Most of them stop short of paranoia, but grade-consciousness, competition, and striving for law review are the rule rather than the exception. The work load is especially staggering in the second semester of first year.

The social life is what you make of it. First year generally means section parties and happy hours. Second and third years involve more frequent bar-hopping.

Student government is not visibly effective, but student participation on faculty committees has increased in past years and appears to be one success story. Although the consensus is that the administration does its job well, the sheer size of the place frequently leaves students with the impression that they are nothing more than a tuition check to the powers that be.

The law school's four-story building is an architecturally nondescript structure sandwiched between the Department of Energy and Route 395 North, nowhere near Georgetown's main campus. There are plans to create a more verdant atmosphere with trees and grass, but the school will never be attractive. What is attractive is the brand-new twenty-million-dollar Edward Bennett Williams Memorial Law Library. The library is one of the best in the country; its collection is rivaled only by the Library of Congress as a Washington legal research center. There are numerous individual and group study rooms throughout the library, as well as a beautiful reading room. The library's many LEXIS and WESTLAW terminals are fully accessible to students.

The law school's classrooms are comfortable and air-conditioned, as is the library. The full-service cafeteria can accommodate several hundred students at one time.

You should know that when Washington employers are looking to hire someone, they come to Georgetown first. And for good reason—the graduates of Georgetown have had a top-notch education. They've also had a very demanding education, so if you're a laid-back-and-mellow type, you'd better keep looking.

George Washington University, National Law Center

Address: **720 20th St., NW, Washington, DC 20052**
Phone: **(202) 994-7230**
Degrees: **J.D., LL.M. (general environmental, international and comparative law, intellectual property, land use, government contracts), M.C.L., J.S.D., J.D./M.B.A.,** **J.D./M.P.H. (public health), J.D./M.A. (international affairs)**
Median LSAT: **41 (full time), 39 (part time)**
Median GPA: **3.43 (full time), 3.39 (part time)**
Applicants accepted: **22%**
Transfers: **12**

Law enrollment: **1682 (1460 J.D.)**
Campus enrollment: **16,000**
Part time: **21%**
Women: **39%**
Minorities: **17%**

Dorm residents: **0**
Library: **392,900**
Student-faculty ratio: **23:1**
Tuition: **$16,752**
Financial aid: **65%**
Apply by: **March 1**

Disabled students: **In one year, six disabled students.**
Placement: **Approximately 77% placed by graduation; approximately 92% employed six to nine months after graduation. Graduates took jobs in South Atlantic (62%), Middle Atlantic (18%), Pacific (9%), New England (3%), East North Central (3%), Mountain (3%), West South Central (2%). Graduates entered private practice (67%), government (11%), judicial clerkships (11%), business (5%), public interest (4%), military (2%). Salary range: $24,800–$85,000.**

GW isn't generally considered to be the top-ranked law school in Washington, but it just may be the one that's most represented in the DC legal community. The Hill, the courts, the agencies, the embassies, the national trade associations, the public-interest groups—all are full of people holding degrees from GW. Many GW grads head for New York, but a phenomenal number stay right in Washington. That tendency is self-perpetuating, of course, so if you want to work in DC, GW is a good choice.

GW *is* the oldest law school in town, and it claims to be the father of the clinical approach to legal education. There's an enormous and varied clinical program to enhance an otherwise extensive curriculum. GW has well-established consumer protection, immigration, and small business clinics where students deal directly with clients, and clinical internship programs for credit in such areas as securities regulation and environmental law.

The course offerings in environmental, government contracts, international, and labor law are some of the most diverse and best taught anywhere. A number of GW's courses are simply unique. A legal activism course, for instance, has catapulted students into advocacy before the U.S. Supreme Court. The patent and intellectual property law program is unsurpassed.

The full-time faculty runs the gamut with respect to teaching talents. The version of the Socratic method where the professor puts you on the spot and lets you twist slowly, slowly in the wind is alive and well here, but it's hardly the exclusive classroom approach.

Any discussion of the faculty must mention the outstanding quality of the part-time professors, most of whom teach specialized subjects related to their professional practices. All are expert and many teach very well.

Although fairly conservative, the GW student body is quite politically and ethnically diverse. Typically, the night students gravitate toward government positions where they fight the big bad corporations, while the day students (or some of them, anyway) would like nothing better than to land a fat-cat position with a big firm.

Competition for grades is keen, but GW still manages to be relatively laid-back for a law school. Book-stealing and the like are unheard of. Although GW is much more than a trade school, many of the students come here expressly for the purpose of receiving more practical training than is available at many law schools. There are, naturally, the requisite courses on legal theory, but the emphasis is definitely on experience.

Much-needed new construction, completed in 1984, significantly expanded the school's facilities.

The opportunity for outside employment in Washington is unsurpassed. The majority of students obtain part-time clerkships by their second year. If you can afford it, you can provide some free labor for a member of Congress and see how the legislative process works. There are also lots of government agencies, legal services, and public-interest groups looking for help. Finally, students work part-time and during the summer for the hotshot lawyers on K, L, and M streets. You can pick up some cash, work experience, and job connections, all at the same time.

Washington is a costly place to live. Food is steep, and housing, though not outrageous as in New York, is prohibitive, with lots of lousy areas that are still expensive. No wonder many are driven to seek out the undistinguished split-levels of suburban Virginia.

The law school is on the main GW campus and has access to all the university's facilities, from the music practice rooms to the gym. These diversions can make the difference between a reasonably balanced existence and utter insanity.

Unless you want to dabble in the arts (and there are an awful lot of museums and performances, courtesy of the government), social life on the town is fairly expensive. There's a rich choice of bars, limited only by the fact that seemingly everywhere one goes, one encounters lawyers or other legal types. If you can avoid these folks, you're in good shape.

GW is in a process of transition, from a good law school to a very good law school. The school—or rather the student body— used to suffer from an abysmal self-image, largely as a result of comparisons with other institutions. The school is now included in most "top twenty-five" lists, prestigious firms court top GW grads, and the school has done fairly well in nabbing federal judicial clerkships.

Unfortunately, a great number of GW students are still not particularly enamored of their school. A major complaint is that the placement office seems to cater only to the top 25 percent of the class. Thanks to various administrative foul-ups, there is a pervasive feeling that student needs and opinions count for little. In recent years, outcry from the student body has begun to buck that trend.

GW's already good national reputation can be expected to grow to match the school's physical expansion. For those with patience for the inevitable frustrating aspects of the place, GW is a law school worth looking at.

University of Georgia School of Law

Address: **Athens, GA 30602**
Phone: **(706) 542-7060**
Degrees: **J.D., LL.M.,**
    J.D./M.B.A., J.D./M.H.P.
    (historic preservation),
    J.D./M.A. (various fields),
    J.D./M.Acc. (accounting)
Median LSAT: **163**
Median GPA: **3.4**
Applicants accepted: **28% (in-state), 11% (out-of-state)**
Transfers: **4–6/35–40**
Law enrollment: **630 (610 J.D.)**

Campus enrollment: **28,000**
Part time: **0**
Women: **38%**
Minorities: **8%**
Dorm residents: **5%**
Library: **440,100**
Student-faculty ratio: **18:1**
Tuition: **$2590 (in-state), $7004 (out-of-state)**
Financial aid: **40% (20% gift)**
Apply by: **March 1, January 31 (aid)**

Disabled students: **Fully accessible. Three wheelchair users in five years.**
Placement: **90% employed six months after graduation. 61% of first-years, 75% of second-years, and 60% of third-years placed by end of spring term. 170 employers on campus in one year; most from Georgia and other Southeast; 90% private firms, 7% government, 3% other. Graduates employed in South Atlantic (86%), Middle Atlantic (3%), East South Central (3%), Foreign (2%), East North Central (1%), other (8%). Graduates entered private practice (67%), government (13%), judicial clerkships (9%), business (5%), academic (3%), public interest (2%), other (1%). Salary range: $16,900–$70,000. Mean salary: $40,234 ($43,677 excluding judicial clerkships). Georgia bar pass rate: 94.7% (statewide average: 65%).**

As a small branch of a large state school, the University of Georgia's Law School offers its students the best of both worlds. Although tuition is almost unbelievably cheap, there is plenty of the quality and flexibility that one usually expects only from a private law school.

In the early 1960s, the Georgia Board of Regents selected several educational areas to develop into "peaks of excellence" within the state school system. One of the areas was law. As a result of this decision, the state has dumped money into U Ga Law School like it's going out of style. The quality of the students, faculty, and facilities has increased to the point that Georgia now boasts one of the finest law schools in the South.

The physical plant is modern and comfortable. The library holdings, including an excellent international law collection, are extensive. A $1.8-million annex, opened in 1981, houses part of the library, as well as offices for student journals and faculty. In 1992, the law school began construction of a multimillion-dollar complex to house the state-of-the-art Dean Rusk Center for International and Comparative Law.

The curriculum is national, not provincial. Only two or three courses emphasize Georgia law; in the others, local cases and statutes get peripheral consideration, and then only when they differ significantly from the norm. The faculty, an unusually large number of whom hold endowed chairs, are mostly a capable lot. Individual quality varies, however. There are famous figures in tax, property, trusts and estates, and international law. The administration is particularly adept at attracting top-name visiting professors and interesting lecturers.

Relations among students, faculty, and administrators are unremarkable. Some professors are extremely cordial and willing to help. Others are a bit more aloof, and a few do a good job at seeming utterly devoid of humanity. Politically, the word for the students is docile.

Most classes range from 20 students up to about 80 for required and fundamental courses. A class of 10 or 20 isn't uncommon, especially for seminars.

In order to graduate, students are required to write an extensive research paper under faculty supervision, or participate in one of the school's two academic journals.

The students' approach to academics is as varied as their aspirations (or lack thereof). At Georgia, the law is largely self-taught, with the faculty acting as facilitators. If one wants to skate by and slide into the family practice back home, Georgia can be a fairly painless place to put in three years.

On the other hand, there are "extras" for the intellectually ambitious. The international and comparative law journal is one of the more respected of its type, but membership in the *Georgia Law Review* carries more weight with employers. Both use writing competitions to select members: the law review attaches equal consideration to grades, and few below the top quarter of the class can make it. The moot court program has achieved national recognition in recent years by sweeping several regional, national, and international competitions. The dual-degree programs with the business school yield highly marketable degrees in law and business or accounting, but the programs are reportedly poorly coordinated between the two schools.

Athens, home to about 70,000 people including the students, is a typical college town with a southern accent. It bears no discernible relation to its ancient namesake. Athens's main claims to fame are the university and (close second) the university football team. Bulldog fever makes the town insufferable on fall weekends unless you are a rabid football fan. The best antidote for an overdose of Athens is a dose of civilization, available without prescription in Atlanta, seventy miles away.

The supply of housing in Athens is adequate; most is modestly priced, though truly low rents are scarce. Avoid the large apartment complexes—they are generally expensive and overrun with noisy undergraduates. The university provides limited cheap housing for both single and married grad students (as well as a more than ample meal plan). If you're interested, apply early.

Parking is a major problem; students arriving at the school after 9:00 A.M. often have difficulty finding a space.

While small-town life has its advantages, such as relatively low expenses, there is one big disadvantage to living in Athens: the local employment picture. Because of the oversupply of student labor, both law-related and non-law-related jobs reportedly pay at or *below* minimum wage. Even law school positions pay badly (except for the rare professor whose publisher has supplied enough money for good research assistant salaries). Some of the most capable law students are lured by the business school for more lucrative teaching and research spots.

For full-time employment, the school's clout is best within Georgia, where many of the students want to be anyway. Most students who want to leave the state find a job with the help of the annual Atlanta employment consortium, which brings firms nationwide to interview students from a group of southeastern law schools. As everywhere, top students have little trouble snagging impressive firm jobs and judicial clerkships.

University of Georgia's law school is a great deal for the money. "A resident wanting to study in-state is crazy not to apply here," says one student, "and it's worth the serious consideration of non-residents too."

Golden Gate University School of Law

Address: **536 Mission St., San Francisco, CA 94105**
Phone: **(415) 904-6830**
Degrees: **J.D., LL.M. (tax), J.D./M.B.A., J.D./M.P.A., J.D./M.S. (tax)**
Median LSAT: **37 (full time), 36 (part time)**
Median GPA: **2.92 (full time), 2.81 (part time)**

Applicants accepted: **42%**
Transfers: **NA**
Law enrollment: **938 (853 J.D.)**
Campus enrollment: **5075**
Part time: **29%**
Women: **46%**
Minorities: **17%**
Dorm residents: **0**
Library: **187,800**

Student-faculty ratio: **21:1**   Apply by: **April 15 (fall),**
Tuition: **$12,624**   **November 15 (spring),**
Financial aid: **85% (33% gift)**   **February 15 (aid)**
Disabled students: **Fully accessible. In one year, five disabled students.**
Placement: **Approximately 88% employed six to nine months after graduation. Graduates took jobs in Pacific (91%), Mountain (4%), South Atlantic (2%), West North Central (1%), West South Central (1%), unknown (1%). Graduates entered private practice (59%), business (17%), government (17%), public interest (4%), judicial clerkships (3%). Salary range: $27,000–$65,000.**

Golden Gate is a modest but ambitious Bay Area law school. Although unable to compete with nationally known Boalt, Stanford, and Hastings, Golden Gate has steadily improved its reputation and visibility in the local legal community over the past few years.

There are many things that set Golden Gate apart from the other Bay Area law schools, and they're not all bad by any means. Because Golden Gate has an evening as well as a day division, it tends to attract students who are seeking second careers as well as recent college grads. The average student age is higher than elsewhere. Many people come to school only to attend classes or to use the library in carefully planned time allotments and then return home to spouses, children, and jobs. There's even a day-care center in the building.

The end product is more than a commuter school; it's a diverse and interesting student body comprised of two distinct generations. The older crowd tends to the business-oriented, real-estate-and-tax-law California conservative type. The dominant group is the younger liberal/radicals, who are heading into public interest and/or criminal defense. Native Californians make up about half or more of the student body, with New Yorkers dominating the remainder.

Golden Gate's commitment to female law students isn't just a phrase in the school catalog. The feminist movement is strong here, and the law review devotes one of its two yearly issues to legal subjects affecting women. The Women's Association keeps a watchful eye over the faculty hiring committee.

Among the most active organizations at GGU is the Lesbian and Gay Law Students.

The administration is seeking more minority group students, but its efforts sometimes reach a dead end at the financial aid office. There just isn't enough money to attract large numbers of working-class students, be they minority or white. Organizations representing students of color work together to promote affirmative action admissions and hiring.

There is plenty of support at Golden Gate for alternative legal work. The school runs extensive clinical programs. You can receive a semester's credit while working full time for a public-interest law office or in a judicial clerkship. Many students clinic with the county public defender's office.

While the most visible of the social and political groups are activist-oriented, classic activities like faculty-student softball games, picnics, and talent shows feature in the extracurricular scene as well.

Golden Gate considers itself a school strong on "student rights." Loosely translated, this means that students participate as full voting members on all the standard faculty committees, like hiring and curriculum. The student government is active, liberal and minority-oriented. The National Lawyers Guild, a politically progressive national organization, has a small but active chapter at Golden Gate that cooperates with chapters from other area schools.

The student mood is described as "supportive, light, and up-beat—with a note of well-founded concern over finding jobs in the Bay Area." You're more likely to run into a study group than an obnoxiously competitive fellow student.

A few classes illustrate the typical Socratic method infused with intimidation, but the faculty generally encourages discussion without requiring participation. Most of the professors communicate on a first-name basis outside of class.

The curriculum is largely litigation-oriented, and what is taught are the basic survival skills—but they're taught well. The faculty is spotty but a cut above adequate. One is best off picking and choosing professors. Student evaluations of individual faculty members are conducted every semester.

The school recently began offering Specialization Certificates to students who focus on international law or public interest. A faculty member helps guide the student's course of study and supervises the writing of a long research paper. Students are also matched up with practicing attorneys in the third year, which can provide some assistance in finding a job.

Since relatively few firms come to Golden Gate to recruit, the placement center is set up to help students find employment for themselves. San Francisco has innumerable opportunities for interesting clerkships during the school year and summer. It also has innumerable law students competing for those opportunities, as well as for permanent positions in the area. Most students like it here enough to want to stay.

There's a lot to like in San Francisco, including Victorian architecture, those steep hills, and generous helpings of local color everywhere you turn. Unfortunately, the allure is a little too strong for the city's own good, and the result is a housing shortage. With no campus housing, Golden Gate students must fend for themselves, many of them ending up in the East Bay area.

Golden Gate not only has no housing, it has no campus either. Located in San Francisco's financial and business district, the law school shares its building with the rest of GGU: an undergrad and graduate school focusing on business, tax, and accounting. There is a small but well-stocked bookstore and a small cafeteria. The YMCA a few blocks away provides the only nearby opportunity for exercise. All in all, the immediate area is less than desirable, but many downtown law offices are conveniently close, as is public transportation.

In any case, people don't choose Golden Gate because they want a quiet, ivy-covered campus where they can bicycle to classes. Plenty of people come here because they didn't get in anywhere else. Others come because it's in San Francisco. But a substantial number choose Golden Gate because it can be a comparatively noncompetitive way of going to law school, in the company of students who are interested in more than money, power, and prestige.

Gonzaga University School of Law

Address: **Box 3528, Spokane, WA 99220**
Phone: **(509) 328-4220**
Degrees: **J.D., J.D./M.B.A.**

Median LSAT: **33**
Median GPA: **3.14**
Applicants accepted: **44%**
Transfers: **4–5**

Law enrollment: **536**
Campus enrollment: **3900**
Part time: **7%**
Women: **32%**
Minorities: **7%**
Dorm residents: **0**

Library: **190,200**
Student-faculty ratio: **23:1**
Tuition: **$10,500**
Financial aid: **90% (15% gift)**
Apply by: **rolling admissions**

Disabled students: **Moderately accessible. In one year, one disabled student.**

Placement: **Approximately 20 employers on campus in one year. Graduates took jobs in Pacific (73%), Mountain (7%), Middle Atlantic (6%), East North Central (4%), West North Central (4%), South Atlantic (4%), New England (1%), West South Central (1%). Graduates entered private practice (70%), judicial clerkships (8%), government (6%), academic (6%), business (5%), military (3%), public interest (2%). Salary range: $20,000–$50,000.**

Gonzaga's students, faculty, and administrators are unanimous on two points: that the school has improved lately, and that they're dedicated to continuing the process.

The law review is bringing the school with it as it gains respect and recognition. The moot court teams' success in interscholastic competition has also helped spread the Gonzaga name, while boosting student morale back home. The library facilities have seen improvements, too.

Gonzaga offers a basic legal education, with an emphasis on practical, down-to-earth courses. Constitutional law is somewhat weak, but the commercial law and tax programs (bolstered by a joint degree with the business school) are good.

The local bar—which includes many GU graduates—is generally cooperative about providing part-time clerking jobs. There is also an extensive internship program that allows third-year students to work in state and federal courts, public defenders' and prosecutors' offices, and other settings. The school's own legal clinic gives a few specially certified third-year students the chance to take cases from the initial client interview to the final judgment, an experience the participating students have found invaluable.

The faculty is mostly young and vibrant. Classes are generally large, but teachers are approachable and friendly, as signified by their unwillingness to rely on the Socratic method; most prefer a more relaxed approach. Several practitioners from the community serve as adjunct faculty and inject a note of worldly experience into the classroom.

Evidence of Gonzaga's Jesuit affiliation seems largely limited to a page in the school catalog. The student population cuts across religious lines. The admissions committee isn't wedded to the LSAT/GPA approach, and its attention to "life experience" results in the acceptance of quite a few older students. Over a third of the student body are Washington residents.

The Student Bar Association is well funded and influences just about every level of law school life. It supports the tutorial program, Women's Law Caucus, intramural sports, and annual Heidelberg celebration. The two legal fraternities sponsor social events as well as community service programs.

Spokane has a small-town, faintly provincial atmosphere and leaves students hard-pressed for any entertainment beyond a few beers at the local tavern. On the other hand, the city is modern, attractive, and extraordinarily clean. This is an area where activities center on the great outdoors. National parks, mountains, lakes, rivers—all are within easy access of the school. A student so inclined can take a study break fly-casting for trout in the Spokane River, which forms a portion of the university boundary.

Law students all live off campus, and while housing costs are rising along with everything else (including tuition), there is a ready market of moderately priced apartments and houses within walking distance of the school. The university cafeteria provides three meals daily, and numerous fast-food factories and a few "home-cooking" restaurants are nearby.

Living expenses in Spokane aren't high, but that can't make up for the fact that salaries for beginning attorneys are embarrassingly low. Students who look to find a ticket out of Spokane find that the school has a growing reputation in Washington, Oregon, Idaho, Montana, and Nevada. The school's recognition factor out of the region lags behind, but some Gonzaga grads do go on to firm jobs, clerkships, and government posts throughout the country. Each out-of-state alum blazes trails for his or her successors, and the placement office has increased communication with employers of all types. Still, if you come to Gonzaga, don't expect to be courted and fought over by campus recruiters. That day still lies in Gonzaga's future.

Hamline University School of Law

Address: **1536 Hewitt Ave., St. Paul, MN 55104**
Phone: **(612) 641-2461**
Degrees: **J.D., J.D./M.B.A., J.D./M.A.P.A. (public administration)**
Median LSAT: **36**
Median GPA: **3.08**
Applicants accepted: **33%**
Transfers: **4–6/10–15**
Law enrollment: **578**

Campus enrollment: **2600**
Part time: **0**
Women: **46%**
Minorities: **8%**
Dorm residents: **NA**
Library: **196,100**
Student-faculty ratio: **20:1**
Tuition: **$10,980**
Financial aid: **90% (20% gift)**
Apply by: **May 15**

Disabled students: **Fully accessible.**

Placement: **Approximately 84% employed six to nine months after graduation. Graduates took jobs in West North Central (70%), East North Central (14%), other (16%). Graduates entered private practice (53%), judicial clerkships (20%), government (13%), business (9%), military (3%), public interest (3%). Salary range: $15,000–$66,000.**

Considering its youth, HUSL has a lot going for it. Applications for admission are increasing, faculty scholarship is solid, and morale is high among students, faculty, and staff.

HUSL was founded in 1972 and formally affiliated with Hamline University in 1976. In 1980, the law school was installed in its own award-winning building on the east side of the 30-acre Hamline University campus.

With entering classes of approximately 200 students, Hamline is the smallest of Minnesota's three law schools. The first-year class is divided into three sections of about 70 students each. There is an amazing sense of solidarity within each section, and although you may occasionally feel lost, you'll never feel alone. Upper-level classes have as few as 10 students and average 50.

The mood among faculty and fellow students is supportive and helpful. Whether working on moot court teams, in client counseling competitions, or as research assistants to faculty members, students find many opportunities to get involved in the life of the school.

HUSL's self-declared purpose is "personal, socially responsive, comprehensive legal education." A solid core of traditional courses is supplemented by electives in specialized areas of legal practice. Over time the school has expanded course offerings in areas such as public law, environmental law, and children's advocacy. Should you wish to reflect on the larger ends and purposes of the law, you can even take courses involving jurisprudential and interdisciplinary approaches to legal thinking. But the focus of the curriculum is primarily practical. A sequenced lawyering skills program of electives allows students to practice their skills in simulated settings, work under the supervision of practitioners in the Practicum program, or practice law in the General Practice Clinic serving refugees in Minnesota.

Student life at HUSL is much like that at other schools. Time is in short supply. The school allows for flexible scheduling during the first year, with some students taking the traditional load of classes on a half-day schedule, or a reduced course load on half-days. Reduced-load students can still graduate in three years by making up courses during the summer or taking advantage of study abroad opportunities. The school produces three competent legal publications: a law review, the *Journal of Public Law and Policy*, and the unique *Journal of Law and Religion*. HUSL has walked away with honors in national and regional moot court competitions. Student organizations are plentiful and run the political, social, and athletic gamut.

One of HUSL's greatest assets is its faculty. Like the school, the faculty is young and most are more interested in being effective teachers than in producing prodigious amounts of scholarship. Many manage to do both. Student-faculty conversations are frequent and informal, whether they take place in the classroom, during office hours, or in the student lounge over lunch. HUSL students also benefit from easy access to their well-liked administrators.

The Twin Cities area is a cultural mecca and has been praised countless times for its quality of life. Even if you're a jaded East or West Coast type, you'll find that you too can survive in Minnesota without culture shock. The Twin Cities offer orchestras, theater, museums, ethnic eateries, professional sports teams, and other trappings of big-city life.

The law center is located midway between the downtowns of Minneapolis and St. Paul in an older, residential neighborhood.

HUSL students come from more than 30 states, and slightly less than half are Minnesotans. The students represent a wide variety of work experience and advanced degrees. Married students are plentiful, and the average age is 27—a bit older than most.

Students insist that HUSL's reputation is spreading. Meanwhile, most appreciate the innovative, progressive spirit of the school, and the overwhelming majority would choose HUSL again.

Harvard Law School

Address: **Cambridge, MA 02138**
Phone: **(617) 495-3109**
Degrees: **J.D., LL.M., S.J.D., J.D./M.B.A., J.D./M.P.P. (public policy), J.D./M.A.L.D. (law and diplomacy), other joint degrees**
Median LSAT: **NA**
Median GPA: **NA**
Applicants accepted: **under 11%**

Transfers: **NA**
Law enrollment: **1797 (1597 J.D.)**
Campus enrollment: **17,000**
Part time: **0**
Women: **41%**
Minorities: **27%**
Dorm residents: **NA**
Library: **1,709,500**
Student-faculty ratio: **28:1**
Tuition: **$16,260**
Financial aid: **70% (40% gift)**
Apply by: **February 1**

Disabled students: **Thirteen disabled students in one year.**
Placement: **90–95% placed by graduation. Graduates took jobs in Middle Atlantic (25%), South Atlantic (23%), Pacific (17%), New England (14%), East North Central (8%), West South Central (6%), Mountain (2%), West North Central (2%), Foreign (2%), East South Central (1%). Graduates entered private practice (60%), judicial clerkships (30%), public interest (5%), government (3%), business (1%), academic (1%). Salary range: $17,000–$105,000.**

Most of what's good and what's bad about Harvard Law School is attributable to the fact that this is the best-known—and one of the largest—of America's law schools. It has more students, more professors, more course offerings, more extracurricular activities, more *everything* than almost anywhere else. Depending on your point of view, life inside this academic horn of plenty can be sheer exhilaration or an ongoing identity crisis.

Harvard's prestige, too, is a mixed blessing. It enables the school to attract as able and distinguished a faculty and student body as can be found anywhere, and it gives its students a considerable advantage in job hunting. But it also engenders a complacency and chauvinism among students and alumni, faculty and administrators. Years later and thousands of miles away, graduates still refer to Harvard casually (and only half-jokingly) as *"The* Law School."

However, the faculty is more ideologically diverse than one would expect of a group whose prerequisites to membership seem to be *magna* at HLS, law review editor, and Supreme Court clerk. (Indeed, major ideological rifts have been known to polarize the faculty in recent years.) And despite a disproportionate number of Ivy Leaguers, the student body shows great variety in racial, ethnic, political, economic, and geographical backgrounds. "The atmosphere here can often be contentious," one student reports, "but it is never dull." There are always several Rhodes Scholars; at the same time, the school is big and confident enough to gamble on a student high on verve and ambition but low on the traditional admissions criteria. The school seems to make a sincere effort to accommodate disabled students.

While the *Paper Chase* image of relentless pressure is no longer apt, first year remains more intense than the next two. Most "One L" classes are still taught by Socratic method, but in some the professor gives advance warning to those who will participate. In others, students can retreat to the vacant seats at the rear of the room—the "back bench"—for immunity from professorial probing. Grading is blind, attendance doesn't count, and it's nearly impossible to flunk out. Still, many first-years are tense because they don't know how they'll stack up against all those Phi Beta Kappas or because they don't believe that half of the law review members really are chosen solely on the basis of a writing competition. (The law review has an affirmative action program as well.)

Half the One Ls are assigned to the experimental sections, which take a more interdisciplinary approach to the standard introductory courses. Students in the experimental sections can expect to be exposed to philosophical trends like critical legal studies, legal realism, and law and economics. People familiar with both places concur that first year at Harvard is generally more rigorous and more intellectually coherent than at Yale.

After a hectic autumn interviewing season, second year consists of going through the motions. And except for a faculty-supervised paper and the occasional stimulating seminar, the only point of third year seems to be to prevent the second year from being the last. The pervasive upper-year apathy toward legal studies manifests itself negatively in reduced class attendance and preparedness, and positively in devotion to clinicals and extracurriculars.

The faculty is strongest in the fields of constitutional law, jurisprudence, tax, criminal law, and international law. Course offerings in environmental law and feminist issues are comparatively sparse. But curricular strengths and weaknesses change as professors quit or go on leave and new faculty or visiting profs arrive. The curriculum is more structured and more practice-oriented than, say, Yale's, but it's far more theoretical than most schools'.

In addition to the law school's own panoply of courses, students may cross-register in courses throughout Harvard University. There are popular joint degree programs with Harvard's business, government, and graduate schools, and with Tufts's Fletcher School of Law and Diplomacy. Harvard College provides a wealth of speakers, but the law students generally treat the undergraduate campus as a walkway to Harvard Square rather than a final destination.

Student-faculty contact is not as rare as the size of the school would suggest. Office doors are open to the intrepid; other students get to know their professors at cocktail parties, in extracurricular activities, or through third-year papers. While individual faculty members can be friendly, the faculty and administration as a whole appear to regard dealing with students as a peripheral and unpleasant aspect of their mission. HLS selects professors for their scholarship more than their teaching ability, and the school is notoriously uninterested in student input about anything other than additions to the awesome law library (reportedly the world's largest). Many students end up feeling completely anonymous; those who thrive are the ones who know what they want, and have the energy and determination to get it.

If you find yourself with time on your hands at Harvard, you'll have only yourself to blame. Clinical programs, both credit and noncredit, are present in the dizzying variety you'd expect of this school, and they are the primary focus of many students' energy and dedication. Student publications include a weekly newspaper with a national audience, a yearbook, the general law review, and specialized journals on civil rights, international law, legislation, environmental law, women's legal issues, and conservative public policy. The law school forum brings in speakers on law, literature, sports, entertainment, and politics (including, in the past, Fidel Castro and Malcolm X). Students write and stage a fall revue and a spring musical comedy rife with inside jokes. Other students enter annual competitions in moot court, international law moot court, and contract negotiation.

Social, cultural, and political organizations exist for black students, Latino students, Asian-Americans, Native Americans, Jews, Christians, women, married students, second-career people, gays and lesbians, French-speakers, Republicans, Democrats, and anyone else you can think of. The Board of Student Advisers runs orientation programs and advises first-year moot court. An active Dorm Council sponsors movies, dances, parties, a video and pinball game room, and intramural sports league. Campus activism has its adherents; for example, in recent years, students have organized to push for greater diversity on the faculty and even sued the school for employment discrimination.

Recreation time is often hard to come by, but places to spend it are not. The law school is one block from Harvard Square's innumerable bars, coffeehouses, ethnic restaurants, bookstores, and trendy shops. Downtown Boston is a fifteen-minute subway ride away. New England skiing and Cape Cod beaches are at the end of a couple of hours' drive. Closer to home, the law school has its own pub. Whatever your tastes, you're sure to find activities catering to them.

Most first-year students live on campus; most of the older and wiser don't. The two old brick dorms have spacious wood-paneled suites complete with fireplaces, but most of the dorm space is in a sterile cinderblock quad that will stand as a lasting embarrassment to the memory of Bauhaus architect Walter Gropius. Rental housing very close to campus is expensive, so many students are willing to walk fifteen minutes or longer to get cheaper accommodations.

It has been said that Harvard Law School turns out two types of people—those who always had the desire to enter large corporate firms, and those who have been converted to it. Actually, every year finds a noticeable minority of students following other paths. The office devoted exclusively to public-interest and government career advice does an amazing job and provides a resource unmatched at most other law schools. The Low Income Protection Plan offers loan forgiveness to graduates in low-paying, law-related jobs.

In the fall, second- and third-year students receive a directory of potential employers the size of a big-city phone book. The job search has gotten a bit tougher for everybody as the market for lawyers becomes glutted. Yet, with the possible exceptions of One Ls and public-interest-oriented third-years, most people get jobs without much difficulty.

The size of the school and a generous endowment enable Harvard to charge a bit less for tuition than some other big-name private law schools. This hardly makes it a bargain, however—particularly in view of the generally high prices in the Boston area.

Harvard Law isn't for everyone, not even for everyone who can get in. Plenty of people say "no thanks" to this school every year. Still, if you're part of the lucky group to find favor in the admissions committee's eyes, most folks will think you strange for turning down such an embarrassment of riches. Whatever its possible drawbacks—pressure, anonymity, snobbery, pervasive success-mindedness—Harvard is still Harvard. For many people, that says it all.

Hofstra University School of Law

Address: **1000 Fulton Ave.,
Hempstead, NY 11550**
Phone: **(516) 463-5916**
Degrees: **J.D., J.D./M.B.A.**
Median LSAT: **160**
Median GPA: **3.2**
Applicants accepted: **29%**
Transfers: **6/45**
Law enrollment: **827**
Campus enrollment: **12,000**

Part time: **0**
Women: **40%**
Minorities: **18%**
Dorm residents: **20%**
Library: **400,000**
Student-faculty ratio: **18:1**
Tuition: **$14,980**
Financial aid: **44% (26% gift)**
Apply by: **April 15**

Disabled students: **Fully accessible. Within five years, one blind student, one deaf, three wheelchair users, five with other mobility problems.**
Placement: **86% employed six months after graduation. 65 employers on campus in one year; 90% from New York; 80% private firms or corporations, 20% government or public interest. Graduates employed in Middle Atlantic (97%), New England (1%), South Atlantic (1%), Pacific (1%). Graduates entered private practice (54%), government (11%), judicial clerkships (11%), public interest (8%), business (7%), other (8%). Salary range: $30,000–$85,000. Average salary: $51,082. New York bar pass rate: 81% (statewide average: 73%).**

In many respects, Hofstra has achieved the kind of excellence one would expect from a nationally recognized law school. In other respects, one can't help being reminded that this is a relatively new law school attached to a university with an essentially local orientation.

The most flattering view of the school is from a purely academic standpoint. "The faculty here is terrific," says one student straightforwardly. Many of the long-term professors are tops in their fields; many are inspiring teachers; and a surprisingly large number fit into both categories. Some of the newer acquisitions are less impressive, but the administration appears willing to recognize who the lemons are and let them go if they don't shape up. All of the faculty members are approachable. Even the meanest tigers in class (and there are some) turn into kittens when you talk to them out of the classroom.

At its founding in the late 1960s, Hofstra intelligently decided to minimize direct competition with other area schools by seeking a less traditional student body. A strong affirmative action program has been in effect from the start. Hofstra has attracted larger than usual groups of older students and of people dedicated to public-interest work. Hofstra quickly became known for having a more cooperative, rather than cutthroat, atmosphere.

As Hofstra's reputation has improved, admissions have become more selective and more traditional, stressing grades and scores. And with the narrowing of the legal job market, Hofstra students have become more competitive, and stories of cheating and stolen outlines can now be heard. But the prevailing atmosphere and the composition of the student body still bear the mark of Hofstra's earlier days.

Hempstead (on Long Island) is far from being the garden spot of New York State. The area's range of things to do and see will leave you underwhelmed—which may be an advantage when you're in law school. New York City, however, is only a half hour away (traffic permitting), and anybody who doesn't take advantage of its proximity at least occasionally is missing out on a social and cultural feast.

While Hempstead isn't the safest place to live, Long Island does provide a number of beautiful spots close enough for student living. Many Hofstra students live in Point Lookout, a popular summer beach community, where school-year rents can be quite reasonable. Hofstra provides on-campus apartments, but they are not elegant. Hofstra's location is an asset because it offers Long Islanders the option of a quality legal education without the hassles of commuting into the city.

The facilities, activities, and campus life at Hofstra University are geared primarily toward the undergraduates. Hofstra is mostly a commuter institution, directing its programs to the local populace. Student life is mainly left in the hands of the law school and its students.

The law school is probably unique on campus in seeking national quality and national attention. This often creates a strain in its relationship with the university administration. But it also makes the law school community cohesive, because students, faculty, and administration are all on the same side when it comes to wanting more money for building, faculty recruitment, and placement. A major construction project, completed in 1990, added a new library, computer facilities, office space, and classrooms.

The tightening of the legal market has hurt Hofstra. Membership on the law review (which is a highly respected publication) is said to be a virtual prerequisite even to get an interview at a major law firm, especially in New York City. "The average student will have difficulty finding traditional legal employment," warns one recent graduate. "Be prepared to be asked over and over again, 'Why did you choose to go to Hofstra?' And be prepared with an answer that sounds intelligent, because the real reason will be that you didn't get into NYU or Columbia."

It's not that students here are any stupider than their compatriots at the two well-known Manhattan schools, or that their education is inferior. It's just that firms know little about Hofstra and the quality of its students, and there aren't enough alumni to spread the school name. Students assert that the placement office will need more staff and more funds before it can overcome these shortcomings.

Still, Hofstra students have every hope that the school's reputation will catch up with its continuing growth and improvement. Given how far the school has come since its founding, anything seems possible.

University of Houston Law Center

Address: **Houston, TX 77204**
Phone: **(713) 749-4816**
Degrees: **J.D., LL.M. (energy and natural resources; international economics; health; comparative; or tax), J.D./M.B.A., J.D./M.P.H. (public health), J.D./M.A. (history), J.D./Ph.D. (medical humanities)**
Median LSAT: **39**
Median GPA: **3.29**
Applicants accepted: **24%**

Transfers: **40**
Law enrollment: **1340 (1251 J.D.)**
Campus enrollment: **30,000**
Part time: **23%**
Women: **45%**
Minorities: **16%**
Dorm residents: **NA**
Library: **327,800**
Student-faculty ratio: **26:1**
Tuition: **$3600 (in-state), $6400 (out-of-state)**
Financial aid: **65%**
Apply by: **February 1**

Disabled students: **Fully accessible. In one year, nine disabled students.**

Placement: **In one year, approximately 250 employers on campus; 80% law firms, 20% government or business. Graduates took jobs in West South Central (93%), Pacific (2%), Mountain (1%), Middle Atlantic (1%), East North Central (1%), South Atlantic (1%), East South Central (1%). Graduates entered private practice (76%), judicial clerkships (9%), business (7%), government (5%), military (1%), academic (1%). Salary range: $31,000–$63,000.**

Oil and water don't normally mix, but for students at UH Law Center, they do. The law school's home, considered the nation's energy capital, is also a port city that ranks in the country's top five. When times are good, both energy and trade provide business for Houston's thousands of lawyers. Many of them graduated from UH.

Among Houston's three law schools, UH is considered tops. A few students even choose this school over its prestigious state-supported competitor in Austin, the University of Texas.

Most of UH's law students commute to school via Houston's crowded freeways. The overwhelming majority of the night students work full time, but most of the day students work also, and many of them are married. Their entering age is a bit older than average. UT–Austin grads comprise a sizable block; there are also a good number of easterners.

Students partake of the usual fare of first-year courses, including contracts, criminal law, legal research and writing, federal civil procedure, property, constitutional law, and torts. Most first-year classes are heavy on Texas law. All are taught in windowless classrooms that hold capacity audiences of 110 or so. In the second and third years, enrollment in many electives drops as low as 15, while the recommended bar courses draw full houses. The Socratic case method predominates in freshman courses, but later offerings mix recitations with lectures.

The faculty roster lists a fair percentage of professors who are also practicing attorneys; many students consider them to be among the school's best. More theoretically oriented Yale and Harvard graduates are represented also.

UH's unique, multimillion-dollar facility places students, faculty, and classrooms in close proximity by the use of two "teaching units" that house offices, study carrels, and lecture halls. It is not unusual to see a professor walking from office to class, followed by several students who have been visiting for a preclass discussion. The coverage of material during class is often rapid fire, so some professors prefer to answer questions outside of the classroom. As many as seventy pages of a casebook have been covered in one first-year class—per day.

UH students have time for study, work, and little else. In their spare time, students can choose from the gamut of fraternal organizations and special interest groups that have offices at the law school, including ones for specific ethnic minorities and academic specialties. The *Houston Law Review,* the *Houston Journal of Interna-*

tional Law, and the award-winning moot court and mock trial teams are popular activities.

The Student Bar Association enlivens the campus with its frequent "arbitrations," or keg parties, and with its hotly contested elections. Although the SBA here has traditionally been low-key, more student involvement in joint faculty committees has been evident recently.

At the Texas Medical Center, minutes from campus, the University of Texas Health Science Center has joined with UH to create the first interdisciplinary teaching facility of its kind, the Health Law Institute. In addition, UH sponsors a Mexican Legal Studies Program every summer in cooperation with the Universidad Panamericana in Mexico City. UH offers several different legal clinics.

The Black Law Students Association and Hispanic Law Students Association work to recruit minority students. At this state-supported law school, enrollment of nonresidents is limited to about 10 percent.

The placement center, founded in 1977, has expanded rapidly and maintains career and clerkship listings and coordinates fall interviews. The school's reputation seems to be beginning to spread across state lines.

UH is known as a fairly difficult school. Some students don't make it through. Among those who do, the majority are satisfied with the legal education they've received.

Howard University School of Law

Address: **2900 Van Ness St., NW, Washington, DC 20008**
Phone: **(202) 806-8008**
Degrees: **J.D., J.D./M.B.A.**
Median LSAT: **33**
Median GPA: **2.81**
Applicants accepted: **23%**
Transfers: **NA**
Law enrollment: **372**
Campus enrollment: **372**

Part time: **0**
Women: **56%**
Minorities: **86%**
Dorm residents: **0**
Library: **234,400**
Student-faculty ratio: **20:1**
Tuition: **$8346**
Financial aid: **approx. 80–90% (60–70% gift)**
Apply by: **April 30, April 1 (aid)**

Disabled students: **Fully accessible. In five years, one blind student.**

Placement: **Graduates took jobs in South Atlantic (69%), Pacific (9%), Middle Atlantic (8%), East North Central (6%), West North Central (4%), New England (2%), Foreign (2%). Graduates entered private practice (34%), government (33%), business (15%), judicial clerkships (8%), military (4%), public interest (4%), academic (2%).**

Howard is the country's foremost predominantly black law school. The school's orientation manifests itself not just in the large numbers of African-American students but also in a serious, thoroughgoing emphasis on civil rights law. Howard has produced some of the finest civil rights lawyers America has ever seen, and many of today's students are inspired by Howard's focus to follow in their footsteps.

In addition to the standard prerequisites of good grades and high LSAT scores, Howard looks for potential leaders who are dedicated to the legal and political needs of underrepresented people. The typical Howard student is aware of the injustices of the past and present and optimistic about creating change in the future.

The students who end up at Howard are generally pleased to be here, because of the training they receive and because of the rapport between students and faculty. The professors' open-door policy affords students an opportunity to learn about and debate every conceivable legal and political issue. Equally valuable is the camaraderie among the students. A feeling of support and shared enthusiasm about law pervades the entire student body.

Although the work load is demanding, there is time to become involved in student government, which is very active in keeping the faculty and administration accountable to the students. On many occasions, the student government speaks out on local, state, national, and even international issues. This energetic awareness of, and participation in, politics is only fitting, given Howard's Washington, DC, location.

The law school is somewhat secluded in Washington's upper Connecticut Avenue area. Still, there are constant reminders that one is studying law where it's made. Students can take advantage of the proximity to the Library of Congress, the federal archives, Congress, and all of the other resources of the nation's capital.

Washington is an international city, with an exciting mix of social and cultural activities, all of which enhance a student's three-year stay at Howard.

The downtown campus of Howard University is separate from that of the law school. For law students willing to make the trip, the main campus (with over 10,000 students) has something for everyone.

The law school has the usual law review and moot court, as well as a student newspaper. Clinical programs cover criminal justice, civil litigation, and labor law. What with the academic, extracurricular, and clinical offerings, a Howard student can easily prepare to become a practicing attorney, professor, politician—or even a Supreme Court justice, like Thurgood Marshall.

Howard's Washington location has two drawbacks you should know about. The cold and snowy winters and unbearably hot and humid summers come as a rude shock to members of the geographically diverse student body who aren't used to one or the other. (On the other hand, spring and fall in Washington are absolutely lovely.) The other problem is a housing shortage. Many Howard students move to neighboring Maryland or Virginia. The cost of living is high in Washington, but it's offset somewhat by Howard's very reasonable tuition.

As an institution founded for African-Americans, Howard faces inevitable prejudice. Job-hunting students sometimes pay the price. Still, Howard has a worldwide reputation for civil rights law. And for black students, as one student put it, "Coming to Howard is coming home."

University of Idaho College of Law

Address: **Moscow, ID 83843**
Phone: **(208) 885-6422**
Degrees: **J.D.**
Median LSAT: **153 (in-state),
160 (out-of-state)**
Median GPA: **3.15 (in-state),
3.11 (out-of-state)**
Applicants accepted: **64% (in-state), 9% (out-of-state)**

Transfers: **1–2/8–12**
Law enrollment: **314**
Campus enrollment: **11,448**
Part time: **0**
Women: **30%**
Minorities: **10%**
Dorm residents: **NA**
Library: **145,800**
Student-faculty ratio: **17:1**

180 | University of Idaho College of Law

Tuition: **$1928 (in-state),**
$5438 (out-of-state)

Financial aid: **NA**
Apply by: **February 1**

Disabled students: **Fully accessible. In five years, two deaf students, one wheelchair user, one with other mobility problems.**

Placement: **80% employed six months after graduation.**
Approximately 15 employers on campus in one year; 95% from Idaho; 48% private firms, 26% government, 13% judicial, 13% other. Graduates took jobs in Mountain (70%), Pacific (20%), South Atlantic (3%), Middle Atlantic (2%), New England (1%), East North Central (1%), West North Central (1%), East South Central (1%), West South Central (1%). Graduates entered private practice (40%), judicial clerkships (25%), government (13%), public interest (8%), military (3%), academic (2%), business (2%), unknown (7%). Salary range: $20,000–$60,000. Mean salary: $28,683. Idaho bar pass rate: 80% (statewide average: 82%).

A common attitude among U of I students is that if you must inflict law school upon yourself, U of I is a bearable place to do it.

The charitable word for U of I's rural location is soothing; less charitable words range from isolated to boring to unprintable. Moscow is the hub of the northern Idaho area known as the Palouse, which consists of wheat fields. Lots of them. The Pacific Northwest deserves its reputation for heavy precipitation; the overcast days outnumber the sunny ones.

Moscow has 18,000 people. Pullman, Washington, eight miles away and slightly more populous, is the home of sprawling Washington State University. The two-city area has a huge student population, which translates into lots of university-sponsored athletic events, concerts, and plays. The cultural offerings of the local farming community are largely limited to a few movie houses, the usual fast-food outlets, some good restaurants, two shopping malls, and numerous drinking establishments, some with dance floors.

The limitless opportunities to hunt, fish, backpack, ski, or just escape civilization are big attractions for U of I students, most of whom are Idaho natives or people who moved here for the woods and mountains.

The law school's handsome and comfortable brick building (completed in 1973) houses a pleasantly small student body. Most law students are friends with each other, and access to the faculty is good, with only a few exceptions.

One disadvantage of the small size is a less-than-varied curriculum. There are few specialized courses, no joint degree programs, and no way of avoiding a particular professor by taking the course from somebody else—because there is nobody else. These problems aren't devastating, because there isn't much time for electives and most of the professors are knowledgeable and capable. Depending on faculty availability, the school does have good offerings in natural resource areas like environmental law, water law, agricultural law, and land-use planning.

Teaching styles range from Socratic-cum-discussion in first year to seminar-style later. Grades are usually issued on the basis of one do-or-die exam given at the end of the semester. (A few upper-level courses have papers instead.) The majority of grades are in the C to B– range. Grades below a C are far from uncommon, and a number of students reportedly flunk out each year for not maintaining the requisite 2.0 average.

Membership on the board of editors of the law review, which publishes three issues a year, is based on academic qualifications and prowess in research and writing. The moot court programs are emphasized at U of I, and their good records in regional and national competitions show it. Under Idaho and Washington law, third-year students may qualify for limited licenses to practice under an attorney's supervision; such licensing is available through legal assistance programs as well as through private practitioners.

U of I has an excellent intramural sports program. The local Blue Mountain Rugby Club and the Women's Dusty Lentils are reputedly two of the best rugby clubs in the Pacific Northwest, so if your taste runs to brutal physical contact and wild parties, you'll be in your element.

Unfortunately, when it comes to student government, the easy-going atmosphere here is indistinguishable from apathy. There are several organizations, like the Phi Alpha Delta legal fraternity, the Student Bar Association, and the Women's Law Caucus, but if you get involved, you'll be in the minority.

The university provides some married student housing and dormitory space, as well as limited space in graduate student residence halls. Most students live off campus and walk or bicycle to school. Students can sometimes find accommodations at local farms.

Because this is farm country, the supply of law students greatly exceeds the area demand for legal researchers and interns. Only a few students find law-related work during the school year (at paltry wages), and almost no one finds summer jobs in the immediate area.

The school placement service assists in locating summer and permanent jobs, but personal effort is a necessity. For all but the very top students, the school's reputation is effectively limited to Idaho and Washington. Although student input is welcomed by the administration, vast improvements in the school's standing are rendered doubtful by the budget (or lack thereof).

U of I students help each other by recommending course outlines, selling used books, and tutoring younger students. This is the kind of place where the administrative secretaries are happy to type your term papers and résumés for you. U of I is a regional law school, though, so make sure you're fond of the region before you sign yourself up.

University of Illinois College of Law

Address: **504 East Pennsylvania Ave., Champaign, IL 61820**
Phone: **(217) 244-6415**
Degrees: **J.D., LL.M., J.S.D., M.C.L., J.D./M.B.A., J.D./M.D., J.D./M.A.S. (accounting), J.D./M.A.P.A. (public administration), J.D./M.A.L.I.R. (labor and industrial relations), J.D./M.Ed. (education), J.D./M.A. or Ph.D. (education), J.D./M.U.P. (urban planning), J.D./D.V.M. (veterinary)**
Median LSAT: **41/160**

Median GPA: **4.43 (on 5.0 scale)**
Applicants accepted: **29%**
Transfers: **1–12/25–30**
Law enrollment: **659 (630 J.D.)**
Campus enrollment: **35,000**
Part time: **0**
Women: **38%**
Minorities: **20%**
Dorm residents: **NA**
Library: **560,000**
Student-faculty ratio: **24:1**
Tuition: **$5010 (in-state), $12,622 (out-of-state)**
Financial aid: **NA**
Apply by: **March 15**

Disabled students: **Fully accessible. Within five years, four blind students, three wheelchair users.**
Placement: **57% placed by graduation; 92% employed six months after graduation. 150 employers on campus in one year; 90%**

from Midwest, 5% West/Mountain, 4% Northeast, 1% Southeast;
83% private firms, 8% government, 8% business, 1% public
interest. Graduates employed in Midwest (83%), West/Mountain
(8%), Northeast (6%), Southeast (2%). Graduates entered private
practice (68%), government (12%), judicial clerkships (9%),
business (5%), public interest (2%), military (2%), academic (2%).
Salary range: $21,000–$83,000. Median salary: $40,000. Mean salary:
$46,471. Illinois bar pass rate: 94% (statewide average: 85%).

The word at U of I is that although the school has never been
ranked in the "top ten," it compares favorably with Northwestern,
Minnesota, and other well-known midwestern law schools. Thanks
to an above-par faculty, student body, and research collection, U
of I's claim to a good reputation seems secure.

The school's faculty includes several noted scholars who, for
the most part, are available for student consultations and even an
occasional drink. But one student notes that with several professors
away recently on leaves or sabbaticals—a frequent prelude in academia to a switch to another school—faculty turnover is always a
possibility.

In any event, the quality of the student body is stable—and
impressive. Particularly for a state school, the numerical profile of
each entering class is admirable. Numbers are the primary concern
of the admissions committee here, but there is also a "plus" in
being a minority, older, or disabled applicant.

Another of U of I's assets is an excellent law library. It is especially noted for its large international collection.

The law school is housed in a functional but unexciting building near the southeastern end of the U of I campus. It is somewhat
removed from the hustle and bustle of undergraduate life, which
is an advantage in itself. Piecemeal remodeling in recent years has
made the school more pleasant and functional. Perhaps the best
thing about the law school's location is that it's less than a block
from the intramural building, where students can relieve the pressures of law school with a game of racquetball, a workout, a swim,
or a few minutes in the sauna.

The Socratic method predominates as a teaching method for
first-year students, who are divided into three sections. Styles do
vary, however, and while some professors ask only for the facts of

a case, others seek legal conclusions, and still others simply open up the classroom as a forum for discussion. During the second and third years, teaching styles differ depending on class size. With courses ranging from small seminars to large groups, professors may ask that students prepare presentations for class or may just call briefly on each student once a semester.

Law students may opt to take up to six credit hours of nonlaw courses to apply toward graduation. Although there are limits on which courses qualify and the grades needed to get credit, most students find these limits not very restrictive.

The law review chooses most of its members according to their first-year grades, but a few students get on board through a writing competition. Students who don't make the review can write case notes for the *Illinois Bar Journal*, a periodical aimed at practitioners more than scholars. In addition, the school has active moot court and international law moot court programs. While U of I's clinical program is still more limited than what is offered at more urban law schools, a well-run trial advocacy program helps third-year students sharpen their litigation skills.

The active Student Bar Association sponsors several social events throughout the year. Students can also participate in basketball and dart leagues within the law school and in the university's intramural program.

The numerous student organizations cater to a wide variety of interests. In addition to three law fraternities, there are support groups for black, Hispanic, and women law students. The International Law Society is one of the many pluses that U of I offers the student interested in international law.

The twin cities of Champaign and Urbana strike big-city types as being literally and figuratively a long way from civilization. In fact, the university provides enough cultural events and social activities for most law students, and downtown Chicago is only a two-and-a-half-hour drive away.

Job-hunting is easier for some students than for others. On-campus interviewers, who come primarily from Chicago and other Great Lakes and Midwest cities, typically set their sights on students in the top third of the class. Those in the bottom two thirds are often left to fend for themselves.

U of I has all the equipment for a first-rate legal education.

And if you keep your grades up, it has the equipment for first-rate placement opportunities, too.

Illinois Institute of Technology, Chicago-Kent College of Law

Address: **565 West Adams St., Chicago, IL 60661**
Phone: **(312) 906-5020**
Degrees: **J.D., LL.M. (tax, financial services, international comparative law), J.D./M.B.A., J.D./LL.M. (tax)**
Median LSAT: **160**
Median GPA: **3.2**
Applicants accepted: **33%**
Transfers: **2–5/20–30**

Law enrollment: **1223 (1145 J.D.)**
Campus enrollment: **NA**
Part time: **31%**
Women: **47%**
Minorities: **15%**
Dorm residents: **5%**
Library: **422,800**
Student-faculty ratio: **16:1**
Tuition: **$15,800**
Financial aid: **78% (33% gift)**
Apply by: **April 1 recommended**

Disabled students: **Fully accessible. Within five years, two blind students, one deaf, five wheelchair users, three with other mobility problems.**

Placement: **91% employed nine months after graduation. 56% of second-years and 76% of third-years employed in legal jobs during the academic year. 80% of first-years and 89% of second-years placed by end of spring term. 111 employers on campus in one year; primarily from Midwest; 76% law firms, 14% government or public interest, 10% business. Graduates took jobs in Chicago (81%), other East North Central (11%), South Atlantic (2%), Pacific (2%), West North Central (2%), Middle Atlantic (1%), East South Central (1%), Foreign (1%). Graduates entered private practice (55%), government (23%), business (13%), judicial clerkships (5%), public interest (4%). Salary range: $23,000–$75,000 (private sector), $18,000–$40,000 (public sector). Average salary: $40,342 (private sector), $29,648 (public sector). Illinois bar pass rate: 90% (statewide average: 85%).**

Chicago-Kent has an extremely varied curriculum by any standards. Although first year consists of the usual required courses (taught

Socratically), almost everything else is elective, and there's a broad range to choose from. But students warn that you shouldn't let the flexible curriculum blind you to the fact that this is a commuter school that aims to turn out competent practicing attorneys. Many of the students view law school as an exercise in preparation for the Illinois bar exam, and they have no trouble finding courses and professors sharing that perspective.

Chicago-Kent is structured for the convenience of its urban clientele. The school offers a full evening division with the same admissions standards and much of the same faculty as the day division. Students can transfer from one division to the other, as their jobs or moods dictate.

Chicago-Kent is distinguished by its strong three-year legal research and writing program. The first year is devoted to the fundamentals of legal research, culminating in the spring with a moot court competition and the opportunity to write a case comment that helps prepare students to compete for law review. The final years are devoted to advanced legal research and drafting skills.

The legal research and writing classes are largely staffed by Chicago area practitioners. So are the excellent trial advocacy courses and many electives. The attitudes of the part-time faculty exemplify Chicago-Kent's emphasis on the practical, rather than the scholarly, side of law.

There are also a number of strong specialty programs. The school's Library of International Relations is one of the largest in the country, serving as one of the few depositories for United Nations and European Economic Community papers. Chicago-Kent has integrated computers into the law school curriculum, with students enjoying 24-hour access to LEXIS and WESTLAW. The Center for Law and Computers develops many programs in conjunction with the American Bar Association. Chicago-Kent's Program in Environmental and Energy Law researches the development of energy resources and efforts to protect the environment.

The law school's location in the Loop (Chicago's business district) puts it close to downtown law firms and courts. Students take advantage of the situation by clerking for private firms, or by participating in the school's clinical programs. Students earn credit for placements with government agencies and federal judges. The school's Law Offices, right in the building, offer supervision and credit for work on criminal defense cases, job discrimination suits, and public-interest cases.

Chicago-Kent's downtown building is about three miles from the main campus of Illinois Institute of Technology. Some housing on the main campus is available for both married and unmarried law students, but few use it.

Many day students are right out of college (University of Illinois grads are plentiful) and live at home with their parents. Among the night students, many are older and live with their spouses and kids. The result is minimal involvement by both groups in school extracurriculars. The Student Bar Association hosts happy hours fairly regularly.

The *Chicago-Kent Law Review* publishes three times a year. One issue carries the widely read Seventh Circuit Review. The Trial Advocacy Team has recently been highly ranked in national competitions. Several trial advocacy classes are taught by sitting judges.

A note about the financial aid picture. If your credentials knock the socks off the admissions committee, this is one school where you stand a chance to get a scholarship on that basis alone. Scholarship dollars are plentiful. Many students receive financial aid here when other local schools offer nothing. A fledgling loan forgiveness program for students taking public-interest jobs is available.

When it comes to finding a job, the school's fall interview program—which lately has attracted over one hundred Midwest employers to campus—can be a big help. But its spring counterpart is much smaller, so by the time Chicago's infamous winters begin to recede, if students are still without job offers they often have to go it alone.

Still, the school's graduates continue to move up in many of Chicago's best firms. The school's rising reputation is symbolized by its brand-new, state-of-the-art building (circa 1992). Chicago-Kent is one of the few places where you're almost sure the school will be more widely known when you graduate than when you started.

Indiana University School of Law—Bloomington

Address: **Law Building, Room 230, Bloomington, IN 47405**

Phone: **(812) 855-2704**

Degrees: **J.D., LL.M., M.C.L., J.D./M.B.A., J.D./ M.P.A., J.D./M.S.E.S. (environmental science), J.D./M.L.S. (library science)**

Median LSAT: **161**

Median GPA: **3.45**

Applicants accepted: **26%**

Transfers: **4–8/30–35**

Law enrollment: **615 (605 J.D.)**

Campus enrollment: **36,100**

Part time: **2%**

Women: **40%**

Minorities: **17%**

Dorm residents: **NA**

Library: **490,000**

Student-faculty ratio: **19:1**

Tuition: **$3929 (in-state), $10,425 (out-of-state)**

Financial aid: **40% (25% gift)**

Apply by: **rolling admissions, March 1 recommended**

Disabled students: **Fully accessible. One wheelchair user in one year.**

Placement: **90–95% employed six months after graduation. 100 employers on campus in one year; primarily private firms from Midwest. Graduates took jobs in Midwest (80%), West (7%), Northeast (6%), Southeast (4%), Southwest (4%). Graduates entered private practice (61%), judicial clerkships (13%), government (11%), business (3%), academic (3%), military (2%), unknown (7%). Salary range: $20,000–$82,000. Median salary: $35,000. Mean salary: $41,192. Indiana bar pass rate: 86.5% (statewide average: 85%).**

Indiana University—Bloomington enjoys a national reputation, and its curriculum reflects its intention to teach legal skills applicable throughout the country. The law school itself has been recently and impressively remodeled, and has a comprehensive research library, complete with extensive computer and legal database facilities.

One aspect of an IU education is unique to Indiana, however. Students attending the law school with an aim toward practicing in-state must satisfy the Indiana Supreme Court's Rule 13 requirements. This rule requires completion of classes from twelve course groupings, which account for approximately half of the student's overall credits. The majority of these can be satisfied with standard first-year courses, and many others are classes most law students would take anyway, such as evidence and tax.

IU has many outstanding teachers, including several recognized authorities, many of whom have written the texts for their classes. In addition, the law school has hired several new faculty in various areas, bolstering in particular the environmental and international law offerings. As with all law schools, some professors are not as good as others. If you plan your schedule carefully, however, core courses are offered often enough that you can usually avoid any professor you wish.

Students interested in a more varied education can pursue joint degrees through the School of Business and School of Public and Environmental Affairs, both of which are highly ranked. For those who are looking for clinical legal experience, the IU law school offers courses such as the Community Legal Clinic and the Student Legal Services Clinic, which allow law students to help city residents and students with legal advice. Other popular "learn-by-doing" courses are Trial Process and Appellate Advocacy. Top "App. Ad." students are eligible to join the moot court team, which has a successful record in regional and national competition. Students can also get hands-on experience on a noncredit basis through the Protective Order Project, which assists victims of domestic violence, and the Inmate Legal Assistance Clinic.

Until recently, the only journal on the law school campus was the *Indiana Law Journal,* traditionally edited by the top students in the class. During the 1992–93 academic year, however, the school launched two new student-edited journals, the *Federal Communications Law Journal* and the *Indiana Journal of Global Legal Studies.*

In addition to academic pursuits, the law school has student groups to cater to almost every interest, including the Public Interest Law Foundation, the Black Law Students Association, the Environmental Law Society, and the Women's Law Caucus. Students are also very active in campus-wide intramural sports.

For those students who hope to get a job upon graduation (namely all of them), IU Law recently expanded its career services office. While only the top students tend to get jobs through the on-campus interview process, the placement office offers plenty of backup assistance in terms of job guides, seminars, and such for those less fortunate in the grade department. Those seeking jobs outside law, however, will often have to fend for themselves.

As a whole, students at IU Law School are open and friendly. Life-styles are relaxed, and most students are glad they're here (a rare sentiment on a law school campus). Though Hoosier natives predominate, the extensive range of undergraduate schools represented, as well as the recent upswing in the number of women and minority students, make for a diverse classroom environment.

The law school is situated on the huge main campus of IU in Bloomington. The campus is hilly and heavily wooded, and the surrounding countryside is worthy of a pastoral poem. When the trees are changing colors in the fall, most IU students couldn't imagine going to school anywhere else. Nearby lakes and national forests beckon invitingly to the prospective biker, backpacker, or cross-country skier.

Besides outdoor activities, the Bloomington campus also has its cultural side. The various arts departments offer frequent concerts, plays, musicals, and operas. Bloomington itself is a college town, home to a wide variety of ethnic restaurants and specialty stores. Indianapolis is less than an hour away.

With its relatively low public school tuition, Indiana's small size, impressive facilities, and comfortable atmosphere make it a tempting choice for prospective law students.

Indiana University School of Law—Indianapolis

Address: **735 West New York St., Indianapolis, IN 46202**
Phone: **(317) 274-2459**
Degrees: **J.D., J.D./M.B.A., J.D./M.P.A., J.D./M.H.A. (health administration)**
Median LSAT: **36 (full time), 37 (part time)**
Median GPA: **3.3 (full time), 3.2 (part time)**
Applicants accepted: **36%**
Transfers: **14**

Law enrollment: **848**
Campus enrollment: **28,000**
Part time: **38%**
Women: **44%**
Minorities: **11%**
Dorm residents: **NA**
Library: **405,900**
Student-faculty ratio: **20:1**
Tuition: **$3581 (in-state), $9850 (out-of-state)**
Financial aid: **44%**
Apply by: **March 1**

Disabled students: **Fully accessible. In one year, one disabled student.**
Placement: **Approximately 77% placed by graduation; approximately 94% employed six to nine months after graduation. Graduates**

took jobs in East North Central (93%), Mountain (2%), Pacific (2%), Middle Atlantic (1%), South Atlantic (1%), West South Central (1%). Graduates entered private practice (55%), business (13%), government (12%), judicial clerkships (11%), public interest (4%), academic (2%), military (1%), unknown (2%).

Like a certain tire manufacturer that people confuse with its blimp-operating competitor, the "other" law school of Indiana University is often ignored or forgotten because of its older brother in Bloomington.

In spite of this identity problem, IU School of Law—Indianapolis has experienced a period of healthy growth since its current building opened its doors in 1970. Ideally located near the business and government districts of Indianapolis, the facility provides a conducive environment for law study. The law library is continually adding to its already good collection.

The curriculum is traditional and very heavy on required courses. Despite some interesting electives that have nothing to do with an Indiana practice (such as sports and entertainment law), the topics of a large number of the courses are dictated by the stringent requirements of the Indiana bar exam. Still, many professors compare Indiana rules of law with rules throughout the country, and they often present the theories behind the law as well as how to apply them, so the school is much more than an Indiana bar review course.

The faculty here includes distinguished scholars and practitioners. Interaction between faculty and students is common, with groups of students and faculty gathering at professors' homes and at various school-sponsored social activities. Professors are generally quite open to meeting and working with students. The Student Bar Association has representatives on nearly all the faculty committees, ensuring that the student viewpoint is at least heard.

Indianapolis is the state's capital and largest city. The school is just a few blocks from the capitol building, home to the legislature and state appellate courts. The Federal District Court for the Southern District of Indiana is also within walking distance, as is the City/County Building, which houses city government, municipal courts, and the offices of the prosecutor and public defender. Private law firms are also close at hand.

Virtually any student who wants to combine employment with classroom education can find a law-related job. The school's full-fledged evening division enhances the opportunity to gain work experience while earning a degree. Another source of firsthand experience is the school's clinical program.

The IU–Indianapolis campus encompasses six professional schools and offers lots of possibilities for interdisciplinary study. The school has a nationally recognized Center for Law and Health which offers interesting programs in cooperation with the IU Medical Center.

The law school was one of the first buildings constructed in an ambitious campus expansion plan. Swimming and track facilities are adjacent to the school. A new tennis stadium, site of the U.S. Clay Courts Championships, is also nearby.

The downtown setting eliminates any chance for a real campus atmosphere, but it also provides a certain number of urban pleasures. Indianapolis has attractions for those interested in sports, the arts, and entertainment of all types.

In addition, the students and various student organizations create their own diversions on a regular basis. The Student Bar Association sponsors a speaker series, seminars, forums, and a variety of social activities.

Other school organizations include an international law society, interest groups for health law and environmental law, organizations for black students and women, and two legal fraternities. The school has two student-edited journals: the *Indiana Law Review* and the *Indiana International and Comparative Law Review*. The moot court program is excellent and has captured regional and national honors. The client-counseling practice program is growing.

IU provides little campus housing for graduate students, except for a dormitory and a few campus apartments. Law students live throughout the Indianapolis metropolitan area or even outside the county, in a variety of living quarters, including apartments, condos, and houses. Transportation isn't a problem, whether you drive or rely on city buses. An additional convenience is a regular shuttle bus between the school and various points downtown.

What IU-Indianapolis may lack in national identity, it makes up for in statewide recognition. The law school on IU's Indianapolis campus is not a "retread" of the Bloomington school. It *is* a place for the future midwestern practitioner to get a basic legal education and pick up some law-related work experience at the same time.

University of Iowa College of Law

Address: **116 Calvin Hall, Iowa City, IA 52242**
Phone: **(319) 335-9071**
Degrees: **J.D., LL.M. (international law), J.D./ M.B.A., other joint degrees**
Median LSAT: **160**
Median GPA: **3.49**
Applicants accepted: **22%**
Transfers: **2–5/25–30**
Law enrollment: **698 (684 J.D.)**

Campus enrollment: **27,500**
Part time: **0**
Women: **43%**
Minorities: **25%**
Dorm residents: **NA**
Library: **699,400**
Student-faculty ratio: **14:1**
Tuition: **$3444 (in-state), $9476 (out-of-state)**
Financial aid: **85% (24% gift)**
Apply by: **March 1**

Disabled students: **Fully accessible. In five years, two deaf students, two wheelchair users, two with other mobility problems.**

Placement: **73% placed by graduation; 94% employed six months after graduation. 268 employers on campus in one year; 23% from Iowa, 13% Illinois, 8% California, 8% Minnesota, 7% Missouri, 6% Washington, DC, 5% Wisconsin, 4% New York, 3% Arizona, 3% Texas, 3% Colorado, 17% other. Graduates took jobs in Iowa (34%), Illinois (15%), Minnesota (13%), Washington, DC (6%), Missouri (4%), Wisconsin (4%), California (4%), Texas (3%), Michigan (2%), Arizona (2%), Florida (2%), Kansas (2%). Graduates entered private practice (54%), judicial clerkships (15%), government (11%), business (8%), public interest (6%), military (2%), nonlegal (4%). Salary range: $19,500–$73,500. Median salary: $42,000. Iowa bar pass rate: 81% (statewide average: 75%).**

Iowans have long been proud of their state's reputation for having high educational standards. This traditional emphasis on education is reflected in the Iowa College of Law, the oldest law school west of the Mississippi. A state-supported institution, it has achieved a degree of prominence despite its relative isolation.

The strongest aspect of the Iowa College of Law (and the one every school either lives or dies by) is the student body. Although the prototypical student is a white male Iowa resident, there are enough out-of-state students (about 30 percent) to make for some variety, and more minority students and women than you might expect. Everyone seems to fit in well. The overall spirit is one of cooperation and camaraderie, and—*mirabile dictu*—most students find their three-year hitch here quite enjoyable.

The law school got a brand-new building in 1986, complete with expanded library facilities. The library is one of the ten largest among public law schools and has a liberal lending policy.

Most professors pride themselves on being open and accessible to students. Teaching is said to be especially good in the areas of contracts, civil procedure, tax, international, and constitutional law.

An important element of the curriculum is a writing program that requires each student to fulfill a total of five legal writing credits as a prerequisite to graduation. The requirement is satisfied upon the successful completion of two legal writing courses and various optional elements (law review, moot court, seminars, etc.). The students agree with administrators that the program is a valuable enhancement to a legal education.

The conventional curriculum consists of a functional blend of large classes, with 90 to 100 students, and smaller courses with 20 to 25 students. Naturally, standard bar exam courses are much sought after, and their size is directly proportional to the demand. A panoply of less traditional courses and seminars offers every student a chance for some more intimate learning experiences.

The Iowa Student Bar Association is the elected arm of student government. It operates a bookstore and a coffee shop and sponsors a broad range of social functions for all students. The ISBA also serves as a liaison between students and administration, and helps oversee student organizations and intramural athletics.

The University of Iowa is a member of the Big Ten Conference, a fact that will not be lost on you if you come here. Be prepared for widespread mourning following a football loss to arch-rival Iowa State. Strong intercollegiate programs in football, basketball, wrestling, swimming, gymnastics, and field hockey offer a ready respite from the drudgery of law school. Intramural programs are also available.

The university provides free busing on the excellent Cambus system, and city bus lines are conveniently routed to provide service to the whole surrounding area. Downtown Iowa City has a surprisingly good selection of restaurants, bars, and theaters. The nearby Coralville Reservoir is a nice place to cool off in hot weather.

The University of Iowa is widely considered a liberal oasis in an otherwise conservative Hawkeye State. But the university gives signs of becoming more conservative, and the state of Iowa is more liberal than most "furriners" tend to believe.

Iowa graduates have a good name in both Iowa and the Midwest generally. But perhaps the best thing about Iowa College of Law is the nonstraitlaced atmosphere. Both students and "townies" are generally tolerant of alternative viewpoints and life-styles—yet this tolerance is not the product of indifference. It's taken as a given here that people are committed to preserving an educational environment that has proven effective, so no one is disturbed if you stir things up a bit. If that isn't what you would have expected from a school in the midst of Iowa's cornfields, think again.

John Marshall Law School

Address: **315 South Plymouth Ct., Chicago, IL 60604**
Phone: **(312) 987-1406**
Degrees: **J.D., LL.M. (tax or intellectual property), J.D./M.B.A.**
Median LSAT: **38**
Median GPA: **3.00**
Applicants accepted: **38%**
Transfers: **approx. 12/21**
Law enrollment: **1283 (1216 J.D.)**

Campus enrollment: **1283**
Part time: **33%**
Women: **36%**
Minorities: **8%**
Dorm residents: **0**
Library: **274,000**
Student-faculty ratio: **24:1**
Tuition: **$12,210**
Financial aid: **approx. 69% (12% gift)**
Apply by: **April 1 (for fall), October 15 (for spring)**

Disabled students: **Moderate/full accessibility. In a recent five-year period, three visually impaired students.**
Placement: **NA**

If your idea of law school is an intimate experience shared with a few hundred other kindred souls, read no further. John Marshall's enrollment places it among the ten biggest law schools in the country.

This is a commuter school, unaffiliated with any four-year college or university, located in the heart of Chicago's Loop (the business and financial hub of the city). While the school draws its students primarily from Chicago, its suburbs, and the surrounding midwestern states, a sizable percentage come from places like New York, New Jersey, Connecticut, Massachusetts, and Pennsylvania.

With the purchase and renovation of the twelve-story Rothschild Building to supplement the adjoining six-story main building, John Marshall enjoys adequate classroom and study space.

Nearly all the professors, both full time and adjunct, have spent many years in practice. Their approach is at least as vocational as theoretical. Most faculty and administrators are helpful and offer the support that older and part-time students especially need.

Each incoming student is assigned to one of the three day sections or to the one evening section, starting in August or January. First-year classes have about 80 to 90 students, but upper-level classes and electives may have as few as a dozen. The Socratic method has all but disappeared. A professor will call on a student—usually without advance notice—but, in the end, the teacher provides the correct answer rather than leaving the student guessing. This method, one student explains, "moves along much more rapidly than the Socratic method, properly used, would permit."

About half the courses are required basics. A four-semester required sequence in "lawyering skills"—legal research, writing, and oral advocacy—is heavily stressed.

John Marshall offers a particularly respected graduate degree in intellectual property (patents, trademark, and copyright). The school hosts an annual conference on intellectual property, as well as offering an unusually comprehensive set of intellectual property courses for J.D. students. In addition to the *John Marshall Law Review*, there is even a *Software Law Journal*.

The school's location offers unique advantages. Close to all major transportation routes, the school sits opposite the federal court building that houses the U.S. attorney's office, the U.S. District Court for the Northern District of Illinois, and the Seventh Circuit U.S. Court of Appeals. Most of the city's law firms—major ones as well as small partnerships—are a short walk away.

Students profit from this proximity to government and private employers by working at part-time jobs to earn money and experience. Many federal judges and some federal agencies use students as unpaid externs. The Illinois Supreme Court permits senior law students to function as lawyers with certain public agencies.

Except for an occasional "apartment for rent" notice on a bulletin board, housing for John Marshall students is a fend-for-yourself affair. The student government has helped by putting together a survey of areas to live in and their going rates. Rents are generally high, especially if you don't want a long commute. (Don't bother bringing a car. Public transportation is more than ample, and parking is expensive.) Some students rent a dorm room at Roosevelt University's Herman Crown Center two blocks away; most get apartments, which are easy to find, especially in the Loop.

The organizations and fraternities at the school sponsor social activities, and many classes hold parties at people's apartments—but in a city the size of Chicago, who really cares? More social life takes place within a mile or two of the lakefront, from the river to Belmont Harbor, than any law student has time to pursue.

Student government exists in the form of the Student Bar Association. The SBA's activities attract the aging campus politico or the budding real-life politician. Few students care about the SBA's inner workings, or about those of the campus ABA Law Student Division chapter.

The school's placement office is relatively new. It's a good source of part-time jobs in the Chicago area, and it has become increasingly active in lending a hand to graduates. Its efforts, combined with those of the law review and several individual professors, have succeeded in placing more and more grads in major firms, judicial clerkships, and federal agencies.

John Marshall isn't a household word on either of the two coasts, or in plenty of places in between, for that matter. But it enjoys a particularly high reputation within the patent bar. Students with a technical, engineering, or scientific background who want to practice patent law can land high-paying starting positions—even with a so-so grade point average—after an education at John Marshall.

University of Kentucky College of Law

Address: **209 Law Building, Lexington, KY 40506**
Phone: **(606) 257-1678**
Degrees: **J.D., J.D./M.B.A., J.D./M.P.A.**
Median LSAT: **160**
Median GPA: **3.4**
Applicants accepted: **30% (in-state), 14% (out-of-state)**
Transfers: **1–3/10–20**
Law enrollment: **459**

Campus enrollment: **25,000**
Part time: **0**
Women: **38%**
Minorities: **6%**
Dorm residents: **NA**
Library: **326,900**
Student-faculty ratio: **19:1**
Tuition: **$3078 (in-state), $8408 (out-of-state)**
Financial aid: **51% (22% gift)**
Apply by: **March 1**

Disabled students: **Moderate/full accessibility. In five years, one deaf student, two wheelchair users, a few with other mobility problems.**
Placement: **95% employed nine months after graduation. Approximately 25% of second-years and 30% of third-years employed in legal jobs during the academic year. Approximately 60% of first-years, 90% of second-years, and 65% of third-years placed by end of spring term. 131 employers recruiting on campus and at off-campus job fairs in one year; 38% from Kentucky, Tennessee, or West Virginia; 23% from other Southeast, 19% East, 11% Midwest, 9% West; 67% private firms, 15% public interest, 12% government, 6% corporations. 70% of graduates remained in Kentucky; 30% went out of state, including Tennessee, Ohio, West Virginia, Washington, DC, New York, Texas, Florida, Georgia, other. Graduates entered private practice (71%), government (12%), judicial clerkships (8%), public interest (3%), business (3%), nonlegal (3%). Salary range: $18,500–$80,000. Median salary: $50,000. Mean salary: $41,000. Kentucky bar pass rate: 96% (statewide average: 84%).**

UK's two greatest assets are its comfortable atmosphere and the marketability of its graduates.

Students and faculty are unanimous in recognizing that fear, anxiety, and a screw-the-next-guy attitude are neither necessary nor helpful parts of a quality legal education. There is certainly competition (class rank has a lot to do with who gets the best jobs), but it takes place in a context of genuine friendliness. If you ask a fellow student for help, you can almost always expect to receive it.

Unlike many of their colleagues elsewhere, most of the professors realize that their obligation to teach extends beyond the classroom. They encourage office visits, and it isn't at all unusual to see professors and students grouped around tables in the law school lounge discussing everything from legal issues to exams to current events.

There are as many different teaching styles as there are professors. Some use a Socratic question-and-answer method, others encourage wide-open class discussions, and still others employ a straight lecture format. The one common denominator is that all the professors insist on thorough preparation for class, but if you're caught napping, your own automatic embarrassment will be more of a punishment than the professor's response.

Between 80 and 90 percent of the students are Kentucky residents, and the number of minority group members is minuscule, so diversity isn't a strong point. On the other hand, students claim that there are many different backgrounds and perspectives to enhance class discussion. Social contact with slightly older fellow students helps cure those directly from college of their undergraduate myopia.

The curriculum here is much like what you'd find at any other law school. That fact calms the fears of many UK students who initially wondered what they might be missing by choosing a state school.

The first-year schedule consists of required courses. As students advance in seniority, there is more latitude to take electives like (in one year) Women and the Law and Business Planning. Many of the electives are small seminars with lively discussion, and most require a substantial research paper. (One such paper is required for graduation.)

UK has long had the kind of practical courses that studies of legal education are now touting as the wave of the future. Within the framework of a traditional curriculum, many students take advantage of courses in legal writing, trial and appellate techniques, legal drafting, and negotiating skills, as well as a variety of clinical programs.

UK is proud of its law journal. Students who don't qualify by having top grades can join by writing a publishable article. The school also has the *Journal of Mineral Law and Policy,* which is part of an entire Mineral Law Center—Kentucky is part of the Coal Belt, after all. The moot court team has been doing very well of late, placing in the top tiers of national competitions.

The Black Law Students Association has an active chapter at UK. With the growing number of women enrolled at the school, the Women's Law Caucus has become especially prominent.

What about life after law school? UK grads say that the school prepared them not only for the practice of law but also for the all-important job search. The placement office is reported to be competent and helpful.

With the job issue clearly in mind, UK students work hard, but they don't neglect the lighter side of life. Since Lexington has a large student population, good restaurants are easy to find. UK basketball and football games are popular entertainment. Nestled among the horse farms of Kentucky's Bluegrass region, Lexington is a very pleasant place (so much so that many UK grads settle here).

While Lexington is too quiet to provide a thrilling nightlife, the law school itself supplies periodic social events. The Student Bar Association and the three legal fraternities can be counted on for several parties each semester. UK students are used to running into their professors at these parties. The event with the biggest draw is the annual Libel Show, the scene of irreverent, light-hearted skits about the faculty. Almost the entire law school—students and professors—turns out for a full evening of laughs and beer. How many law schools can get their students out of the library and into a just-for-fun activity? UK is definitely a touch more relaxed than the average school.

Lewis and Clark College, Northwestern School of Law

Address: **10015 S.W. Terwilliger Blvd., Portland, OR 97219**
Phone: **(503) 768-6613**
Degrees: **J.D., LL.M. (environmental and natural resources), J.D./M.P.A.**

Median LSAT: **161**
Median GPA: **3.22**
Applicants accepted: **27% (in-state), 73% (out-of-state)**
Transfers: **15–25/40–50**
Law enrollment: **688 (682 J.D.)**

Campus enrollment: **3200**   Library: **317,700**
Part time: **34%**   Student-faculty ratio: **23:1**
Women: **42%**   Tuition: **$13,050**
Minorities: **13%**   Financial aid: **80% (40% gift)**
Dorm residents: **1%**   Apply by: **March 15**

Disabled students: **Moderate/full accessibility. Within five years, one
blind student, one deaf, one wheelchair user.**

Placement: **89% employed several months after graduation. More
than 50 employers on campus in one year; from Oregon, other
Pacific, Nevada, Guam, Washington, DC; 60% private firms, 19%
government, 13% public interest, 8% business. 85% of graduates
remained in Pacific region. Graduates entered private practice
(50%), government (18%), business (17%), judicial clerkships
(7%), other (3%). Salary range: $15,000–$70,000. Median salary:
$32,000. Mean salary: $33,240. Oregon bar pass rate: 76%
(statewide average: 72%). Washington bar pass rate: 89%
(statewide average: 78%).**

Northwestern School of Law (not to be confused with Northwestern *University* School of Law) was founded in 1884. It went into a
slump as the University of Oregon Law School flourished. Then
Lewis and Clark College, an aspiring private institution, decided to
make an educational investment in the declining, but historically
significant, old law school. It bought Northwestern in 1965, and
the school gained full accreditation in 1973.

Lewis and Clark is now the only law school in Oregon with an
evening division. The "night school" is a full-fledged program
taught by the school's regular profs. The evening division is further enriched by the interchange between the somewhat more
academic day students, who take many of their advanced courses
in the evening, and the more down-to-earth evening students,
who've already established themselves in the outside world.

The environmental law program at L & C has a national reputation. Course selections in land-use planning are excellent; the
school houses the Natural Resources Law Institute; the law review,
Environmental Law, is open to all students through a writing competition. The school has an externship program that allows students
to spend one or two semesters working for a federal or public-
interest environmental agency. Many of the professors are avowed

or "closet" environmentalists, but some students wish the faculty were more politically active on environmental issues.

About 40 percent of L & C students are married, and many have jobs while they're in school. Not only do the evening students work full time, but the second- and third-year day students generally work from fifteen to twenty hours a week. Some students work out of economic necessity, others to get a foot in an employer's door, but in both cases, course work may be neglected in the process. One student writes, "In many instances, second- and third-year classes are characterized by the students' lack of preparation."

Active extracurricular activities include the Minority Law Students Association, Women's Law Caucus, Environmental Law Caucus, Phi Alpha Delta, and National Lawyers Guild. L & C students learn each other's names, become friends, and help each other generously with class outlines, notes, books, and advice. There is a strong feeling of being in the same academic boat, and competitiveness is virtually unknown.

This is a commuter school, located on the fringe of Dunthorpe, Portland's "old money" neighborhood. Architecturally, the school is a combination of early bomb shelter and auto showroom glassworks. But the windows look out into a 600-acre wooded state park, and many students take advantage of the extensive nature trails during lunch breaks.

Commuting from ten minutes to half an hour is a way of life here. Parking is a problem, exacerbated by the continuing battle between the local envirofreaks and the motorheads. Bus transportation from the downtown area is more than adequate, but few students take advantage of it. Housing of all descriptions is reasonably plentiful at moderate prices.

Lewis and Clark's main campus half a mile away houses the undergrads and a few graduate programs. Most law students visit it only for the bookstore or the gym. (The outdoor pool is a favorite in the summer.)

Most of the law school professors are excellent. The pleasant Portland surroundings and an initial core of high-quality professors have enabled the school to attract first-rate faculty members. Downtown practitioners are regularly hired to bring a whiff of practicality into the academic air. Many of the practitioners are interested and energetic instructors, but some are, in one student's words, "too pooped to pop." Classes typically have 40 to 80 students, although many seminars enroll fewer than 20. Some of the professors are approachable on a first-name basis; student-faculty socializing is rare.

L & C trains general practitioners in a locale where the market for them is particularly thin. Part-time and full-time internships (with private firms, public defenders, and prosecutors) are easy to get, because L & C is the only law school in Portland. When it comes to finding postgraduate employment, it's a different picture. Only a few L & C grads each year wind up behind desks at the "big four" Portland firms; graduates of high-prestige national schools have a competitive edge over the homegrown product.

The fact that L & C students lament their difficulties in getting the best jobs in Portland indicates what a delightful place it is. This is a large city with small-town attributes such as friendliness, clean air, green space, and civic pride. L & C's idyllic surroundings make it appealing even for the student whose interest in the environment extends only to his or her own.

University of Louisville School of Law

Address: **Louisville, KY 40292**
Phone: **(502) 588-6364**
Degrees: **J.D., J.D./M.B.A.,**
   J.D./M.Div. (divinity)
Median LSAT: **35/156 (in-state), 38/157 (out-of-state)**
Median GPA: **3.25 (in-state), 3.24 (out-of-state)**
Applicants accepted: **52% (in-state), 9% (out-of-state)**
Transfers: **2/5**
Law enrollment: **532**

Campus enrollment: **23,000**
Part time: **20%**
Women: **45%**
Minorities: **5%**
Dorm residents: **NA**
Library: **220,000**
Student-faculty ratio: **18:1**
Tuition: **$2960 (in-state), $8290 (out-of-state)**
Financial aid: **78% (32% gift)**
Apply by: **February 15**

Disabled students: **Fully accessible. In five years, one visually impaired student, two wheelchair users.**
Placement: **40% placed by graduation; 86% employed six months after graduation. 34 employers on campus in one year; 70% from Kentucky, 7% Tennessee, 7% West Virginia, 7% Ohio, 6%**

Indiana, 3% Georgia; 70% private firms, 17% business, 7% government, 3% public interest, 3% judicial. Graduates took jobs in Kentucky (78%), other Southeast (3%), Midwest (9%), other (10%). Graduates entered private practice (52%), government (10%), judicial clerkships (9%), business (7%), public interest (3%), military (2%). Salary range: $18,000–$83,000. Median salary: $30,000. Mean salary: $29,089. Kentucky bar pass rate: 84% (statewide average: 84%).

The University of Louisville School of Law is located near the heart of a city that combines elements of the Midwest, the South, and the East. The students here are also an interesting blend, with varied attitudes, backgrounds, and ambitions. The night division enables the school to attract people who already have established careers or family responsibilities. The school is even stepping up recruitment of minority students and faculty, whose numbers have lagged.

All the same, don't forget that this is a state school, required by law to restrict "foreigners" to a limited percentage of the enrollment. (That percentage represents a fair number of states and colleges, though.) It is also a commuter school. Although some campus housing is available, it's not popular, and the students who rent nearby in the attractive, renovated Old Louisville neighborhood are outnumbered by those who commute from surrounding areas.

Though the law school is on the main campus of the University of Louisville, most students don't stray from the confines of the law school complex (which includes a large addition completed in 1982) except for an occasional trip to the bookstore or the cafeteria. Louisville has very good physical facilities, including plenty of study space in the library. The law students tend to be an insular group, relying on the comradeship of fellow law students and on the social activities planned by law school organizations.

Fortunately, the organizations don't shirk their solemn duties. The Student Bar Association is truly a major force on campus, planning "everything from orientation to graduation," in the words of one student. Recently, the SBA organized a ski trip, and each year it hosts "Libel Night," when students get to lampoon their professors.

As at most commuter schools, the more specialized student activities don't always succeed in attracting much student interest. An exception, of course, is the law review, which takes the form here of *The Journal of Family Law*. Membership is based on a combination of writing and academic abilities. The *Journal of Law & Education* is less competitive because it has more positions to fill.

The school's basic curriculum revolves around the traditional law courses presented in semi-Socratic style, combining student discourse with lecture. Class participation is often counted into a student's grade. Freshman courses and other core subjects have an average of about 65 per class, while seminars enroll 15 to 20.

While the University of Louisville has good in-depth seminars and only an average number of required courses, students complain that scheduling conflicts and class size restrictions operate to curtail access to specialized, non-bar-related classes. First- and second-year students are placed in sections, and for each subject they want to take, they are limited to the specific course, professor, and time allocated for their section. The result is a frustrating lack of scheduling flexibility.

Students report that academic pressures create a moderate but noticeable attrition rate. The enforcement of stringent academic policies leads to some occasional ill will between students and the administration. However, the administration is willing to listen to student ideas, as evidenced by students with voting positions on most law school committees and two votes at all faculty meetings.

Student-professor relationships are good, and it is not unusual for professors (and even deans) to have lunch with students.

In the senior year, students can gain experience in criminal law through internships with the county prosecutor or public defender, among other internship offerings. Civil counseling and litigation experience are available through the legal aid clinical program. The large metropolitan legal community offers lots of paid part-time and summer positions, though their quality varies greatly. Louisville is one of the few law schools that require students to fulfill a public service requirement before graduation.

With few "theory" courses, the University of Louisville seems to turn out legal generalists with a practical bent. Students accuse the school of inadequate emphasis on placement. The placement office is a relatively recent addition to the school. The school's reputation is regional, though many graduates have succeeded in finding jobs elsewhere.

But if you expect to be on the rail for the Kentucky Derby every year simply because you go to school in Louisville, you should think again. The administration has had the nasty habit of scheduling at least one day of final exams after the annual spring horse race. Those who want to enjoy watching the ponies run have to plan ahead—which is not a bad life lesson, when you think about it.

Loyola University of Chicago School of Law

Address: **1 East Pearson St., Chicago, IL 60611**
Phone: **(312) 915-7170**
Degrees: **J.D., LL.M. (health law), J.D./M.B.A., J.D./M.S.W. (social work), J.D./M.A. (political science), J.D./M.H.R.I.R. (industrial relations)**
Median LSAT: **160**
Median GPA: **3.3**
Applicants accepted: **38%**
Transfers: **8–10/60**

Law enrollment: **739 (719 J.D.)**
Campus enrollment: **17,000**
Part time: **26%**
Women: **56%**
Minorities: **17%**
Dorm residents: **NA**
Library: **273,000**
Student-faculty ratio: **24:1**
Tuition: **$12,702**
Financial aid: **63% (40% gift)**
Apply by: **April 1**

Disabled students: **Fully accessible. In one year, one student with mobility problems.**
Placement: **92% employed six months after graduation. 155 employers on campus in one year; 68% from Illinois; 79% private firms, 12% government or public interest, 8% corporations. 90% of graduates remained in Illinois, 4% other Midwest, 2% East, 2% West, 2% Southeast. Graduates entered private practice (67%), government or public interest (18%), business (9%), judicial clerkships (6%). Salary range: $22,000–$85,000. Median salary: $44,000. Mean salary: $46,951.**

The law school at Loyola University of Chicago, like many other urban law schools, enjoys the advantages of a location close to the heart of a thriving legal community.

Loyola's downtown campus, set next to the historic Chicago Water Tower, is a brisk fifteen- to twenty-minute walk from the heart of Chicago's Loop. Such a location is an obvious plus for students who want part-time law firm work, as well as for the hearty souls who find the time and energy to work a full-time job during the day and tackle law school at night. Proximity to state and federal courts provides additional opportunities to supplement book learning with exposure to the actual practice of law.

For a long time, the price for Loyola's great location was a mediocre physical plant. The school moved into a new building, one block from the old one, in 1980. The design of the new facility is excellent. Particularly noteworthy are the three courtrooms, complete with videotaping equipment. The new building is important not only for its improved facilities, but because it signals the university's commitment to the quality of the law school. Plans for further expansion are in the works.

By far most Loyola students are from the Midwest, and a majority hail from Chicago. There's a large commuter population (inevitable at a school with a sizable evening student contingent). The school is accessible by bus, subway, and suburban railway, as well as by private wheels. Many students whip in and out each day, staying little longer than their classes force them to.

Still, a number of the students come from other parts of the country, including both coasts. Their employment backgrounds are diverse, and undergrad majors range from philosophy to engineering to business, with a smattering of CPAs.

Loyola students are hard workers. Many have financed their own education, often with help from a local banker. Freshmen are strongly dissuaded from taking jobs, as the first-year class schedule makes employment next to impossible. But most second- and third-year students take part-time clerkships with the many firms located in the city. Salaries vary, depending on the employer and the job; the educational rewards, however, are almost always great.

Most faculty members are well qualified and dedicated to teaching. Pedagogical approaches differ according to the professor and the course. Loyola students encounter the pure Socratic method and the pure lecture method as well as various amalgamations of the two. Easy access to faculty members gives students legal training in informal discussions as well as in the formal classroom set-ting. First-year classes have up to about 75 students; many advanced courses limit enrollment to fewer than 30.

A unique subgroup of the Loyola faculty are those who teach the trial advocacy program, offered as both a semester course and a one-week intensive session. The trial advocacy faculty are experi-enced trial lawyers, many of them with terrific professional reputa-tions. Most maintain full-time practices in addition to their faculty duties, so they bring practical insight to bear on their teaching. Students largely credit the trial advocacy faculty for the success of the school's trial teams in regional and national competitions.

You'll find all the usual extracurriculars here, such as various moot court competitions and a law journal. Externships with vari-ous government agencies are available. The students seem satisfied with the administration's handling of the clinical and externship programs.

Chicago can boast of two law schools with top-notch national reputations. Loyola isn't one of them. Although the bar exam preparation is good and Loyola students on law review and in the top 10 percent of the class compete for the same jobs as students at the University of Chicago and Northwestern, the school's name is mainly local (with the possible exception of the health law pro-gram, which is recognized as particularly strong). Of course, as local areas go, this one has a lot more to offer than many.

Loyola University School of Law—New Orleans

Address: **7214 St. Charles Ave., New Orleans, LA 70118**
Phone: **(504) 861-5575**
Degrees: **J.D., J.D./M.B.A., J.D./M.A. (communications or religious studies)**
Median LSAT: **NA**
Median GPA: **3.4**
Applicants accepted: **34%**
Transfers: **1–2/27–30**
Law enrollment: **778**

Campus enrollment: **4900**
Part time: **25%**
Women: **45%**
Minorities: **13%**
Dorm residents: **NA**
Library: **219,700**
Student-faculty ratio: **26:1**
Tuition: **$12,710**
Financial aid: **approx. 63% (34% gift)**
Apply by: **May 1 recommended**

Disabled students: **Fully accessible.**

Placement: **Approximately 64% employed six to nine months after graduation. In a recent class, 75% of graduates remained in Louisiana. Salary range: $18,000–$71,500.**

If you tell people you go to law school in New Orleans, they'll assume you mean Tulane. It's a minor annoyance that Loyola–New Orleans students learn to accept.

There are advantages to attending a lesser-known law school. A primary one is that admissions criteria at Loyola are less demanding than at a big-name school. Standards have been rising lately, but a student with a less-than-impressive GPA and LSAT score is not yet rejected summarily.

Loyola's curriculum emphasizes the practical basics, with less emphasis on electives. Because Louisiana is a civil law jurisdiction (the rest of the country relies on common law), Loyola offers a civil law curriculum for home-state students as well as a common law curriculum for out-of-staters. The common law students make up half of the day division, while the civilians constitute the remainder, as well as the total night division population.

The two groups attend many classes together. A few students compare the two legal systems by supplementing common law courses with civil law courses or vice versa. The common law students represent a wide variety of undergraduate schools but are mostly Northerners.

Students find that the faculty and deans are readily accessible for both academic and social purposes. The Socratic method prevails over other approaches, and professors expect students to prepare for class and to produce high-quality work. Grade inflation hasn't hit here yet; Cs seem to predominate. The professors manage to sustain a relaxed and friendly mood in class that carries over into the attitudes of the students themselves.

This relaxed atmosphere may be attributable in part to Loyola's location in the city of Mardi Gras. The school is in a new facility which opened in 1986 six blocks from the main Loyola campus. New Orleans is a city of fine French and Creole restaurants and an active nightlife, ideal for the overworked, nervous law student. Although the carnival season officially lasts a mere two months, its spirit of revelry seems to pervade the city throughout the year.

New Orleans also has the problems of any urban center, and more than one Loyola student has begun to tire of jazz and jambalaya by the time three years are up.

Loyola students need not resort to the French Quarter for respite from the rigors of academia. The Student Bar Association sponsors diverse activities in which both common law and civil law students participate, including the law school newspaper, a Halloween dance, a spring formal, picnics, and several TGIFs a year. The SBA does a good job of establishing a feeling of community. The legal fraternities organize social activities of their own.

In addition to active groups for women and minority group students, Loyola has a noteworthy lecture series. The moot court teams in both national and international law have chalked up terrific competitive records, and students and faculty are proud and supportive of them. Loyola's advocacy offerings have expanded to include mock trial and client counseling programs.

Loyola also has a legal clinic that enables students, under the supervision of practicing attorneys, to represent indigent clients in court. It's a good way to earn credits and practical experience while offering a service to the community.

For those more interested in writing and research than litigation, there's the *Loyola Law Review*. The review is basically an honors program, but there's also a writing competition each year for all interested students. Another option is clerking for a federal judge in the New Orleans area.

The law school's affiliation with Loyola University is advantageous. The university's modern, well-equipped sports facility is open to, and frequently used by, law students.

Loyola's dorms house both undergraduate and graduate students. They provide a convenient and worthwhile choice for the first-year law student. Most students, however, take advantage of the abundant affordable off-campus housing nearby, ranging from an anonymous-looking apartment complex to a genuine New Orleans shotgun. The streetcar line offers convenient transportation between the university and the downtown area.

How about life after Loyola? The school has a strong reputation in Louisiana. Many Loyola students are recruited by local firms, and some have become important Louisiana public figures. The common law student who wishes to return to his or her home state to practice has a harder time of it, since the school doesn't have enough of a national name to draw interviewers from far away. With extra effort, the common law student can usually line something up. "Unfortunately," one student writes, "Loyola's placement office is not one of its stronger points; however, it is presently making great efforts to diversify its services, both locally and nationally."

Loyola has a lot to offer, and its students are generally satisfied with the education provided them. As one recent grad puts it, "Since Harvard wasn't in the realm of possibility, Loyola was certainly a good alternative."

University of Maryland School of Law

Address: **500 West Baltimore St., Baltimore, MD 21201**
Phone: **(410) 328-3492**
Degrees: **J.D., joint degrees**
Median LSAT: **39**
Median GPA: **3.25**
Applicants accepted: **24%**
Transfers: **29**
Law enrollment: **851**
Campus enrollment: **5000**
Part time: **27%**

Women: **53%**
Minorities: **24%**
Dorm residents: **NA**
Library: **316,600**
Student-faculty ratio: **16:1**
Tuition: **$5945 (in-state), $10,411 (out-of-state)**
Financial aid: **70% (gift: 65% of full-time students)**
Apply by: **February 15**

Disabled students: **Fully accessible. Eight disabled students in one year.**

Placement: **Approximately 84% employed six to nine months after graduation. Graduates took jobs in South Atlantic (71%), Middle Atlantic (6%), New England (1%), East North Central (1%), West South Central (1%), Pacific (1%), other or unknown (19%). Graduates entered private practice (29%), judicial clerkships (19%), government (14%), public interest (4%), military (2%), academic (2%), other or unknown (30%).**

Since 1816, the University of Maryland School of Law has been nestled in the heart of what residents fondly refer to as "Bawlmer, Merlon."

The law school shares its downtown campus with Maryland's

schools of medicine, dentistry, social work, nursing, and pharmacy. Except for occasional parties and pubs, there's not much interaction among the schools. The other students would be easy to ignore if they didn't wear their white coats everywhere.

The law school itself is an architectural potpourri. Two L-shaped main buildings containing classrooms and faculty and student group offices were built in 1965. Adjoining them is the modern Thurgood Marshall Library, completed in 1980. Also part of the law school is a renovated three-hundred-year-old church, rectory, and cemetery complex (Edgar Allan Poe is buried here); the law review and a meeting room are in this complex.

Getting to and from the school is easy. A subway is two blocks away, as is a light-rail line connecting Baltimore to the suburbs.

A significant segment of the student population is in the night division. Many of the night classes are taught by local legals who've made it big. The student-faculty ratio is excellent, and most professors are very approachable.

First-year students can expect plenty of competition, one small class with a faculty member (no teaching assistants at Maryland), and 60 to 75 people in the rest of their classes. The faculty never fails anyone, but good grades are hard to come by.

The course menu is meat and potatoes, with more than a few extras like environmental, health care, and business law. There are legal clinics in various areas of practice, including landlord-tenant, juvenile, criminal, and environmental law. There is also a required first-year clinical course that has received mixed reviews. Some students say the relatively new offering suffers from lack of organization and a bias toward public-interest law practice.

The student body is a nice mixture. Many day students left jobs to come to law school, and many night students are still working. the average student age in one recent year was twenty-five for day students and thirty for evening. An entering class recently included an astrophysicist, a former Olympic athlete, and a political organizer. The school actively encourages applications from minority group members.

In a typical year, the largest percentage of students are graduates of the University of Maryland in College Park; second place goes to Johns Hopkins, and after that it's one from here and two from there, with a surprisingly diverse student body for a state institution.

Needy students can be sure of getting enough aid to attend Maryland, but the grant/loan balance varies. Baltimore is cheap. It's possible to live in the most charming part of town for exactly half of what the same place would cost in Washington. UM's tuition is a bargain, too.

Most people in most places aren't quite sure what to think when you present a degree from Maryland. But UM grads are well received throughout the mid-Atlantic region, in New York, Annapolis (the state capital), and DC. If your intention is to live in Baltimore, this school is recommended over Harvard. In response to student criticism, the school has recently switched to a lottery system to assign on-campus interviewing slots.

As a rule, students are firmly aimed toward careers and aren't too interested in socializing. Most social events are casual and revolve around beer. Extracurricular groups and clubs, including the Maryland Public Interest Law Project, are thriving.

Baltimore is about an hour's drive from both DC and Annapolis. The city offers a cultural smorgasbord, including theaters and a symphony orchestra. Bars cater to every crowd, from jazz to country, from good-timey undergrad to gay pickup.

There is a large black population (some well off, some poor), a sizable suburban Jewish community, and many smaller ethnic neighborhoods, each with one or two good places to eat. The summer and fall months are crowded with downtown ethnic festivals. Inner Harbor is a very successful urban renewal project that features the National Aquarium and an enticing array of shops and restaurants. And don't forget the always-exciting Baltimore Orioles.

The thirteenth largest city in the country is not headquarters for many things, but almost everything has a branch office here. If you're thinking of settling in this area, you could do worse than spend your law school years in Baltimore.

Mercer University, Walter F. George School of Law

Address: **1400 Coleman Ave.,**
    Macon, GA 31207
Phone: **(912) 752-2605**
Degrees: **J.D., J.D./M.B.A.**
Median LSAT: **156**

Median GPA: **3.11**
Applicants accepted: **23%**
Transfers: **2/10–15**
Law enrollment: **405**
Campus enrollment: **6104**

Part time: **1%**
Women: **40%**
Minorities: **13%**
Dorm residents: **NA**
Library: **240,900**

Student-faculty ratio: **16:1**
Tuition: **$12,600**
Financial aid: **70% (24% gift)**
Apply by: **April 1**

Disabled students: **Fully accessible. In a five-year period, one deaf student, four wheelchair users.**

Placement: **70% placed by graduation; 88% employed six months after graduation. 85 employers on campus in one year; 100% from Southeast; 93% private firms, 6% government, 1% public interest. Graduates took jobs in Georgia (63%), Florida (15%), other Southeast (11%), unknown (9%). Graduates entered private practice (73%), government (12%), judicial clerkships (10%), military (2%), public interest (2%), business (1%). Salary range: $17,800–$66,000. Median salary: $30,000. Mean salary: $32,941. Georgia bar pass rate: 93%.**

The Walter F. George School of Law of Mercer University is located in Macon, Georgia. You now know its weakest point. Macon is a sleepy southern town of 110,000 located on the Ocmulgee River in central Georgia. Fortunately, Atlanta, seventy-five miles to the north, is wide awake.

The school's strongest point is its small class size. Each entering class numbers about 150 and is divided into two sections for the required courses; one first-year course is taught in "small sections" of 25; and upper-level courses rarely have more than 50 students.

Teaching at WFG generally follows the casebook method, with one exam per course. Because the student body is so small, it's easy to get to know the faculty members, most of whom are genuinely interested in helping students with academic as well as personal problems. The school hasn't been afraid to experiment with the curriculum—for example, by introducing unorthodox courses like statutory analysis, sales, and "Jurisdiction and Judgments" during the second semester of first year.

For the most part, the students are from Georgia, the Carolinas, and Florida, although geographical diversity is growing in keeping with an admissions policy that seeks a variety of backgrounds. The students reflect a wide range of ages and temperaments.

The students generally know each other, fraternize easily, and show a true southern appreciation for a good ol' time. The Student Bar Association and the legal fraternities sponsor rounds of parties. The Law Spouses group promotes gatherings for students with families. Women and minority law students have very active on-campus associations.

Faculty members often turn up at various school social functions. The student government sponsors meet-the-faculty keg parties in the fall that help set the friendly tone.

Macon boasts several nightclubs, but students tend to pass them up and gather instead for beer-drinking sessions at the local bars. The town also offers some good restaurants and several plays produced by local amateur groups as well as touring companies. Serious devotees of the arts can make pilgrimages to enjoy Atlanta's bountiful cultural resources. Macon itself hosts some diversions, like the annual Cherry Blossom Festival.

Nearby Lake Tobesofkee provides a pleasant escape for those who like the sun and water. Indoor health and exercise facilities are available for the athletically inclined. The law school features intramural football, basketball, and softball. There is also a strong following for Atlanta's professional sports teams.

WFG isn't part of the Mercer undergraduate campus but is located in a large, beautifully appointed building in Macon's historic district. Lots of students find apartments in the restored historic homes nearby. Rents are generally reasonable, except for the really elegant mansions, where you can live out your *Gone With the Wind* fantasies. The law school has some apartments for rent that are very comfortable and affordable.

WFG's law review (the oldest in the state) selects its members on the basis of grades or through a writing competition conducted in the summer. The moot court and appellate advocacy programs are said to be strong. Interested students can staff Student Bar Association committees on faculty relations, curriculum matters, and visiting speakers. Students also publish a newspaper.

In the last several years, the placement office has made notable progress in bringing more prospective employers to interview on campus, but a large number of students still find their jobs the hard way—by sending out lots of application letters and hoping for the best. While Mercer's reputation is growing, it remains a regional school.

Mercer has some advantages. The students are friendly and the faculty supportive. Although the atmosphere is competitive, WFG is spared the pressure of larger, higher-powered law schools. Nevertheless, the school's geographically limited reputation should make students planning to settle outside the Southeast think carefully before enrolling at WFG.

University of Miami School of Law

Address: **P.O. Box 248087, Coral Gables, FL 33124**

Phone: **(305) 284-2523**

Degrees: **J.D., LL.M. (estate planning, inter-American law, international law, ocean and coastal law, real property development, tax)**

Median LSAT: **approx. 158**

Median GPA: **3.3**

Applicants accepted: **33%**

Transfers: **10/50**

Law enrollment: **1365 (1292 J.D.)**

Campus enrollment: **14,700**

Part time: **14%**

Women: **41%**

Minorities: **20%**

Dorm residents: **0**

Library: **376,623**

Student-faculty ratio: **23:1**

Tuition: **$15,428**

Financial aid: **83% (22% gift)**

Apply by: **rolling admissions, March 8 recommended, March 1 (aid)**

Disabled students: **Moderate/full accessibility. In five years, four wheelchair users, three with other mobility problems.**

Placement: **83% employed six months after graduation. 20% of second-years and 35% of third-years employed in legal jobs during the academic year. 20% of first-years, 40% of second-years, and 72% of third-years placed by end of spring term. 120 employers on campus in one year; 80% from Florida, 15% other South Atlantic, 5% Middle Atlantic; 70% private firms, 15% public interest, 10% government, 5% business. Graduates took jobs in South Atlantic (88%), Middle Atlantic (6%), New England (2%), East South Central (2%), other (2%). Graduates entered private practice (61%), government (26%), business (7%), public interest (4%), academic (1%). Salary range: $23,200–$74,500. Median salary: $40,000. Mean salary: $41,822. Florida bar pass rate: 88.2% (statewide average: 74%).**

The University of Miami School of Law is located on the main campus of the University of Miami, which is known far and wide as "Suntan U." Unfortunately, this image is often incorrectly applied to the law school.

In fact, Miami is on its way to becoming one of the nation's better law schools. The law library is excellent. Experts from other high-quality schools have arrived as new faculty members, and admissions standards are becoming more demanding each year. The graduate programs in taxation and estate planning are well known as superb.

The school's concerted effort to produce superior lawyers has a price: rigorous academic standards. In the sink-or-swim first-year program, students are flooded with work—six courses a semester, including a demanding writing and research course and a highly theoretical course in legal reasoning. Things let up a bit in the second year, but failing grades aren't unusual, and more than one student has flunked out for failing to maintain a C average.

The first-year class is split into sections of about 100 students each. Each section stays together and has the same round of required courses. The exception to this rule is the writing and research tutorial, taught by recent law school grads to sections of 30 students.

During second and third year, Miami students have to fulfill fairly extensive distribution requirements and take two seminars or workshops. The elective courses cover a broad range of subjects, with a particular emphasis on tax and international law. After the first year, classes generally get smaller and the sometimes intimidating Socratic method begins to give way to lectures. As a rule, professors are helpful, friendly, and available.

Upper-level students can take advantage of an intensive trial advocacy program to practice their litigation skills under simulated trial conditions. Also available are various clinical programs that offer hands-on experience in internships with the public defender, state attorney, U.S. attorney, legal aid, and other local, state, federal, and private groups.

Miami's students represent a wide variety of undergraduate colleges and come from all over the United States, but most are from the Northeast or Florida. There is a large number of Jewish students. A sizable international contingent is attracted by the unusually varied graduate program.

The students here take school seriously but manage to be congenial, down-to-earth, and fond of a good time. First year is especially competitive, but a good orientation program and frequent parties help friendships develop quickly. Everyone seems to fit in with at least one clique.

All five buildings in the law school quadrangle are air-conditioned, a must in the Miami heat. The surrounding University of Miami campus has an Olympic-size pool, a weight room, running track, softball fields, and tennis, basketball, and racquetball courts. All these facilities are available to the hardworking law student. The law school itself has a softball league and annual tennis and golf tournaments.

The city of Miami is a bit dull, but the surrounding area (Coral Gables is a suburb) has plenty of fun and excitement if you can find the time and money. Dog-racing, horse-racing, and jai alai abound for those with gambling in their blood. There is no shortage of nightlife. Fort Lauderdale, Key West, and plenty of beaches and fishing are nearby. On Friday afternoons, the law school usually has beer parties. When the kegs run dry, you can walk over to the Rathskeller for happy hour with the undergrads, but most law students assiduously keep their distance from undergraduate activities.

One warning: Miami weather may seem appealing from a distance of a thousand miles due north, but for the unaccustomed, it can get uncomfortable during the early fall and late spring. Summers are spent running from air-conditioned car to air-conditioned building, and the humidity is unbelievable. (On the other hand, who can complain about a place where you'll wear shorts in January?)

There is no on-campus housing for law students. The shrewdest approach, students say, is to arrive about a month before school begins and find a three-bedroom apartment to share with two roommates. The apartments in the area are fairly expensive, but many have recreational facilities and almost all are air-conditioned.

Transportation is a dilemma here. Most apartments require a drive of ten minutes or so, and public transportation is nonexistent. However, if you're not in the school parking lot by 8:00 A.M., you can forget about finding a space, even if you have invested in a parking decal. Student government has had no success in confronting this problem; although the Student Bar Association is highly effective as the organizer of the softball league and beer and wine parties, it doesn't make much of a dent on administration policy.

Students concur in finding the placement office deficient for all but those on law review or in the top third of the class. Unless your credentials are impeccable, don't expect an offer out of the on-campus recruiting process. Students hunting for jobs are generally left to their own letter-sending and pavement-pounding devices. First-years hardly ever get legal employment unless they know someone, and even part-time clerkships during the term are the object of severe competition.

Given the tight market in Miami, many students return home (i.e., north) to look for summer and permanent jobs. Unfortunately, Miami's national reputation hasn't yet caught up with its many recent improvements. As word gets out that this is anything but a play school, the job picture should improve. In the meantime, if you're looking for a combination of high standards and high temperatures, look at Miami.

University of Michigan Law School

Address: **312 Hutchins Hall, Ann Arbor, MI 48109**
Phone: **(313) 764-0537**
Degrees: **J.D., LL.M., M.C.L., J.D./M.B.A., J.D./Ph.D. (economics), J.D./M.A. (various)**
Median LSAT: **166 (in-state), 168 (out-of-state)**
Median GPA: **approx. 3.7**
Applicants accepted: **23% (in-state), 19% (out-of-state)**
Transfers: **25/100–150**

Law enrollment: **1135 (1065 J.D.)**
Campus enrollment: **36,600**
Part time: **0**
Women: **43%**
Minorities: **24%**
Dorm residents: **NA**
Library: **738,500**
Student-faculty ratio: **23:1**
Tuition: **$10,178 (in-state), $18,152 (out-of-state)**
Financial aid: **85% (35% gift)**
Apply by: **February 15**

Disabled students: **Fully accessible. In five years, three blind students.**
Placement: **96% employed six months after graduation. 90% of first-years, 98% of second-years, and 91% of third-years placed by end of spring term. 940 employers on campus in one year; 16% from**

California, 12% Washington, DC, 11% Michigan, 10% New York, 8% Illinois, 5% Ohio, 5% Texas, 4% Florida, 3% Minnesota, 3% Pennsylvania, 23% from 27 other states and Foreign; 91% private firms, 6% government or public interest, 3% corporations.
Graduates took jobs in Michigan (19%), Illinois (14%), California (12%), New York (10%), Washington, DC (9%), Ohio (5%), Texas (4%), Massachusetts (3%), Pennsylvania (3%), 25 other states and Foreign (21%). Graduates entered private practice (72%), judicial clerkships (17%), government or public interest (6%), business (3%), other (2%). Salary range: $24,000–$84,000. Median salary: $60,000. Mean salary: $55,954.

Michigan Law students claim they have the finest law school in America. Certainly no one can dispute that the faculty, student body, and academic programs put U of M in the top ten. And the Michigan student will add: Where else can you and 105,000 other people spend Saturday afternoon watching the best in college football?

Of course, the average student here has a great LSAT score and superior undergraduate grade point. But there's more to the admissions standards than meets the eye. For one thing, roughly half of each class is composed of in-staters (who still must meet stringent admissions requirements). For another, while about half of the students are accepted on the basis of stellar academic qualifications alone, the others are products of a "diversity program." This means that all applicants whose "magic numbers" exceed a certain LSAT and GPA cutoff are thrown into an applicant pool, from which they are admitted on the basis of extracurricular activities, previous jobs, special talents, geographical and racial diversity, and so forth. This dual system has resulted in a student body of talented and interesting people as well as superbrains.

Also, note that one quarter of the first-year class gets a head start by beginning in the summer. Although the thought of starting classes two weeks after college graduation makes most seniors cringe, the relaxed atmosphere and reduced course load help to relieve the pressure of starting law school. Moreover, many older students who are returning to academia find the summer term a nice transition.

The faculty's tremendous reputation is probably the school's top asset. Although scholarship, unfortunately, does not always translate into teaching ability, the faculty is large and talented enough so that most students can avoid ever having to take a boring class. One can discuss Norse Viking dispute resolution in the morning and the legal battle to preserve Chicago's Comiskey Park in the afternoon. A past problem—that not enough business law classes were offered—has been resolved, students report. Professors are generally eager to meet with students, and while all of them have office hours, many might prefer to talk over a casual lunch or a couple of beers.

Like all of the elite schools, Michigan stresses legal theory rather than laws themselves. The school teaches legal skills—how to think and write like a lawyer—and leaves the rote learning to your favorite bar review course and on-the-job training.

First-year classes are split into four sections of about 90 students each. Most first-years take five classes—three classes with their entire section and two in small sections of about 20. One of these, Writing and Advocacy, is taught by third-year students, so the quality of instruction varies from superb to utterly useless. In addition, each year one of the four sections is designated the "new section" and takes an interdisciplinary focus. At the core of the "new section" is the standard curriculum—but special lectures, readings, and writing assignments, as well as a unique teaching effort, are aimed at demonstrating how property, contracts, constitutional law, torts, and civil procedure are interrelated. Most students in the "new section" find the program an interesting, progressive addition to a first-year legal education.

First-year students at Michigan are less competitive than at certain other top schools. Sharing of notes and study outlines is fairly commonplace. Although most students spend countless hours in the library, they do so in part for the social benefits—the Main Reading Room may be the best place on campus to find a date for Friday night (no wonder campus wags call it the "Breeding Room"). In any event, the first-year work load is manageable.

After first year, the last vestiges of competition seem to melt away as students' concerns shift from the classroom to the all-important job interviews. Suffice it to say that as befits an extremely well-regarded national law school, Michigan's placement office is tremendous and students get top jobs and clerkships all over the country.

In between "fly-backs" for job interviews, upperclass students do attend class on a semiregular basis. Upperclass course work is virtually entirely elective. Usually, second- or third-years take four courses per semester, varying in size from 10 to 200 students; varying in content from Indian Law to Corporate Finance to Moral Reasoning; and varying in testing format from a single term paper to a multiple-choice in-class exam to a forty-eight-hour take-home essay. When called on in class, many students politely decline to respond if unprepared. The school permits students to take a generous number of credit hours on a pass/fail basis. For many courses, you can even elect the pass-fail option up to 5 minutes before the exam.

The law school gives credit for up to three non–law school courses, and some students opt to take classes in U of M's other excellent graduate programs, like the Business School and the Institute of Public Policy Studies.

The fact that most first-years live in the Lawyers Club, adjacent to the law school, is one of the unique aspects of life at Michigan. This can cut both ways—it's very easy to make friends when classmates live in such close proximity, yet it's also possible to have an anxiety attack around finals because someone else's study lamp is always turned on. Although many first-years get stuck in triples, most enjoy the feeling of tradition in the hundred-year-old rooms complete with stone fireplaces and carved wood. Students living in the Lawyers Club eat in the attached dining hall, which serves typical dorm food in majestic Gothic surroundings.

Most upperclass and married students live off campus in houses or apartments. Rents are reasonable and a diligent search will yield a nice place to live within a few blocks of the school.

Most upperclass energy flows to extracurricular activities, which are in abundant supply. The school's most prestigious publication, the *Michigan Law Review,* boasts a superb national reputation. Membership on the review, coveted by some as a ticket to success and by others who are truly interested in legal scholarship, is earned through a combination of top first-year grades and a writing competition. The *Journal of Law Reform, Journal of International Law,* and *Journal of Gender and the Law* choose members entirely on the basis of writing ability and offer a less rigorous alternative to the law review. For past debaters and future litigators, the Campbell Moot Court Competition offers the opportunity to argue a case before a panel of judges that usually includes a U.S. Supreme Court justice. Several legal clinics provide a healthy balance to the more theoretical course work by giving students the responsibility of handling their own cases ranging from petty theft to prisoner rights to child advocacy.

Campuswide intramurals, as well as law-school-sponsored tournaments, receive a lot of attention, with favorites being softball, Ultimate Frisbee, and basketball. Law students also work out at one of the two nearby sports complexes. More than a few upperclass students have been known to skip afternoon class for golf at the U of M course or cross-country skiing during the extremely long and snowy winters.

The Law School Student Senate's official function is helping set law school student policy. Its most important role, however, is sponsoring social events such as the Tropics Party and the Halloween Party.

Where the official social events end, unofficial ones begin. Michigan law students throw a party for any and all occasions, ranging from weekly football pregame grillouts to the annual hundred-bottle Tequilafest. In addition, the members of a social club, The Barristers, host bar hops, a skiing trip, and the annual Law School prom, called Crease Ball.

Not everyone thinks that Michigan is socially like high school. Some people insist it's more like junior high. The students go to classes together, eat together, party together, and closely observe each other's lives. For those who are truly motivated, the campus is large enough to provide escape from the feeling of living in a fishbowl.

Ann Arbor is home to a wide variety of restaurants and bars suiting every pocketbook and palate. This small city of 100,000 is widely known as a cultural hub of the Midwest. Whether you're into the Vienna Philharmonic or the Grateful Dead, the Bolshoi Ballet or the Dance Theatre of Harlem, Bill Cosby or Def Comedy Jam, you'll be in your element. In addition, U of M is a socially conscious and politically active campus: in any one semester you might find an antiapartheid demonstration, a gay/lesbian rights march, the great marijuana "hash bash," and rallies for presidential hopefuls.

By this point, you may be wondering how you'll pay for all of this. If you're from Michigan, the school is relatively inexpensive, but it's next to impossible to obtain in-state status merely by being a full-time Michigan student. Tuition is almost twice as much for out-of-staters. Don't despair, though; there's plenty of financial aid available.

U of M's law school is a beautiful Gothic oasis in the midst of a vast university. Its multimillion-dollar, award-winning library provides a stimulating environment for legal study. Perhaps more important, the hard work is made bearable by the midwestern friendliness of the place. Jerks and snobs are few and far between. The law school community is very close—everyone seems to know everyone else. And they like it that way.

University of Minnesota Law School

Address: **229 19th Ave. South, Room 290, Minneapolis, MN 55455**
Phone: **(612) 625-5005**
Degrees: **J.D., LL.M., J.D./M.B.A., J.D./M.P.A., other joint degrees**
Median LSAT: **163**
Median GPA: **3.55**
Applicants accepted: **26%**
Transfers: **5/25**
Law enrollment: **796**

Campus enrollment: **53,000**
Part time: **0**
Women: **42%**
Minorities: **16%**
Dorm residents: **3%**
Library: **800,000**
Student-faculty ratio: **19:1**
Tuition: **$6418 (in-state), $12,146 (out-of-state)**
Financial aid: **85% (20% gift)**
Apply by: **March 1, February 15 (aid)**

Disabled students: **Fully accessible. Within a five-year period, five blind students, one wheelchair user, two with other mobility problems.**

Placement: **96% employed six months after graduation. 129 employers on campus in one year; 50% from Minnesota, 22% other Midwest, 14% West, 14% East; 85% private firms, 6% government, 6% business, 2% judicial. Graduates took jobs in Minnesota (62%), other West North Central (7%), Pacific (11%), East North Central (7%), South Atlantic (4%), Mountain (3%), West South Central (2%), New England (2%), Middle Atlantic (1%), East South Central (.5%), Foreign (.5%). Graduates entered private practice (64%), judicial clerkships (17%), business (9%),** government (5%), public interest (4%), other (1%). Salary range: $24,000–$83,000. Mean salary: $45,162. Minnesota bar pass rate: 97.35% (statewide average: 88%).

Nestled on the shores of the Mississippi River, on the "West Bank" of the University of Minnesota campus, is U of M Law, a thriving state law school.

The multimillion-dollar law building, opened in 1978, is worthy of full description. It houses one of the largest law libraries in the United States, which occupies four stories. What the building lacks in aesthetic eye-appeal (it was purportedly modeled after the state penitentiary), it makes up for in efficiency. Classrooms are horse-shoe-shaped in order to maximize student participation and in-crease faculty recognition of the inevitable classroom confusion. There are several hundred wooden study carrels in the library—complete studying microenvironments—which some students can reserve on a semester basis. The largest classroom is an acoustically perfect auditorium in which the Eighth Circuit U.S. Court of Ap-peals and the Minnesota Supreme Court occasionally convene for the edification and enjoyment of the student body. Other features of the building include private group-study rooms, research and instruction computers, two student lounges, and a self-sufficient bookstore.

Although the law school is situated in the mainstream of the campus, the law student body tends to be isolated. Law student contact with the rest of the university seems to be confined to conflicts in property rights—over law library space or stools at local eating and drinking establishments, the more compelling arguments (based on the extent of use) made for the latter. The social lives of law students tend to become quickly intermeshed, almost certainly because of the time engaged in the study of law to the exclusion of other activities. There are, however, a number of students who manage (and much prefer) to remain detached from the social world of the law school.

According to one student, the professional and academic mood of the school is strongly divided. It ranges from blatantly cynical to hypermotivated. There are annual skirmishes between faculty and students over curriculum, faculty hiring, examinations, and arbitrary grading, with the dean's office assuming the role of mediator. The controlling sector of the faculty is the more formal, conservative faction, this student reports, and generally, as the years progress, students tend to become disenchanted with the faculty as a group. The relationship among students themselves is characterized as a sort of boot-camp camaraderie, although competition among students is at times fierce, especially in the first year.

The work load of U of M is as varied as the student body. Although many students contend that grade averages are inversely related to the number of hours of preparation, most admit to a fairly rigorous study schedule. About three quarters of the student body is at some time involved in study groups, and many form close-knit groups that last throughout their law school careers.

The Socratic method, in more or less strict form, commands a slight edge over other, less intimidating forms of instruction. Classes range in size from 100 for many first-year and bar-required courses to as few as a half-dozen in seminars. Even in large classes, U of M professors are usually very approachable on a one-to-one basis.

Employment placement is a concern at most law schools, and the University of Minnesota is no exception. Nevertheless, the law school is nationally known and respected, and its graduates are generally much preferred over the state's two other accredited law schools. Students report that the placement director makes a valiant effort to meet their needs.

A comparatively large number of organized activities are available to U of M law students. Official ones include the Women's Law Student Association, Third World Caucus, Jewish Caucus, Christian Legal Society, Environmental Law Society, American Bar Association (Law Student Division), and National Lawyers Guild. Law school sports are all coed and extremely popular. They include touch football, volleyball, tennis, golf, squash, and softball.

The governing body of the school is the Law School Council, which consists of a president and three representatives from each class. *Minnesota Law Review* membership is limited to students selected in their second and third years. *Law and Inequality: A Journal of Theory and Practice* publishes legal scholarship on issues of race, class, gender, sexual orientation, and the environment, primarily from a leftist perspective. Moot court and trial practice are available for blossoming oral advocates (both for credit).

Clinical programs, also for credit, are available to provide practical experience for interested students. The Legal Aid Clinic provides civil legal assistance to low-income clients. LAMP (Legal Aid to Minnesota Prisoners) puts students to work with inmates in the state penitentiary on both criminal and civil matters. There are also salaried positions for second- and third-year students as legal writing and appellate advocacy instructors.

If you can put up with cold, snowy winters, Minneapolis is a lively, culturally active place to be. Minnesota residents have a good deal going for them in U of M Law. If you're an out-of-stater, you might well be attracted here too, but you'll have to fight for one of the seats left over after the in-state quota is filled.

University of Missouri—Columbia School of Law

Address: **103 Hulston Hall,** **Columbia, MO 65211**
Phone: **(314) 882-6042**
Degrees: **J.D.**
Median LSAT: **157**
Median GPA: **3.35**
Applicants accepted: **25%**
Transfers: **3–5/20–25**
Law enrollment: **441**
Campus enrollment: **23,300**
Part time: **5%**

Women: **45%**
Minorities: **10%**
Dorm residents: **5%**
Library: **250,000**
Student-faculty ratio: **25:1**
Tuition: **$5436 (in-state),** **$10,700 (out-of-state)**
Financial aid: **75% (45% gift)**
Apply by: **March 1** **recommended**

Disabled students: **Fully accessible. In five years, two blind students, one deaf, eight wheelchair users, four with other mobility problems.**

Placement: **90–95% employed six months after graduation. 5% of first-years, 15% of second-years, and 20% of third-years employed in legal jobs during the academic year. 4% of first-years, 45% of second-years, and 65% of third-years placed by end of spring term. About 85 employers on campus in one year; 90% from Missouri; 70% private firms, 15% government, 5% corporations, 10% other. 75% of graduates stayed in Missouri; remainder in 10 other states. Graduates entered private practice (60%), judicial clerkships (20%), government (10%), other (10%). Salary range:**

$22,000–$80,000. **Median salary: $26,000. Mean salary: $34,000.
Missouri bar pass rate: 90.8% (statewide average: 89%).**

Established more than a hundred years ago on the campus of the
first state university west of the Mississippi, UMC Law enjoys a
reputation that's solidly established in this region. The law school
is situated in the heart of the campus, which features beautiful
ivy-covered Georgian brick buildings, many of them national land-
marks. A new law building, completed in 1988, tripled the school's
space.

The geographic location of the school combines a favorable
academic environment with practical advantages for the law student. Columbia is a city of 69,000 in the center of Missouri (and
of the country), about a hundred miles from both St. Louis and
Kansas City, the large urban centers on the east and west borders
of the state. Jefferson City, the state capital, is a thirty-minute drive
to the south. This proximity permits students to participate in and
observe legislative, executive, and judicial activities.

State officials are frequent lecturers at the school, and faculty
members are actively involved in the development of Missouri law.
The faculty of the law school consists almost entirely of full-time
teachers, most of them experienced as legal practitioners.

Almost all the students are from Missouri and plan to stay there
after graduation. Other than the admissions boost for in-state students, the reasons for this are threefold. First, fees are substantially
cheaper for residents. Second, graduates of the school are well
prepared for the Missouri bar exam. Finally, UMC has an excellent
reputation among employers in the state—many of whom are
themselves alumni.

The *Missouri Law Review* is well regarded by academics and
practitioners. Students also edit the *Journal of Dispute Resolution,*
recognized nationally for its studies of alternative dispute resolution. The members of both publications are chosen from among
the second- and third-year classes on the basis of class rank or
writing competition.

The Board of Advocates is the supervising body for both intra-
and interscholastic moot court competition. It is composed of
second- and third-year students who were stars in appellate advocacy during their first year.

As the student government, the Student Bar Association coordinates student activities and provides a medium for faculty-student communication. The SBA's programs are fairly typical—speakers, a student book pool, and social functions.

The Women's Law Caucus and the Black Law Students Association are said to be active. The legal fraternities sponsor a number of activities, both scholastic and social.

Clinical programs for credit have been increasing in popularity lately. During the second and third years, students have the opportunity to work as clerks for state supreme court justices, the state attorney general, the county prosecuting attorney, the public defender, legal services, and other state and local agencies.

There are seminars to cover specialized fields that take students beyond the four walls of the classroom. In a representative year, law and medical students donned gowns to witness open-heart surgery at the University Medical Center, and communications law students studied at the renowned University of Missouri School of Journalism.

There is no absence of social life in Columbia. As a matter of fact, the campus is reported to be a vibrant place, jumping with things to do. The Missouri Tigers are members of the Big Eight Conference, and all the major spectator sports are here for the watching. In the fall, the football team is the center of attention. The university, as well as nearby Stephens and Columbia colleges, all produce plays and sponsor noteworthy speakers. Restaurants, movie theaters, and bars abound and are hubs of activity on the weekends.

For the athletic and health-conscious, university facilities include an indoor track, outdoor lighted tennis courts, indoor and outdoor swimming pools, basketball and racquetball courts, and soccer, football, and baseball fields, as well as a golf course. The surrounding countryside is perfect for hiking, there are several nearby rivers suitable for floating on inner tubes, and the bluffs along the Missouri River provide a challenge for climbers and rappellers.

There is enough housing to go around, including married students' campus housing, dorm rooms for single students, and apartments in Columbia. All are reasonably priced.

UMC's small size, combined with the predominance of in-state students, could make the school a bit confining for some people. But most of the students here enthusiastically praise the friendliness and camaraderie, and are satisfied with things as they are.

University of New Mexico School of Law

Address: **1117 Stanford Dr. NE, Albuquerque, NM 87131**

Phone: **(505) 277-2146**

Degrees: **J.D., J.D./M.B.A., J.D./M.P.A., J.D./M.A. (Latin American studies), other joint degrees**

Median LSAT: **34**

Median GPA: **3.14**

Applicants accepted: **18%**

Transfers: **NA**

Law enrollment: **334**

Campus enrollment: **24,000**

Part time: **0**

Women: **54%**

Minorities: **42%**

Dorm residents: **NA**

Library: **330,800**

Student-faculty ratio: **12:1**

Tuition: **$2010 (in-state), $6810 (out-of-state)**

Financial aid: **50%**

Apply by: **February 1**

Disabled students: **Fully accessible. Three disabled students in one year.**

Placement: **Most graduates remained in New Mexico. Graduates entered private practice (57%), government (21%), judicial clerkships (15%), public interest (6%), unknown (1%). Average salary: $29,800.**

UNM School of Law has a lot to offer, not the least of which is some of the best weather—for studying or for relaxing—that you could hope to find anywhere. Fortunately or unfortunately, the word on UNM is out, which makes getting in here no easy matter.

Thanks to its climate and generally pleasant atmosphere, UNM appeals to large numbers of applicants. Competition for entrance is tough for state residents, but it's even tougher for nonresidents. UNM is the only law school in the state, so 90 percent of the places are reserved for New Mexicans.

A state school usually means a homogeneous school, but UNM is an exception. There's plenty of evidence of the state's multicultural nature in the law school student body, as there is throughout the university campus and the entire city of Albuquerque. Minority recruitment and admissions are taken seriously here, and Hispanics and Native Americans are especially plentiful on campus. Women are well represented in the student population.

Admissions are based on the standard criteria of LSAT and GPA, but the admissions committee also looks at experience and motivation. The result is a diverse student body that enters at an average age of twenty-eight in a representative year, with a wide variety of graduate degrees and work experiences.

Transfers are admitted on an ad hoc and limited basis, generally only at the beginning of the second year and then only to fill any vacancies in the existing class.

Current students give high marks to the administration for listening, discussing, and generally helping—whether the problem is obtaining financial aid, locating job possibilities, battling main-campus bureaucracy, or remedying registration problems. The administrators are also reportedly open to student suggestions on curriculum and class scheduling.

The faculty is for the most part excellent. Although research, community service, and legal consultation go on, the faculty members see themselves primarily as teachers. The professors maintain an open-door policy and are nearly always available for discussion, tutoring, bridge, Ping-Pong, or whatever. If you make a little effort, you can get much of your legal education on a one-to-one basis, which students here claim is infinitely preferable to having a big-name prof you never see except behind the lectern. Of course, many students don't want to become that involved, and they keep their distance. First-year courses run about 55 to a class, but after that it's rare to be in a class larger than 30.

One of UNM's greatest assets is a general feeling of cooperation and rapport. Differences of opinion exist, but there's an open forum for communication among students, faculty, and administration. And as for intense competition—well, maybe at the top of the class and at the beginning of the first year; otherwise, teamwork is the name of the game, beginning with an orientation program that features a barbeque given by the dean.

The social life varies from student to student. Many are married, and many come from Albuquerque. These people often continue whatever social lives they had before law school. The school itself has regular organized social events, and private parties take place close to continuously at certain times of the year.

The Student Bar Association is charged mainly with social activities and the orientation of students into the state bar. Its executive board is the main communication link between the faculty and administration and the student population. Special-interest organizations are very much alive here, particularly the Mexican American Law Students Association, American Indian Law Students Association, Women's Law Caucus, and Black Law Students Association. Each of these groups is active in recruiting and orientation.

The moot court teams benefit from abundant encouragement and have done well in recent years both regionally and nationally. UNM students put out two legal journals, the *New Mexico Law Review* and the *Natural Resources Journal.* Membership is determined by writing competition, not grades.

Academics are solid—but if UNM were in Alaska, you probably wouldn't want to drop everything to come here. One student cautions that strictly bar-oriented types may find that the curriculum committee, in its enthusiasm for providing a diversity of course offerings, sometimes consigns core courses to a secondary role. However, the basics are there for the student who plans accordingly.

The first-year curriculum definitely is basic, complete with an intense required legal research, writing, and advocacy program. The last two years are at the student's discretion, with only constitutional law, an ethics course, and six hours of clinical work required. The clinical program enables a student to practice (with supervision) in the New Mexico courts. The six clinical hours must be earned in the clinical programs run by the school. Additionally, students can arrange internships for law school credit with private lawyers or governmental agencies.

Although UNM has traditionally had a good in-state placement record, the tightening job market for lawyers has taken its toll. Employment opportunities in Albuquerque and Santa Fe seem to be shrinking.

Asked to describe UNM, one student said, "Mostly it's a fun and beautiful place to spend three years learning the law." What else is there to say?

City University of New York Law School at Queens College

Address: **65-21 Main St., Flushing, NY 11367**
Phone: **(718) 575-4210**
Degrees: **J.D.**
Median LSAT: **30**
Median GPA: **2.87**
Applicants accepted: **19%**
Transfers: **0**
Law enrollment: **459**
Campus enrollment: **approx. 17,000**

Part time: **1%**
Women: **53%**
Minorities: **30%**
Dorm residents: **0**
Library: **179,300**
Student-faculty ratio: **13:1**
Tuition: **$4993 (in-state), $7372 (out-of-state)**
Financial aid: **66% (51% gift)**
Apply by: **May 1**

Disabled students: **Thirteen disabled students in one year.**

Placement: **Approximately 80% employed six to nine months after graduation. 97% of graduates remained in Middle Atlantic. Graduates entered public interest (43%), private practice (26%), government (19%), judicial clerkships (10%), unknown (2%). Salary range: $18,000–$42,000.**

Founded in 1983, dedicated to the mission of "law in the service of human need," CUNY is one of the nation's most unusual law schools.

The unusual approach starts with admissions. Rather than hinging on grades and LSAT scores, the main requirement is an interest in public-interest law. This criterion, together with CUNY's goal of bringing so-called nontraditional students into the study of law, results in a student body radically different from what you'll find at most law schools. For instance, in a typical year, the median age of entering CUNY students is thirty-one, there are more women than men, and about a third are minority group members; about 75 percent of students are from New York State, however.

The diverse student body and the similarly diverse faculty ensure that the traditional voice of law—white, male, and straight—does not predominate at CUNY. Most faculty elicit and respect students' experiences and perspectives, and some attempt to integrate critical legal theory into the study of legal doctrine. Classroom discussions are often heated, as students master rules and methods of law while attempting to critique them at the same time.

The curriculum at CUNY attempts to balance the often competing tasks of teaching the theory of law and the practice of law. Some of the lecture courses combine more than one traditional legal subject—such as criminal law and torts in Responsibility for Injurious Conduct—in order to compare them side by side. This approach is unique to CUNY and helps to conceptualize the law in an integrated way.

The centerpiece of the CUNY curriculum is the Office system. The Office is meant to replicate a law office—twenty students share a small classroom with one professor, who functions as the "senior attorney." The work consists of a series of simulations which involve legal issues drawn from the lecture classes, as well as practical writing and communication projects typically experienced by lawyers. Along with legal skills, the Office teaches students to weigh the consequences of the lawyering choices they make.

The Office experience can be intense, as the simulations often deal with emotionally charged issues, like battering and gay families. However, the skills gained in Office are invaluable, the simulations make the law come alive, and the simultaneous emphasis on theoretical perspectives and lawyering as a process helps place legal issues in a social context.

CUNY attempts to minimize competition among students. Lecture courses are graded on a pass/fail basis, although exams, which were once anathema at CUNY, play an increasing role in the curriculum. Office work is evaluated according to seven "Competencies." There are no grades and no class rank. Even so, students typically experience a high degree of stress surrounding academics. With time-consuming clinical work as well as classroom courses, students sometimes feel they are trying to cram two legal educations into one. Third-year students choose between an on-campus clinic and an off-campus two-day-a-week placement, in addition to regular classes.

Most students come to CUNY because they are committed to public-interest law, and large numbers seek out jobs at Legal Aid and other public-interest groups. But a significant number seek work in firms, many take judicial clerkships, some become staff members to legislators, and quite a few are interested in teaching, writing, and legal scholarship. The placement office is expanding its on-campus interviewing program and puts out a regular newsletter on job openings and job-seeking skills. CUNY students are eligible for grants to subsidize summer public-interest jobs.

The Black Law Students Association, Asian Pacific American Law Students Association, Gay and Lesbian Law Students Association, a Latino students' organization, and many other student groups are active at CUNY. There is even a group for students who have served time in jail. Students regularly organize conferences on progressive themes. Because CUNY is a commuter school, most groups meet during the daytime, but there are occasional parties in the evening. Social life mainly takes place on campus, although a major gripe of students is the lack of a cafeteria selling hot food. Flushing boasts some very good ethnic restaurants, and the Queens College campus, across a field from the law school, offers concerts, lectures, and a gym that is a popular destination for law students. For nightlife, Manhattan is a subway ride away.

CUNY has not been without its growing pains. The school earned full ABA accreditation in 1992. The low bar exam pass rates of the early classes of graduates provoked a major controversy between the law school and the higher-ups in the City University administration. After some soul-searching, the law school is tackling the problem head-on with special weekly bar review classes for third-year students.

CUNY is not for the confirmed traditionalist who wants the security of a tried-and-true legal education. Those who elect to come here to study the law in a social and ethical context have generally found the experience stimulating, challenging, and rewarding. And even skeptics have to admit that the school is doing its best to create a new breed of lawyers.

State University of New York at Buffalo School of Law

Address: **O'Brian Hall, Amherst Campus, Buffalo, NY 14260**
Phone: **(716) 636-2061**

Degrees: **J.D., J.D./M.B.A., J.D./M.S.W. (social work), J.D./M.A. or Ph.D. (policy studies, political science,**

philosophy, economics, other)
Median LSAT: **38**
Median GPA: **3.35**
Applicants accepted: **32%**
Transfers: **8**
Law enrollment: **767**
Campus enrollment: **26,000**
Part time: **0**

Women: **47%**
Minorities: **19%**
Dorm residents: **NA**
Library: **431,700**
Student-faculty ratio: **21:1**
Tuition: **$4200 (in-state),**
  $8850 (out-of-state)
Financial aid: **88%**
Apply by: **February 1**

Disabled students: **Fully accessible. In one year, twenty-one disabled students.**

Placement: **Approximately 78% employed six to nine months after graduation. Graduates took jobs in Middle Atlantic (81%), South Atlantic (9%), New England (2%), East North Central (2%), West South Central (2%), Foreign (2%), Pacific (1%), other or unknown (2%). Graduates entered private practice (52%), government (18%), judicial clerkships (9%), public interest (9%), business (6%), academic (4%), military (2%), unknown (1%). Salary range: $19,000–$85,000.**

Now in its second century of existence, SUNY—Buffalo is often described as a humane place. A school that somehow seems to feel personally responsible to its students, SUNY—Buffalo puts the emphasis on the individual. The admissions process welcomes a wide variety of people, including older students, and there is a unique program to admit and tutor disadvantaged students. The vague grading system keeps competitiveness under control. The wide selection of clinics and other academic programs lets students pursue their own interests.

SUNY—Buffalo Law has a noticeable leaning toward a progressive, policy-oriented approach. The strength of the faculty lies in its diversity, not only in terms of race and gender, but also in approaches to the law. Many of the law professors are trained in the social sciences and other disciplines, and the curriculum reflects this interdisciplinary perspective. A recent year's offering of upper-level courses included Law and Marxism, Feminist Theory, Internal Union Democracy, and Indian Law. In addition, the school's Baldy Center offers a joint Ph.D./J.D. program in social policy.

But if you're corporate-minded, don't let the progressive orientation turn you off. Some of Buffalo's most outstanding teachers are in commercial law and tax.

Buffalo is a word that strikes terror in the hearts of sun-lovers, but the city offers a pretty good selection of cultural events to compensate for its abysmal winter weather. Concerts are especially plentiful. City funds have been pumped into revitalizing the downtown theater district and improving the transit system.

Most first-year students work their tails off. All their courses have about 80 students, with the exception of the demanding full-year research and writing course (the grading of which is pass/fail with a written evaluation). Most professors make at least some use of the Socratic method, but not in its most intimidating form.

What really sets Buffalo apart is a wealth of clinical programs. The range is impressive and includes education law, legal services for the elderly, immigration law, low-income housing development, and community economic development. Other special programs include a trial technique course that culminates in a day-long simulated trial in front of a real judge and jury. A small number of students clerk for area judges for academic credit; entry into this program is competitive.

The administration is reported to be accessible and helpful. The placement office is aggressive and does a good job helping students write résumés, develop interviewing techniques, focus their career goals, and get job leads. Special guidance is available to help the many students interested in finding public-interest jobs. The Buffalo Public Interest Law Program (a student organization) and the school's Public Service Fellows Program offer funding for summer internships in public-interest agencies.

The law review chooses students on the basis of grades and writing. As at most schools, there's a schoolwide moot court competition as well as teams that participate in intermural contests in moot court. In addition to the popularly elected Student Bar Association, active student organizations include the National Lawyers Guild, the Association of Women Law Students, the Black Law Students Association, Latin American Law Students Association, a law fraternity, and a student newspaper.

Social activities range from those with serious sociopolitical value to plain heavy-duty partying. The Distinguished Visitors

Forum brings in speakers on important issues. The Student Bar Association organizes several theme parties, in addition to which there's usually at least one unofficial student party per weekend. For those who like to sweat together, the SBA sponsors an annual Race Judicata, and there are intramural volleyball and softball leagues.

Housing is plentiful and cheap around both the Amherst campus (where the law school is) and the university's Main Street campus. There are buses between the two campuses every five or ten minutes.

The law school's location in the midst of a large university helps keep students from developing tunnel vision. Besides the seven-floor law library, there are two large university libraries on either side of the law school. Student concerts, theater performances, and movie screenings are close by or on the Main Street campus. It's easy to cross-register for courses in almost any field.

Sometimes called the Berkeley of the North, Buffalo Law turns out students whose education has gone way beyond memorization, and students concur that it's a friendly place. But remember: a tolerance for extremely cold, windy, and snowy weather will stand you in good stead here.

New York University School of Law

Address: **40 Washington Square S., Room 419, New York, NY 10012**
Phone: **(212) 998-6000**
Degrees: **J.D., LL.M. (tax, corporate, international, trade regulation, general), J.S.D., M.C.J. (comparative jurisprudence), J.D./ M.B.A., J.D./M.P.A., J.D./ M.U.P. (urban planning), J.D./M.S.W. (social work), J.D./M.A. (various)**
Median LSAT: **167**
Median GPA: **3.6**

Applicants accepted: **18%**
Transfers: **25–30/125–150**
Law enrollment: **1650 (1200 J.D.)**
Campus enrollment: **45,000**
Part time: **0**
Women: **43%**
Minorities: **22%**
Dorm residents: **60%**
Library: **845,000**
Student-faculty ratio: **15:1**
Tuition: **$19,220**
Financial aid: **80% (40% gift)**
Apply by: **February 1**

Disabled students: **Moderate/full accessibility. Within five years, two blind students.**

Placement: **96% employed six months after graduation. 95% of first-years, 98% of second-years, and 92% of third-years placed by end of spring term. 910 employers on campus in one year. Graduates took jobs in New York (64%), New Jersey (6%), Washington, DC (6%), California (5%), Pennsylvania (3%), Massachusetts (2%), Illinois (2%), other states (11%), Foreign (1%). Graduates entered private practice (66%), judicial clerkships (18%), government (7%), public interest (3%), academic (3%), business (2%), other (2%). Salary range: $26,700–$87,500. Mean salary: $62,609 (mean law firm salary: $76,025). New York bar pass rate: 93.7% (statewide average: 73%).**

If you asked a group of NYU law students why you should attend NYU Law, they would probably come up with two very good reasons. First, NYU is reputed to be one of the top ten law schools in the country, and that counts in this prestige-obsessed profession. Second, and probably more important, NYU's location, curriculum, and atmosphere offer unique educational opportunities.

Thanks to its location, NYU draws on the talents of some of the nation's top practicing attorneys, in addition to its own full-time faculty. The curriculum is therefore extremely rich, offering something for everyone. Traditionally very strong in tax, copyright, and patent law, the school has more recently made a conscious attempt to become a leader in law and philosophy, public-interest law, and clinical legal education.

The clinical program, one of the most extensive in the country, offers third-year students (and a few second-years) academic credit for work in urban, criminal, family, environmental, civil rights, juvenile rights, and government and corporation counsel projects. There are also two elaborate civil and criminal litigation simulation courses. In recent years, budget constraints have led some faculty members to advocate a reduction in "real" clinics in favor of simulations, which are cheaper and are said to provide more controllable learning experiences. Students have strongly opposed "real" clinic cutbacks, however. It seems fair to say that while the clinical program is likely to undergo significant revisions as time goes on, the changes will be careful and well-planned. It's also worth remembering that, the clinics notwithstanding, a host of local and national public-interest and governmental organizations eagerly seek NYU law student volunteers for what may prove to be path-breaking litigation.

The Root-Tilden-Snow program offers three-year, two-thirds tuition scholarships and summer public-interest stipends to about ten entering students who have demonstrated a commitment to public-interest law. An additional three or four scholarships are awarded at the end of the first year. (Roots who ultimately cannot resist the lure of the private sector are under a moral obligation to repay their scholarships, with interest.) The Root program also sponsors interesting speakers and forums. And the school has traditionally funded forty-odd summer stipends for non-Roots pursuing public-interest internships. Perhaps most important of all, the school has in recent years succeeded in attracting several outstanding public-interest-oriented faculty members.

For all its public-interest and clinical focus, NYU is nonetheless a fairly conventional law school, particularly in its first-year curriculum. First year consists of traditional bread-and-butter courses and 15-person sections of legal analysis, research, and writing. The administration has the sense to assign first-semester classes to faculty members who try to minimize collective panic. If you have questions about your course work, what you're doing in law school, or the meaning of life, you're likely to be able to find a professor willing to discuss things with you during office hours or over coffee. The faculty has also established a teaching assistants' program in which second- and third-year students hold regular review sessions for those who find themselves growing progressively more entangled in the seamless web.

After first year all courses, except constitutional law and professional responsibility, are electives. Other prerequisites for graduation include two writing requirements. Classes are a mixture of lecture and discussion, with all but a small minority of teachers reverting occasionally to the Socratic method. The predominant approach to the material is geared to the needs of a practicing attorney, though some classes take a more theoretical view.

NYU students are bright, ambitious, and hardworking—although the pressure is more internal than external. While the Ivies are well represented, and a majority comes from the Northeast, there are students from all over the country. Many follow the well-trodden path into corporate firms, but those who are public-interest-conscious comprise a vocal and ever-growing bloc. The first-rate placement staff runs an extensive on-campus recruiting program, as well as employment forums in other cities. The placement office library is excellent. The new Public Interest Center facilitates the search for public-interest jobs. In general, NYU grads with strong records do as well in New York City as graduates from just about any other institution, and NYU students obtain desirable placements all over the country.

The student government has evolved into an outspoken, but not necessarily powerful, force. The Student Bar Association sells coffee and doughnuts in the lounge and plans social events, including a widely enjoyed sports program. It has limited impact, however, on policy issues like faculty hiring and tuition increases. The administration seems interested in student views, but its actions don't always prove the sincerity of the interest.

Other conspicuous student groups include the National Lawyers Guild, Black Law Students Association, Lesbian and Gay Law Students, Latino Law Students Association, Law Women, and Jewish Law Students. This is New York; it's hard to think of a type of person you can't find here.

Ah yes, New York. After three years here, you might hate it or you might swear you'll never leave, but you won't be indifferent. The four law school buildings, along with the rest of NYU, are clustered around Washington Square Park, which offers some greenery, some concrete, and lots of free entertainment ranging from jogging to street musicians. Greenwich Village is short on skyscrapers and the frenetic pace of midtown Manhattan, and long on restaurants, theaters, movies, bookshops, and coffeehouses. In the 1960s, this was a political and artistic center unlike any other. The area is still filled with people the likes of whom you'd be hard-pressed to find west of the Hudson River.

Nearby, there are galleries in SoHo, dim sum in Chinatown, pasta in Little Italy, and jazz everywhere, all within walking distance. And there's Lincoln Center, Broadway, the Metropolitan Museum . . . the list goes on and on.

Unfortunately, to enjoy the Village and the rest of the city, it helps to have money and free time, scarce commodities among law students. There are always a few university dances and events, but most people escape to off-campus attractions. Although law school friends are easy to make and there's some sense of community, there is little dating among law students and even less contact with the rest of the university. A good number of students are married.

A traditionally poor housing situation at NYU has improved dramatically. New construction has made nearby dorm living a viable alternative, though not an inexpensive one. Although the NYU off-campus housing office offers a good listing of nearby apartments, Manhattan housing prices are very steep, assuming you can even find a place. Apartments at slightly less wallet-busting prices are available in Brooklyn, but you may want to think twice about living far from Washington Square and relying on the subways. Another advantage of living near the law school: promixity to the new, well-equipped, and heavily used Coles Sports Center.

Most surveys place Columbia higher in prestige than NYU. More than one employer has remarked, however, that NYU recruits are more interesting folks than Columbia alums. And more than one NYU student will tell you that Greenwich Village beats Morningside Heights any day.

University of North Carolina School of Law

Address: **Van Hecke-Wettach Hall, Campus Box 3380, Chapel Hill, NC 27599**
Phone: **(919) 962-5106**
Degrees: **J.D., J.D./M.B.A., J.D./M.P.A., J.D./M.P.H. (public health), J.D./M.R.P. (regional planning), J.D./ M.P.P.S. (public policy studies)**
Median LSAT: **163 (in-state), 164 (out-of-state)**
Median GPA: **3.52 (in-state), 3.61 (out-of-state)**
Applicants accepted: **24% (in-state) 13% (out-of-state)**

Transfers: **0–7/30–40**
Law enrollment: **695**
Campus enrollment: **24,000**
Part time: **0**
Women: **45%**
Minorities: **14%**
Dorm residents: **NA**
Library: **350,000**
Student-faculty ratio: **18:1**
Tuition: **$1350 (in-state), $9600 (out-of-state)**
Financial aid: **49% (17% gift)**
Apply by: **February 1**

Disabled students: **Fully accessible. In five years, one deaf student, two wheelchair users, two with other mobility problems.**

Placement: **89% employed twelve months after graduation. 175–200 employers on campus in one year; from 22 states, Washington, DC, and 2 foreign countries. Graduates took jobs in 21 states, Washington, DC, and 1 foreign country; 59% remained in North Carolina, 22% other South Atlantic. Graduates entered private practice (66%), judicial clerkships (11%), government (9%), business (9%), public interest (3%), advanced degree (2%), academic (.5%). Salary range: $19,600–$84,000. Median salary: $37,000. North Carolina bar pass rate: 92% (statewide average: 78%).**

For the money, UNC is one of the best buys available in legal education.

By school policy, about three fourths of the students are Tarheels. A large number attended college right in Chapel Hill, but there are plenty of people from NC State, Duke, and other schools, mostly in the Southeast and East. This local flavor gives UNC a relaxed, friendly, and down-to-earth atmosphere. UNC's student body is nonetheless diverse, as reflected in the broad range of thriving student organizations, including the National Lawyers Guild, Christian Legal Society, Black Law Students Association, Women in Law, and Environmental Law Project. These organizations sponsor a number of guest speakers and discussions, as well as occasional social activities.

The Student Bar Association is generally very active. Among its many activities, the SBA sponsors a successful satirical skit and a popular intramural athletic program. The formal fête of the year is the annual Barristers' Ball.

Second- and third-year students may participate in moot court competition in the fall and spring. The Holderness Moot Court Bench includes winners of the spring advanced competition, the international competition, and the client counseling competition.

With a few exceptions (easily identified through the school grapevine), the faculty is able, interested in its work, and open to students. The property and constitutional law professors are excellent, and there are stars in such fields as environmental law, evidence, taxation, criminal law, and trial advocacy. The curriculum is very solid in core subjects, and occasional sorties are made into innovative areas like Law and Literature. Although specialized courses are sometimes limited, UNC students may fill the gaps by taking courses at nearby Duke or North Carolina Central at no extra charge.

The clinical opportunities include a Civil and Criminal Law Clinic, as well as an Appellate Defenders seminar, conducted on a clinic format. Typically, all interested third-year students have been squeezed in, but the list is long. The consensus is that the program is well worth the work involved.

A number of four-year joint degree programs are available, including law and public health, regional planning, and public policy. The M.B.A./J.D. program is popular, probably because of the business school's high quality. In addition, law students may take one nonlegal course for credit in any of the university's graduate departments.

Grading can be strict. About 40 percent of the first-year class will get Cs, due to the infamous mandatory C-curve. As at any law school, first year here is rigorous. Exams are emphasized from day one, and pressure is inevitable in the scramble to grade onto the law review. The top 10 percent of the first-year class is offered a staff position on the respected *North Carolina Law Review,* and the top 15 percent is offered a place on the *Journal of International Law and Commercial Regulation.* The masses comprising the remaining 85 percent are given an additional chance by entering writing competitions sponsored by both journals. For those interested in more creative journalism, there is an award-winning monthly newspaper.

Of the five mandatory first-year courses, four are large classes, with 80 to 100 students each. The fifth class is a "small section" of about 20. The small section serves as the forum for first-year orientation and study groups, and often remains the basic social foundation throughout law school. Most classes are taught using the Socratic method.

The law school is housed in a spacious contemporary building about a quarter of a mile from the main campus. The woodsy setting on the east edge of campus gives the law school a sense of separateness from the rest of the university. A prefab annex adjoining the faculty parking lot, added in the spring of 1990, houses the snack bar and a number of student organizations, allowing for more lockers and office space in the main building. The snack bar is well stocked but pricey, and the law school is some distance from any local eating establishments. Microwaves are provided, however, so brown-baggers can suit themselves.

The library is well stocked and the staff is capable and extraordinarily courteous. Unfortunately, a major architectural compromise allowed athletic fields to bound the building on two sides, subjecting students to the nearby thuds, grunts, and yells of jocks in training, as well as marching band practice.

Chapel Hill is the quintessential college town, with a long and venerable history. It is set in the midst of North Carolina's rolling Piedmont country. The beach and mountains, at least three hours away in opposite directions, are euphemistically referred to as "equally close." The thickly wooded Piedmont is not without its own charms, however.

Housing is a mixed bag. A recent explosion of condo and apartment building has glutted the apartment market, so housing is plentiful, though not always cheap. Although some law students live in Craige Dormitory, a grad student dorm, it is not a prestigious address. The *Village Advocate,* a biweekly advertising paper, is an excellent source of listings.

Parking is a problem; 261 expensive parking permits are distributed by the SBA among over 700 law students. Those living within two miles aren't even eligible, except in cases of "hardship." Nearby churches permit some parking, but policies fluctuate. Many of those living in nearby Carrboro brave the hazards of bicycling, but remember that Chapel Hill was aptly named.

Jobs are available in local law firms. Though Chapel Hill employers pay low wages compared to larger cities, competition is nonetheless stiff. Work options at the law school include research assistantships and library jobs. Nonlaw jobs are also available throughout the area. The nearby Research Triangle is riding the crest of high-tech prosperity, and part-time opportunities can be found.

The law school selects its students by a "modified rolling admissions" system. Numbers (GPA and LSAT) determine the fate of the majority of candidates, while those whose scores and grades place them at neither the top nor the bottom of the numerical ladder get closer scrutiny. The committee does give serious consideration to unique work or service experience. Two or three letters of reference and discreet examples of creative initiative are considered, but flooding the office with letters of praise, videotapes, and manuscripts tends to alienate the committee, according to one student.

UNC offers a solid legal education in a very attractive environment, among students who are surprisingly diverse for a state university. The school has its share of minor problems, but it's got energy and an openness to change. Its reputation promises to continue expanding beyond its regional boundaries.

North Carolina Central University School of Law

Address: **Durham, NC 27707**
Phone: **(919) 560-6333**
Degrees: **J.D., J.D./M.L.S.**
  (library science)
Median LSAT: **27 (full time),**
  37 (part time)
Median GPA: **2.93 (full time),**
  3.12 (part time)
Applicants accepted: **42%**
Transfers: **NA**
Law enrollment: **321**

Campus enrollment: **5000**
Part time: **22%**
Women: **52%**
Minorities: **48%**
Dorm residents: **NA**
Library: **169,200**
Student-faculty ratio: **16:1**
Tuition: **$1133 (in-state),**
  $7471 (out-of-state)
Financial aid: **NA**
Apply by: **April 15**

Disabled students: **Moderate/full accessibility. One disabled student in one year.**
Placement: **Approximately 67% employed six to nine months after graduation. Graduates entered private practice (39%), government (16%), judicial clerkships (11%), public interest (11%), business (2%), military (2%), academic (2%), unknown (16%). Average salary: $26,000.**

Students are satisfied that the North Carolina Central University School of Law—founded in 1939—has experienced an exciting rebirth. The school greeted the 1980s with a new administration and a just-built $4-million building. Admissions standards, although they wouldn't be confused with their counterparts at a prestigious private school, are improving. The library and computer facilities are growing and meet students' needs.

NCCU is a predominantly black state university. In the past, the law school's mission has been to train minority students and the underprivileged, primarily from North Carolina. While that task is still taken seriously (in-state residents are roughly 80 percent of the total, and African-Americans are often a majority), the primary emphasis now appears to be on getting entering classes with a broad range of backgrounds. Students' ages range from the early twenties to late fifties. Many are just out of college, but most seem to have spent a few years working in the outside world at a variety of tasks. The differences in viewpoint make for interesting discussions, in class and out.

With its tiny student body, NCCU enjoys an extremely favorable student-faculty ratio. Classes are unusually small for a law school— from 12 to 45 students—so you'd better be prepared to be called on.

Parties attract a much larger number, whether the occasion is a picnic at a professor's house or the annual postexams barbecue sponsored by the legal fraternities. Student-faculty relations are excellent, with frequent impromptu round-table discussions in the student lounge or lobby. The administrators, like most professors, maintain an open-door policy.

The NCCU curriculum offers the basics and some typical electives. Students may take other courses at the nearby law schools of Duke University (also in Durham) and the University of North Carolina (twenty minutes away). This cross-pollination among the three law schools is a reciprocal arrangement, and participation requires only the dean's permission.

For those who must work full time or prefer not to interrupt their careers, NCCU offers a fully accredited evening program. The night school permits a student to earn a J.D. by attending classes for four to five years.

Clinical programs allow students to work with the local district attorney or legal services. Although some clinical courses are offered in the summer, most full-time students interested in summer school enroll at the University of North Carolina. By attending two summer sessions and carrying a heavy load the rest of the time, one can graduate a semester early, but current students don't recommend it.

The big break from the books comes in April, when the school celebrates Law Day with activities for alumni and students. The celebration starts with a talent show (more fun than talent) featuring faculty, staff and student skits. The weekend of seminars and luncheons culminates with the annual banquet, at which students and faculty are presented with awards for outstanding accomplishments.

Despite the low tuition, many NCCU students are hard-pressed financially, and that creates problems. The law school has research assistantships allowing students to work with faculty members in various capacities, but the number of positions is limited. Due to the large student population in the Durham area, other part-time jobs are hard to find. Even when students do get work, it can eat away at much-needed study time. Students say this might be one reason for the school's history of so-so bar pass rates, but they are confident that improvements at the school (coupled with careful financial planning by students themselves) will bring bar results up in the future.

Although it's been shaping up lately, the school's record for permanent job placement has been weak in the past. North Carolina has five accredited law schools, and most NCCU graduates plan to stay in-state, so competition for spots is stiff. Since visits by recruiters are at a minimum, the students who bang on the most doors generally get the best jobs.

Many NCCU students feel a special loyalty to the school since they were rejected by, or couldn't afford, bigger-name institutions. Because NCCU is more willing than most to give someone with an unimpressive record a crack at a legal education, the attrition rate is higher than at some other schools. But many of the students on whom the admissions committee has taken a gamble go on to become highly successful attorneys and judges. It is in these cases that NCCU feels it has fulfilled its mission.

University of North Dakota School of Law

Address: **University Station, Grand Forks, ND 58202**
Phone: **(701) 777-2104**
Degrees: **J.D.**
Median LSAT: **31**
Median GPA: **3.1**

Applicants accepted: **63%**
Transfers: **5**
Law enrollment: **374**
Campus enrollment: **11,000**
Part time: **0**
Women: **45%**

Minorities: **3%**

Dorm residents: **NA**

Library: **217,400**

Student-faculty ratio: **25:1**

Tuition: **$2566 (in-state),**
    $6358 (out-of-state)

Financial aid: **90%**

Apply by: **April 1**
    recommended

Disabled students: **Moderate/full accessibility.**

Placement: **Approximately 94% employed six to nine months after graduation. Graduates entered private practice (50%), judicial clerkships (28%), government or military (9%), academic (6%). Salary range: $17,000–$32,000.**

When most people think about North Dakota (if they ever do), what comes to mind are howling blizzards and forty-below-zero temperatures. Locals insist this sort of weather is great for keeping out the riffraff and shouldn't be the key factor in deciding whether to attend UND Law.

Something here attracts a student body that is roughly 25 percent out-of-staters. It's not the cosmopolitan location. Grand Forks has 49,000 people. That's considered big, because it's the second largest city in the state. The school is 150 miles from Winnipeg and 315 miles from Minneapolis. That's considered close, because the area is so sparsely populated.

Most law students manage to avoid the elements by spending all their waking hours in the law school building. It's not hard to do, since the school lounge has a TV, card tables, junk food vending machines—all the necessities of life.

The Memorial Student Union is right next door to the law school and has two cafeterias where you can usually find groups of law students taking coffee breaks. The UND fieldhouse—for running track, pumping iron, etc.—is only a short distance away.

Many law students take advantage of the nonlaw activities at UND, such as theater productions and sports events. First-year students are a notable exception to that rule. Credit is permitted for nonlaw courses, if you can dream up a legitimate reason for taking the course and prove that it relates in some way to law.

It is possible to survive in Grand Forks without a car, but only if you live on or near campus. North Dakota winters are not conducive to extended outdoor strolls.

UND is a small law school, and the student-teacher rapport is good. The instructors are generally young (many students will find that they're older than their professors), or at least young at heart. Beyond the first year, intimidation doesn't play a role in classroom dynamics. Most instructors will put in an appearance at a law school kegger at one time or another, and it's not rare for students and faculty to be on a first-name basis.

There's a flip side to the small-school coin, though. When teachers know students personally, they are apt to notice who doesn't show up for class. Also, because the numbers of students and instructors are so limited, many courses can be offered only every other year. In some cases, a course is offered one time only; take it now or forever hold your peace.

Students complain from time to time that there aren't enough practical courses, but they're quick to add that the school has a number of clinical and internship-for-credit programs. There are also a few research fellowships available in criminal justice and agricultural law.

UND offers the usual activities. Law review and moot court are the most active and attract the most participation. There's also the Law Women's Caucus and Student Bar Association. UND has three legal fraternities that provide activities ranging from the reasonably intellectual to the totally hedonistic.

The law school puts on an annual musical, which enjoys overwhelming student participation and attendance. Sports are also strong here, with intramural teams called Assault and Battery, Nuisance Per Se, and the Joint Tortfeasors. The law students' softball, football, hockey, and basketball teams all draw spectators and get support from the law school's own kazoo marching band.

UND law students value sports as an all-too-necessary break from the books. It's the first-years who need that break most of all; second- and third-year students (*especially* third-year students) aren't as driven to study constantly. A student who makes it through the first year here is well nigh guaranteed to make it through the next two.

The UND student body represents a variety of backgrounds. Many have taken time off after college, and undergraduate majors range from economics to home economics. But despite the diversity in their pasts, UND students share a common future, at least geographically. Although the school's job-referral service does a good job listing full-time and summer positions and coordinating interviews, the reputation of this school remains thoroughly regional.

Northeastern University School of Law

Address: **400 Huntington Ave., Boston, MA 02115**
Phone: **(617) 437-2395**
Degrees: **J.D., J.D./M.B.A., J.D./M.S. (accounting)**
Median LSAT: **38**
Median GPA: **3.28**
Applicants accepted: **23%**
Transfers: **7**
Law enrollment: **557**

Campus enrollment: **39,200**
Part time: **0**
Women: **62%**
Minorities: **22%**
Dorm residents: **NA**
Library: **152,800**
Student-faculty ratio: **19:1**
Tuition: **$15,000**
Financial aid: **83%**
Apply by: **March 1**

Disabled students: **Fully accessible. No disabled students in one year.**
Placement: **Approximately 85% employed six to nine months after graduation. Graduates took jobs in New England (69%), Pacific (10%), Middle Atlantic (9%), South Atlantic (6%), East North Central (2%), Mountain (2%), West South Central (1%), Foreign (1%). Graduates entered private practice (50%), judicial clerkships (26%), public interest (10%), government (7%), business (1%), unknown (8%). Salary range: $22,000–$68,000.**

Northeastern is not a typical law school. While many schools provide limited-enrollment clinical programs as an afterthought, Northeastern requires extensive periods of full-time work experience for everyone.

Under Northeastern's unique "cooperative" plan, first-year students complete nine months of traditional course work and then alternate three-month periods of work and study for the next two years. Northeastern students achieve the J.D. in the same thirty-three months it would take elsewhere, but at the end they have had seven academic quarters and four work quarters. Instead of seasonal vacations, there is a one-week break after each quarter.

During each co-op quarter, a student must successfully complete at least eleven weeks of law-related work under the supervision of a practicing attorney. Students are free to find co-op jobs on their own, but the school maintains a file of over four hundred regular co-op employers and actively assists job-seekers. While many of the positions are in the Boston area, Northeastern students can be found all over the country, including Alaska, Hawaii, and Puerto Rico.

Co-op jobs are available in almost every area of legal practice, including private firms, corporations' legal departments, public-interest groups, and government agencies. Students' experiences range from pure research and writing to frequent court appearances. The co-op program exposes students to a wide variety of real-life employment opportunities and frequently leads to permanent offers.

The co-op program is just one example of Northeastern's innovative approach to legal education. Grading in all classes is pass/fail. Both professors and co-op employers submit written evaluations that become part of each student's official transcript. There is no class ranking.

Classes at Northeastern are relatively small. First-years have one class with 30 students and the remainder with about 100 students. Because the second- and third-year students are divided into two sections, one of which is out on co-op during any given quarter, there are never more than about 130 upper-level students attending classes. Second- and third-year courses usually range from 15 to 50 students.

The school's curriculum includes all the standard subjects familiar at other law schools, including several clinical courses. Although there are comparatively few classes in specialized legal areas, those that are offered have been developed in response to student interest and are sometimes on subjects you wouldn't find elsewhere.

The classroom environment is described as informal and relaxed. Seating charts are rarely used, and most students and professors are on a first-name basis. Most of the faculty members are young; all are actively involved in the daily life of the school and are very accessible to students.

Northeastern's admissions policy reflects its pragmatic approach to legal education. Motivation and experience are more important, and LSAT scores and GPAs less important, than at many other schools. Most students arrive here by way of several years of employment or postgraduate study. The large female enrollment includes many women who have raised families.

The political climate at the school is lively. Although the dean and faculty have ultimate control over school policy, there are student representatives on all the administrative committees, and students participate—often vociferously—in the decision-making process.

Professors and students alike are concerned about inequities in the national legal system, and political issues are regularly addressed in class and out. An interesting legal practice course is part of the required first-year curriculum.

Students are active in a number of law school organizations such as the Black Law Students Association, Asian Law Students Association, Environmental Law Forum, Domestic Violence Project, Women's Caucus, and Lesbian and Gay Caucus. The Equal Justice Foundation and National Lawyers Guild have strong chapters here, and many students find time to work on national and community issues while in school.

Law students have access to all the facilities of Northeastern University, including tuition-free courses in other departments.

The recently renovated law building is in the heart of Boston, which has advantages and disadvantages. On the plus side, the Museum of Fine Arts, the Boston Symphony, Fenway Park (home of the Red Sox), and innumerable other attractions are within walking distance. The school is easily accessible by public transit, and parking is available for commuters.

On the minus side, Boston is as noisy and occasionally unsafe as any northeastern city. Also, the law school offers little housing, and rent and other necessities are very expensive.

Tuition is high, too, as befits a private law school. Financial aid is mainly in the form of guaranteed student loans and work/study aid; scholarship funds go primarily to the entering class. Most co-op jobs are salaried, which can help pay the bills, but few are really lucrative. The emphasis is on experience, not cash. The school provides some money for unsalaried co-op jobs.

Northeastern is definitely an unusual and exciting place to go to law school. The school is still growing and making mistakes, but it's flexible and innovative enough to make the necessary changes. In the meantime, there are few places that offer such a successful combination of a congenial atmosphere, practical experience, and a commitment to social change.

Northern Kentucky University, Salmon P. Chase College of Law

Address: **Nunn Hall, Highland Heights, KY 41076**
Phone: **(606) 572-5384**
Degrees: **J.D., J.D./M.B.A.**
Median LSAT: **152**
Median GPA: **3.37**
Applicants accepted: **21%**
Transfers: **4–5/19**
Law enrollment: **411**
Campus enrollment: **12,000**
Part time: **42%**

Women: **47%**
Minorities: **5%**
Dorm residents: **3%**
Library: **233,000**
Student-faculty ratio: **21:1**
Tuition: **$2980 (in-state), $8310 (out-of-state)**
Financial aid: **63% (32% gift)**
Apply by: **March 1, February 1 (aid)**

Disabled students: **Fully accessible. In five years, one blind student.**
Placement: **65% employed six months after graduation. 15% of first-years, 40% of second-years, and 63% of third-years employed in legal jobs during the academic year. 30% of first-years, 70% of second-years, and 50% of third-years placed by end of spring term. 27 employers on campus in one year; 67% from Ohio, 30% Kentucky, 4% West Virginia; 66% private firms, 15% corporations, 19% government. Graduates took jobs in Kentucky (60%), Ohio (35%), other (5%). Graduates entered private practice (60%), judicial clerkships (12%), government (12%), business (12%), military (3%), academic (1%). Salary range: $17,000–$68,000. Mean salary: $32,763. Kentucky bar pass rate: 81.6% (statewide average: 84%). Ohio bar pass rate: 90.7% (statewide average: 83%).**

Chase College of Law has had a long and shaky history. In recent years, it has solidified its programs and is working to establish a distinct identity.

Chase originated in 1893 as Cincinnati's night law school, affiliated with the YMCA. For years, it served those who held down other jobs while training to become lawyers, and practitioners composed its faculty. After World War II, however, the school began hiring full-time faculty to keep up with accreditation requirements. It finally affiliated with Northern Kentucky University in 1972.

Today, the school's future is no longer in question. A full-time program is thriving along with the night program. The administration is working to improve fund-raising, to increase scholarships, and to hire faculty dedicated to publishing as well as teaching. But Chase is still struggling to compete with schools that are more established and have bigger endowments.

The school is on a modern campus on a hill overlooking downtown Cincinnati five miles away. That is probably its biggest drawback, because the school is not part of Cincinnati, nor is it truly identified with Kentucky. The high quality of life in the Cincinnati area—and its traditional cliquishness—make high-paying local jobs hard to come by for those not in the top 10 percent of their classes. The result is that those who stay in the area often start with small, low-paying firms. Outside Kentucky and Ohio, average Chase graduates have difficulty getting jobs because the school is simply not known.

With both a day and night program, Chase attracts students with diverse backgrounds, particularly older students. GPAs and LSAT scores are the primary considerations for admission, but workplace experience and accomplishments play a strong role.

First-year students all take Introduction to Law, a pass-fail class that teaches how to read and brief cases, gives a short history of the American legal system, and tells students how to study for and take a law school exam. A midterm exam, followed by lots of faculty feedback, helps first-years figure out what is expected of them. No one is left to flounder without guidance.

Chase demands more required courses of its students than do many law schools. For example, Federal Tax, Secured Transactions, and Commercial Paper are required in the last two years of school. In addition, every student must take a "breadth and perspective" class such as Comparative Law, Jurisprudence, History of Anglo-American Law, and so on. Finally, each student is required to write an upper-level paper.

Elective courses range from Coal Law to Admiralty, Entertainment Law, and Environmental Law. Students receive class credit and a letter grade for work on law review and moot court. Apart from the J.D./M.B.A. program, NKU refuses to grant credit for courses in other departments.

Class attendance is mandatory and attendance is taken at each class. Classes are small (usually 60 to 80 students), so the professors get to know the students by name. The professors are readily accessible for assistance and discussion and seem genuinely interested in the students' academic success.

The clinical program is in flux as the school scrambles to meet the ABA's strict new accreditation requirements concerning faculty participation. A federal trial practice course gives students credit for working with one of the local federal judges, and it may be expanded to include work with state judges.

The Cincinnati region is a dynamic cultural area. All types of entertainment are available: pro baseball and football; huge festivals from March through October; a wonderful symphony, playhouse, and ballet. Good nightlife can be had, too, including all the top national rock concerts. Campus life and programs are unimpressive because NKU is unquestionably a commuter-oriented school. Students warn that NKU dorm rooms are small and dilapidated.

The Student Bar Association provides a vehicle for relaying student concerns to the administration, arranges some social activities (College Night at the Reds, Barristers' Ball, and Libel Night), and publishes a student phone and address directory. The Women's Law Caucus, Young Democrats, and Young Republicans are also active.

The placement program has become very active only recently, but it has accomplished a lot in a small amount of time. Large Cincinnati and Kentucky law firms come to campus to interview. The military, attorney general's office, and a few corporations also visit. Mock interviews and seminars help students prepare for the rigors of the job hunt.

Most students seem to go to Chase because they're tired of their old jobs and want to become practicing attorneys. The school gears its curriculum and programs toward that end. Chase is recognized for providing a practical education—but for the moment, it is only recognized at all in the immediate geographical area.

Northwestern University School of Law

Address: **357 East Chicago Ave., Chicago, IL 60611**
Phone: **(312) 503-8465**
Degrees: **J.D., LL.M., S.J.D., J.D./M.M. (management), J.D./Ph.D. (social sciences)**
Median LSAT: **NA**
Median GPA: **NA**
Applicants accepted: **15%**
Transfers: **6**
Law enrollment: **609 (591 J.D.)**

Campus enrollment: **NA**
Part time: **0**
Women: **38%**
Minorities: **19%**
Dorm residents: **NA**
Library: **554,900**
Student-faculty ratio: **14:1**
Tuition: **$16,386**
Financial aid: **70%**
Apply by: **February 1**

Disabled students: **Fully accessible. In one year, one disabled student.**

Placement: **Approximately 96% placed by graduation. Graduates employed in East North Central (59%), Pacific (13%), Middle Atlantic (9%), South Atlantic (8%), West North Central (4%), New England (3%), West South Central (2%), Mountain (1%), Foreign (1%). Graduates entered private practice (77%), judicial clerkships (14%), public interest (4%), government (4%), business (1%). Salary range: $30,000–$80,000.**

Northwestern is clearly a law school on the rise. During the early 1980s, the school added several nationally recognized professors and built a $30-million multistory addition to house the national headquarters of the American Bar Association as well as a new law library, classrooms, and offices.

School administrators make no bones about their goal: to push Northwestern from its current position as one of the country's reputed top fifteen or so law schools to somewhere in the top half-dozen. But Northwestern students don't spend three years discussing how their law school ranks with the others, or the fact that many of them came here as a second or third choice. They realize that their school is among the best, and that's enough.

Most of the professors are earnest legal scholars and engaging teachers. And almost all make it a point on the first day of classes to tell first-years that Northwestern is not like *The Paper Chase;* students will be challenged, not terrorized or humiliated.

Since Northwestern is a national law school, many courses focus on federal law, and those that deal with state law are taught so that concepts learned here are applicable anywhere. Few students plan on going into public-interest law; the majority by far are interested either in business litigation or corporate work. Nonetheless, the school has its own outstanding legal clinic, with many students competing for a small number of spots.

During first year, all but two courses are required, with students choosing a "perspective" elective such as legal history, law and social science, or law and economics. After first year, only one semester of ethics is required. The school also has a writing requirement, to be fulfilled through two seminar papers, in-depth independent study, or a combination of work on one of the three legal journals and a seminar paper.

Northwestern University is famous for its beautiful suburban Evanston campus. The law school isn't on it. However, the law school's location in downtown Chicago on the lakefront just east of the "Magnificent Mile," is ideal. The downtown legal community is minutes away in the Loop, and a wealth of entertainment is available by foot or bus in the city's famous Rush Street and Lincoln Avenue areas. Nonetheless, the school's small campus is so self-contained that students sometimes feel they are living in a city within a city and forget what the outside world looks like.

Although the Chicago campus also contains the university's medical and dental schools, most law students frequent only the law school itself and the two campus dormitories. Abbott Hall, the cheaper of the two, is an eighteen-story building with small institutionally furnished rooms and shared bathrooms. The Lake Shore Center dorm used to be an exclusive men's club and features a student bar and grill, gymnasium, racquetball and handball courts, and a large swimming pool. The Lake Shore facilities are available to all students.

Off-campus housing close to campus is expensive and somewhat difficult to find due to the school's "Gold Coast" location. Consequently, many students live in apartments fifteen or twenty minutes away by bus.

The law school itself is small enough so that red tape is kept to a minimum in the admissions, financial aid, and dean's offices. Despite some inevitable annoyances in dealing with the law school administration, students find it infinitely preferable to taking on the impersonal main-campus bureaucrats.

The Student Bar Association monitors the actions of the faculty and administration, and sponsors several social events. A Women's Caucus hosts discussions and films on current issues, and the Black Law Students Association also has a regular slate of activities. The weekly school newspaper is eagerly awaited for tidbits of law school gossip and general information about law school activities. But the most popular activity may well be Bar Review, where a hundred or more students show up at a preselected bar each Thursday night to hoist a few and chat with the regular handful of professors who drop by.

Back at school, an organization called Student Funded Public Interest Fellowships works to counterbalance the corporate law firm influence on the summer job market. SFPIF collects a small donation from those who want to contribute and then awards stipends to students who have found summer jobs with public-interest organizations. With the exception of first-years, those seeking summer or permanent positions with traditional law firms don't need much help from anybody, thanks to the high volume of on-campus recruiting.

Serious complaints about the school are rare. A few faculty members have mean and/or pompous streaks, and a couple of rookie professors have been known to have trouble expressing legal concepts to their classes. Few students complain about the social life (or lack thereof). As at all top law schools, students study very hard—numerous first-years have been known to work around the clock on one of their major legal writing assignments.

On the other hand, students have quite a bit to boast about. Despite the school's hefty tuition, each class maintains a fair degree of diversity. A recent legal clinic case was argued before the U.S. Supreme Court, and current and former Supreme Court justices regularly preside over the final round of the yearly moot court competition. Moreover, the school offers a popular joint degree in management with the superb business school on the Evanston campus.

Administrators are eager to spread this upbeat attitude about the school on recruiting tours, and applications to Northwestern have jumped dramatically in the last few years. And why not? Students looking for a challenging legal education at a rapidly improving school could do much worse.

University of Notre Dame Law School

Address: **P.O. Box 959, Notre Dame, IN 46556**
Phone: **(219) 239-6626**
Degrees: **J.D., LL.M., J.D./ M.B.A., other joint degrees**
Median LSAT: **41**
Median GPA: **3.4**
Applicants accepted: **NA**
Transfers: **11**
Law enrollment: **574 (552 J.D.)**

Campus enrollment: **9500**
Part time: **0**
Women: **37%**
Minorities: **14%**
Dorm residents: **NA**
Library: **298,200**
Student-faculty ratio: **16:1**
Tuition: **$14,095**
Financial aid: **65%**
Apply by: **April 1**

Disabled students: **Fully accessible. Three disabled students in one year.**

Placement: **Approximately 95% employed six to nine months after graduation. Graduates employed in East North Central (36%), Pacific (13%), Middle Atlantic (13%), South Atlantic (10%), West North Central (10%), West South Central (7%), New England (4%), Mountain (4%), East South Central (1%), Foreign (1%). Graduates entered private practice (74%), judicial clerkships (10%), government (5%), business (4%), military (4%), public interest (1%), academic (1%), unknown (1%). Average starting salary: $55,000.**

Notre Dame's emphasis on the individual begins with the application. The school has implemented a "whole person" admissions process that produces incoming classes with a wide variety of ages, backgrounds, ethnic affiliations, and home states. About half the students are Catholic. This is America's oldest Catholic law school, and while the religious affiliation is more than mere tradition, humorless Bible-thumping is nonexistent.

Its community atmosphere is one of Notre Dame's strengths. The school's small size plays a part, but the attitude of students, professors, and even the administration is the key. Upperclass students provide notes, outlines, and help to anyone who asks; "missing" library materials and uncooperative attitudes are not tolerated by fellow students.

The administration fosters a collaborative version of competition with a policy that combines the fight against grade inflation with a refusal to publish class rank. Though some law firms find the lack of ranking a bit irritating, the vagueness can be used to advantage, and it does accomplish the purpose of limiting rivalry between individuals. Despite the camaraderie and supportiveness, however, human nature and the intrinsic qualities of law school create enough pressure and competition to satisfy any stress addict.

Professors are committed to the school's open-door policy, and even the busiest are available at a knock throughout the week—no appointment needed. The professors' philosophies and pedagogical approaches run the gamut, which in one or two cases is not an advantage. However, the vast majority display both an admirable knowledge of the subject matter and the ability to convey what they know to the students. Several are described by students as among the finest they have encountered. Faculty and staff participate in school life beyond the academic. Alongside students, they play basketball and volunteer at a local homeless center.

First-year classes contain 75 or fewer students and are taught in a gentle variation on the Socratic theme. Especially appreciated by first-years inundated with four substantive courses plus Legal Writing and Legal Research (taught as separate courses on the theory that a specialist in each should lead the learning process), as well as Ethics, is the practice exam held in early November. Graded by the faculty for diagnostic purposes only, these exams greatly reduce the anxiety level.

Numerous required courses give Notre Dame its "tough" reputation; however, they comprise the sequence of study chosen by most would-be lawyers at any school. Among the most popular electives are Trial Advocacy, Negotiation, and Complex Litigation. The National Institute for Trial Advocacy is located at Notre Dame. Its director and several instructors are professors, which accounts for the school's good reputation in litigation.

The law school's location in South Bend has been characterized as "Mecca in the cornfields." The fact that the university is the second most popular tourist attraction in Indiana (after the Indianapolis Motor Speedway, home of the Indianapolis 500) speaks volumes about both the fame of the institution and the character of the area surrounding it. However, Chicago, an hour-and-a-half drive away, provides culture transfusions for those in need. The "Mecca" part of the description is appropriate because Notre Dame is the home of Fighting Irish football. Football season is a time when the outfits sported by alumni remind one that all colors are not found in nature, no matter how varied the fall foliage display. Notre Dame offers more than football, but you may forget that when the Fight Song wafts through the leaded-glass windows of the library as the marching band parades by on Friday afternoons.

The school has benefited from an aggressive library acquisitions program and recent additions to its physical plant. Furthermore, over two dozen LEXIS and WESTLAW terminals along with Macintosh and MS-DOS personal computers provide one of the best computer database facilities in the country.

With an open-stack library and its computer facility available to students 24 hours a day, 365 days a year, and most students living either in nearby apartment complexes or on campus in dorms and apartment-style units, life centers around the law school. Studying takes up most of a student's week, but more interactive activities are available. Intramural sports for both men and women are popular. Basketball, football, soccer, hockey, boxing, golf, and Thursday night beer bowling are among the annual offerings. Friday afternoon means happy hour in the law school lounge, with the Student Bar Association sponsoring more formal parties several times each year. Students find that their significant others and/or children are welcome at most social events.

Besides law review, students have an opportunity to work on three specialized journals. Affiliated research foundations like the Center for Civil and Human Rights and the Center on Law and Government bring outstanding speakers to the law school. Other extracurricular legal activities include the opportunity to get involved with legal aid, including some criminal work (nearby Michigan allows certified students to handle criminal cases with supervision), to do research for professors, or to work for local judges and attorneys.

After passing first-year examinations, the major concern of law students everywhere is finding the right job. The placement office here is efficient and helpful. It attracts a large number of firms for on-campus interviews. Many are from the Midwest, but New York and LA are represented. With the school's strong national reputation, a little effort by students has resulted in on-site interviews in the city of their choice. Second-year students interested in summer jobs in difficult-to-crack legal markets like Boston, Seattle, and San Francisco report a good response to letter-writing campaigns, even if they were not on law review.

No description of Notre Dame is complete without mentioning the school's London campus. Courses are taught by American and English professors during the school year and summer. Electives as well as a few required courses are offered by this ABA-accredited facility. Additionally, students in London can be members of the law review or any of the other journals and can win a place on the moot court team. A second year spent in London can be just what the doctor ordered for the law student interested in international law—or even for the student who's just looking for a change from South Bend.

Nova University, Shepard Broad Law Center

Address: **3305 College Ave., Fort Lauderdale, FL 33314**
Phone: **(305) 452-6100**
Degrees: **J.D., J.D./M.B.A., J.D./M.S. (psychology)**
Median LSAT: **151 (full time), 150 (part time)**
Median GPA: **3.02 (full time), 3.19 (part time)**
Applicants accepted: **23%**
Transfers: **2–5**

Law enrollment: **830**
Campus enrollment: **2000**
Part time: **3%**
Women: **40%**
Minorities: **21%**
Dorm residents: **NA**
Library: **254,000**
Student-faculty ratio: **22:1**
Tuition: **$14,080**
Financial aid: **80%**
Apply by: **March 1**

Disabled students: **Fully accessible. Sixteen disabled students in one year.**
Placement: **80% employed six to nine months after graduation. Graduates took jobs in South Florida (90%), Central Florida (1%), Southwest Florida (1%), Northeast including Washington, DC (5%), Midwest (2%), West (1%). Graduates entered private firms (60%), government (16%), self-employed (6%), judicial clerkships (3%), nonlegal jobs (7%), business (2%), military (1%),**

public interest (1%), advanced degree (2%), unknown (2%).
Salary range: $15,000–$59,000.

Nova, as its name suggests, is one of the country's newer law schools. The school received full ABA accreditation in 1982 and in 1992 moved into a pristine, custom-designed $8.6-million building.

Nova's youth has more advantages than disadvantages. There are no stodgy traditions. The atmosphere is relaxed. The professors, are, for the most part, young, dynamic, and excited about the law. Many of them welcome informal discussion with students on legal or nonlegal topics.

The students here are an atypical group. Many are older, local people beginning a supplemental or new career. You'll also find just-out-of-college enrollees from all over the country, but predominantly from the East and Midwest. The school has a large number of Spanish-speaking students, too.

Nova's curriculum follows the pattern of most law schools, but the school is not afraid to add new courses to reflect emerging areas of the law.

The entering class is divided into unusually small sections of about 45 students each. Members of each section take all their classes together and develop strong loyalties to section-mates. After first year, classes continue to be reasonably small, with the exception of certain subjects required for the bar exam.

Although the school does encourage competition and hard work, it hasn't yet fostered the cutthroat rivalry of law school legends. Many students form study groups and willingly share class notes, outlines, and study aids.

The law library houses a very good collection; it is one of the few depository libraries for United Nations documents. The Law Center is minutes away from the county and federal courts and the center of downtown Fort Lauderdale.

The school has expanded its in-house clinical program recently. In addition, through externship programs, students work for the state's attorney, public defender, legal aid, and state or federal judges for up to nine hours of classroom credit. Under Florida law, clinical students may be certified to practice and can find themselves on their own in the courtroom, a terrifying but enlightening experience.

The admissions requirements at Nova are based on a typical magic number system that emphasizes GPA and LSAT. Some weight is given to diversity factors like work experience, social and economic background, and extracurricular activities. The school seems willing to make the admissions process flexible to accommodate disabled students.

For applicants who otherwise wouldn't make it, there is a chance for admission through the conditional acceptance program. This means you take two courses during the summer, and if you rack up a 2.5 average on a 4.0 scale, you're automatically in.

There are a number of active student organizations at Nova. The largest is the Student Bar Association, to which all students automatically belong. It sponsors guest speakers, organizes law week in the spring, and throws wine and beer parties throughout the school year. Elected student representatives sit on all faculty committees.

The Moot Court Society is very active and runs a competition for first-year students during second semester. The *Nova Law Review* bases membership on writing ability and scholarship.

There are also an award-winning school newspaper, a chapter of the American Trial Lawyers Association, the legal fraternities, and groups for women, black students, and Spanish-Americans, plus interest groups in international law and entertainment law. For the size of the school, that's a lot to choose from.

Nova's placement office does a creditable job. Its main role is to provide information on potential employers, as well as guidance and other reference materials. There is some on-campus interviewing, but not enough to permit students to sit back and wait to be recruited.

The law center's new building is on the main Nova University campus. Surrounded by palm trees and adjacent to a small campus lake, the school is within walking distance of the university cafeteria, bookstore, a dormitory, and campus apartments.

But campus life isn't really necessary when you have eternal summer, beautiful beaches, and great restaurants and nightclubs on every other block. If you're going to spend three years at law school, why not spend it where you can come out from behind the books for a little sunshine?

Ohio State University College of Law

Address: **1659 North High St., Columbus, OH 43210**
Phone: **(614) 292-2631**
Degrees: **J.D., J.D./M.B.A., J.D./M.P.A., J.D./M.H.A. (hospital administration), other joint degrees**
Median LSAT: **161**
Median GPA: **3.46**
Applicants accepted: **30%**
Transfers: **3–8/20–30**
Law enrollment: **650**

Campus enrollment: **54,000**
Part time: **0**
Women: **43%**
Minorities: **17%**
Dorm residents: **approx. 40%**
Library: **564,900**
Student-faculty ratio: **18:1**
Tuition: **$4584 (in-state), $11,298 (out-of-state)**
Financial aid: **70% (40% gift)**
Apply by: **March 15, March 1 (aid)**

Disabled students: **Fully accessible. In one year, one blind student, two with temporary mobility problems.**

Placement: **70% employed six months after graduation; 86% employed nine months after graduation. 30% of second-years and 50% of third-years employed in legal jobs during the academic year. 50% of first-years, 85% of second-years, and 60% of third-years placed by end of spring term. 100 employers on campus in one year; 90% from Ohio; 90% law firms, 7% corporations, 3% government. Graduates took jobs in 18 states, including Ohio (60%), Illinois (5%), Indiana (2%), Pennsylvania (2%). Graduates entered private practice (66%), judicial clerkships (13%), government (11%), business (6%), other (4%). Salary range: $20,000–$80,000. Mean salary: $43,346. Ohio bar pass rate: 93% (statewide average: 83%).**

Ohio State University, as almost everyone knows, is a mammoth institution. The university's size is imposing, but for its students, the benefits are legion. Ohio State law students have the use not only of one of the country's biggest law libraries, but of some thirty other university libraries as well. The university athletic quarters offer everything from an indoor Olympic-size pool to tennis, racquetball, and even roller-skating facilities. Law students can get up to eight hours of credit in the thousands of nonlaw courses offered by other university branches (accounting and real estate are popular choices).

At the same time, the College of Law is completely self-contained and has only a midsize enrollment. The students here are the product of fairly demanding admissions criteria; even in-state residents face competition among their own, since this is the best school for the money in Ohio. Grade point average and LSAT scores rule the admissions process, but the school seems genuinely to look for minority applicants, older students, women, and disabled candidates.

Ohio State is definitely a midwestern school. Law students' political views range from slightly left to slightly right of middle-of-the-road. The local version of the work ethic is to work hard and play hard. Intramural athletics are so widespread that there are specialized "serious" and "nonserious" leagues for some sports. The Student Bar Association sponsors numerous happy hours in campus bars (of which there are many) and occasional parties.

Students here are not caught up in the race for the competitive edge. Books on reserve in the library don't disappear, class notes left unattended are there when their owner returns, and nobody tries to confuse or sabotage anyone else.

Members of both faculty and administration regularly participate in social events and intramural sports. Says one student, "Slaughtering the faculty basketball team is second in enjoyment only to embarrassing the pants off the faculty team at the Annual Law School Trivia Contest." The faculty and administration also take part in the yearly talent show, a showcase for both the spectacularly talented and spectacularly talentless.

Though they receive SBA funding, the other student organizations are completely independent. They include a National Lawyers Guild chapter, environmental law association, and groups for black students and women. There are also three chapters of national legal fraternities.

First-year classes, as elsewhere, are rather large (75 to 100 students) and are conducted in the universally unpopular Socratic style. The work load borders on the intolerable. Second and third years, class sizes shrink (10 to 75 students), teaching becomes more informal, and the academic burden grows considerably more bearable.

Though there is a significant emphasis on well-taught business-related courses like tax, securities, and commercial law, the curriculum by no means stops there. Interesting and unusual seminars, most of them designed to develop research and writing skills, are offered each semester so that upperclass students can satisfy the seminar requirement. One popular seminar in legislative planning is offered in cooperation with the Ohio legislature. The active clinical program lets second- and third-year students put their legal know-how to work on real clients' problems.

While the curriculum would suffice to prepare almost any type of lawyer, students say that midsize law firms are the most typical destination for Ohio State grads. The school enjoys a reputation among Ohio employers as the best in the state. Prestigious firms from Ohio as well as other cities across the country recruit here regularly, but they generally limit their interviews to law journal members and the top 20 percent of the class. The placement program is improving, but those with modest achievements and modest goals face a tightening job market.

Columbus, although a bit slow-paced, is a good town for students. Abundant off-campus housing is available within walking distance of the College of Law; just watch out for "student slums" and unsafe areas. The cost of living is low here. Public transportation is good, traffic minimal, and outside entertainment plentiful. While other northern cities have struggled to stay afloat, Columbus has maintained economic stability and is even growing as a center for corporate headquarters. If you're not intimidated by being in the midst of a megauniversity, perhaps you should say hello to Columbus.

University of Oklahoma College of Law

Address: **300 Timberdell Rd., Norman, OK 73019**
Phone: **(405) 325-4699**
Degrees: **J.D., J.D./M.B.A.**
Median LSAT: **33**
Median GPA: **3.33**
Applicants accepted: **42%**
Transfers: **4**
Law enrollment: **688**
Campus enrollment: **22,000**

Part time: **0**
Women: **42%**
Minorities: **12%**
Dorm residents: **NA**
Library: **250,000**
Student-faculty ratio: **19:1**
Tuition: **$2665 (in-state), $7915 (out-of-state)**
Financial aid: **66%**
Apply by: **March 15**

Disabled students: **Fully accessible. Five disabled students in one year.**

Placement: **Approximately 95% employed six to nine months after graduation. Graduates employed in West South Central (89%), Pacific (5%), Mountain (3%), East North Central (1%), South Atlantic (1%), Middle Atlantic (.5%), West North Central (.5%), East South Central (.5%). Graduates entered private practice (71%), government (13%), nonlegal jobs (4%), business (3%), judicial clerkships (3%), public interest (3%), military (2%), academic (1%). Salary range: $20,000–$80,000.**

The University of Oklahoma College of Law is located in the middle of a field, south of the main campus of U of O. To the arriving first-year student, the starkly modern building (completed in 1976) may look like an ominous fortress, but the Law Center is described as an informal and friendly place.

The school features a three-story library housing the most comprehensive legal collection in the state. One problem with the building is chronically inadequate parking space.

The student body comes from academic backgrounds ranging from accounting to music to nuclear physics. Students' ages range from 21 to 50, with the average in the mid-twenties. The state requires that at least 85 percent of each incoming class be from Oklahoma. The school has a special program called Admission by Performance, for about 30 applicants each year who show potential but don't offer academic records meeting regular standards.

Although no school can claim that every professor is a gem, U of O's faculty can boast of many members who have distinguished themselves in and out of the classroom, particularly in the areas of securities, taxation, oil and gas, constitutional, estate planning, and Indian law. The office staff is generally competent and helpful, although class scheduling often creates problems for students trying to find time for jobs.

The curriculum regularly includes internship programs, practice court, a legal aid clinical program, client counseling seminars, and a prisoner legal assistance program. The Continuing Legal Education department provides a variety of practical skills courses that students may take alongside practicing attorneys. A number of students work with the Legal Research Board doing research projects for area lawyers. For those who can't bear to see school end in May (and who are well provided for financially), the school offers summer courses in Oxford, England.

The work load is moderate to heavy; a student making average to low grades usually studies twenty to thirty hours a week. Exams are conducted under the honor code and grading is anonymous.

Students may elect to become members of one of the three legal fraternities. Student government buffs can go for the Student Bar Association or the American Bar Association Law Student Division. Each spring, second-year students organize Gridiron, a semi-formal BYOB bash that consists of skits and a dance. As for intramural sports, law school teams compete with each other and other student groups in softball, golf, basketball, tennis, flag football, and racquetball.

Women, black students, and Native Americans have their own organizations. The College of Law is home to the *Oklahoma Law Review* and the *American Indian Law Review*. The school holds competitions in moot court and appellate advocacy, client counseling, and trial practice; prizes are awarded during the annual Law Day celebration. U of O's extensive Enrichment Program regularly brings nationally known speakers to the Law Center.

Because Norman is a university town, most students have little difficulty finding entertainment. On autumn Saturday afternoons, football is king. Many law students manage to avoid the Sooner madness; many others find it easier just to join in.

Norman can be frigid in the winter and scorching in the summer. It's a quiet community of young to middle-aged adults. Oklahoma City is twenty miles to the north.

Norman's cost of living is low. The university dorms are within two to five blocks of the Law Center, and married student housing is right across the street. Apartments abound in Norman, but they have waiting lists. Most students stay put once they locate a reasonable place to live.

Employers in Oklahoma and the surrounding states respect a degree from U of O. The placement office is active, but some students complain that on-campus recruitment consists primarily of large employers interested only in the top 10 percent of the class. Most students use the placement office as a resource but ultimately find jobs through their own hard work.

University of Oregon School of Law

Address: **Eugene, OR 97403**
Phone: **(503) 346-3846**
Degrees: **J.D., J.D./M.B.A.,
J.D./M.S. (environmental
studies)**
Median LSAT: **40**
Median GPA: **3.11**
Applicants accepted: **19%**
Transfers: **6**
Law enrollment: **446**
Campus enrollment: **16,500**

Part time: **0**
Women: **36%**
Minorities: **13%**
Dorm residents: **NA**
Library: **262,800**
Student-faculty ratio: **19:1**
Tuition: **$5018 (in-state),
$9446 (out-of-state)**
Financial aid: **67%**
Apply by: **March 15, March 1
(aid)**

Disabled students: **Fully accessible. In one year, four disabled
students.**

Placement: **69 employers on campus in one year. Graduates took
jobs in Pacific (76%), Mountain (7%), South Atlantic (7%), East
North Central (5%), West North Central (2%), Foreign (2%), New
England (1%). Graduates entered private practice (49%), judicial
clerkships (20%), government (18%), public interest (6%),
business (4%), military (1%), academic (1%), unknown (1%).**

Some students come to U of O because it has the lowest law school
tuition in Oregon. Others come because the law school harbors a
blend of sincere students, eccentrics, artists, innocents, and wast-
rels, all in a congenial medium-pressure environment.

One of the best reasons to come to U of O is Eugene. This is
an active, proud, university-oriented community of about 110,000,
nestled in the fertile Willamette Valley. Within a seventy-mile radius lie the dramatic Oregon coast and sand dunes, the majestic
Cascade Mountains, the state capital, and tall forests that yield
most of the nation's timber. For big-city types, Portland is two
hours away, Seattle is about six. Be forewarned, though: in the
winter, months may go by before you see a sunny day.

Oregon's political climate is generally progressive, especially in
Eugene. The initiative and referendum ballot were introduced in
Oregon at the turn of the century; nonreturnable beverage bottles
and flip-top cans were banned in 1971; Oregon was the first state

to decriminalize possession of small amounts of marijuana; and a ban on disposable diapers has been proposed.

The first-year class at U of O is divided into two sections of about 90 students. All their courses are required and run-of-the-mill, with the exception of a nonconventional course in legislative and administrative processes. The sections are further divided into groups of about 20 for the legal research and writing class. All that's mandatory after the first year are an ethics course and some writing requirements.

The larger classes are usually taught by Socratic method. As a rule, responsive answers are admired; lack of preparation is understood; and insecurity is accepted, especially in the first year. "Every student is expected to speak at least once per class per semester," writes one correspondent—hardly a taxing standard.

Every rule has exceptions, and there are some professors who do demand rigorous preparation for class discussion. Others forgo the Socratic method altogether or combine it with lectures.

U of O has four different clinics—civil, environmental, criminal defense, and criminal prosecution. The clinics and trial practice classes are very popular, so those who want that kind of experience are well advised to sign up early. During the third year, law students can be certified to appear in court.

Many students are attracted to U of O's environmental program, which is unusually extensive. The school offers programs leading to a certificate in ocean and coastal law or environmental and natural resources law.

A recent poll revealed that the typical first-year student here studies five hours a day, with the range between one and twelve hours. Students are competitive, with an eye toward maximizing chances for future jobs, but most of them have too many other interests in the community to let grades determine their lives. Membership on the law review and moot court team is based on a competition, not grades.

Classroom dress is comfortable, although toward the third year the tendency increases to dress as though headed for a job interview. The student population is environment-conscious and healthy. Students lobbied successfully for a basketball hoop just outside the front steps of the school. Joggers will find company here; so will vegetarians. Alcohol and caffeine are the most used drugs; more people smoke marijuana than tobacco.

Elected students govern the Student Bar Association, which provides coffee, doughnuts, bagels, free phones, intramurals, and occasional keggers. Extracurricular opportunities include a great speaker's program and an in-house newspaper. The walls of the building are littered with announcements for events and community activities.

The law building (completed in 1970) is modern and pleasant, but suffers from poor design (bad air circulation, echoes, etc.) in places. The student lounge is a friendly place to spend an hour between classes reading, conversing, playing cards, or dining à la vending machine. There are also various restaurants and taverns within walking distance.

The law library is a reasonably comfortable spot. Seating space is adequate; shelf space, less so. The students are represented by a strong library committee. One persistent complaint: the library staff is frequently made up of undergrads who don't have the foggiest notion where that book you can't do without is located.

The quality of the faculty varies markedly. Some approach excellence; others are innovative; others merely adequate. Students report a high proportion of novice teachers. Fortunately, the school seems eager to improve teaching quality and to attract good professors and administrators. There are faculty evaluations on file that give an idea of who's worth taking and who's not. The Student Bar Association also puts out a grade distribution report each term, so students can learn how merciful or merciless the different professors are.

Financial aid is available for those in need—but get your application in early. The law school itself administers some aid, but the major portion comes through the main University of Oregon financial aid program, which can be bureaucratic and frustrating.

Many law-related jobs are available for those on work-study. Most second- and third-year students do part-time research or clerking in local law offices. The placement office can be quite helpful in making up résumés, pointing out employment opportunities, and arranging interviews, but don't count on them to get you a job.

U of O grads have no trouble passing the Oregon bar exam, and the majority of them settle in the state. Given the agreeable atmosphere in Eugene, it's no wonder they want to stay.

University of the Pacific, McGeorge School of Law

Address: **3200 Fifth Ave., Sacramento, CA 95817**
Phone: **(916) 739-7105**
Degrees: **J.D., LL.M. (tax; business and tax; or transnational business practice), J.D./M.B.A., J.D./M.S. (accounting, computer science), J.D./M.I.S. (management information), other joint degrees**
Median LSAT: **157 (full time)**
Median GPA: **3.14 (full time)**
Applicants accepted: **35% (full time)**

Transfers: **0–5/5–15**
Law enrollment: **1255 (1225 J.D.)**
Campus enrollment: **1255**
Part time: **31%**
Women: **43%**
Minorities: **12%**
Dorm residents: **15%**
Library: **379,100**
Student-faculty ratio: **26:1**
Tuition: **$14,098**
Financial aid: **97% (25% gift)**
Apply by: **May 1**

Disabled students: **Fully accessible. In five years, one blind student, two deaf, five wheelchair users, two with other mobility problems.**
Placement: **86% employed six months after graduation. 162 employers on campus in one year; 90% from California; 74% private firms, 20% government, 4% corporations, 2% judicial. 88% of graduates remained in California. Graduates entered private practice (65%), government (11%), business (7%), judicial clerkships (6%), public interest (6%), military (3%), academic (2%). Salary range: $22,000–$82,000. Median salary: $42,000. Mean salary: $44,569. California bar pass rate: 80% (statewide average: 55%).**

Grades are the primary concern of most McGeorge students. Grade inflation has not happened at McGeorge yet, and there are no signs of it on the horizon. New students are told that they're obviously not used to getting Cs (or they probably wouldn't be here), but that they'd better get used to it fast. Sure enough, As and Bs are hard to come by. If, at the end of first year, you have under a 2.0 average, you will be "academically excluded." That's a polite way of saying flunked out. (You can petition for readmittance, though.) The first-year attrition rate in a recent year was a significant 8 to 10 percent.

No one knows for sure how much work you have to do to avoid being bounced, so most err on the safe side and study an enormous amount. It helps that everyone else is in the same boat, but the school is nevertheless a stressful place.

Actually, academics are one of the brighter spots in the picture here. The professors are generally very well organized and lucid in their presentation of the material. Teaching methods range from almost total lecture to straight student recitation supplemented by lecture when required. The professors are usually cooperative and easy to reach if you need help. First-year classes are large, with about 95 students.

The school offers a unique summer study program in Europe. The extremely varied clinical offerings would make students at many other schools feel deprived in comparison.

Since most students are preoccupied with their grade averages, student government doesn't get overwhelming support. You're lucky if you can find someone who knows who the student-body officers are. In one student's words, "Why give a damn about what the administration does, as long as they do a competent job of running the school and let me stay in it?"

Despite the prevailing apathy, the Student Bar Association manages to put together a number of social activities, including the well-attended annual talent show. Intramural sports are also big, especially football, volleyball, and softball. Curtis Park, two blocks from the school, is full of McGeorge students taking an afternoon study break to run, play tennis, or join a softball game.

The day class at McGeorge tends to be fairly young; the evening section has a number of older and married students. Both groups are on the conservative side of the political spectrum. Few are interested in public-interest law; most want to get their diplomas and make money in a mainstream law firm.

The university's main campus is in Stockton. The McGeorge campus in Sacramento has a pub, pool, sauna, weight room, basketball court, and a couple of pool tables to provide mild temptation.

Sacramento is very flat with lots of fields—more like the Midwest than like most people's vision of California. The city has little in the way of entertainment, but Lake Tahoe, San Francisco, and the wine country are all within two hours by car.

Despite their complaints, students here readily concede that the school functions pretty well, if you regard the prime function of a law school to be the production of competent attorneys. The school's pass rate on the notoriously difficult California bar exam is enviable, perhaps because of all that pressure to study. McGeorge enjoys high esteem in southern California and is well thought of in most of the state. Good moot court and law journal programs are helping the school's reputation to grow, but graduates still have a tough time elbowing into the crowded San Francisco-area legal community, largely a Stanford-Hastings-Berkeley club. A growing number of out-of-state students may suggest the beginnings of a national reputation, but at this stage it's hard to say. The job placement service is good, and the Sacramento location means easy access to some government jobs.

Whoever said that life in California is laid back wasn't thinking of McGeorge. You can get a very good job graduating from here. But the school requires a lot of work, and if you don't do it, you may not survive to see graduation day.

University of Pennsylvania Law School

Address: **3400 Chestnut St., Philadelphia, PA 19104**
Phone: **(215) 898-7400**
Degrees: **J.D., LL.M., M.C.L., S.J.D., J.D./M.B.A., J.D./M.C.P. (city planning), J.D./M.A. or Ph.D. (economics or public policy analysis), other joint degrees**
Median LSAT: **43**
Median GPA: **3.61**
Applicants accepted: **21%**

Transfers: **15**
Law enrollment: **798 (743 J.D.)**
Campus enrollment: **22,000**
Part time: **0**
Women: **42%**
Minorities: **22%**
Dorm residents: **NA**
Library: **511,500**
Student-faculty ratio: **18:1**
Tuition: **$17,176**
Financial aid: **75%**
Apply by: **February 1**

Disabled students: **Fully accessible. Two disabled students in one year.**
Placement: **Approximately 96% placed by graduation. Graduates employed in Middle Atlantic/New England (57%), South Atlantic**

(25%), Pacific/Mountain (7%), East North Central/West North Central (2%), West South Central (1%), unknown or other (2%). Graduates entered private practice (74%), judicial clerkships (13%), government (5%), business (1%), public interest (1%), military (1%). Salary range: $28,000–$82,000.

Penn has at times had a bit of an inferiority complex as a so-called lesser member of the Ivy League. That complex is even less deserved by the law school than it is by other branches of the university. Most people would place Penn's law school within the top ten. The school's serious-but-friendly atmosphere doesn't show up on rankings, but it's a big plus.

Penn's admissions office makes a strong effort to assemble a diversified class and succeeds, although the East Coast and the Ivy colleges remain disproportionately well represented. A sizable group of students have been out of school for a while. Penn is small enough to avoid anonymity—in fact, the administrative staff seems to know everybody—but not so small as to be incestuous.

Currently, the first-years are split into two sections of about 115 people each. An increase in class size is planned, which will likely result in three sections of about 90 students each. The first-year curriculum consists of eight classes, each lasting a semester, instead of the standard year-long dose. Students are exposed to some subject areas, such as constitutional law and labor law, that other schools often save for later years. One first-year course is an elective. First-years also take a legal writing course, which is taught in small groups by qualified third-year students.

All courses in the second and third years are elective, except for a required class in professional responsibility.

Upper-level classes vary from seminars of 10 or 12 to lectures of 150, but the average is about 50, few enough to permit some discussion. Most seminars and classes with limited enrollments are filled by lottery, sometimes with preference given to third-year students. All the standard business and property law courses are offered regularly, and there's a good selection in constitutional law and in criminal and procedural areas. Very popular classes in appellate advocacy and trial advocacy are taught by experienced practitioners. The school has a special reputation for commercial, labor, and criminal law, as well as legal philosophy.

Penn's curriculum stretches beyond the law school's walls. Both criminal and civil clinical programs are available, but enrollment is limited, necessitating a lottery every year. The law school will grant credit for a limited number of courses in other schools in the university. An externship program automatically awards credit for a semester spent working part time for a public-interest agency in Philadelphia or full time at one of several designated public-interest groups.

The new Public Service Program requires each second- and third-year student to devote thirty-five hours each year to public service legal work. Students may, for example, work at agencies that provide legal services to the poor. This program is designed to expose students to career possibilities outside large private firms and emphasize the importance of *pro bono* work by all attorneys.

The Penn faculty runs the gamut from terrific to learned but dull. Some of the best people teach the first-year classes. Class participation is fairly relaxed; no one stands up to recite, and professors generally avoid putting people on the rack.

If students are willing to make the effort, the faculty is easy to get to know. The professors can usually be found in their offices and are amenable to students dropping by and asking questions.

Penn students tend to be obsessed in their second and third years with the job hunt, often to the point where such worldly matters eclipse any intellectual interest in the law. The placement office uses a computer system to allocate interviews with the hundreds of employers visiting the campus. This ensures that no firm can refuse to see anyone on the basis of grades alone. It also means that some students spend hours in interviews that lead only to polite letters of rejection.

Although the placement office recognizes a variety of professional goals, on-campus recruiters are predominantly the large private firms. Penn has no inherent bias toward corporate firm practice, but interviews arranged by the school are so much easier than writing letters or pounding the pavement that many students—here as elsewhere—are inevitably influenced in that direction. Of course, many students arrive here with that orientation already in place, as evidenced by the popularity of the joint degree with Penn's top-rated Wharton School of Business Administration.

A group of committed students can usually be depended on to organize public-interest-oriented programs and activities. A student organization currently provides grants to students who take low-paying public service summer jobs. The Public Interest Loan Repayment Assistance Program, which aids students who enter public service jobs after graduation, is being evaluated by students and administrators and is likely to become more expansive and generous in the future.

In the early 1990s, the school's crowded but pleasant facilities were treated to an expansion. The new building, containing a library, classrooms, and space for student activities, was designed to furnish the most modern of facilities. The law dorms were sacrificed to make way for the new building, but university housing remains available in the Graduate Towers, one block from the law school.

Most law students, especially second- and third-years, live off campus, either in West Philadelphia (the neighborhood surrounding the university) or in Center City. Both areas have their charm and are accessible to the law school, but crime is something to think about these days, especially in West Philly.

Students are active in a variety of organizations. Some clubs focus on areas of legal interest, such as international, health, or environmental law. There are associations of women, black, Asian, Latino, and gay and lesbian students. Student performers contribute their talents to the annual Law Revue and Law School Light Opera Company productions. Other activities range from two semiformal dances to faculty-student volleyball games. Intramural sports are also popular diversions.

The *University of Pennsylvania Law Review,* one of the oldest and best-respected in the country, is, of course, entirely student-run. Students are invited to join on the basis of a writing competition and first-year grades. Two other student-run journals, the *Journal of International Business Law* and the *Comparative Labor Law Journal,* provide additional opportunities for students to contribute to legal scholarship.

The rest of the university offers ample social, recreational, and cultural activities. Philadelphia itself has an ever-growing number of good restaurants, a world-famous symphony with cheap "rush" tickets, museums, sports events, and one of the largest inner-city parks in the country. The city is made up of many small neighborhoods and different ethnic groups. Although this is the nation's fifth largest city, the downtown area is a manageable size.

People at Penn work hard, and the library is full on Sunday

afternoons. Still, students here speak of a prevailing "humaneness" and a "sense of perspective." Yes, they crack the books, but there's always time for a game of softball or a cappuccino.

University of Puget Sound School of Law

Address: **950 Broadway Plaza, Tacoma, WA 98402**
Phone: **(206) 591-2252**
Degrees: **J.D.**
Median LSAT: **39/159**
Median GPA: **3.27**
Applicants accepted: **34%**
Transfers: **10–20/20–30**
Law enrollment: **875**
Campus enrollment: **4037**
Part time: **19%**
Women: **48%**
Minorities: **13%**
Dorm residents: **0**
Library: **291,800**
Student-faculty ratio: **22:1**
Tuition: **$12,480**
Financial aid: **86% (31% gift)**
Apply by: **April 1, March 1 (aid)**

Disabled students: **Fully accessible. In five years, two visually impaired students, four wheelchair users, one with other mobility problems.**

Placement: **78–88% employed six months after graduation. Approximately 5% of first-years, 50% of second-years, and 50% of third-years employed in legal jobs during the academic year. 20% of first-years, 75% of second-years, and 60% of third-years placed by end of spring term. 60–90 employers on campus in one year, primarily from Pacific; 66% private firms, 24% government, 8% business, 2% public interest. Graduates took jobs in Pacific (86%), Southwest (5%), Washington, DC (3%), other (6%). Graduates entered private practice (59%), government (16%), judicial clerkships (9%), business (8%), military (3%), public interest (3%), advanced degree (3%). Salary range: $25,000–$67,000. Mean salary: $36,122. Washington bar pass rate: 81%.**

In the fall of 1980, the UPS School of Law moved to a brand-new, innovative complex in downtown Tacoma. The huge law center put one roof over the law school, the large law library, a legal aid clinic, office space for practicing attorneys, and the state court of appeals.

The law center symbolizes and enhances the pragmatism of the legal education available at UPS. You can expect traditional course material and teaching methods here, but with a more practical flavor than at many other law schools. Legal internships are readily available, some of them for clinical credits that count toward graduation.

The first-year curriculum is entirely required and consists of the usual basics. Four of the six classes last both semesters. You will appreciate this system, if at all, only after it's over.

The average enrollment in the introductory courses is slightly under 100; numbers decline significantly by second year.

The permanent teaching staff is of a reasonably high caliber, especially considering the tender age of the school. There are also a number of adjunct professors. Students appreciate the practical insights of these local practitioners but are less than enthusiastic about their teaching skills. The students have a voice in hiring new faculty members.

The professors make heavy use of the Socratic method. They have office hours and are usually open to class-related conversation.

UPS is a commuter school. Students choose from houses, apartments, and condominiums in Tacoma, south to Olympia, or as far north as Seattle. If you're a social type, you'll be disappointed. Although the Student Bar Association sponsors keggers regularly, and student organizations have occasional get-togethers, most students spend little time at the school aside from attending classes. It can be difficult to get to know fellow students, and you'll be forced to create your own social diversions.

The main UPS administration does exert control over budget and policy decisions at the law school, but it isn't felt as a presence on the law school campus. Although students can drive to the main campus (about three miles from the law center) to use the gyms, fieldhouse, and library, many feel it's not worth the trouble.

Life in the Pacific Northwest is casual and slow-paced. While the Puget Sound area is home to over 1 million people, the rest of Washington is sparsely populated. To the immediate east are the Cascade Mountains, and to the west the Olympic Mountains and rain forest. People here enjoy sailing, skiing, backpacking, and other outdoor activities. (Once classes start, however, there's little time for such things.) It's a great area—but be sure you have the ways and means to escape downtown Tacoma, where the local pulp mills do an odoriferous number on the mountain air.

The students here represent a wide variety of geographic areas, but about 70 percent of them are Washingtonians. There is a sizable Alaskan enrollment. Many of the students have part-time legal jobs, or (in the case of evening students) full-time employment.

The students' academic credentials have risen with each incoming class. The school makes academic scholarships available for top entering and continuing students. The grading system is very stringent. For the lucky few who reach the top after first year, the law review beckons. The moot court program and law review have grown and prospered in the last few years.

The employment picture for UPS grads is improving but has a long way to go. Graduates are welcomed by some of the top firms in the Northwest, but in other areas the school doesn't have much of a name.

No view of UPS would be complete without a glance at the substantial price tag. But the school is moving in an interesting direction, and you just might decide it's worth the cost.

Rutgers University School of Law—Newark

Address: **15 Washington St., Newark, NJ 07102**
Phone: **(201) 648-5557**
Degrees: **J.D., J.D./M.A. (political science or criminal justice), J.D./ Ph.D. (philosophy), J.D./ M.C.R.P. (city and regional planning)**
Median LSAT: **162**
Median GPA: **3.32**
Applicants accepted: **21%**
Transfers: **6/50**

Law enrollment: **820**
Campus enrollment: **9700**
Part time: **30%**
Women: **44%**
Minorities: **35%**
Dorm residents: **14%**
Library: **395,000**
Student-faculty ratio: **23:1**
Tuition: **$6055 (in-state), $9282 (out-of-state)**
Financial aid: **50% (5% gift)**
Apply by: **March 15, March 1 (aid)**

Disabled students: **Fully accessible. In five years, three blind students and one wheelchair user.**
Placement: **81% employed six months after graduation. Graduates took jobs in Middle Atlantic (90%), South Atlantic (4%), Pacific (3%), West South Central (1%), New England (1%), East North**

Central (.5%). Graduates entered private practice (39%), judicial clerkships (26%), business (8%), government (4%), public interest (3%), academic (2%). Salary range: $21,000–$85,000.

For a long time, Rutgers—Newark has had a special admissions program. Originally designed to ensure that at least 25 percent of each class would be minority students, the Minority Student Program has been expanded: up to 30 percent of the class can now be admitted this way, and disadvantaged whites can qualify. However, efforts to create additional special admissions slots for gays and lesbians and disabled candidates have so far not met with success.

Partly because of the MSP, and partly because of the generally enlightened admissions policy, Rutgers can boast of a student body that is diverse in fact and not just in theory. (An exception: 70 to 80 percent claim to be New Jerseyans, but that figure may be exaggerated because of the substantial difference between resident and nonresident tuition.) The median age of the entering day division is close to thirty, making for lots of varied "life experience." Rutgers should be commended for making a particular effort to attract women, especially those entering law from other careers.

Pressure is relatively low, with the exception of the mania of the first year. However, Rutgers students are achievement-oriented, and many work very hard.

The students here have a well-deserved reputation for political activism, but some students nevertheless complain that moderation wins out far too often. A student with an interest in politics and social change will have many intellectual choices at Rutgers. These choices range from researching a topic with a faculty adviser to litigating a case in one of the many legal clinics.

The Student Bar Association has increased its effectiveness as the voice of the student body, particularly on behalf of the evening students. All student organizations receive their funding through SBA budget hearings.

The first-year classes are standard in both subject matter and (as one student put it) "the incredibly tired, counterproductive, and archaic Socratic approach." All other courses are electives, and not all are offered each term. In a recent year, seminars included Affordable Housing, Control of Toxic Chemical Pollution,

Hate and The First Amendment, Unconstitutional Conditions, and Women and the Criminal Law. The upper-division classes are more informal than the first-year ones—there's more lecturing and less Socratic method, and the professors appear to be less upset by the sight of an unprepared student. The problem-solving approach is also widely used, particularly in code courses such as tax.

Rutgers is deservedly noted for its strong in-house clinical programs. Some samples from a recent course offering are clinics in constitutional litigation, animal rights, environmental law, urban legal problems (including landlord-tenant), and women's rights litigation. The Environmental Law Clinic has participated in major litigation against some of New Jersey's largest polluters. Students working in the clinics learn how to file suits and the appropriate papers as the suit progresses. This is an invaluable experience and possibly the only real legal work students get to do in law school. Some students spend several semesters on waiting lists before getting into a clinic. There are also externship programs through which a small number of students get credit for outside placements.

Rutgers has three major law journals, satisfying the diverse legal interests of its students. The law review and the computer and technology journal have a write-on competition to select members. The *Women's Rights Law Reporter* is the alternative law journal at Rutgers. The *WRLR* does not have any competition for membership. In addition to producing their publications, the journals organize special events like the *WRLR*'s symposium on "Ecofeminism: The Woman/Earth Connection."

Students report that the quality of teaching is markedly uneven. Some professors are renowned scholars and excellent teachers; some leave so much to be desired that class attendance is a burden to be avoided at all costs. Practicing attorneys teach many courses as adjunct professors, and the quality of their instruction ranges from very good to awful. The classroom atmosphere is loose; the professors are generally approachable and will answer questions after class.

Although Rutgers people are friendly, open, and relaxed, there is virtually no school social life. This is a commuter school where a large number of students have families and other non–law school responsibilities, so most socializing ends with the day's last class.

The SBA and the Public Interest Legal Foundation (PILF) throw end-of-term parties and occasionally sponsor entertainment programs, but few of the evening activities succeed in attracting much of the student body.

The law school building also houses the School of Criminal Justice and the Center for Dispute Resolution. The large lounge on the main floor is a popular gathering place. The cafeteria and pub are located in a dingy basement but offer a decent menu.

The graduate school, business school, and several other divisions of Rutgers University are located a few blocks from the law school. From time to time, they offer films, lectures, and musical events.

Public transportation to Newark is good, especially from Manhattan. This enables students to live in New York City, as well as the Newark suburbs and the Princeton and New Brunswick areas.

You wouldn't want to live in Newark, but Rutgers is located on one of the nicest streets of the main business district. The school is flanked by the Newark Public Library and the Newark Museum and sculpture garden and is across the street from a pleasant park, all of which offer distractions from the casebooks. The surrounding neighborhood, like business districts of many large cities, empties after six o'clock. Caution is a must.

Rutgers has an excellent reputation among New Jersey firms and government agencies. A few employers west of Philadelphia look here when they want lawyers from the exotic East. A growing number of New York City firms are also interested in Rutgers grads, but pretty much the only route to Wall Street is via law review.

Rutgers can best be described as "a politically progressive mainstream law school." If you can deal with Newark, the school offers a relaxed, collaborative environment for learning the law.

Saint Louis University School of Law

Address: **3700 Lindell Blvd., St. Louis, MO 63108**
Phone: **(314) 658-2800**
Degrees: **J.D., LL.M. (health law or foreign),**

J.D./M.B.A., J.D./M.H.A. (health administration), J.D./M.A. (urban affairs or public administration)
Median LSAT: **156**

Median GPA: **3.2**

Applicants accepted: **approx. 35%**

Transfers: **2–5/10–15**

Law enrollment: **818**

Campus enrollment: **11,703**

Part time: **33%**

Women: **39%**

Minorities: **14%**

Dorm residents: **2%**

Library: **360,000**

Student-faculty ratio: **23:1**

Tuition: **$12,400**

Financial aid: **85% (20% gift)**

Apply by: **March 1 preferred**

Disabled students: **Fully accessible. In a five-year period, two wheelchair users.**

Placement: **92% employed six months after graduation. During the academic year, 10% of first-years, 65% of second-years, and 65% of third-years employed in legal jobs. 20% of first-years, 90% of second-years, and 50% of third-years placed by end of spring term. 60 employers on campus in one year; 95% from Midwest; 85% private firms, 5% government, 5% corporations, 5% public interest. Graduates employed in West North Central (67%), East North Central (10%), South Atlantic (5%), New England (2%), Middle Atlantic (2%), East South Central (2%), West South Central (2%), Mountain (2%). Graduates entered private practice (73%), business (10%), judicial clerkships (10%), government (5%), public interest (2%). Salary range: $22,000–65,000. Median salary: $37,000. Mean salary: $34,000. Missouri bar pass rate: 86% (statewide average: 89%).**

St. Louis University School of Law was founded in 1842 as part of the oldest university west of the Mississippi. For a long time, that was its only claim to fame. Things are looking up, however. The completion of a new library in the early 1970s, a new law building in 1980, and a new addition in 1990 signify the school's high hopes for future development.

The facilities are beautiful—fully carpeted, air-conditioned, and professionally decorated. Lounge areas and classroom space are ample. The library is quiet and well supplied with comfortable spots for studying.

The school's revitalization has not been limited to its physical facilities. The Jurist-in-Residence program has succeeded in attracting increasingly prominent judges to come to the school for a week each spring to rub elbows with students and faculty. The school has a national reputation for its Health Law Studies Center, considered to be one of the most sophisticated of its kind. The Center for Employment Law, established in 1987, also has received kudos. There are criminal and civil clinics, a judicial clerkship program, and a foreign studies program.

The faculty and administration like to think of SLU as a national law school, but native midwesterners predominate. The admissions committee considers the normal criteria—undergraduate GPA and LSAT score—and also seems to give heavy emphasis to work experience, especially where it's law-related, and to writing skill.

The curriculum has a lot of variety and is strong in most areas. One exception: the first-year legal research and writing program is reportedly poorly organized. The joint degrees get reviews based on the quality of the other branch of SLU involved; thus, the business degree is poor, the master's in public administration or urban affairs is fair, and the health administration degree is good.

Of course, the success or failure of the law curriculum turns on the faculty, and some of them should be turned out to pasture. Fortunately, their reputations precede them, and careful advance planning permits you to give them the wide berth they deserve. Several promising new professors have been added recently. In general, a personal meeting with a faculty member is as simple as making an appointment during office hours.

SLU's grading system will take some getting used to if your undergrad school had any grade inflation. Be prepared to work very hard for a C or C+, particularly first year. Some students shop around for courses that will pad their GPAs, but employers are increasingly taking note of gut courses and relying on class rank.

Academic competition runs high. Students consider grades and schoolwork important, and most find that the work load pushes them to their limits. However, one of the best things about the school is the amount of mutual assistance that goes on. Every first-year student is assigned two upperclass student advisers, who inevitably prove to be lifesavers.

The university housing has improved thanks to recent dormitory construction. However, most law students live in off-campus apartments. Accommodations of varying quality and price are available in the immediate vicinity. Since the university is in midtown St. Louis, security and parking are occasionally problems.

The university's recreation center offers an athletic escape from law school life. Thursday nights are sacred for law school pilgrimages to neighborhood bars. On Fridays and Saturdays, you can drive about fifteen minutes to the entertainment district of St. Louis, if you have the money and a car. Although seriously bad-mouthed almost everywhere else, St. Louis actually has its share of restaurants, culture, and hedonistic diversions. In addition, the spectacularly picturesque Ozarks are within easy driving distance.

School extracurriculars include the normal social affairs sponsored by the professional fraternities and the Student Bar Association. The SBA holds a cost-cutting book sale at the beginning of the year and appoints student representatives to several important school committees.

SLU School of Law is not a household word in the legal circles of New York, Washington, or L.A., but it's well regarded in the Midwest. In addition to arranging some on-campus interviews, the placement office gives résumé advice, interviewing tips, and career counseling—but it remains the students' responsibility to conduct their own job search.

SLU uses the same casebooks, teaching methods, and (in most cases) caliber of faculty as many bigger-name schools. The differences: your education will cost you a bit less than at some of those places, and you'll encounter greater recognition problems if you try to move out of the Midwest.

St. Mary's University School of Law

Address: **One Camino Santa Maria, San Antonio, TX 78228**
Phone: **(512) 436-3424**
Degrees: **J.D., J.D./M.B.A., J.D./M.P.A., J.D./M.Econ. (economics)**
Median LSAT: **36**
Median GPA: **3.0**
Applicants accepted: **36%**
Transfers: **2**
Disabled students: **Fully accessible.**

Law enrollment: **722**
Campus enrollment: **2600**
Part time: **0**
Women: **43%**
Minorities: **14%**
Dorm residents: **NA**
Library: **267,600**
Student-faculty ratio: **21:1**
Tuition: **$11,450**
Financial aid: **75%**
Apply by: **March 15**

Placement: **94% of graduates remained in Texas. Graduates entered private practice (65%), judicial clerkships (15%), business (9%),**

government (9%), military (1%), public interest (1%). Salary range: $20,000–$55,000. Texas bar pass rate: 93% (statewide average: 79%).

There are a lot of law schools in Texas, and St. Mary's is one of the easier ones to get into. It's also one of the smaller ones, and one of the more pragmatic in approach.

The admissions committee here uses a rolling admissions policy. As soon as an application is completed, it is reviewed by the admissions committee, and qualified students are accepted according to the number of places available. The moral of the story is: get your application in early.

The median LSAT and GPA for St. Mary's students are less than forbidding. Even if your numbers are low, you stand a chance of being accepted here, thanks to the emphasis the admissions people put on various subjective factors. Among them are indications of leadership, evidence of interest in a law career, an appropriate prelaw curriculum, good recommendations, extracurriculars, work experience, and demonstrated ability to overcome financial, social, and personal problems. Acceptance, however, is no guarantee of academic success. The attrition rate is quite high.

The majority of students are from Texas, although there's a smattering of people from all over the country. The school is small enough so that everyone knows or at least recognizes most of the students before long. It's also small enough to get to know the professors. Although there is a certain amount of competitiveness among the students, many are willing to help each other succeed.

St. Mary's enjoys a reputation as a "lawyer's law school." The focus here is on preparing for practice by offering "core" and "bar" courses, supplemented by electives and clinical programs. The school has definitely broadened its horizons in recent years: upper-level requirements have been reduced, the selection of specialized seminars has expanded, and joint degrees are now offered. Nevertheless, those who crave an innovative, philosophical legal education may find St. Mary's wanting.

Beginning students attend all their classes with a group of about 100 other students. Later, elective courses get as small as 10 students.

Points are taken off your final grade for any absence over the permitted number designated in the catalog. Most teachers require students to present oral summaries of the assigned cases. No matter what the professor's teaching style, students are expected to be prepared every day. If they're not, the professor may deduct points from the final grade.

The law school campus is composed of three attractive buildings constructed in 1968, plus a newer law library.

Aspiring legal scholars have an opportunity to write for the *St. Mary's Law Journal*, which is limited to the top entrants in a writing competition plus those who qualify on the basis of a weighted average of the writing competition and their first-year grades.

Extracurricular activities provide a refreshing break from the coursework. St. Mary's offers students a selection of legal-specialty associations (criminal, family, international, education, etc.), special-interest organizations (for minority, women, and married students), and legal fraternities. The student-managed Board of Advocates holds eight moot court and mock trial competitions throughout the academic year. All students are members of the Student Bar Association, represented by the Student Senate. The Senate is the students' liaison to the administration and selects students to serve as voting members on faculty committees. In addition to community service projects, tutoring, and guest speaker programs, many of these organizations sponsor a variety of social events.

San Antonio is the third-largest city in Texas, but it doesn't have an intimidating big-city feeling about it. Still, there are plenty of big-city attractions, including a mix of cultural and festive events such as Fiesta, a week-long party held each April. For sports fans, there are the San Antonio Spurs and the San Antonio Missions, a minor league baseball team. San Antonio has several military bases, universities, and colleges, which means lots of young people, lectures, and entertainment. St. Mary's Street, named for the university, is lined with clubs and restaurants and offers respite from the rigors of law school.

Students are able to select from a large number of apartments and houses to fit any budget. Most students prefer to live near the sprawling medical center located twenty minutes away in the northwest part of the city.

As you would expect from a large city, San Antonio has a number of law firms, many of which hire law clerks during the school year. The placement office keeps an up-to-date list of the various openings for permanent jobs and coordinates the on-campus interviews each semester. Most firms that interview on campus are based in Texas, but many have offices located in other parts of the country. For students interested in working for the courts, the judicial clerkship committee is instrumental in placing a number of graduates in positions at both the state and federal levels.

Texas employers frequently remark that St. Mary's graduates are better prepared for daily life in the office than are graduates of other Texas law schools. If you seek a legal education oriented toward the practical, St. Mary's can give it to you.

University of San Diego School of Law

Address: **5998 Alcala Park, San Diego, CA 92110**
Phone: **(619) 260-4528**
Degrees: **J.D., LL.M. (tax, general), M.C.L., J.D./M.B.A., J.D./M.I.R. (international relations), J.D./M.I.B. (international business)**
Median LSAT: **161**
Median GPA: **3.27**
Applicants accepted: **30%**
Transfers: **10–20/50–70**

Law enrollment: **1055 (977 J.D.)**
Campus enrollment: **6100**
Part time: **26%**
Women: **42%**
Minorities: **16%**
Dorm residents: **NA**
Library: **304,500**
Student-faculty ratio: **18:1**
Tuition: **$15,500**
Financial aid: **75% (18% gift)**
Apply by: **February 1**

Disabled students: **Moderate/full accessibility. In five years, one blind student, one deaf, four wheelchair users, one with other mobility problems.**

Placement: **More than 90% employed six months after graduation. Approximately 60% of second-years and 60% of third-years placed by the end of spring term. More than 200 employers recruiting on and off campus in one year; 80% from West; 85% law firms, 15% government. Graduates took jobs in Pacific (86%), Mountain (6%), West South Central (3%), East North Central (2%), South Atlantic (2%), New England (1%). Graduates entered private practice (76%), government (14%), business (6%), judicial**

clerkships (2%), public interest (2%), academic (.5%). Salary
range: $40,000–$70,000. Mean salary: approximately $55,000.
California bar pass rate: 76.1% (statewide average: 55%).

USD sits majestically on a hill overlooking San Diego and magnificent Mission Bay. Students here are fond of saying it's the top law
school in town. Seriously, the school enjoys a good reputation in
the area and has advantages beyond the spectacular view.

On the whole, the teaching staff is capable and hardworking.
The school has attracted a few distinguished senior experts, adding
to USD's local and statewide prestige. Most of the professors are
accessible and sympathetic. In fact, many take time to instruct first-
years in exam-taking techniques and to give extra review sessions.

First-year classes are all required and inflict the Socratic method
on their victims. The remaining required courses take up about
half of second year. Electives are varied in subject matter, teaching
approach, and grading method (regular exams, take-homes, or
research papers). Everyone must fulfill a writing requirement—
usually either a paper for a seminar or a law review comment.

Clinics offered in a recent year included immigration, civil,
criminal, mental health, and environmental law. Numerous judicial internships are available in state and federal courts, at both
the trial and appellate levels. Unfortunately, several key courses
(including some required ones) restrict admission by lottery; too
many students want the best professors.

The Center for Public Interest Law is a plus for students interested in consumer rights and administrative law. Students in the
Center monitor administrative agencies, testify at agency meetings,
and write for the quarterly *California Regulatory Law Reporter*.

The law school shares its small campus with the undergraduate
and nursing schools. As all three have expanded in enrollment,
the university has suffered from growing pains. Fortunately, the
law library has recently more than doubled in size.

Student government consists of the Student Bar Association
and class representatives. General awareness of and participation
in their doings are minimal. By contrast, the year-round intramural
sports are a perennial favorite. Other typical campus organizations,
like law review, moot court board, and two legal fraternities, are
here.

On-campus housing is hard to obtain, but there are reasonably priced apartments in nearby communities. There is a wealth of things to see and do in San Diego, including beaches, parks, theater, and trips to Mexico and Las Vegas. San Diego's climate permits scuba diving, sailing, and lying in the sun all year long.

Through its diversity admissions policy, the school seeks out disadvantaged and minority candidates. Most students accepted under the diversity policy are required to attend summer school before their first year, and they receive tutorials and plenty of moral support throughout.

Considering the temptations of sun and surf so close at hand, many USD students are surprisingly ambitious, even continuing law studies through the summers to graduate one semester early. There is a minimum of cutthroat competitiveness, though. Study groups are popular.

USD's placement office is helpful and adequate, but California, and especially San Diego, suffer from a lawyer glut. Still, those who want jobs find them on their own or through personal connections.

One last note: USD is a private Catholic school. This means that, compared to the California state law schools, it is quaint, conservative—and very expensive.

Santa Clara University School of Law

Address: **Santa Clara, CA 95053**
Phone: **(408) 554-4800**
Degrees: **J.D., J.D./M.B.A.**
Median LSAT: **159**
Median GPA: **3.31**
Applicants accepted: **24%**
Transfers: **10–15/50**
Law enrollment: **869**
Campus enrollment: **7800**

Part time: **21%**
Women: **47%**
Minorities: **31%**
Dorm residents: **5%**
Library: **201,000**
Student-faculty ratio: **27:1**
Tuition: **$14,204**
Financial aid: **50% (30% gift)**
Apply by: **March 1**

Disabled students: **Moderate/full accessibility. Within five years, one deaf student, one wheelchair user, three with other mobility problems.**

Placement: **Approximately 84% employed six months after graduation.**

80 employers on campus in one year; 95% from California, 5% Hawaii; 90% private firms, 5% public interest, 5% other. 90% of graduates remained in California; 10% took jobs in Hawaii, Arizona, Oregon, or Nevada. Graduates entered private practice (72%), judicial clerkships (8%), nonlegal jobs (8%), government (5%), business (4%), other (3%). Salary range: $29,700–$75,000. California bar pass rate: 74.3% (statewide average: 55%).

Law school at Santa Clara is a relaxed experience. The atmosphere is friendly rather than competitive, cooperative rather than high-pressured. While most Santa Clara students originally wanted to go elsewhere, almost all are glad they're here.

The student body has relatively high proportions of women, minority students, working night students, and people returning to school to start a second career. Former classics majors sit next to real estate brokers and homemakers entering the job market. Student attitudes are similarly diverse, but you'll find the student body solidly liberal by most standards and middle-of-the-road for California. At one time, the students were drawn almost entirely from California and the West. Now, it is increasingly common to find transplanted New Yorkers and midwesterners.

Law-related student groups abound, and they're very energetic. The feminist and minority groups are well organized and effective. The law review (which chooses its board by a research and writing competition) and moot court are demanding but draw many contenders. Not surprisingly in fitness-conscious California, athletic teams (including men's rugby) are big.

While the law school administration is generally responsive to the voice of student government, some feel that this is not an indication of real student power. In any case, the administrators are very approachable, and they try to meet student demands while attempting to expand and upgrade on a tight budget.

The work load at Santa Clara differs markedly from year to year and from student to student. During first year, the academic burden is heavy indeed, but thereafter the load depends on how much you wish to apply yourself. One constant is that the school requires a handful of bar-related courses in the upper years.

The Socratic method is rarely used even during first year. After that, it's always up to the students to volunteer for answering questions. The seminars encourage lively discussion, while the lecture courses sometimes resemble spoon-feeding.

The faculty is generally young, well trained, and enthusiastic. The school makes an effort to bring in recognized specialists as visiting professors each year. The student-faculty ratio could be better, but the accessibility and concern of the professors more than make up for this. The large class size first year is eased by dividing the students into smaller sections for legal research and writing.

Public-interest law, tax and business law, and especially clinical work are the high points of the faculty and curriculum. Judicial externships with federal and state court judges are encouraged. Credit is also given for work with various local legal agencies. The school runs a nearby legal clinic where students can gain practical experience and up to six credits. Summer programs abroad, each with a different focus, are offered in England, France, Switzerland, Hungary, and the Far East.

Santa Clara's combined J.D./M.B.A. program is pragmatic and job-oriented, and the business school is good. The program offers a specialty in agribusiness, the graduates of which are well recruited. Equally marketable are J.D./M.B.A. grads with a technical background; the Silicon Valley companies are nearby.

The law school started expanding enrollment dramatically in about 1970, and despite renovations, the facilities remain overcrowded.

With the exception of the athletic facilities, few law students take advantage of the nonlaw aspects of the Spanish-style campus. There is little on-campus housing for law students, but reasonably priced rental houses and apartments are readily available within walking distance. The Santa Clara Valley is suburbia par excellence. Some students escape by living in the Santa Cruz Mountains, Palo Alto, San Francisco, or points between. The school is located on the major bus and train routes of the peninsula. A car opens up the varied enticements of San Francisco Bay Area for exploration.

Social life usually takes the form of informal small gatherings, often disguised as study groups. The school, various clubs, and even professors sponsor parties and receptions of differing degrees of decorum.

The placement office is very helpful in locating summer jobs, but the word is that most students find postgraduation employment through their own efforts. Santa Clara has a good reputation in the Bay Area and is known throughout California, Nevada, Hawaii, and Alaska. Since the school expanded only in the early 1970s, its reputation needs time to grow. More and more Santa Clara students are venturing out of state after graduation.

Santa Clara is gradually gaining a geographically broader reputation. Meanwhile, if you're attracted to the sun-ripened California life-style, Santa Clara could be a good choice.

University of South Dakota School of Law

Address: **414 East Clark St., Vermillion, SD 57069**
Phone: **(605) 677-5443**
Degrees: **J.D., J.D./M.B.A. other joint degrees**
Median LSAT: **approx. 34**
Median GPA: **3.3**
Applicants accepted: **27%**
Transfers: **1**
Law enrollment: **224**
Campus enrollment: **7200**
Disabled students: **NA**
Placement: **NA**

Part time: **0**
Women: **34%**
Minorities: **3%**
Dorm residents: **NA**
Library: **142,100**
Student-faculty ratio: **12:1**
Tuition: **$2929 (in-state), $4734 (out-of-state)**
Financial aid: **75% (25% gift)**
Apply by: **March 1**

An obvious reason for attending USD Law School used to be that graduates were automatically admitted to the South Dakota state bar. Well, the "diploma privilege" has been scrapped in favor of a multistate bar exam administered at the end of the second year of school, but you still might find reasons to come here. For instance, tuition is unbelievable cheap.

A good reason for *not* attending USD is Vermillion. Even the most loyal South Dakotan has to admit that this town, which has only slightly more residents than the university has students, leaves much to be desired. Winters are very cold and snowy, and summers are extremely hot. There's good duck and pheasant hunting in the fall, but that can hardly make up for the rest of the year. There are a few places to dance, some fair places to eat, and a couple of movie theaters and bars worth frequenting. For shopping, it's best to head for Sioux City, forty minutes away, or Sioux Falls (the state's largest city, 100,000 people), about an hour away.

No wonder USD law students rely heavily on their own parties. There are also school plays, concerts, movie series, speakers, and athletic events. The university runs a full-fledged intramural sports program, with lots of law students and their spouses participating.

The Dakota Dome, completed in the early 1980s, houses facilities for everything from football to track, including an Olympic-size swimming pool and racquetball courts.

Students can live in graduate dorms or university married-students' housing. The rents are low, but the quarters are neither spacious nor luxurious. The quality of off-campus housing is often poor. Many returning students sign leases for the following fall by April, so an entering student should start the apartment search early. It takes some time and patience, but most people manage to find something within walking or biking distance of the law school. Many students, including off-campus residents, take advantage of the university cafeteria meal plans.

At last count, the curriculum at USD consisted of forty-five required credit hours out of the ninety needed to graduate. With only three semesters of electives, it's next to impossible to focus on an offbeat specialty. First-year courses are tough and require conscientious preparation because the classes are smaller than at many schools. Although attendance policies are strictly enforced, the second and third years feature a lighter work load, and reduced use of the Socratic method in advanced courses makes lack of preparation less traumatic.

Seniors can take advantage of a clinical program. A student can earn credit interning in a law office during the summer or either semester. Clinical jobs are full time and with firms outside of Vermillion.

USD is a small law school, and it offers many small classes. Even in the "large" courses of 65 people, the professors make some effort to get to know the students.

Racial diversity is distressingly low among faculty. Diversity is not big among students either. As a state-sponsored institution, USD naturally attracts primarily in-state residents.

The student mood is relaxed and not particularly competitive.

Morale was boosted by completion of the current law building in 1981.

Both the moot court and client counseling teams have been extremely active and successful. There's also a law review, of course.

The Student Bar Association is active. Its committees sponsor various projects affecting law school life, including the annual Barristers' Ball and the fall and spring barbecues. The SBA also conducts the Dean's Advisory Committee meetings—an open forum where students can voice concerns directly to the dean.

USD is the only law school in the state, so someone looking to work in South Dakota need look no further. The school is strongly slanted toward producing practicing attorneys, although judicial clerkships are an increasingly popular first stop after graduation. According to one correspondent, South Dakota private practitioners are still nonplussed by female candidates for lawyer jobs.

The student who applies to USD should be seeking a small school in a safe, friendly community. He or she should be willing to be known by name among all the professors and administrators, and should not be too interested in an exotic specialty. And it definitely helps to be headed for a South Dakota practice.

University of Southern California Law Center

Address: **University Park, Los Angeles, CA 90089**
Phone: **(213) 740-7331**
Degrees: **J.D., J.D./M.B.A., J.D./M.P.A., J.D./M.A. (international relations, economics, communications, religion), J.D./M.S.W. (social work), J.D./M.B.T. (business tax), J.D./M.R.E.D. (real estate development), J.D./Ph.D. (economics)**
Median LSAT: **165**

Median GPA: **3.4**
Applicants accepted: **20%**
Transfers: **10/150**
Law enrollment: **585**
Campus enrollment: **25,000**
Part time: **0**
Women: **40%**
Minorities: **28%**
Dorm residents: **5%**
Library: **330,000**
Student-faculty ratio: **15:1**
Tuition: **$18,260**
Financial aid: **70% (30% gift)**
Apply by: **February 1**

Disabled students: **Fully accessible. Three deaf students and six with mobility problems in five years.**

Placement: **82% employed six months after graduation. About 250 employers on campus in one year. Graduates took jobs in California (60%), other Pacific (30%), South Atlantic (4%), Mountain (1%), unknown (5%). Graduates entered private practice (60%), judicial clerkships (8%), government (6%), business (4%), public interest (2%). Mean salary: $65,750.**

Not too many years ago, USC Law Center was the scene of the following drama: while stifling in the Los Angeles heat, a group of USC law students wearing T-shirts and cutoffs gazed longingly into a nearby classroom where a noticeably different breed of students, clad in khaki pants, crewneck sweaters, and Topsiders, listened attentively as their instructor berated them on the fine points of promissory estoppel. The instructor was John Houseman, the class was Contracts I, and the students were actors being filmed for the TV series *The Paper Chase.*

Although the film crews are long gone, this incident typifies the USC Law Center. The school has largely succeeded in its struggle to achieve national status like its eastern counterparts, but it still can't quite shake its southern California ambience. An inordinate number of students plan to go into entertainment law, and on sunny days there are apt to be as many students outside the Law Center working on a tan as inside the library working on torts.

Although the Law Center will probably never be the Harvard of the West, it provides an excellent legal education, especially for those students who want to remain in southern California. USC has loyal contacts for employment. The good old boys who make up the Law Center alumni rank prominently in LA's most important firms and courtrooms. Out-of-state firms do recruit, but many of them believe that no one bright enough to be hired would leave all this sunshine for the slush-filled streets of New York or Washington. Nevertheless, a fair number of students each year accept jobs throughout the rest of the country.

Most of the students here were born and reared in California, but there are substantial numbers of easterners and midwesterners attracted to the obvious advantages of a stint in the Golden State.

In fact, the administration actively recruits out-of-state students and just being from someplace out of the area seems to tip the scales in favor of a borderline applicant. Politically, the students span the entire spectrum, although the presence each year of a number of vocal free-market types lends a definite conservative tone to some class discussions.

The faculty is one of the Law Center's biggest assets. Its members are typically young and energetic, ideologically diverse, and generally regarded as the rising stars in legal education. They are so well regarded, in fact, that the Law Center has problems holding on to them, and several have been wooed away by more prestigious schools.

The Law Center is on the beautiful USC campus, which is located in one of the most undesirable portions of Los Angeles. Because of this geographical fact, most students live away from campus and commute, despite the price of gas and the abundance of freeway traffic. USC does provide some graduate dorm rooms, as well as a nearby apartment building reserved especially for law students.

Maybe it's just the sunshine that brings out the smiles, but the students at least look as if they enjoy attending the Law Center. The school is smaller than many others. The administration maintains friendly relations with its charges and lacks the aloofness found in most academic settings.

Classes are difficult and demanding, and most of the students work hard at staying prepared. The level of preparedness, however, correlates inversely with the number of years that the student has been in law school.

The Law Center offers a thorough clinical and judicial externship program, which many students rank among their best experiences here. Law review is a big deal, and most of the review members think it's worth it. There is also an honorary moot court program for second-year students, which attracts enthusiastic participation.

Even if you're not interested in getting a tan, the level of education here is first-rate, the students bright and enthusiastic, and the job opportunities promising. If you have to attend law school, USC is one of the more pleasant places to do it.

Southwestern University School of Law

Address: **675 South Westmoreland Ave., Los Angeles, CA 90005**
Phone: **(213) 738-6717**
Degrees: **J.D.**
Median LSAT: **34**
Median GPA: **3.21 (full time), 3.18 (part time)**
Applicants accepted: **35%**
Transfers: **2**
Law enrollment: **1156**

Campus enrollment: **1156**
Part time: **32%**
Women: **47%**
Minorities: **19%**
Dorm residents: **0**
Library: **312,000**
Student-faculty ratio: **26:1**
Tuition: **$13,660**
Financial aid: **83% (31% gift)**
Apply by: **June 30, June 1 (aid)**

Disabled students: **Fully accessible. Approximately five to ten disabled students in one year.**

Placement: **Approximately 50% placed by graduation; approximately 92% employed six to nine months after graduation. Graduates took jobs in Pacific (83%), Mountain (4%), Middle Atlantic (3%), South Atlantic (3%), East North Central (2%), New England (1%), West North Central (1%), East South Central (1%), West South Central (1%), Foreign (1%). Graduates entered private practice (70%), government (13%), business (11%), judicial clerkships (3%), academic (2%), public interest (1%). Average salary: $50,000.**

Law school can be boring, demoralizing, and hazardous to your health. One way to avoid the worst symptoms of law studentitis is to get yourself into a relaxed law school. The next best thing is to find a law school whose surroundings are conducive to letting off steam. Southwestern falls into the second category.

Southwestern is located right off Wilshire Boulevard, in the heart of fast-paced Los Angeles, a city that provides innumerable diversions from legal tunnel vision. Forty minutes away is the Santa Monica beach, where you can boat, surf, and fish. The Los Angeles County Art Museum is only fifteen minutes away, and the open-air rock and classical concerts at the Hollywood Bowl and Greek Theater are also close. The Hollywood Hills and nearby Sierra Nevadas provide ready escapes from the law school trauma.

One of Los Angeles's greatest cultural assets is the diversity of its population. Little Tokyo, Chinatown, and the Mexican mood of Olvera Street are all within an easy fifteen-minute trip by bus or car. There are Armenian, Jewish, Chinese, Japanese, Mexican, and Thai restaurants within walking distance.

Southwestern's student body mirrors the diversity that characterizes L.A. A significant minority are from out of state. This is one of the ten or so largest ABA-accredited schools in the country. No matter what your background or interests, student organizations exist to help you find your niche.

Thanks to its size, Southwestern can offer more programs than a small school. For instance, you can get your J.D. here in one of four ways. The full-time day program, which enrolls a majority of the students, follows the traditional legal education model. There's an evening program that lets students who need to work full time take four years to finish law school. A part-time day program schedules all classes between 10 A.M. and 2 P.M.

But what really sets Southwestern apart is the SCALE program. The initials stand for Southwestern's Conceptual Approach to Legal Education, one of the only two-year J.D. programs in the country. If you're in a hurry to get law school over with, SCALE enables you to buzz in and out in two full calendar years. But before you decide that SCALE is for you, remember that you'll have absolutely no time for part-time or summer employment.

The SCALE program is a departure from the traditional law school approach in that it's not organized by subject (e.g., torts, contracts, criminal law) but rather by concept (e.g., negligence, strict liability, intent). SCALE features an interdisciplinary study of how legal concepts apply to problems in the real world.

Professors at Southwestern have extensive backgrounds in the subjects they teach and are very willing to help students. Some came to Southwestern with decades upon decades of practical legal knowledge and share their wisdom with students who can benefit from their firsthand insights.

Established in 1911, Southwestern has had a significant impact on the Los Angeles legal community. Many members of the local bar—including some California luminaries—got their degrees here. Alumni of the school like to hire other alumni, so Southwestern can offer terrific access to employment opportunities after graduation.

Recognizing that a large number of its students plan to practice in the area, the school rounds out its list of electives with such L.A. specialties as entertainment, natural resources, and sports law.

The advantages of the alumni network pay off even for currently enrolled students. Thanks to cooperation from the local bar, opportunities for externships are numerous. Summer externships for credit with a judge, district attorney's office, or other placements are popular.

Southwestern isn't a mellow place. A mandatory first-year grading curve ensures that some students will flunk out. The SCALE program is particularly intense. Still, this isn't necessarily bad. "Times are tough and jobs are scarce," one student points out. "The many skills you will learn in the unique environment that is Southwestern will prepare you for the real world. 'Struggle to survive' and 'grit your teeth and bear it' are two of those skills, and you will be a better person for them."

Stanford Law School

Address: **Stanford, CA 94305**
Phone: **(415) 723-4985**
Degrees: **J.D., J.S.D., J.S.M. (jurisprudence), M.L.S. (legal studies), J.D./M.B.A., J.D./M.P.A., J.D./M.A. (economics, history, political science, international studies), other joint degrees**
Median LSAT: **44**
Median GPA: **3.64**
Applicants accepted: **8%**

Transfers: **9**
Law enrollment: **568 (536 J.D.)**
Campus enrollment: **13,000**
Part time: **0**
Women: **44%**
Minorities: **39%**
Dorm residents: **NA**
Library: **395,000**
Student-faculty ratio: **16:1**
Tuition: **$16,722**
Financial aid: **70%**
Apply by: **March 1**

Disabled students: **Fully accessible. Twelve disabled students in one year.**

Placement: **Approximately 88% employed six to nine months after graduation. More than 350 employers on campus in one year. Graduates took jobs in Pacific (58%), Middle Atlantic (13%), South Atlantic (13%), East North Central (6%), New England**

(3%), West North Central (2%), Mountain (2%), West South
Central (2%), Foreign (1%). Graduates entered private practice
(56%), judicial clerkships (19%), government (6%), business (2%),
public interest (2%), unknown (15%).

Any ranking of law schools is to some extent in the eye of the
beholder. Yet regardless of who's doing the computing, the excellence of Stanford's physical facilities, faculty, and student body
ensures that Stanford Law will receive a very high rating.

Just where Stanford falls among the so-called top five is a trivial
issue compared with the unique academic environment that prevails here. We all know that, generically speaking, law school is a
compulsive-neurotic experience. The better qualified the students,
the more the school resembles a Hobbesian war of all against all.
Stanford has altered this essentially East Coast phenomenon to fit
the socially and climatically temperate zone of the San Francisco
Bay Area.

Stanford attracts students who work hard (sometimes very hard,
as a library tour will attest), but who take time off to enjoy the
recreational opportunities the area offers. The faculty's intellectual
powers are used as pedagogic assets, not as weapons to reduce the
student body to a mass of quivering gray matter. Competition for
its own sake, public ridicule in the service of inflated egos—though
no law school can claim the total absence of these irritants—are
kept at a bare minimum.

Never underestimate the influence of day after day of warm
sunshine. Stanford students must endure a brief winter rainy season, but even then the daytime temperature normally remains
above fifty. Nestled between the San Francisco Bay and the Santa
Cruz Mountains, the Stanford area is suburban California at its
hilly, palm-shaded best. Although jogging, tennis, and "catching
rays" are major pastimes, those who thrill at skimming descents
down powder slopes should not despair; Lake Tahoe is within a
few hours of scenic driving.

The nearest community, Palo Alto, is primarily residential with
little in the way of college-town character. Consequently, daily student activities are centered at Stanford, especially for students living on campus and lacking personal transportation into town. (San
Francisco is readily accessible by train or bus, however.)

Completed in 1975, the school's facilities are a modern triumph—at once beautiful, comfortable, and functional.

Many law students living on campus are housed in Crothers Hall, a law dorm that's a two-minute walk from classes and is "great for socializing." Others prefer to live in the newly constructed Rains Apartment Complex, which provides more privacy than the dorm environment. Off-campus living is also popular. With a little work, suitable rentals can be found within bicycling distance of school. However, houses and apartments are both expensive and in short supply.

Stanford is delightfully small, leading easterners to compare it to Yale more often than to Harvard. The first-year class is divided into groups of about 30. Although not a panacea for the pressure that plagues professional schools, this system ensures at least some opportunity for personal relationships.

The variety in the student body ensures that southern charm and eastern chutzpah add spice to the pervasive (and sometimes soporific) mellowness of California life. Student tastes vary as much as backgrounds, so be prepared for discussions of Johnny Cash as well as John Coltrane, and the stock market as well as the short story.

The students are friendly, approachable, and eager to offer help and advice. No social barriers exist among students in the three classes, and everyone seems to have ample time to participate in social events like dinners, dances, card games, and good-natured athletic meets.

For the athletically inclined, Stanford offers the opportunity for year-round participation in outdoor sports (including three outdoor pools), as well as the myriad indoor sporting facilities common to large modern campuses. Especially important to the budding lawyer is Stanford's nationally rated golf course, where you can hone the skills most necessary to a successful professional life. For the spectator, Stanford has nationally ranked baseball, basketball, swimming, and volleyball teams.

Stanford also offers other forms of diversion. The university boasts three art galleries and frequent drama productions, and several campus organizations present regular film series. Additionally, theater, opera, and ballet are available in San Francisco and on the Peninsula.

For the organization person, the law school offers more possibilities than can be mentioned here. Participation in any of the many scholarly publications refines writing skills and provides an opportunity to see one's work in print. Black students, Latinos, Native Americans, women, and gays and lesbians have their own organizations, which have been instrumental in raising community awareness and promoting recruitment of women and minority students. A number of groups provide hands-on legal experience while supplying valuable services to the community.

Second-semester students have some elective options, and the curriculum is entirely elective after the first year. Relative to the law school enrollment, there is an exceptionally wide variety of courses to choose from. The school has a number of clinical courses that demand considerable time from students but are much sought after for the opportunity to work with outstanding faculty members. The school has also instituted a business curriculum, as well as a law and social change course sequence. If the curriculum has any weakness, it is that the small student body dictates that more exotic courses be offered only every other semester or year.

To expand your horizons, you can earn eleven credit hours from courses outside the law school. If you want to escape the law school for an entire term, various externships are available in Washington, DC, Switzerland, England, or wherever else you can arrange a position.

Teaching styles are as many and varied as the courses. The traditional Socratic method has largely been supplanted by lectures and clinical instruction. Regardless of teaching style, most professors maintain an open-door policy and encourage students to drop in to discuss anything from federal jurisdiction to the correct form for a jump shot. They make an effort to attend social functions, and in the case of some young instructors, even initiate them.

Despite the lawyer glut, the employment outlook for Stanford Law graduates is bright. One student writes that there are ten job offers for every candidate; whether or not that is hyperbole, you get the idea. Stanford is widely viewed as number one in California and is respected in urban centers everywhere. Among the on-campus recruiters are many midsize and small western firms. Firms from cities outside the area also make their annual pilgrimages to Stanford, but they tend to be larger and more selective.

Although the placement office is primarily geared to arranging careers with private corporate law firms (the emphasis is partly due to the fact that public-interest employers on tight budgets can't handle yearly interviewing trips, and partly due to the desires of the student body), its staff works hard to provide information about career alternatives. In recent years, Stanford has averaged two or three U.S. Supreme Court clerks annually, as well as scores of clerks in the prestigious federal courts of appeals.

The students who get into Stanford Law are very, very smart. So are the students at many other schools. What sets Stanford students apart is that they accept the futility of outright competition in such a uniformly capable group. They keep studying but stop worrying. What's the use of fretting about grades when you're virtually guaranteed a great job—and when there are so many better ways to spend a sunny day?

Suffolk University Law School

Address: **41 Temple St.,
  Boston, MA 02114**
Phone: **(617) 573-8144**
Degrees: **J.D., J.D./M.B.A.,
  J.D./M.P.A.**
Median LSAT: **158**
Median GPA: **3.3**
Applicants accepted: **25%**
Transfers: **2–10/75–100**
Law enrollment: **1710**

Campus enrollment: **5000**
Part time: **40%**
Women: **52%**
Minorities: **11%**
Dorm residents: **NA**
Library: **300,000**
Student-faculty ratio: **26:1**
Tuition: **$13,190**
Financial aid: **80% (20% gift)**
Apply by: **March 1**

Disabled students: **Moderate/full accessibility. In five years, two
  blind students, one deaf, two wheelchair users, five with other
  mobility problems.**
Placement: **84% employed six months after graduation.
  Approximately 30% of first-years, 60% of second-years, and 90%
  of third-years employed in legal jobs during the academic year.
  40% of first-years and 70% of second-years placed by end of
  spring term. 100 employers on campus in one year; 60% from
  New England; 58% private firms, 7% corporations, 25%**

government or public interest. **Graduates took jobs in New England (75%), Middle Atlantic (10%), South Atlantic (8%), Pacific (8%), Mountain (1%), Foreign (1%). Graduates entered private practice (48%), business (19%), government (17%), judicial clerkships (10%), academic (2%), public interest (1%), unknown (3%). Salary range: $25,000–$85,000. Mean salary: $40,000. Massachusetts bar pass rate: 85% (statewide average: 78%).**

When you think of going to law school in Boston, you probably think of Harvard. That's not your only choice.

Founded as a law school in 1906 (by Gleason Archer, who reputedly gave law lectures in his bedroom), Suffolk University continues to be primarily concerned with legal education. The law school is housed in a fairly new building on Beacon Hill, behind the State Capitol.

Suffolk is located in the heart of one of the largest legal centers in America. Six law schools are located in the Boston area (including the one in Cambridge), which is both a blessing and a curse. The number of law students increases the fierce competition for jobs, especially with large firms, but it creates an atmosphere conducive to the study of law.

If you asked most entering students why they came to Suffolk, they would tell you it was because they didn't get into their first choice. However, ask returning students why they came back, and they'll say that Suffolk offers a practical introduction to law, both in its course offerings and in its emphasis on providing work experience.

Suffolk students spend two years, not one, in required courses designed to give them a sound, functional background. In the third year, the school offers a good diversity of electives. More than three quarters of the students participate in one or more of the clinical programs, which work with state government and nonprofit agencies to provide criminal and civil representation for the needy.

The faculty is highly rated and includes some who made big names elsewhere. All of the faculty have practiced law (some continue to do so), and they use this background to expose students to real-life problems and issues. The large adjunct faculty is uneven in quality, boasting some eminent lawyers, legislators, and judges who can teach effectively and others noted only for their easy standards.

Competition is rare at Suffolk. With a Supreme Court clerkship unlikely to be awaiting any graduate, the law students tend to be friendly and concerned about one another. Class sections socialize frequently, in and out of school, in bars and on playing fields.

The day sections include many graduates of Massachusetts and Rhode Island colleges who plan to work in Boston or its environs. The evening sections are mostly older married people who hold full-time jobs. Overall, the students are middle class and less diverse than at some other urban law schools, although there are several organizations that recruit and represent black, Asian, and Hispanic students. There has been some visible effort by the administration to attract minority students and faculty members.

The administration is often responsive to student views. It allows members of the Student Bar Association to sit in on the faculty meetings, and sometimes makes changes in curriculum and class scheduling to accommodate student preferences.

Boston is a town for students—thousands of them. There are plenty of apartments, but most are not cheap. It is a good idea to find a roommate. The best times to look for apartments in Boston are August and January. Living outside the city limits can be far less expensive, and most areas are served by bus, train, or trolley.

The law library is the focal point of law school social and scholastic life. Because of Suffolk's location, lawyers frequently use the library to supplement the materials in nearby state and federal libraries. Both the collection and the facilities are very good.

The placement office is striving to expand its services. Unfortunately, Suffolk students face a market already overcrowded with other qualified lawyers. In general, large, well-established firms are not interested in Suffolk grads. Second-year summer jobs are easier to find in Boston than permanent positions.

The tuition at Suffolk is low for a Boston-area law school. The annual cost of the evening section is even lower, and the class schedule allows students to hold down full-time jobs, making it an excellent choice for those with few financial resources and a lot of drive.

Syracuse University College of Law

Address: **Syracuse, NY 13244**
Phone: **(315) 443-1962**
Degrees: **J.D., LL.M. (tax), J.D./M.B.A., J.D./M.P.A., other joint degrees**
Median LSAT: **155**
Median GPA: **3.2**
Applicants accepted: **30%**
Transfers: **4/22**
Law enrollment: **816 (811 J.D.)**

Campus enrollment: **approx. 15,000**
Part time: **2%**
Women: **41%**
Minorities: **28%**
Dorm residents: **NA**
Library: **318,800**
Student-faculty ratio: **19:1**
Tuition: **$16,304**
Financial aid: **70% (46% gift)**
Apply by: **April 1**

Disabled students: **Moderate/full accessibility. One blind student in one year.**

Placement: **48% placed by graduation; 93% employed six months after graduation. 75 employers on campus in one year; 56% from New York, 22% Washington, DC, 5% New Hampshire, 4% Connecticut, 3% New Jersey, 3% Ohio, 3% Pennsylvania, 2% California, 1% Wisconsin, 1% Maryland; 67% private firms, 25% government, 7% public interest, 1% business. Graduates took jobs in New York City (21%), other New York State (38%), other Middle Atlantic (10%), Washington, DC (11%), New England (6%), Sunbelt (4%), other (11%). Graduates entered private practice (63%), government (12%), judicial clerkships (9%), business (5%), academic (5%), military (3%), public interest, (2%). Salary range: approximately $20,000–$80,000. Median salary: $40,000. Mean salary: $34,912.**

Life at SU Law is a mixture of advantages and disadvantages. First, the bad news. At various times, students have complained that the administration is unresponsive; that the financial aid office isn't as helpful as it should be; that the placement office is struggling to overcome a history of having a marginal existence at best; and that finding safe parking near the law library at night is next to impossible.

On the good side, the faculty is well above average in teaching ability and other desirable traits. The professors are intelligent, well informed—and more politically liberal than the student body.

deliberate deemphasis of grades. First-term courses are graded pass/
fail, easing dramatically what is at other law schools a time of
terror. After first term, students receive grades of Honors, Pass,
Low Pass, and Fail. But this increases pressure only slightly. Everyone gets at least a Pass (the dean has been known to tell his torts
class that no one is allowed to fail); getting Honors isn't terribly
important unless you want to clerk for the Supreme Court; and
there is no such thing as class rank.

Moreover, unlike almost all the other law reviews, the *Yale Law
Journal* does not select its members on the basis of grade performance. The selection process varies from year to year, but generally includes a writing sample and proof of editing skills. Students
can also join the *Journal* by completing a publishable "note," a
heavily researched piece of legal scholarship. Writing a note is a
grueling process, usually consuming lots of time and effort and
involving much haggling with student editors. Those who go
through with it gain prestige, a published work, and a great experience in legal writing and editing. The school's many specialized
journals—covering topics like feminism, international law, law and
the humanities, regulation, and public policy—are also popular.

Finally, there's the job security conferred by a Yale Law School
diploma. To put it bluntly, nearly every Yale student can have
whatever kind of job he or she wants after graduation. Top grades
or participation on the law review are just not necessary. In part,
this is because Yale's low-key grading system and voluntary law
journal don't tell much about student performance. Mostly it's
due to the traditional magic of the Yale name, the proliferation
of Yalies in influential places, and recognition of Yale's selectivity.
Only Harvard can rival Yale's nationwide clout among legal employers—and there are only a third as many students at Yale as
Harvard, making Yalies that much more sought after.

The Yale myth holds that the school is a breeding ground for
academics, judges, government administrators, and public-interest
attorneys, and Yalies continue to be heavily represented in these
fields. An extraordinary number land judicial clerkships. But most
Yale graduates end up on the more traditional and high-paying
path to the big-city corporate law firms, primarily in New York,
Washington, and Los Angeles. Public-interest-oriented students
have banded together and have succeeded in gaining increased

attention from the placement office; they have also organized a nonprofit foundation for funding postgraduate public-interest projects and a fund that awards grants to students taking public-interest jobs in the summer. The school offers loan repayment assistance for graduates in low-paying careers.

Yale is one of the most selective law schools in the country. A rising tide of applications threatens to swamp the admissions office, due in part to several national surveys (of questionable scientific validity) that have deemed Yale to be "number one" in legal education. The medians here are very, very high; but Yale seems to look behind applicants' statistics for nonnumerical evidence of creativity and drive.

The students are an interesting group, with a variety of backgrounds and interests. Once at Yale, their high energy level is evident in rapid-fire intellectual debates that take place almost constantly in class and out, as well as the willingness of small groups of students to form new extracurricular organizations (or transform the old ones) to reflect their wide-ranging interests. Intimidation is far more likely to arise from listening to the other students talk than from worrying about meeting the professors' expectations.

The main reason that almost half of those accepted by Yale choose not to attend is New Haven. New Haven is definitely not Cambridge or Palo Alto or Chicago. Then again, it's not Bridgeport, Connecticut, either. Shopping and eating in New Haven are good and improving, there are lots of movies around, and theater is excellent, featuring two of the country's finest repertory theaters. Street crime is a major problem, although the security-minded administration provides free round-the-clock transit to students. Because of New Haven's size, interesting part-time jobs or volunteer positions are harder to find than in some larger cities.

Yale University is a cultural mecca. Campus life is clearly centered on the 5,000 Yale undergraduates. With some effort, law students who so choose can involve themselves in university politics, athletics, theater, singing groups, and other cultural and social activities. There are always the law school's own dances, a capella singing group, basketball league, and satirical end-of-year "law revue."

The law school building, an impressive Gothic structure, is near the center of the Yale campus. It provides housing which is roomy and has Old World charm. But living in the dorm can get claustrophobic, and after first year most students live off campus. The library is terrific. In 1992, the administration announced an ambitious plan to renovate the facilities, no doubt a lengthy process.

In recent years, Yale has been thrust into the limelight to an unprecedented degree. Virtually the only thing that Bill and Hillary Clinton, Jerry Brown, Paul Tsongas, Pat Robertson, Clarence Thomas, and Anita Hill all have in common is that they were Yale Law graduates—a fact not lost on the national press. Amid the routine of daily classes, the air at Yale is filled with excitement and a sense of the school's role in shaping—and training its students to shape—American law and public policy. Perhaps the greatest dangers the institution now faces are arrogance and complacency.

Yet, as law schools go, Yale is as friendly, free, thoughtful, and provocative a place as you can find. And maybe that *is* a kind of Wonderland.

PLUME

GET YOURSELF ORGANIZED

☐ **NOT FOR PACKRATS ONLY** *How to Clean Up, Clean Out, and De-Junk Your Life Forever!* **by Don Aslett.** America's top cleaning expert has developed a sure-fire clutter clean up program that will rid you of your piles of junk stashed in your offices, garages, and homes. (265932—$10.00)

☐ **FINDING THE HAT THAT FITS by John Caple.** This upbeat, inspiring guide helps you achieve a meaningful, valuable, rewarding life by going beyond conventional career and employment counseling and bringing you close to ideas that can make a difference in your life. Whether you are starting out . . . starting over . . . or ready to move on . . . it's time to pursue your passions, to live your dreams, this is the book for you. (269962—$11.00)

☐ **GOING THE DISTANCE** *Finding and Keeping Lifelong Love* **by Lonnie Barbach and David L. Geisinger.** Filled with inspiring case histories and practical advice, this essential guide shows you how to leave behind old habits and defenses that make you unhappy in the past, and provides a blueprint for the kind of long-term monogamy that promotes growth and nourishes the best in each of us. (269482—$10.00)

Prices slightly higher in Canada.

Most of them are experienced teachers but still young, and they are easy to communicate with about legal and nonlegal problems. More than one student has found the faculty to be the school's saving grace.

For those interested in international law, the international legal studies program includes an appellate argument team, the *Journal of International Law and Commerce,* and a limited summer study program in London. An International Legal Studies Certificate can be earned by completing a special sequence of international law classes in the second and third years.

Syracuse also boasts a superb moot court program, with both intra- and intermural competition. Together with the international law team, specialized teams for interscholastic contests include the trial advocacy and tax teams.

The law review's annual issues include the unique *Survey of New York Law,* which summarizes the year's developments in state law. The course offerings, however, do not unduly emphasize the law of New York. Most courses take a federal law perspective, which doesn't appear to disadvantage those who remain in New York to practice. Students at SU are primarily from the New York/New Jersey area; however, in recent years the school has made an effort to diversify.

First-year courses are all required. In addition to the usual subjects, all new students take a year-long Law Firm class, which teaches basic lawyering skills in a mock law firm setting. Syracuse's emphasis on real-world skills carries over into its strong clinical program. Students may select from among four in-house clinics: criminal, civil, housing and finance, and public interest. Externships with judges and governmental law offices are also available.

The Legislative Research Bureau lets students undertake research projects referred by public and political bodies on both the federal and state levels.

The city of Syracuse is an acceptable place to live while attending law school. To those from large cities, Syracuse may seem small-townish, but it has something to offer to anyone with the time and desire to pursue cultural activities.

The worst part of Syracuse is the weather. The winters are extremely long and brutally cold. If you can put up with the ice and snow from November to April, you may find that SU's pros outweigh its cons.

Temple University School of Law

Address: **1719 N. Broad St., Philadelphia, PA 19122**
Phone: **(215) 787-8925**
Degrees: **J.D., LL.M. (law and humanities, clinical legal education, tax, or comparative law), J.D./M.B.A.**
Median LSAT: **35 (full time), 34 (part time)**
Median GPA: **3.32 (full time), 3.23 (part time)**
Applicants accepted: **27%**
Transfers: **3**

Law enrollment: **1361 (1286 J.D.)**
Campus enrollment: **approx. 15,000**
Part time: **29%**
Women: **45%**
Minorities: **16%**
Dorm residents: **NA**
Library: **413,400**
Student-faculty ratio: **25:1**
Tuition: **$6626 (in-state), $12,118 (out-of-state)**
Financial aid: **70%**
Apply by: **March 1**

Disabled students: **Fully accessible. Twenty-two disabled students in one year.**

Placement: **95% employed six months after graduation. More than 150 employers on campus in one year. Graduates took jobs in Middle Atlantic (80.5%), South Atlantic (9%), Pacific (5%), New England (2%), East North Central (2%), Foreign (1%), West North Central (.5%), East South Central (.5%), West South Central (.5%). Graduates entered private practice (50%), judicial clerkships (14%), government (13%), nonlegal jobs (8%), public interest (6%), business (4%), academic (4%), military (1%). Salary range: $18,500–$82,000. Average salary: $41,605.**

There are lots of urban law schools with day and evening classes, a commuter ambience, and a mainly local reputation. Temple is a fairly good one. Also, Temple does not make second-class citizens of its evening students: the same admissions standards and curriculum offerings apply, and the same full-time faculty teach in both the day and evening divisions.

Thanks to a generally enlightened admissions policy, students with a stimulating variety of backgrounds come to Temple. Grades and LSATs aren't all that count; work experience—not necessarily law-related—carries weight, too, and a substantial number of the students have taken time off after college. There's an extensive special admissions program for students (of all races) who have high academic achievements but low board scores.

Although it's affiliated with the state, Temple doesn't give admissions preference to Pennsylvania residents. Still, many students are from the area, if only because it's so convenient to get to Temple—by subway, bus, trolley, commuter line, or car—from most parts of Philadelphia and its suburbs.

Temple's location may be convenient, but it's far from picturesque. The law school borders the main campus of the undergraduate school, in gritty North Philadelphia. There are some areas of the campus that are actually quite lovely—in the spring anyway—but they can't make up for the neighborhood. When you wander around after dark, you feel you're taking your life in your hands. No wonder most students prefer to live elsewhere. Nevertheless, the law school makes the best of the urban location; upwards of two thousand cases a year from the immediate community are handled by the Temple Legal Aid Office.

Housing is not too hard to come by, and it's quite inexpensive in the Germantown and West Philadelphia areas. Center City is more expensive, but certainly nothing comparable to Washington, Boston, or New York.

Temple's functional eight-story building offers lots of study space—carrels for solitary types, tables for the more social, and a smoking section. One correspondent describes the library as "well-stacked." The excellent book collection includes numerous copies of the most frequently used volumes, and the library staff is reported to be cooperative and well informed.

One of Temple's greatest strengths is its faculty. As at most law schools, the professors have impressive credentials, but here they're especially willing to discuss both academic and personal issues with students.

The law school has a fairly well-balanced curriculum. The first-year class is divided into sections of about 35 students each. Most of the first-year courses (all of which are assigned) combine two sections. Some, like legal writing, have fewer students; others have more.

Upper-level students choose all their courses from a wide variety of electives. Public-interest courses are numerous. The consensus is that, unlike situations at most law schools, the work load remains fairly even in the upper years.

Teaching is generally Socratic, but whereas some professors tend toward the theoretical (which should appeal to those inclined to follow an academic career), others have a refreshingly practical approach (for those interested in the day-to-day practice of law).

Temple can boast of a fine clinical program in both civil and criminal law. Students can spend a semester with the Philadelphia district attorney, the public defender, the U.S. attorney, small claims mediation, housing court, legal aid, or Community Legal Services. Temple students may also take year-long judicial clerkships.

The undergraduate school offers little social activity for law students. For those who like sports, Temple has an excellent basketball team, and lately the football team is improving. The university drama department is outstanding and produces shows regularly.

Philadelphia itself offers a panoply of sights and events, including theaters, sports contests, and terrific restaurants and bars. Not all the activities are expensive. The art museum is a delightful place to spend an afternoon. Gallery seats are available for reasonable prices at the Academy of Music. Many of the historical sites charge no admission at all. W. C. Fields's jibes notwithstanding, Philly is a livable place.

Should one become sated with the delights of Philadelphia, Temple Law has innovative summer sessions in Italy, Greece, and Israel.

The Student Bar Association is unusually active not only in the governance of the school but in planning for the students' social needs. Although students go their own ways at the end of most days, happy hours and wine and cheese parties are regularly scheduled and well attended. Indeed, some first-year students use the wine and cheese gatherings to reduce their grocery bills substantially.

Despite the school's size, the mood is warm. Most students are friendly and there is very little backstabbing. The fact that students live all over the city tends to create small, close-knit study groups rather than universal camaraderie.

Except for occasional student discontent with specific administrative actions, student-administration relations are basically good and reportedly have been getting even better in recent years.

Temple is not exempt from the first-year panic and the third-year boredom that are the source of jokes at all law schools. It also has its share of less than satisfactory courses. Finally, it suffers all the special problems of a commuter school. But Temple seems to make a good-faith effort to counter its problems or to use them to advantage, and you can get a good education here.

University of Tennessee College of Law

Address: **1505 W.
Cumberland Ave.,
Knoxville, TN 37996**
Phone: **(615) 974-4131**
Degrees: **J.D., J.D./M.B.A.,
J.D./M.P.A.**
Median LSAT: **36**
Median GPA: **3.39**
Applicants accepted: **26%**
Transfers: **NA**
Law enrollment: **463**

Campus enrollment: **24,000**
Part time: **0**
Women: **40%**
Minorities: **9%**
Dorm residents: **NA**
Library: **325,800**
Student-faculty ratio: **17:1**
Tuition: **$2450 (in-state),
$6040 (out-of-state)**
Financial aid: **NA**
Apply by: **February 1**

Disabled students: **Moderate/full accessibility.**
Placement: **Approximately 72% placed by graduation; approximately 96% employed six to nine months after graduation. Graduates took jobs in East South Central (73%), South Atlantic (16%), West South Central (6%), Middle Atlantic (2%), West North Central (2%), Mountain (1%), New England (1%). Graduates entered private practice (64%), government (17%), judicial clerkships (7%), business (6%), military (3%), public interest (2%), academic (2%). Salary range: $18,500-$97,500.**

Most state law schools are designed to produce competent members of the state bar. University of Tennessee College of Law (known as GCT because it's located in the George C. Taylor Law Center) is no exception. About four fifths of the students here are Tennessee residents; most of them plan to enter Tennessee practices; and the majority of the recruiters are Tennessee firms.

Still, the law students benefit from the efforts of a hardworking placement office staff, and every year some of them end up in law firms, governmental agencies, and corporations throughout the country. In addition to on-campus interviewing, students can attend the Southeastern Placement Consortium in Atlanta to interview with national law firms.

Most of the faculty members are good instructors, and a few are well known in their fields. A great deal of faculty time is spent preparing work for publication, which results in frequent job opportunities for student researchers. The faculty generally emphasizes Tennessee law. The result: GCT students often have a higher pass rate on the Tennessee bar than their competitors from more prestigious Vanderbilt. First-year classes are taught on the Socratic model, but upper-level courses are more relaxed.

Grade inflation never hit GCT, and a 3.0 average here is likely to put you in the top 10 percent of the class. After fulfilling the first-year requirements, students must take an additional five required courses. Course offerings vary from year to year.

The legal clinic program is outstanding. Clinic students earn course credit for representing indigent clients, frequently in court.

All second-year students having at least a 2.0 grade point average are eligible to write their way onto the *Tennessee Law Review*. Successful candidates must complete two acceptable drafts of a case note for membership, and a final draft is required for academic credit. GCT has a national reputation for moot court excellence, and the intraschool Advocates' Prize competition annually draws a distinguished group of judges.

The minority enrollment here has historically been low, but the school is making an effort to rectify matters. Some disadvantaged students who don't meet formal admissions standards are admitted for fall after attending summer classes elsewhere.

The Black Law Students Association is fairly active, as is the law women's group.

The relationship between students and faculty is excellent. Teachers are always accessible outside of class and often show up at school beer busts. The students display typical irreverence toward particular faculty members through the school newspaper, the *Forum*. On the whole, the students seem genuinely to like the professors and the school.

The administration gets high marks for its unbureaucratic approach to problems. Students have input through the Student Bar Association, Dean's Advisory Committee, and various student-faculty committees.

The students here tend to be an outgoing, friendly, close-knit bunch. Despite the presence of quite a few people from smaller cities and towns in Tennessee, students insist that the mood is not hick.

The SBA throws beer busts and periodic holiday parties. Anyone can join the two legal frats, and nonmembers are always welcome at their parties.

On Thursday nights, many law students commune at a nearby bar to celebrate Rump Court. Knoxville has good clubs, bars, and restaurants, a number of them on the Cumberland Avenue "Strip" that runs by the law school. The UT campus has superb recreational facilities, as well as a good film series and some of the best theaters to be found on any college campus.

The Smokies are only a short drive away; you can take a short hike, or you can backpack for days in unspoiled wilderness. There are TVA lakes for fishing and waterskiing, too.

The dorms here are OK as dorms go, and the university high-rises near campus are a bargain. Just off campus is the Fort Sanders neighborhood, made up mainly of old and sometimes charming houses divided into apartments, densely packed with students. Rent is high but affordable; some houses are in worse shape than others; watch out for landlord ripoffs. To be sure of finding a decent place, get here in August.

The road from GCT to Wall Street, although not entirely untraveled, is considerably less direct than the road from Harvard or Columbia. But you can get a good legal education here, and you'll make lifelong friends, all without developing ulcers.

University of Texas School of Law

Address: **P.O. Box 149105, Austin, TX 78714**
Phone: **(512) 471-3207**
Degrees: **J.D., LL.M., M.C.J. (comparative jurisprudence), J.D./M.B.A., J.D./M.P.A.**

Median LSAT: **42/162 (in-state), 44/164 (out-of-state)**
Media GPA: **3.52 (in-state), 3.61 (out-of-state)**
Applicants accepted: **30% (in-state), 13% (out-of-state)**

Transfers: **5–10/40–60**
Law enrollment: **1540 (1527 J.D.)**
Campus enrollment: **49,800**
Part time: **0**
Women: **42%**
Minorities: **23%**

Dorm residents: **1%**
Library: **823,800**
Student-faculty ratio: **20:1**
Tuition: **$4250 (in-state), $7850 (out-of-state)**
Financial aid: **67%**
Apply by: **February 1**

Disabled students: **Fully accessible. In five years, six blind students, one deaf, one wheelchair user, two with other mobility problems.**

Placement: **83% placed by graduation; 90% employed six months after graduation. 316 employers on campus in one year; 66% from Texas, 9% Midwest, 8% Washington, DC, 7% California, 3% South, 3% West; 92% private firms, 4% government, 2% corporations, 2% judicial. Graduates took jobs in West South Central (75%), Pacific (9%), South Atlantic (6%), East North Central (3%), Mountain (3%), Middle Atlantic (2%), West North Central (1%), unknown (1%). Graduates entered private practice (81%), judicial clerkships (8%), government (5%), business (4%), military (1%), public interest (1%), academic (.5%). Salary range: $17,000–$75,000. Median salary: $54,000. Mean salary: $56,000. Texas bar pass rate: 91% (statewide average: 88%).**

Since its inception in 1883, the University of Texas School of Law has been characterized by conflicting goals. The constitutional mandate for a "university of the first class" inspired visions of a school contributing to the legal life of the nation, but a provincial bar has sought to restrict the school to the needs of the state's good-old-boy network. The latter approach found expression in the complaint of a powerful alumnus about the faculty's emphasis on legal theory over local law: "What y'all want to do is make UT into a Harvard."

Like Harvard, UT places primary emphasis on big-firm, corporate law practice. Fulfilling its acknowledged role as one of the top fifteen or so law schools in the nation, Texas serves as a training ground for some of the nation's most influential private and government attorneys. In addition to hosts of federal and state judges, Texas has begun to graduate future law professors in healthy numbers. But true to its state affiliation, UT also prepares lawyers for the varying demands of a local practice.

The large student body includes an 85-percent contingent of Texans, a quota imposed by the state government. While this requirement limits the potential diversity of the students, the law school benefits from an exciting mixture of political, racial, intellectual, and economic backgrounds. The admissions committee actively recruits qualified minority candidates.

The imposing effect of the law school's size is effectively diminished by the division of the freshlaws into five sections. The freshlaw receives academic advice and instruction in legal research and writing from "teaching quizmasters" selected from the upper classes.

Beyond the first year, UT law students can select from a huge variety of courses, ranging in a typical year from oil and gas law to international business transactions. Once the student masters the intricacies of the computer registration forms (usually by the third year), it's not too hard to get into first-choice courses. The law faculty has traditionally been strong in the fields of torts and products liability, oil and gas, federal courts and procedure, and commercial law. In recent years, the criminal law faculty has become nationally prominent, and an emphasis on international law has been developed. Students can participate in a half-dozen or so assorted clinics.

In addition to first-year requirements, students must take advanced constitutional law, professional responsibility, and a writing seminar in order to receive the J.D. Second- and third-year students may do an independent research project under the guidance of a professor. In addition, law students may take graduate-level courses from other departments at the university for up to six hours of credit.

Because of their geographic isolation—the law school is located in the northeast quadrant of the enormous UT campus—and their spelunkerlike study habits, law students don't participate much in the cultural and entertainment offerings of the university. The typical law student's time is divided among the Tarlton Law Library, the student legal publications, and parties sponsored by the Student Bar Association.

The law building has been treated to a series of renovations. The library, resplendent in its new location, is one of the nation's largest. Particular strengths of the library are its selections of Latin American statutes and case law, and its huge collection of legal art.

Along with the prestigious *Texas Law Review*, the legal publications here include the *Texas International Law Journal*, the *Review of Litigation*, the *American Journal of Criminal Law*, the *Texas Environmental Law Journal*, the *Texas Journal of Women and the Law*, the *Texas Intellectual Property Law Journal*, and the *Hispanic Law Journal*.

When time permits, students enjoy exploring Austin, a city they praise enthusiastically. Located in the Texas hill country, Austin is blessed with lush, green recreational areas. The leisurely pace of life and the friendliness of Austinites compensate for the muggy summers and heavy pollen saturation in the spring. The university students contribute significantly to the city's population and political life but don't dominate either one. Austin entertainment includes great country-western, jazz, and popular music, movie theaters, and countless restaurants, some of them specializing in the famous "Texas barbecue" or "Tex-Mex" cuisine.

The bottom line for law students at Texas, as elsewhere, is to get a job. The placement office is good at helping students get employment by sponsoring interviews and job fairs. As in most places, minority and women students have a harder time breaking into the big Texas private firms than their white male counterparts.

UT is cheap for state residents and relatively inexpensive even for out-of-state students. A few out-of-state students manage to wangle Texas status for themselves after first year is over, but it's not easy.

One of UT's major drawbacks, which it shares with many state schools, is that the university is often at odds with its board of regents and with the Texas legislature. The law school is partially insulated from the friction, because it has an independent source of financing, the Law School Foundation.

If UT's future resembles its recent past, it will remain an excellent place to get a legal education.

Texas Tech University School of Law

Address: **Box 40004, Lubbock, TX 79409**
Phone: **(806) 742-3985**

Degrees: **J.D., J.D./M.B.A., J.D./M.P.A., J.D./M.S. (agricultural economics)**

Median LSAT: **37**

Median GPA: **3.27**

Applicants accepted: **28%**

Transfers: **8–10/30–40**

Law enrollment: **621**

Campus enrollment: **25,000**

Part time: **0**

Women: **36%**

Minorities: **13%**

Dorm residents: **5%**

Library: **226,500**

Student-faculty ratio: **21:1**

Tuition: **$3376 (in-state),**
$4966 (out-of-state)

Financial aid: **60%**

Apply by: **February 1**

Disabled students: **Moderate/full accessibility. In five years, one blind student.**

Placement: **Approximately 60% placed by graduation; approximately 80% employed six to nine months after graduation. 98% of graduates remained in West South Central, 1% Mountain, .5% East North Central, .5% West North Central. Graduates entered private practice (90%), judicial clerkships (8%), business (5%), government (1%), military (1%). Salary range: $17,000–$64,000.**

Texas Tech School of Law is in Lubbock, an isolated Texas Panhandle city of 185,000 people and occasional dust storms. While that bit of information may not entice a prospective law student to enroll here, there are compensations if you're interested in pragmatic career preparation.

Situated on the edge of the Texas Tech University campus, the school of law is housed in a modern facility that has won several awards for its architectural design and efficiency. Students are satisfied with the building's atmosphere and resources. The library has the necessary core collection to meet most research needs.

Admission is becoming a bit difficult because of the school's growing reputation combined with the administration's desire to limit enrollment. Besides the regular fall admissions program, Texas Tech has an entering summer class of 20 students whose applications reveal special qualities that compensate for marginal LSAT records. The student body includes people fresh out of undergraduate school, as well as a large number who have been working full time for several years.

On-campus housing is available, but most law students prefer to live off campus. The apartment situation can be tight just before the start of the fall semester, so it's a good idea to contact the

Lubbock Apartment Association or the Student Bar Association for vacancy notices.

Job opportunities for spouses are abundant. Pay is low, but so is the local cost of living. Jobs at the law school and elsewhere are available for second- and third-year law students, but again, wages are on the low side.

The students and administration get along with a minimum of conflicts. Still, the Student Bar Association yearly dues are a worthwhile investment. The SBA provides such services as free check cashing, discount prices for used books and school supplies, and a channel for voicing ideas to the administration and faculty. The SBA also coordinates many social activities such as get-acquainted, Halloween, and TGIF parties.

Texas Tech's three legal fraternities (for men and women) all do their part in promoting social events. The fall-term frat parties are open to all students and provide a way to meet members of other classes in a social setting. Rush and initiation parties for first-year students and interested "veterans" are held during the spring.

Texas Tech University is known as a good party school. In winter, Lubbock's proximity to the New Mexico mountains enables students to enjoy superb skiing. During the school year a wide range of intramural sports is offered by the main campus, including racquetball, football, baseball, tennis, and swimming. The single male student will find an active social life at Tech. Married law students (who are estimated by one student at half of the total) have their own social group, the Law Partners, in addition to those open to all students.

Even though there are opportunities to take part in extracurricular activities, the average Tech law student finds little time to participate. The total load requirement at the school of law is ninety hours, including an independent research project, making a full semester between fourteen and sixteen hours. Students are restricted to required courses during their first year. Furthermore, six required courses covering commercial law, income tax, corporations, wills and trusts, criminal procedure, and other areas must be completed by the advanced student. Although these courses may be taken any time during the latter two years, most students fulfill them in the second year in order to take advanced electives that have prerequisites. Some students find the required courses burdensome, but the resulting emphasis on general legal practice seems to appeal to many employers.

The entering class is divided into three sections. Most first-year and advanced required courses have 80 to 90 students. Enrollment for electives is usually much smaller, and students report that class size and space availability present no major problems.

Selected students are eligible to become members of the *Texas Tech Law Review*, the Board of Barristers, and the Legal Research Board.

From a regional viewpoint the faculty is well respected. Course evaluation surveys indicate that students are satisfied with the availability of professors for private conferences. The teaching style is principally the case method; however, several statutory courses such as commercial law and income tax are taught by the problem method, where students practice applying the law to specific fact situations.

The placement office is aggressive and efficient. However, if you are not in the top 25 percent of your class by the end of your first year, the office's assistance diminishes, according to one student. Texas Tech is mainly geared toward producing competent practicing attorneys for Texas and (to a lesser extent) neighboring states.

Probably the most attractive feature of the school is the low price tag. On the other hand, it should be remembered that Texas law restricts out-of-state enrollment to 10 percent of the entering class. While the curriculum is somewhat limited, Texas Tech can offer a good grounding in the legal basics.

Thomas M. Cooley Law School

Address: **P.O. Box 13038, Lansing, MI 48901**
Phone: **(517) 371-5140**
Degrees: **J.D.**
Median LSAT: **28**
Median GPA: **2.8**
Applicants accepted: **82%**
Transfers: **8/12**

Law enrollment: **1536**
Campus enrollment: **1536**
Part time: **93%**
Women: **31%**
Minorities: **5%**
Dorm residents: **0**
Library: **292,100**
Student-faculty ratio: **27:1**

Tuition: **$10,538**   Apply by: **rolling admissions**
Financial aid: **75% (31% gift)**
Disabled students: **Moderate/full accessibility. Within five years, three blind students, four wheelchair users, five with other mobility problems.**
Placement: **90% employed six months after graduation. 18 employers on campus in one year; primarily Michigan private firms. Graduates took jobs in Michigan (35%), Pennsylvania (7%), New York (5%), New Jersey (4%), Florida (4%), Illinois (3%), other (42%). Graduates entered private practice (47%), government (17%), judicial clerkships (10%), business (13%), academic (4%), public interest (2%), unknown (5%). Salary range: $10,000–$80,000. Median salary: $30,000. Mean salary: $32,400. Michigan bar pass rate: 80% (statewide average: 75%).**

Thomas M. Cooley Law School, named for a former Michigan jurist, was founded in 1972. As a young institution, it has had to struggle with Michigan's four longer-established law schools for recognition. Today, Thomas M. Cooley seems secure in its niche as a tough law school with modest admissions standards and an emphasis on the practical.

Thomas M. Cooley has increasingly succeeded in attracting law students from all across the country, as well as Michigan. The school offers electives on court procedure in Arizona, Florida, Indiana, Illinois, New Jersey, New York, Pennsylvania, Texas, and Wisconsin. A growing number of Cooley graduates return to their home states to work, helping the school to make the transition to national recognition.

Many of the faculty are excellent. The tuition is lower than at some private schools offering a comparable education.

Cooley's classrooms are housed in a beautifully renovated former Masonic temple, complete with a grand-balconied auditorium and tiered classrooms. The school is located in downtown Lansing, within a few blocks of the state capitol, courts, and government offices. The location facilitates student internships. It also permits big names like the state attorney general and justices of the state supreme court to teach courses—and recruit students for positions at their offices.

Cooley has a new $10.2 million library. In addition to the state-of-the-art computer resources and comprehensive state and federal materials, the library benefits from a very dedicated and helpful staff.

Cooley is a private school, unaffiliated with any university. Most students structure their social lives around the numerous activities sponsored by the 32 active student organizations. Lansing provides concerts, professional and amateur theater, and art centers, as well as nightclubs and restaurants. Michigan State University is about two miles away in East Lansing. It offers a college-town atmosphere with arts, entertainment, and Big Ten sports.

Cooley's classes are scheduled year-round, during three terms. Entering freshmen begin in September for the morning program, in January for the afternoon division, and in May for evening division. Since the work load is spread out over the entire year, there is less work each term. It's common for Cooley students to maintain substantial jobs all year long while they're taking classes. On the other hand, an exceedingly brief summer break does not permit students to take full-time summer jobs.

The curriculum at Thomas Cooley is firmly aimed at "practical scholarship in the law." Students praise the quality of the school's clinical program (limited to the Sixty-Plus Elderlaw Center), moot court, and client counseling training.

The school's placement office is professional and efficient. A growing reference library, including audio and video resources, job postings for full-time and part-time positions, and a 24-hour job hot line all assist current students and graduates alike. However, large firms and corporate employers are not banging down the doors to compete for Cooley graduates.

Rules are strict here. Students may be barred from taking the final exam in a course if they miss too many classes or have been late too often without an excuse. The school recently adopted an Honor Code drafted by a committee of students and faculty. Required courses on basic subjects are so numerous that Cooley students are almost necessarily legal generalists. Students are reconciled to these restrictions as a way to enhance the school's credibility.

Thomas Cooley is a place to obtain a basic, practice-oriented legal education even if your grades and scores couldn't get you into the University of Michigan. Ease of admission has always been one of this school's main attractions, but it is counterbalanced by the strict rules and requirements that make being a student here anything but easy.

University of Toledo College of Law

Address: **Toledo, OH 43606**
Phone: **(419) 537-4131**
Degrees: **J.D., J.D./M.B.A.**
Median LSAT: **36 (full time),
34 (part time)**
Median GPA: **3.00 (full time),
2.88 (part time)**
Applicants accepted: **52%**
Transfers: **NA**
Law enrollment: **688**
Campus enrollment: **24,000**

Part time: **27%**
Women: **38%**
Minorities: **7%**
Dorm residents: **0**
Library: **263,700**
Student-faculty ratio: **20:1**
Tuition: **$4353 (in-state),
$8435 (out-of-state)**
Financial aid: **87%**
Apply by: **March 15**

Disabled students: **Fully accessible. Three disabled students in one year.**

Placement: **Approximately 90% employed six to nine months after graduation. Graduates took jobs in East North Central (86%), South Atlantic (7%), Middle Atlantic (5%), New England (1%), Pacific (1%). Graduates entered private practice (52%), business (20%), government (12%), judicial clerkships (9%), academic (4%), military (2%), public interest (1%). Salary range: $18,000–$62,000.**

The University of Toledo College of Law does a good job at the magical transformation of wide-eyed students into qualified lawyers. Bar exam preparation, complete with several multiple-choice exams resembling the multistate bar exam, is taken seriously here.

The admissions committee typically considers a student's undergraduate GPA and LSAT score, reportedly placing a little more emphasis on the LSAT. Toledo admits a sprinkling of humanities and science students to leaven the homogeneous blend of political science and business majors drawn to a legal career. Since UT is largely a commuter school, a significant portion of the law student body is comprised of older working people and homemakers from the Toledo area. Most students, however, hail from other parts of Ohio, Michigan, New York (Buffalo is well represented), and Pennsylvania.

The atmosphere of the law school is perhaps one of its most attractive features: Toledo is simply a nice place to go to school (insofar as this is compatible with legal education). The students are for the most part warm, friendly people who eschew competitiveness and cultivate camaraderie. The faculty also are pleasant and some go out of their way to get to know students personally.

As for social activities, the most popular seem to be the fall pig roast and the spring golf tournament. Every year the Student Bar Association arranges a Monte Carlo Night to raise money for the scholarship fund. Other activities are planned throughout the year by the Black Law Students Association and the Women Law Students Association.

Beyond the law school walls, the city of Toledo has much to commend it, including ample housing, good medium-priced restaurants, an excellent metro-park system, a fine symphony orchestra, and a noteworthy art museum. For those who are used to the cultural benefits of a large college town, Ann Arbor, Michigan, is only forty-five minutes away up Route 23. Unfortunately, at UT a car is practically a necessity.

The curriculum of the law school has no outstanding strengths or glaring weaknesses, though the clinical program enjoys a good reputation. The faculty is generally solid, and there are several exceptional instructors who would stand out at any law school (as well as one or two tenured incompetents).

Students at UT are diligent but tend not to take themselves too seriously. Many law students arrange their schedules so that they can clerk at local law firms during their second and third years.

Where job placement is concerned, UT's reputation with employers is good as far as it goes, but for the most part it goes only as far as Ohio and the surrounding states. Graduates have gotten jobs with the highest-paying firms in Detroit, Cleveland, Chicago, and even New York, but "The University of Toledo" is not yet a magic password to Wall Street. As at most schools, members of the law review usually do better in the job market than other graduates.

UT is a worthwhile, pleasant place to go to law school, but

prospective students should expect to exert a bit of effort if they hope to obtain jobs later in large metropolitan firms.

Tulane Law School

Address: **New Orleans, LA 70118**
Phone: **(504) 865-5930**
Degrees: **J.D., LL.M. (general, admiralty, or energy and environment), M.C.L., S.J.D., J.D./M.B.A., J.D./M.H.A. (health administration), J.D./M.S.P.H. (environmental health), B.A./J.D., other joint degrees**
Median LSAT: **160**
Median GPA: **3.3**

Applicants accepted: **29%**
Transfers: **15–20/50**
Law enrollment: **1005 (970 J.D.)**
Campus enrollment: **11,000**
Part time: **0**
Women: **42%**
Minorities: **24%**
Dorm residents: **NA**
Library: **470,000**
Student-faculty ratio: **21:1**
Tuition: **$18,185**
Financial aid: **70% (35% gift)**
Apply by: **May 1, March 1 (aid)**

Disabled students: **Moderate/full accessibility. In one year, some students with temporary mobility problems.**

Placement: **85% employed six months after graduation. 250 employers on campus in one year; 65% from Louisiana; 65% private firms. Graduates took jobs in West South Central (54%), South Atlantic (12%), Pacific (7%), East South Central (4%), Mountain (4)%, Middle Atlantic (4%), East North Central (2%), West North Central (2%), Foreign (2%), New England (1%), unknown (8%). Graduates entered private practice (66%), government (13%), judicial clerkships (13%), business (4%), public interest (1%), military (.5%), unknown (3%). Salary range: $18,000–$80,000. Mean salary: $43,795. Louisiana bar pass rate: 74% (statewide average: 62%).**

Tulane Law School (pronounced TOO-lane by all self-respecting southerners) is in the throes of change. Faculty hiring has been stepped up. The course selection available to juniors and seniors is expanding. The school's student body and reputation have become more national in scope. And the school broke ground for a brand-new building in 1992. Literally and figuratively, Tulane is a law school on the rise.

Perhaps the biggest misconception people have about Tulane concerns the curriculum. No (to all of you who remember Stanley Kowalski's raving about his rights to his sister-in-law's property), Tulane does not teach the Napoleonic Code. Yes, a person accused of a crime in Louisiana is innocent until proven guilty, just as in the rest of the country.

What Tulane students can study (if they wish) is the Louisiana Civil Code. This code does have roots in French and Roman antecedents, but the influence of the law in the other forty-nine states, which has English common law origins, has been pervasive. Few areas of Louisiana law are based on principles different from those that hold sway in the rest of the country.

A Tulane student never has to look at the Civil Code; one chooses between the civil law curriculum and the common law curriculum. Either way, you're mainly learning how to think like a lawyer. Your education won't suffer from studying common law principles in a state governed largely by civil law. On the contrary, the exposure to a civil law system at Tulane can be helpful for comparative purposes, since the majority of the world's countries have a civil code. If you want to practice in Louisiana, Tulane is a natural.

Aside from the two curricula, Tulane's course offerings are similar to those of other schools its size. There are a few extras worth noting. The school has clinical programs in which seniors actually represent indigent and juvenile clients. There's also a judicial clerkship program that permits students to work for federal district court judges. Tulane also was the first school in the nation to institute a community service obligation, requiring every student to devote twenty hours to providing free legal assistance.

Tulane has one of the best admiralty (maritime law) programs in the country. If you like Melville, the smell of the briny deep, and the thrill of wind in the sails, but your pragmatic side is pulling you into the legal profession, consider Tulane's admiralty offerings, which include a graduate degree program and a legal journal.

Classes here are heavy on the Socratic method, but professors' teaching styles vary considerably. First-year classes typically consist of over 100 students and a professor who practices the art of intimidation. A first-year student can expect to do about five to eight hours of homework a night and then face the chance of being called on at random from a seating chart.

Southerners no longer make up the majority of Tulane students (only about 25 percent come from Louisiana). There's a substantial contingent from the Northeast, as well as others from across the country and a few foreign lands. Although most come from families sufficiently well off to afford the hefty tuition, they don't all travel in the same social circles. There are Jewish students from Long Island who have every intention of going back there after graduation; there are New Orleans "gentlemen" whose families have lived in the same home for a hundred years; and there are jazz aficionados who spend whatever free time they can find in the French Quarter clubs. The minority enrollment has increased, and the administration seems committed to admitting and retaining minority students.

The job market for Tulane grads varies according to one's place in the class. The top quarter of the class has little trouble finding jobs, some of them even ending up in New York or Washington. A student graduating in the lower half of the class may have somewhat more difficulty. One exception to this rule: if you've got a strong background in admiralty law, you have a good chance with an admiralty firm in any of the major port cities. One student in the bottom half of his class managed to land a job with an admiralty firm on Wall Street.

Housing around Tulane is difficult to find and often overpriced; get here about a month before school starts to look over what's available. The graduate and married students' housing is in a six-story, drab, institutional-looking building, although close to campus and relatively cheap. If you want a taste of life in New Orleans, campus housing isn't the place to live.

There's more nightlife here than anyone can handle—although you'll probably be tempted to try. Many clubs in the French Quarter never close, and it's not hard to forget the wrong answer you gave in contracts class when people are dancing with wild abandon all around you. Temporary oblivion is surely one of the most useful weapons that law students can have at their disposal.

University of Utah College of Law

Address: **Salt Lake City, UT 84112**
Phone: (801) 581–6833
Degrees: **J.D., LL.M. (energy law), J.D./M.B.A., J.D./M.P.A.**
Median LSAT: **40**
Median GPA: **3.5**
Applicants accepted: **30%**
Transfers: **3**
Law enrollment: **393 (382 J.D.)**

Campus enrollment: **25,000**
Part time: **0**
Women: **37%**
Minorities: **11%**
Dorm residents: **NA**
Library: **260,800**
Student-faculty ratio: **14:1**
Tuition: **$2843 (in-state), $6476 (out-of-state)**
Financial aid: **75%**
Apply by: **February 1**

Disabled students: **Fully accessible. Two disabled students in one year.**

Placement: **Approximately 90% employed six to nine months after graduation. Graduates employed in Mountain (69%), Pacific (15%), New England (5%), West South Central (4%), South Atlantic (2%), Foreign (2%), Middle Atlantic (1%), East North Central (1%), East South Central (1%). Graduates entered private practice (53%), government (26%), judicial clerkships (17%), business (4%), public interest (1%). Salary range: $15,000–$85,000.**

For a long time, the University of Utah was a "sleeper" among law schools. While highly rated among state-supported schools, it failed to receive the kind of publicity that would make more people aware of its existence.

Well, that is changing. Applications are soaring and the school is increasingly successful in attracting highly qualified students from throughout the United States and several foreign countries. The bargain-basement tuition—even for nonresidents—may have something to do with the school's dramatic increase in popularity.

The high-quality faculty and student-friendly atmosphere are the school's main attractions. Students say that the professors are talented and hardworking but try to create a mostly noncompetitive atmosphere for learning the law. Many of the faculty are

332 | University of Utah College of Law

nationally distinguished scholars and most encourage close association with students and have "open door" policies rather than
limited office hours.

Utah is rare in having an administration and staff who are
student-oriented and work hard to make student life easier. Students say the personalized attention, whether it be in registering
for classes or putting together a customized, interdisciplinary
course of study, makes a big difference in the quality of their
education.

Under the auspices of a Department of Education grant, the
curriculum underwent a major overhaul a few years ago. Called
Cornerstone-Capstone, the curriculum is designed to provide each
year of legal education with a distinctive purpose. All students start
out with a week-long Introduction to Law course. The remaining
first-year courses focus on typical foundation subjects and employ
the traditional case method of study. First-year classes range in size
from 10 to 65 students.

The second and third years diverge from the norm with unique
offerings and opportunities involving extensive research and writing. Other writing opportunities are offered by the moot court
programs and the several student-published scholarly journals. Although the student body is small, there's a surprisingly diverse
menu of advanced courses, most of which are elective. A few of
the newer faculty members are into high-tech classroom presentations and use state-of-the-art video-computer projection equipment
installed in all of the major classrooms.

The environmental, natural resources and energy law program
has established itself as a leader and offers more related courses
than you can jam into three years. Qualified students can write
for the *Journal of Energy, Natural Resources and Environmental Law,*
or the *Western Energy Bulletin.* The law school program even offers
a graduate research degree in energy law.

The school also has strong academic programs and co-curricu-
lar activities that support public-interest law, responding to height-
ened student interest. There are several summer stipend programs
for public-interest summer employment, a student loan forgiveness
program for graduates who enter public service, and the Public
Interest Law Organization (PILO).

The school is only a mile from downtown Salt Lake City, so

there are extensive "live" clinicals in civil and criminal law offices and agencies. Third-year law students in Utah can actually conduct their own civil and criminal trials if supervised by a licensed attorney. There are many opportunities to clerk for federal and state judges while enrolled as a student, and an unusually high percentage of the graduating class accepts judicial clerkships after graduation.

The University of Utah name is best known for job placement, in the intermountain area and along the West Coast, but those with out-of-region ambitions aren't left wanting, thanks to long-standing recruitment ties with some major firms and government agencies. About half of the graduates start out with jobs in Utah. Salaries in Utah may be lower than in some other places, but so is the cost of living and stress level. The excellent placement center also houses a customized database service that allows student résumés and transcripts to be sent directly to employers selected by students from a national and international network list.

The university—known as the place "where intellect and environment meet"—is in the foothills of the Wasatch range, which boasts the "Greatest Snow on Earth." Well within an hour of the law school, you can ski at internationally known resorts like Deer Valley, Park City, Alta, and Snowbird; local favorites include Solitude, Brighton, and Park West. The state's five national parks are within range for weekend outings.

Students can take advantage of excellent recreational facilities on the 1500-acre campus, which also serves as the state's official Arboretum. The fieldhouse is conveniently located just east of the law school parking lot and is free to students. The law school is active in university intramurals and has several sports tournaments of its own. Since the law school is small, making friends or joining activities—such as the fourteen different law student organizations—is easy.

Salt Lake City offers quite a range of social and cultural activities for a city of its size. The Utah Symphony, Ballet West, Pioneer Memorial Theater (along with numerous other dance and theater companies) provide high-quality performances. The enormous, new Delta Center is home to the acclaimed Utah Jazz basketball team and the Golden Eagles hockey team.

334 | Vanderbilt University School of Law

Most people find life healthy, safe, and pleasant here, which explains why outstanding faculty members stick around and the school continues to attract new faculty "stars." After three years at the University of Utah College of Law, you may find yourself happily settling down to an in-state job—even if you came with no intention of staying.

Vanderbilt University School of Law

Address: **Nashville, TN 37240**
Phone: **(615) 322-6452**
Degrees: **J.D., J.D./M.B.A., J.D./M.Div. (divinity), J.D./M.T.S. (theological studies), J.D./M.A. or Ph.D. (various)**
Median LSAT: **164**
Median GPA: **3.61**
Applicants accepted: **21%**
Transfers: **6–9/35**

Law enrollment: **550**
Campus enrollment: **9000**
Part time: **0**
Women: **38%**
Minorities: **20%**
Dorm residents: **1%**
Library: **303,000**
Student-faculty ratio: **17:1**
Tuition: **$16,800**
Financial aid: **75% (40% gift)**
Apply by: **February 1**

Disabled students: **Fully accessible. Within five years, two wheelchair users.**

Placement: **92% employed six months after graduation. 75% of first-years, 97% of second-years, and 80% of third-years placed by end of spring term. 400 employers on campus in one year; 94% private firms, 6% government. Graduates took jobs in Southeast (50%), West and Southwest (22%), Northeast (15%), Midwest (12%), Foreign (1%). Graduates entered private practice (71%), judicial clerkships (22%), academic or other (3%), government (2%), public interest (1%), business (1%). Salary range: $26,000–$85,000. Median salary: $56,000.**

Vanderbilt seems to manage a healthy balance between academic achievement and a livable atmosphere.

The school's location in Nashville, the state capital, gives students the opportunity to intern in state or federal courts, help draft legislation through the school's Legislative Reference Bureau, and participate in the well-developed civil, criminal, and juvenile clinical programs. The local legal community strongly supports the law school. Attorneys serve as instructors in moot court and trial advocacy classes, and law firms offer part-time work during the year as well as summer clerkships.

The entering class of about 180 is divided into two sections with different professors and schedules. Legal writing and appellate advocacy are taught in smaller groups of about 30. The level of instruction and work load varies from group to group, depending on the professor. The second- and third-year course offerings include seminars with just a few students, but some basic classes such as corporations or evidence are much larger.

Student-faculty relations are generally excellent. Students sit on most faculty committees, working on such questions as admissions and placement. Professors maintain an open-door policy, and informal contact with professors is as frequent as students desire. Many work one-on-one with faculty members, as research assistants or on individual projects. Vanderbilt has had increasing success in retaining its high-caliber established professors and attracting young on-the-rise types as well.

Vanderbilt is academically rigorous and its students work hard. Many arrive unprepared for either the time constraints imposed by studying or the pressure (largely self-imposed) to perform in class. Nevertheless, the atmosphere here is far less competitive than at some comparable schools. Students are willing to help each other out and exchange outlines, even during finals. "Misshelving'" essential library books and other examples of law-school-induced paranoia are almost unheard of and would be subject to universal condemnation, not to mention prosecution under the student-enforced Honor Code.

Widespread student opposition succeeded in eliminating class ranking and changing the grading system from ruthlessly precise numbers to vaguer letter grades. The *Vanderbilt Law Review* and *Vanderbilt Journal of Transnational Law* select their members on the basis of first-year grades and performance on a writing competition.

The relatively noncompetitive atmosphere is nurtured by the biweekly school-sponsored beer busts (which even professors attend), frequent parties, and events such as the annual Barrister's Ball. The southern locale guarantees a moderate climate permitting outdoor activities until December.

Vanderbilt's placement office gets high marks. Recruiters from hundreds of law firms nationwide visit the campus each year, luring prospective associates with unreasonably high salaries. However, students with weaker academic records may have to settle for something less than their dream job.

Contrary to popular belief, Vanderbilt is not a regional law school. Half the students come from outside the South, and many leave the area after graduation. But for an academically challenging national law school, Vanderbilt is able to maintain a surprisingly pleasant environment, thanks to its unmistakable southern charm.

Vermont Law School

Address: **P.O. Box 96, South Royalton, VT 05068**
Phone: **(802) 763-8303**
Degrees: **J.D., M.S.L. (environmental law)**
Median LSAT: **158**
Median GPA: **3.1**
Applicants accepted: **24%**
Transfers: **4–6/15–25**
Law enrollment: **533 (496 J.D.)**

Campus enrollment: **533**
Part time: **0**
Women: **44%**
Minorities: **6%**
Dorm residents: **6%**
Library: **165,100**
Student-faculty ratio: **20:1**
Tuition: **$14,065**
Financial aid: **79% (27% gift)**
Apply by: **February 15, January 15 (aid)**

Disabled students: **Moderate/full accessibility. No disabled students in five-year period.**
Placement: **78% employed six months after graduation. 45% of first-years, 96% of second-years, and 40% of third-years placed by end of spring term. 50 employers on campus in one year; 60% from New England, 40% Mid-Atlantic; 50% private firms, 20% government, 20% public interest, 10% other. Graduates took jobs in New England (37%), Mid-Atlantic (25%), South Atlantic (10%), West (3%), Midwest (3%). Graduates entered private practice (45%), judicial clerkships (13%), government (9%), public interest (4%), military (3%), business (3%), academic (1%). Salary range: $16,000–$80,000. Median salary: $31,175. Mean salary: $32,500. Vermont bar pass rate: 69% (statewide average: 74%).**

Vermont Law School is not in Burlington (the state's largest city), nor is it affiliated with the University of Vermont. With those popular misconceptions dispelled, we can look at what VLS *is*.

One of the keys to understanding VLS is its location in a quaint, rural New England village. With a Laundromat, hardware store, and bars and restaurants you can count on the fingers of one hand, South Royalton has less to do than almost anywhere except its neighboring towns. More than one student has gotten a severe case of cabin fever in "So Ro."

For those who prefer a wider range of activities—and this includes everyone but the wildlife—several excellent downhill ski areas and countless cross-country trails are within striking distance. Within about forty-five minutes of South Royalton are Montpelier (Vermont's capital and a good source of summer jobs), Woodstock, Vermont (with its restored nineteenth-century homes and inns and its moneyed vacationers), and Hanover, New Hampshire (home of Dartmouth, the preferred destination of escaping VLS students). There is definitely more to do here than walk the mountain meadows; all it takes is some imagination and a car.

In any event, many students thrive on the serenity. They come to VLS to avoid the pressures of the big city. Most of the students have taken some time off between college and law school. In general, the mood is relaxed.

There is some school-owned housing, and a range of off-campus options is available, from modern apartments to shared space on nearby farms. Rent is high for Vermont but unbelievably cheap by Boston standards. Some students prefer to commute from outside the immediate area; they thereby enjoy some respite from the sensation—common at VLS—of living in a fishbowl.

First-year students are divided into two sections of about 70 students each. Their courses are all required and cover the usual subject matter. After the first year, class size drops in all but the most fundamental bar-exam-related courses. The work load is moderate to heavy, requiring at least one hour of preparation for each hour of class time.

The choice of courses is fairly limited due to the school's small size. There is an excellent selection of environmental courses, and the clinical programs get high ratings. One major problem is the inevitable schedule changes that take place between course registration and the beginning of the semester, forcing students to scurry to add and drop classes at the start of each term.

Students interested in subjects not covered by the course catalog may devise independent study courses with a faculty member of their choice. This option was made more popular by the administration's adoption of an advanced writing requirement. The faculty is generally young, enthusiastic, and readily available outside the classroom.

In keeping with its small-town flavor, VLS offers an optional General Practice Program, which is designed to train attorneys who want to practice solo or in a small firm. Students take a series of courses providing the basics any general practitioner would need, and can test out their new skills in externships outside the classroom.

VLS has its share of on-campus activities, including an environmental activist group and a women's group. Friday afternoon kegs appear with some regularity. The otherwise invisible Student Bar Association funds a yearbook and a newspaper and runs rugby, soccer, Ultimate Frisbee, and field hockey teams, and basketball and softball leagues. Members of the Vermont Legal Research Group, who are selected on the basis of an annual writing competition, do research for practicing attorneys and write summaries of recent Vermont Supreme Court decisions for publication in the Vermont Bar Association newsletter. The law review has a surprisingly good reputation, considering its rather grudging funding by the administration.

VLS has only been around since 1972, and naturally, it is still building its reputation. While the school is best known in Vermont, its national recognition got a big boost when the school was ranked number one for environmental law two years in a row in *U.S. News & World Report*'s annual survey of law school deans and faculty.

In recent years, the career services office has aggressively sought to improve outreach to public and private employers, foster awareness of public-interest careers, and assist students seeking judicial clerkships. However, students can still be heard to complain that the placement process is primarily successful for the top-ranked portion of the class.

Aside from its strength in environmental law, VLS's main distinguishing feature is its bucolic setting. It is a mellow and scenic, if sometimes stifling, place to spend three years.

Villanova University School of Law

Address: **Villanova, PA 19085**
Phone: **(215) 645-7010**
Degrees: **J.D., LL.M. (tax), J.D./M.B.A., J.D./Ph.D. (clinical psychology)**
Median LSAT: **40**
Median GPA: **3.43**
Applicants accepted: **29%**
Transfers: **NA**
Law enrollment: **953 (702 J.D.)**

Campus enrollment: **12,000**
Part time: **0**
Women: **51%**
Minorities: **9%**
Dorm residents: **less than 1%**
Library: **396,600**
Student-faculty ratio: **25:1**
Tuition: **$13,175**
Financial aid: **64%**
Apply by: **January 31**

Disabled students: **Moderate/full accessibility. Two disabled students in one year.**
Placement: **Approximately 93% employed eleven months after graduation. Graduates entered private practice (61%), judicial clerkships (17%), government (11%), business (6%), academic (3%), public interest (1%), unknown (1%). Salary range: $16,000–$75,000.**

Villanova was founded in the early 1950s, and it quickly established a good reputation in the Philadelphia area for turning out competent and knowledgeable lawyers. Many local employers compare the school favorably to others in the region, including Penn.

Situated along Philadelphia's Main Line, Villanova's location is close to ideal—a quick and convenient twenty-five-minute train ride into Center City Philadelphia, yet with the advantages of a safe, tree-lined suburban setting.

Villanova's student body is drawn mainly from the Northeast. The majority of students rent apartments near the school, which are plentiful and reasonably priced. Others, strapped for funds, live with their parents in various communities along the Main Line. Because students are scattered over the area, social life is limited. There are occasional beer parties and movies, and student groups bring in speakers. Still, most law students just get together with groups of friends and party in the suburbs.

Although Villanova is a Catholic university, there is little to remind students of that fact, except the crucifix that adorns every room in the building.

Villanova's curriculum offers a traditional approach strongly emphasizing a fundamental legal education. The Socratic method is trotted out for many first-year classes, but it is much less common in the second and third years. The course offerings have traditionally been strongest in business law fields. The criminal law program has been strengthened, and offerings in public and environmental law areas have increased. Second- and third-year students can choose from an expanding variety of clinical and practical skills courses.

Teaching seems to be the main interest of the professors. Most are available for help and conversation; it's a rare student who doesn't get to know at least one professor well. What's more, the faculty members take a strong interest in student affairs, involving themselves in most student organizations.

Along with traditional academic organizations (like the law review, moot court board, and the relatively new environmental law journal), Villanova offers many clubs geared toward students interested in particular areas of law. Additionally, groups such as the Black Law Students Association and the Women's Law Caucus maintain active chapters at Villanova.

On the less academic side, the law school sponsors a theatrical group as well as several very popular intramural athletic leagues. Students have access to the university's modern athletic and recreational facilities. The law school itself offers softball, volleyball and highly competitive basketball.

While Villanova is mainly considered a local law school, some students every year do land jobs outside the Philadelphia-New York area. The placement office can help with job search skills, but no one will confuse Villanova with Ivy League schools when it comes to the number and variety of on-campus interviews.

Due to Villanova's class rank system and its comparatively tough grading policy, a competitive atmosphere is unavoidable. Nonetheless, the prevailing attitude is friendly and helpful, with study aids freely exchanged. Each first-year student is assigned two upper-level students and a faculty member as advisers. First-year courses are scheduled with an hour break between classes, which allows students to get to know each other a bit. All these things make Villanova well worth considering, particularly if you are interested in earning a diploma with primarily local appeal.

University of Virginia School of Law

Address: **Charlottesville, VA 22901**
Phone: **(804) 924-7351**
Degrees: **J.D., LL.M., S.J.D., J.D./M.B.A., J.D./M.P. (planning), J.D./M.A. (economics, philosophy, history, sociology, marine affairs), J.D./M.A. or Ph.D. (government and foreign affairs), J.D./M.S. (accounting)**
Median LSAT: **43**
Median GPA: **3.59**

Applicants accepted: **16%**
Transfers: **NA**
Law enrollment: **1193 (1137 J.D.)**
Campus enrollment: **16,000**
Part time: **0**
Women: **40%**
Minorities: **13%**
Dorm residents: **NA**
Library: **631,900**
Student-faculty ratio: **22:1**
Tuition: **$4858 (in-state), $11,538 (out-of-state)**
Financial aid: **59%**
Apply by: **January 15**

Disabled students: **Fully accessible. Six disabled students in one year.**
Placement: **Approximately 92% placed by graduation. Approximately 90% of second-years placed by end of spring term. Graduates took jobs in South Atlantic (47%), Middle Atlantic (17%), Pacific (12%), New England (7%), East North Central (5%), West South Central (5%), East South Central (4%), West North Central (1%), Mountain (1%), Foreign (1%). Graduates entered private practice (65%), judicial clerkships (17%), government (4%), business (2%), public interest (2%), academic (1%), military (1%), unknown (8%). Salary range: $25,000–$85,000.**

The University of Virginia School of Law is tucked away at the foot of the Blue Ridge Mountains in the quintessential college town of Charlottesville. As a state school, UVa must reserve 55 percent of its places for Virginians. Still, that's lower than resident figures at many other state schools, and quite a few of the "instate" students are transient Washington, DC, suburbanites or out-of-staters who established residency at Virginia colleges. Nonresidents in each entering class typically come from over thirty-five states and several foreign countries. UVa was designed to be, and is, a national law school.

Except for the fact that Virginians get a big admissions boost, the admissions process here is as much of a mystery as anywhere. High numbers are important, but the fact that UVa is among the few schools to grant interviews is one indication that you can compensate for mediocre grades and scores with an interesting personality. The entering class is always filled with multitalented, unusual people. "Unfortunately," says one student, "Virginia's prevailing corporate bent tends to mold the diverse group into a startlingly uniform graduating class. A well-rounded student at UVa is someone who has developed his or her softball skills along with the social polish necessary for a large corporate firm." To be fair, it should be noted that the placement office has recently added a staff position dedicated exclusively to servicing public-interest job-seekers.

The basic courses are taught in large (100-plus students) classes. There are a number of small seminars and courses with fewer than 20 enrolled. First-year students have at least one "small section" course (with about 30 members), which serves as the basis for lasting social ties. In some cases you can arrange for independent study. After first semester, requirements are few.

Frequent complaints are that many classes are too large, basic courses are too difficult to get into, and scheduling is a nightmare. The administration's approach to the problems has been to curtail course adding and dropping privileges somewhat. Virginia has only grapevine counseling on course selection, and available course descriptions are reportedly out of date and inaccurate.

Unusual academic specialties available here include law and psychiatry, and oceans law and policy. Professors tend to emphasize underlying theoretical issues over nuts-and-bolts aspects of law. Law and economics is a common ideological perspective among the faculty, and students who question the supremacy of the free market may find themselves in the minority.

UVa has an honor system, which is supposed to ensure that you can leave your notes, books, and coats in the library and not worry about whether they'll be there when you get back—and for the most part you can. But the administration has had to face reality, and certain hallways are now locked during off-hours. Another benefit of the honor system—total freedom to schedule your own exams—has been cut back a bit: a few of the most popular classes now have scheduled exams. Because the penalty for violating the honor system is expulsion, the whole system is the source of great controversy.

The student body tends to pride itself on its laid-back, beer-and-softball atmosphere. Most UVa students quickly realize that constant studying is not necessary, so other activities are popular. Charlottesville is amply supplied with bars for every taste. The university campus always has a lot of cultural events, but few students venture beyond attending the classic movies. The law school has an extremely well-subscribed softball league and occasional official parties and events. In the annual Libel Show, students stage skits and songs poking fun at faculty members and law school life in general.

The weekly graduate school happy hour on the main campus provides invaluable contacts for the young and restless male law student but provokes yawns from most of his female classmates. The law school also has its own Thursday happy hour, known as "Bar Review." But the real focuses of law school social life are large private parties and dating. The active gossip network, together with the daily presence of all the students in one building, makes the whole thing slightly high-schoolish.

Student publications include journals in international law, tax, and environmental law, in addition to the law review. The moot court program is so popular that it might as well be a requirement. There are courses and programs available for students interested in client contact under attorneys' supervision. Organizations appealing to those with special interests include several singing groups, the law school newspaper, and associations for black students, women, and gay and lesbian students.

Student government exists at a rock-bottom level of effectiveness. Student unity is nonexistent, and consequently the student body has little voice in policy matters. The school officials do maintain an open-door policy, but when it comes time to make decisions, faculty demands tend to take priority over those of students.

The law school building (completed in 1979) is a modern structure with a 400-plus-seat auditorium, an audiovisual center, and a very extensive library collection. The law school has plans to expand the facility.

Placement is perhaps Virginia's greatest pride. Graduates enjoy the benefits of a "top-ten" reputation that extends far beyond the state borders. Unlike their peers at many other schools, a vast number of first-years land summer jobs in law firms.

UVa is facing the same financial aid crunch as all law schools, so money will be increasingly tight. Still, the school will probably continue its policy of making sure no one leaves for lack of funds. If grants and loans are insufficient or unavailable, there are many part-time jobs to be had, either through the school or with private firms.

Tuition at UVa is among the cheapest you'll find for a school of this caliber. The cost of living is high for a small town but moderate by all other standards. University housing is available right across the street from the law school, but it's hard to get into, and you'd better not object to living on top of three other people. After first year, many students move to houses overlooking the surrounding countryside.

If you can clear the admissions hurdle, you have plenty to look forward to at UVa. Virginia has a well-deserved reputation for being a relatively relaxed law school. Students study a lot, but the small percentage who overdo it have only themselves to blame. Class participation rarely counts in term grades; exams don't bear the students' names; and there's no class rank. Nearly everyone gets Bs, and no one flunks out unintentionally. Another reason for the relaxed atmosphere is the lovely campus and the surrounding Blue Ridge countryside, which provides a terrific physical environment, decent weather, and a disincentive for studying. But perhaps the most obvious explanation for the mood is also the truest: students here know that this is one of the country's top schools—and they know that employers know it.

Washburn University School of Law

Address: **1700 College, Topeka, KS 66621**
Phone: **(913) 231-1185**
Degrees: **J.D.**

Median LSAT: **153**
Median GPA: **3.2**
Applicants accepted: **32%**

Transfers: **2–3/10**

Law enrollment: **435**

Campus enrollment: **6600**

Part time: **0**

Women: **41%**

Minorities: **15%**

Dorm residents: **2%**

Library: **250,500**

Student-faculty ratio: **16:1**

Tuition: **$4579 (in-state),**
 $6063 (out-of-state)

Financial aid: **92% (42% gift)**

Apply by: **March 15**

Disabled students: **Fully accessible. In five years, five deaf students, five wheelchair users, two with other mobility problems.**

Placement: **89% employed six months after graduation. Approximately 50% of second-years and 80% of third-years employed in legal jobs during the academic year. 52 employers on campus in one year; majority from Missouri and Kansas; 90% private firms, 10% government or public interest. 83% of graduates took jobs in Kansas or Missouri. Graduates entered private practice (51%), government (32%), business (7%), nonlegal jobs (7%), public interest (3%). Salary range: $18,000–$51,000. Median salary: $29,000. Kansas bar pass rate: 86.5% (statewide average: 85%).**

If you're attracted to the atmosphere of a friendly, conservative midwestern town, Washburn University in Topeka may be the answer to your law school prayers. Topeka is the state capital and the third-largest city in Kansas, but its mood is slow-paced.

Washburn boasts one of the finest law buildings in the country after a 1991 expansion project added 33,000 square feet of library, classroom, and office space. The addition includes a 30-station computer lab that is available to students for legal research as well as word processing. The well-appointed courtroom is used for trial skills courses and has hosted the Tenth Circuit U.S. Court of Appeals and numerous state agency hearings, which students are invited to observe.

The area surrounding the university is residential. Reasonably-priced housing is easy to find within walking distance of the campus. On-campus housing for both single students and families is available on a limited basis.

Washburn permits a small number of students to enter in the spring semester. About 60 percent of each entering class is from Kansas, but the remainder is surprisingly diverse, with students from throughout the United States and several foreign countries. To those who come from outside the Farm Belt, the people here seem extraordinarily friendly. Students share outlines and lecture notes and frequently form cooperative groups to study for exams.

Professors encourage active class participation, so preparation is a must. Most of the first two years is spent on required courses and distribution requirements. Basic courses are midsized—generally less than 80 students. First-year students will be in at least one class of approximately 25. Although professors use the case-study Socratic method in most of the required courses, electives are characterized by more varied and creative teaching styles. Most professors pride themselves on their accessibility to students and often attend student functions and participate in student activities.

Studying law in the state capital has its advantages. The Kansas Supreme Court, Court of Appeals, U.S. District Court, Federal Bankruptcy Court, and the Kansas District Court are all located in Topeka. The state law library, housed in the Kansas Judicial Center in downtown Topeka, is available to students. The majority of students obtain part-time and summer positions with the courts, legislature, private firms, and corporations, or various state agencies and departments. Students can also work with faculty members as research assistants.

Washburn was one of the pioneers in clinical legal education and remains at the forefront. It has a fully staffed legal clinic located in a separate building adjacent to the law school. Third-year students can earn a generous amount of credit representing indigent clients. More than half of the students participate in clinical education and most say the experience is invaluable for those interested in entering private practice. In addition to the clinical offerings, the school has a rural law center and offers certificates in Law and Mental Health and Tax Law.

For those who want their résumés to show something other than name, rank, and grade point average, there are numerous activities. The *Washburn Law Journal* selects students to write and edit based on grades and an annual writing contest. Washburn students also have the opportunity to serve on the staff for the American Bar Association *Family Law Quarterly*. Students can try out for moot court competitions, trial advocacy, negotiation, and client counseling teams.

Student-sponsored activities and special-interest student groups abound, ranging from environmental to international law issues. The student newspaper, *The Legal Brief,* has experienced a rebirth in the past couple of years with enthusiastic new editors. Washburn's student government actively, and often successfully, advocates for student interests. In addition to Student Bar Association dances and picnics, there are intramural basketball and football teams, racquetball and golf tournaments, and parties hosted by the three legal fraternities. Washburn enjoys a high level of student participation in these events.

The career services office provides a variety of student services including arranging some on-campus interviews for permanent, summer and part-time positions. It also offers workshops on résumé writing, interviewing techniques, "dressing for success," and nonlegal careers. Alumni often participate in career planning workshops.

Topeka's cultural attractions include museums, concerts, plays, dance performances, an active community theater, as well as a unique zoo. The parks provide numerous recreational opportunities. The usual cluster of college bars is only a block from campus. Some students regularly drive the short hour to Kansas City for jazz, sporting events, and other activities. Nevertheless, Washburn's surroundings are calmer and quieter than what you'd encounter at a law school in a larger metropolis. And for many Washburn students, that's just fine.

University of Washington School of Law

Address: **1100 N.E. Campus Parkway, Seattle, WA 98105**
Phone: **(206) 543-4078**
Degrees: **J.D., LL.M. (Asian law or marine affairs), J.D./M.B.A., other joint degrees**
Median LSAT: **163**
Median GPA: **3.5**

Applicants accepted: **19%**
Transfers: **5/50**
Law enrollment: **500 (450 J.D.)**
Campus enrollment: **30,000**
Part time: **0**
Women: **50%**
Minorities: **37%**
Dorm residents: **NA**

348 | University of Washington School of Law

Library: **434,000**

Student-faculty ratio: **13:1**

Tuition: **$3500 (in-state),**
$8900 (out-of-state)

Financial aid: **75% (50% gift)**

Apply by: **January 15**

Disabled students: **Fully accessible. In five years, four blind students,
two wheelchair users.**

Placement: **93% employed six months after graduation. 50% of first-
years, 70% of second-years, and 40% of third-years placed by end
of spring term. 103 employers on campus in one year; 80% from
Seattle area, 5% other Washington, 15% other Pacific; 75%
private firms, 25% government or public interest. Graduates took
jobs in Seattle area (80%), other Pacific (10%). Graduates entered
private practice (72%), judicial clerkships (12%), government
(10%), business (3%), academic (2%), public interest (1%). Salary
range: $27,300–$70,000. Washington bar pass rate: 90% (statewide
average: 78%).**

The allure of the University of Washington School of Law is attributable to its Seattle location, relatively inexpensive tuition, and
top-notch faculty and library.

Often rated one of the most livable cities in the U.S., Seattle
is a green, hilly city on the water and close to the mountains. The
best transport is by bus, bike, or ferry. A car is useful only for
getting out of town. Even when it's raining (which is most of the
time), Seattle's urban personality shines through. The city doesn't
disappoint those who enjoy theater, film, readings by celebrated
authors, gallery openings, professional sports, and music festivals.
However, UW students rarely have the time or money to take full
advantage of the cultural offerings.

The UW law school is located in a business and residential area
three miles north of downtown Seattle. The area is dominated by
the university, whose enrollment (one of the largest on the West
Coast) puts a strain on the local housing market. The cost of living
is fairly high. Those students who succeed in living nearby begin
the search early and with plenty of money in hand. Good public
transportation makes it possible to find attractive housing outside
the university district.

The law school building is three blocks west of the main campus. The school has its own administration and only minimal con-

tact with the huge university and its red tape. This isolation contributes to solidarity among the law students but also makes it easy to spend three years without sampling the many recreational and cultural resources the main campus has to offer. Students have complained that the university bureaucrats are stingy with funding for the law school.

The first-year curriculum is definitely demanding and leaves little time for anything else. After first year, the load lessens only slightly, but students seem to develop better methods for coping with it and manage to take on jobs and other outside activities. Competition for law review and moot court is noticeable during the first year. All three years, Seattle's wet weather creates an atmosphere conducive to indoor study for those who aren't hardy.

Second- and third-year courses are almost all electives. The business and comparative Asian law programs are particularly strong. International, environmental, and Native American law courses are also popular. Students can get good experience through programs like law review, moot court, and judicial and legislative externships. Thanks to budget cuts, UW is not the place to come for in-house clinical practice opportunities.

Although students grumble that the law school building is ugly, there is general agreement that the library is superb. Knowledgeable, helpful, and friendly librarians help students get the most out of the vast collection.

The faculty has excellent scholarly credentials, and most are very good teachers. Strong progressive and conservative factions of the faculty contribute to lively policy discussions about the governance of the school. The low student-faculty ratio is a definite plus.

The student body tends to lean left of center, though the right wing makes its presence known. The Law Women's Caucus brings in feminist speakers. The Minority Law Students' Association is quite active, especially in student recruiting. The gay, lesbian, and bisexual students meet and socialize fairly often.

The students here set a typical Pacific Northwest standard: Work hard, play hard, and don't take yourself too seriously. There is competition, but it's kept at a reasonable level by the presence of a number of people who run, bike, hike, ski, and sail all year round. Intramural sports and Ultimate Frisbee are popular. Some students are politically active, others devote themselves to literature or music. Older second-career types seem to fit in.

The placement service arranges on-campus interviews, but most students have to arrange outside interviews on their own to find a part-time or summer job. The placement service's listing of jobs in local firms is a helpful starting place. Students heading for the nonprofit sector reportedly get little help. UW does not have a large national following, for the reason that most UW grads prefer to stay in the Seattle area.

Seattle offers a life-style that many people find very attractive. The good news is that if you go to UW, you'll be the envy of your friends at law schools in much less appealing locations. The bad news is that getting into this school is not easy; admission to UW is extremely competitive.

Washington University School of Law

Address: **One Brookings Drive, Box 1120, St. Louis, MO 63130**
Phone: **(314) 889-4525**
Degrees: **J.D., LL.M. (tax), J.S.D., J.D./M.B.A., M.J.S. (juridical studies), J.D./M.S.W. (social work), J.D./M.H.A. (health administration), J.D./M.A. (Asian studies), other joint degrees**
Median LSAT: **160**
Median GPA: **3.3**

Applicants accepted: **48%**
Transfers: **5–10/20**
Law enrollment: **687 (651 J.D.)**
Campus enrollment: **11,000**
Part time: **0**
Women: **42%**
Minorities: **13%**
Dorm residents: **0**
Library: **470,000**
Student-faculty ratio: **18:1**
Tuition: **$16,750**
Financial aid: **70% (20% gift)**
Apply by: **March 1**

Disabled students: **Moderate/full accessibility. Three to four wheelchair users attended in five years.**
Placement: **85% employed six months after graduation. 40% of second-years and 60% of third-years employed in legal jobs during the academic year. 50% of first-years, 65% of second-years, and 43% of third-years placed by end of spring term. 57 employers on campus in one year; 65% from Missouri, 25% Illinois, 2% Kentucky, 2% Tennessee, 2% Washington, DC, 2% Florida, 2%**

Nebraska; 81% private firms, 14% business, 5% government. Graduates took jobs in West North Central (48%), East North Central (18%), South Atlantic (17%), Pacific (5%), Middle Atlantic (4%), West South Central (3%), Mountain (3%), New England (1%), East South Central (1%). Graduates entered private practice (56%), government (16%), judicial clerkships (14%), business (5%), public interest (2%), military (1%), nonlegal (6%). Salary range: $23,000–$83,000. Mean salary: $39,000. Missouri bar pass rate: 92% (statewide average: 89%).

Washington University's campus rests in a suburban area bordered on one side by a large, well-groomed park. The law school is housed in a Kafkaesque nightmare of a building apparently designed to embody some architect's distaste for law students. But securing a new building is a major priority of the administration.

Upper-middle-class whites from the East and Midwest dominate the student body. A large majority take their studies seriously. Fortunately, this studiousness does not take the form of vicious competition. A feeling of camaraderie manifests itself in shared outlines and notes and first-year study groups.

The faculty represents the usual mix of bright young professors and few older distinguished specialists. Most are quite capable teachers; several could give Socrates a run for his money. The best aspect of the faculty members is their accessibility outside of class. They often, for example, join in the Friday afternoon beer parties thrown by the Student Bar Association.

The curriculum reflects the interest of the students in practicing with small to medium-size private firms, businesses, and government. Washington U's reputation is strongest in the heartland, although East Coast placements are by no means uncommon.

The curriculum is a little thin outside the traditional private law areas (personal, business, and tax). In public law subjects, with the exception of labor law and criminal law, there is rarely more than one course in any area, although environmental courses are coming on strong. The course in trial techniques, a practical laboratory in trial procedure and argument, is very popular and well run. Students caution that some subjects are not offered at all or only in summer school, and that many specialties are dominated by one professor.

The first-year classes, which enroll 75 or more students, together make for a challenging sixty- to seventy-hour work week. Contrary to most expectations, the second year is more time-consuming than the first: the reduction in time spent studying is more than compensated for by a part-time job, moot court, and/or law review.

All second- and third-year students must fulfill a writing requirement by participating in a seminar, supervised research, moot court, or one of the law reviews. The moot court program is outstanding in all respects. It is one of the largest and best-organized in the country and is judged by prominent lawyers and judges from the St. Louis area. The *Law Quarterly* and the *Journal of Urban and Contemporary Law* both select new members on the basis of either grades or a writing competition.

Those who participate in the clinical program often feel strongly either that it is very good or a waste of time. In addition to legal services, the local U.S. attorney's office, and a few judicial clerkships, clinical placements are expanding to include the EEOC and other choices.

Wash U is said to be the only law school in the country to have a congressional internship program. Each spring, about 24 third-year students spend their last semester working in Washington for a congressional office. The success of the program varies depending on how much effort and energy the student puts into the position.

Wash U's immediate surroundings have relatively little in the way of restaurants and nightlife. You can walk to only one decent bar from campus. However, several other areas of the city have experienced a renaissance. If you look hard enough and know someone with a car, you can find jazz clubs, riverboat restaurants, good dive bars, nice shops, even a good play, concert, or ballet. Forest Park, which borders Washington University to the east, contains the art museum, the opera house, the famed St. Louis Zoo, and other attractions. St. Louis hosts major-league baseball and hockey teams.

Attractive housing in the area is relatively cheap. Some neighborhoods are safe; others are not. Come early and plan to spend up to two weeks to find a place. You can get by without a car except for grocery shopping. The on-campus housing is expensive and very difficult to get.

Washington University is neither in the exciting metropolis of Washington, DC, nor in the fresh mountain air of Washington State. Still, Wash U's Gateway-to-the Midwest location is a boon if you plan to practice in this part of the world.

Washington and Lee University School of Law

Address: **Lexington, VA 24450**
Phone: **(703) 463-8504**
Degrees: **J.D.**
Median LSAT: **164**
Median GPA: **3.46**
Applicants accepted: **20%**
Transfers: **2–3/20**
Law enrollment: **375**
Campus enrollment: **2000**
Part time: **0**

Women: **41%**
Minorities: **13%**
Dorm residents: **20%**
Library: **294,200**
Student-faculty ratio: **11:1**
Tuition: **$12,830**
Financial aid: **80% (50% gift)**
Apply by: **February 1 recommended**

Disabled students: **Fully accessible. One blind student and one deaf in five years.**

Placement: **95% employed six months after graduation. 212 employers on campus in one year; 25% from Virginia, 51% other Southeast, 8% Washington, DC, 8% Northeast, 2% West, 1% Midwest, 1% Southwest, 4% other. Graduates took jobs in South Atlantic (67%), West South Central (9%), Middle Atlantic (7%), New England (4%), East South Central (4%), East North Central (2%), Mountain (2%), Pacific (2%), Foreign (2%). Graduates entered private practice (60%), judicial clerkships (24%), government (4%), military (3%), academic (4%), other (5%). Salary range: $20,000–$80,000. Mean salary (excluding judicial clerkships): $47,000. Virginia bar pass rate: 85% (statewide average: 77%).**

Washington and Lee offers the benefits of a small student body, a great physical plant, and a picture-postcard location. It is in Virginia's Shenandoah Valley, nestled between the Blue Ridge and Allegheny mountains. The area is heavily forested and laced with fresh-running trout streams. The Appalachian Trail passes within twenty miles of the school, creating a perfect hiking and backpacking retreat from the rigors of a legal education. Goshen Pass and

Crab Tree Falls are a short drive away and offer "tubing" and swimming in crystal-clear waters.

The town of Lexington is small (7,000 permanent residents), rural, remote—and old. Thanks to the town's strong commitment to architectural restoration, many buildings from the eighteenth and early nineteenth centuries remain standing and serve as homes, offices, restaurants, and museums.

It is picturesque—*not* lively. If you seek recreation other than what the natural beauty of the area can offer, you're out of luck. Lexington has four main streets, two movie theaters, a dozen restaurants, and several bars. Law students' social lives tend to center around the Student Bar Association's weekly parties. Private parties of all types also materialize, celebrating anything from meeting a major brief-writing deadline to a full moon.

The nearest metropolitan areas are Roanoke and Charlottesville (home of the University of Virginia), each about an hour's drive. Both Washington and Lee and the "other" school in town (Virginia Military Institute) sponsor cultural activities, but few law students seem to take advantage of them. W & L undergrad is heavily into frats.

In between parties, many W & L students participate in extracurricular activities. Intramural sports keep students fit throughout the academic year. Active organizations include the law school newspaper, Black Law Students Association, Women's Law Student Organization, International Law Club, and the Federalist Society (a politically conservative group). The legal fraternities undertake some community service activities.

The law school also sponsors several academic extracurriculars. *The Washington and Lee Law Review*, judicial clerkships, and the Virginia Capital Case Clearinghouse provide research and writing experience. Moot court, mock trial, negotiation, and client counseling competitions, as well as clinical programs, help students acquire real-world skills.

The law school facilities here are among the best in the nation. Lewis Hall, a $7-million gem, opened its doors in 1976. Every student has a personal study carrel; they're frequently noisy but provide the perfect place to store the ungodly number of books a law student inevitably accumulates. Library space is superabundant, and the library staff is always willing to go the extra mile to help you find the book you're looking for.

The library also houses computer terminals, complete with wordprocessing software, for students to use to type papers or outlines. Unlike most schools, the library and computer room are open 24 hours a day, 365 days a year.

The university furnishes fully equipped offices for all student activities, including law review and the clinical programs. The videotape facilities help in improving oral advocacy skills.

W & L students come from most parts of the country (with an emphasis on the East), and their backgrounds vary. Many have taken time off after college for work, travel, and self-exploration. While the student body is diverse, it historically has included few minority group members. Fortunately, the number of students of color attending W & L is growing.

A small school, W & L also has small classes. First-year classes (all of which are, as usual, required) never have more than 60 students. Second- and third-year courses average 30 to 40 people, and seminars range from 5 to 30. Professors—and classmates—expect everyone to attend every class and be prepared to discuss the course material in detail. Because classes are small, professors readily recognize students' problems and can be helpful; they also recognize lack of preparation and can be demanding.

The courses offered in the upper years cover a broad range of subject matter, but many are focused on corporate, commercial, and litigation practice areas. Few faculty members cultivate pressure or pretense in the classroom. Most go out of their way to remain accessible and promote friendly, informal relations with students. A recent push to expand the size of the faculty has resulted in as many as three new faculty members a year, and most seem to get along quite well with students. The student-to-faculty ratio has dropped to one of the lowest in the nation, but annual tuition hikes to pay for the new staff have met with predictable objections from students.

Student government is handled by an active, university-wide Executive Committee. Law students send two representatives to this twelve-person body and are eligible to run for its three leadership offices. The EC has jurisdiction over financial and extracurricular matters. It also administers the student-run honor system, an unwritten code that, in one student's words, "succeeds in fostering honesty, trust and respect." Cynics, take note.

The university housing is a good choice for first year, largely because the apartments are about one minute away from the law school. Most students move off campus in the second year. Apartments in Lexington are cheap by any standard, and many of them are within walking distance of the law school. For those who fancy themselves country squires, there's the option of renting in the countryside for not much more.

There's no question that Washington and Lee's strongest reputation—and it is strong—is in the Southeast, where the majority of earlier graduates went on to practice. During the 1970s, however, as the student body diversified and the placement office pushed for greater recognition, the school began to place graduates with major firms in cities throughout the country.

The placement office concentrates on attracting large urban law firms with corporate clients, because that's what most of the students want. Consequently, students looking for small firms or public-interest groups must often initiate contact with employers on their own.

Washington and Lee offers an excellent education in surroundings free of concrete, chrome, traffic, and tumult. The pace is slow, and people learn to appreciate the beauty and tranquillity of the country. But if you're an urbanite who feels lost without a half-dozen nightclubs to choose from, don't choose Washington and Lee.

Wayne State University Law School

Address: **468 West Ferry Mall, Detroit, MI 48202**
Phone: **(313) 577-3937**
Degrees: **J.D., LL.M. (tax, labor, or corporate), J.D./M.A. (history, public policy), other joint degrees**
Median LSAT: **38**
Median GPA: **3.35 (full time), 3.39 (part time)**
Applicants accepted: **36%**
Transfers: **10**
Law enrollment: **879 (751 J.D.)**

Campus enrollment: **29,000**
Part time: **27%**
Women: **49%**
Minorities: **17%**
Dorm residents: **NA**
Library: **415,700**
Student-faculty ratio: **27:1**
Tuition: **$5057 (in-state), $10,975 (out-of-state)**
Financial aid: **30%**
Apply by: **March 15**

Disabled students: **Fully accessible. In one year, two disabled students.**

Placement: **Approximately 95% employed six to nine months after graduation. Graduates took jobs in East North Central (93%), West South Central (1%), Mountain (1%), Pacific (1%), New England (1%), Middle Atlantic (1%), Foreign (1%). Graduates entered private practice (65%), business (15%), government (8%), judicial clerkships (8%), public interest (3%), academic (1%).**

Wayne State lies in the heart of Detroit's Cultural Center. It draws its students primarily from Michigan, including a good many from Detroit. Sometimes regarded as being in the shadow of nearby University of Michigan, Wayne nevertheless deserves a second look.

The faculty at Wayne is generally far better than most incoming students think. Many members are leading scholars; others have developed innovative teaching techniques and curricula. Nearly all are accessible to and interested in the students, and student-faculty relations are good. The part-time faculty includes prominent judges and attorneys.

Wayne State used to be one of the largest law schools in the country. Then, a few years back, the school made a conscious decision to reduce enrollment in order to maintain high admission standards. The majority of the class is admitted solely on the basis of high undergraduate grades and LSAT scores. For the remainder, the admissions committee is free to look at other criteria. The number of applications has grown in recent years, permitting the school to become increasingly choosy.

The curriculum here is similar to that of any national law school. The first-year courses, all required, are typical. The first-year legal writing program is an outstanding introduction to research and to oral and written advocacy. After the first year, all courses are elective, with the exception of constitutional law and professional responsibility. A well-organized tutorial program helps students in academic difficulty.

A portion of the student body is composed of people who have been away from school for a while. Some are married, some have children, and a good number are employed throughout their law school careers.

Wayne is primarily a commuter school. Some university housing is available, as is a limited amount of nearby off-campus housing. With students scattering to their homes at the end of the day, there's not much organized social life, except for occasional parties and activities sponsored by the law school's Student Board of Governors or by the various law fraternities.

Academic extracurriculars are more popular. Because of its urban location, the school can offer a wide variety of clinics and internships. Students work with the legal aid clinic, the City of Detroit corporation counsel, the county prosecutor, the U.S. attorney's office, and the federal courts, to name just a few.

The *Wayne Law Review* is one of the largest in the nation in staff and pages printed. The law review is particularly well known for its annual survey of Michigan law. Wayne State's excellent moot court program competes with major law schools all over the country.

Wayne is considered prestigious by Michigan employers, and the graduates' pass rate on the Michigan bar exam is usually high. The school isn't as well known outside the state, but there is hope that the increase in applications will soon be mirrored by a growth in national prestige. Word has already begun to leak out that this school, in its new, smaller incarnation, is much improved.

Western New England College School of Law

Address: **1215 Wilbraham Rd., Springfield, MA 01119**
Phone: **(413) 782-1406**
Degrees: **J.D.**
Median LSAT: **155**
Median GPA: **3.1**
Applicants accepted: **28%**
Transfers: **6/30**
Law enrollment: **809**
Campus enrollment: **2990**

Part time: **36%**
Women: **48%**
Minorities: **6%**
Dorm residents: **2%**
Library: **275,000**
Student-faculty ratio: **26:1**
Tuition: **$11,140**
Financial aid: **81% (6% gift)**
Apply by: **rolling admissions; March 15 recommended**

Disabled students: **Fully accessible. In five years, one deaf student, three with mobility problems.**
Placement: **Approximately 74–84% employed six to nine months after graduation. 30 employers on campus in one year; 45% from**

Massachusetts, 45% Connecticut; 95% private firms or businesses. Graduates took jobs in New England (79%), Middle Atlantic (15%), South Atlantic (2%), other (4%). Graduates entered private practice (52%), business (15%), judicial clerkships (15%), government (15%), public interest (3%). Salary range: $20,000–$70,000.

Western New England's law school has been around since 1919, but in its present form it's one of the newer law schools in the country. For years, it had only evening classes and part-time faculty. In 1973, a full day division was added, and the little-known college embarked on a high-powered effort to transform its law program virtually overnight.

The $3.8-million S. Prestley Blake Law Center, completed in 1978, is an amazing facility. It boasts a courtroom (complete with judge's chambers and jury room), spacious classrooms, and lounge areas which easily accommodate the entire student body. The law library comprises 40 percent of the building.

Western New England students are tremendously proud of these strides forward. Many of them grew up in lower-middle-class households and are the first in the family to attend professional school. They come from over two hundred colleges and universities and from undergraduate programs ranging from liberal arts to pharmacy. Most are from Massachusetts, Connecticut, New York, and other New England and mid-Atlantic states.

For many of Western New England's students, this school was a second or third choice, resorted to after rejections from more prestigious schools. This phenomenon is especially prevalent among the generally younger, full-time day students. The evening student is typically older and looking for a career change.

The mood of students at Western New England follows a predictable year-by-year pattern. First-years tend to be tense and worried about class preparation and exams. Second-years study less and participate actively in various student organizations. By the third year, many students have little interest in classes and are primarily concerned with finding a job and passing the bar exam.

Student life at Western New England is generally more relaxed than at many schools. Students here feel that the school has prospered from some, but not too much, competitiveness. Most of them aren't grinds, although those in the top half of the class (class rank is computed after first year) are considerably more driven than those below.

The curriculum at Western New England is undergoing expansion thanks to the addition of new faculty members. There's a good choice of seminars available in specialized fields.

The Socratic method is the primary teaching technique, especially in the first-year classes. These have about 100 students each. Upper-level electives range from 5 to 75 students.

Most of the full-time professors are very accessible. (The adjunct faculty members, with active practices in the area, are harder to get hold of.) The faculty is predominantly on the young side, enthusiastic, and supportive. The whole faculty, as well as the deans, are invited to most social events, and most welcome informal contact with students.

For the student who wants practical experience, there are several possibilities. Western New England competes against other area schools in regular and international law moot court, as well as in client counseling and trial advocacy competitions. Various internships and clinical offerings are available. The law students handle actual cases, and in some instances, represent their clients in court.

The law school is on the main college campus, but the undergrad division has little to offer law students except for excellent athletic facilities. The law students take part enthusiastically in intramural sports. The Student Bar Association hosts the Annual Invitational Law School Basketball Tournament.

The SBA is practically ubiquitous on campus, thanks to its huge budget. To supplement the private parties held almost every weekend, the SBA stages well-attended social functions such as monthly beer blasts and the annual spring banquet. The organization also runs a particularly vigorous speakers' program, faculty evaluations, freshman orientation, and used-book sales. Students appointed by the SBA are voting members of most of the faculty committees, and two students attend faculty meetings with full voting privileges.

Springfield is a large town in ambience and a small city in its cultural offerings. There are always symphony concerts, plays, and current movies. Whatever Springfield lacks, it makes up for by its central location, midway between Albany and Boston and a half hour from Hartford, Connecticut. You can get to the Berkshires, Vermont, New Hampshire, or New York City quickly and easily.

Finding comfortable, inexpensive housing in the area is a breeze if you start looking early. There are large apartment complexes within walking distance of the law school, and the surrounding communities offer many houses and apartments for rent.

The employment search isn't quite so easy. Graduates are fully able to pass the bar exam in any state and assume any type of practice, but there's a name-recognition problem outside New England. The school's small career counseling office is diligent, but graduates have mainly found jobs by passing the bar exam and then knocking on doors or starting their own practice. As Western New England's reputation spreads, things should get much better.

Willamette University College of Law

Address: **900 State St., Salem, OR 97301**
Phone: **(503) 370-6282**
Degrees: **J.D., J.D./M.M. (management)**
Median LSAT: **157**
Median GPA: **3.15**
Applicants accepted: **41%**
Transfers: **0–3/0–3**
Law enrollment: **480**
Campus enrollment: **2400**

Part time: **0**
Women: **39%**
Minorities: **10%**
Dorm residents: **NA**
Library: **133,400**
Student-faculty ratio: **13:1**
Tuition: **$12,035**
Financial aid: **80% (25% gift)**
Apply by: **April 1, February 1 (aid)**

Disabled students: **Fully accessible. In five years, one deaf student, three wheelchair users.**

Placement: **65% employed six months after graduation. 20% of first-years, 35% of second-years, and more than 50% of third-years employed in legal jobs during the academic year. 50% of first-years, 75% of second-years, and 35% of third-years placed by end of spring term. 55 employers on campus in one year; from Oregon, Washington, Alaska, Nevada, and Hawaii. Graduates took jobs in Pacific (86%), Mountain (7%), East North Central (2%), South Atlantic (2%), West North Central (1%), West South Central (1%), Foreign (1%). Graduates entered private practice (51%), government (25%), business (12%), judicial clerkships**

(10%), public interest (1%), academic (1%). **Salary range: $12,000–$53,000. Mean salary: $33,993. Oregon bar pass rate: 88%. Washington bar pass rate: 73%.**

Before you start your legal education in the Pacific Northwest, set your biorhythms back to negative ten, bring a large collection of progressive jazz records, and be prepared to spend a hefty sum on camera equipment and rain gear. Oregon is beautiful and wet. (Locals sometimes worry that they'll develop webbed feet, or at least moss on the north side of their nose.)

Situated in Salem, the state capital, Willamette is the oldest law school in the Pacific Northwest. Unfortunately, except for a few bars offering atmospheres from redneck to countercultural, and a burgeoning selection of espresso bars, Salem is devoid of diversions. The town is midway between Portland and Eugene, and from what anyone can gather, it has remained in their shadows.

Salem blossoms for six months every two years, only to wilt away again after the adjournment of the state legislature. The town's primary economic sustenance is the state bureaucracy, which provides numerous internship opportunities for law students. (Oregon has adopted the student appearance rule, which allows third-year students to argue before both trial and appellate courts.) However, the professional state workers tend to commute from the more urban areas: hence Salem's staid ambience.

Living in such a climate has its advantages: distractions are minimal, and job opportunities abundant. If one is fortunate enough to work in the public sector, wages and benefits are quite tolerable.

Housing is relatively cheap by metropolitan standards and plentiful, at least during off-legislative years. However, prevailing market prices are rising steeply. The university administration makes only a token effort to provide on-campus housing, so the law student must look to neighboring residential areas for shelter. Most students find accommodations within walking or biking distance. If you yearn for the countryside, there are some old farmhouses for rent within ten or fifteen miles. But beware: insulation and storm windows were unheard of until recently.

Due to a lack of cultural stimulation, the students tend to fall into two groups: those who never take their heads out of the casebooks for three years, and those who find solace in the spectacular nearby mountains and coastal areas. Cross-country and downhill skiing are favorite winter pastimes, not to mention backpacking, fishing, clamming, and rafting when the weather permits. Athletic facilities at the university are outstanding: indoor swimming pool, tennis courts, racquetball and basketball courts, etc. Bring your jogging shoes.

The college-age population of Salem is divided between Willamette's undergraduates, the local bible college, and a relatively new community college. All three are equally inaccessible to law students.

A cross section of the law student population indicates a predominant western bloc. Sprinkled in between are disaffected northeasterners, at-heart easterners from the Midwest, and a strong contingent from Hawaii and Alaska. "Unfortunately," one student reports, "Willamette has not succeeded in attracting and/or retaining significant numbers of African-American students and faculty."

Both admissions and curriculum policy are geared toward traditional students (those straight out of college). Teaching styles depend upon the professor. Most students are exposed to the Socratic method as well as the lecture format. The latter tends to predominate. The faculty currently favors classroom instruction over practical skills training. Recent curriculum changes involve eliminating the audit option for class credit and a change to a standard 4.0 grading system.

Willamette offers a moot court program and thorough areas of concentration in tax and contract law. The school continues to "stress the written word" by demanding a third-year writing requirement as a prerequisite to graduation.

Most traditional first-year courses are divided into two sections, with 75 students in each. The course load for the first-year student is heavy, with a significant emphasis placed on a research and writing course.

The relatively low-key atmosphere here, combined with the small size of the school, permits students to know each other and members of the faculty on a first-name basis. However, the atmosphere has become less intimate since a major reconstruction project, completed in 1992, doubled the school's space.

Traditionally, Willamette has been thought of as a "meat-and-potatoes" school. To counteract this image, Willamette has instituted a few new courses in fields like environmental law and international law. However, at the heart of the program stand the conventional bar-exam-related courses, highly emphasized and religiously taken.

Willamette has produced a sizable portion of the Oregon state judiciary, not to mention the practicing bar. The institution is well thought of within the area legal community, so when jobs are available, Willamette grads have a good chance for them. The placement office has traditionally been neglected, one student warns.

Most students are too involved with academics and their personal lives to pay much attention to student organizations, but there are several worthy of note. Among them are the National Lawyers Guild, the Women's Law Caucus, the Multi-cultural Law Student Association, Environmental Law Society, and the student paper, which sponsors a yearly home-brewed beer contest.

The student government selects students to serve on faculty-student committees, organizes faculty evaluations, and arranges social activities. The last-named are not too frequent—a few drunken brawls a year—due to limited student motivation.

Willamette sees some competition for law review and the prestigious clerkships. Nevertheless, the degree of mutual affection, respect, and admiration among Willamette students is refreshing—even if a little incestuous.

College of William and Mary, Marshall-Wythe School of Law

Address: **P.O. Box 8795, Williamsburg, VA 23187**
Phone: **(804) 221-3785**
Degrees: **J.D., LL.M. (American law or tax), J.D./M.B.A., J.D./M.P.P. (public policy), J.D./M.A. (American studies)**
Median LSAT: **165**

Median GPA: **3.3 (in-state), 3.5 (out-of-state)**
Applicants accepted: **23% (in-state), 15% (out-of-state)**
Transfers: **0–5/30–50**
Law enrollment: **563 (545 J.D.)**
Campus enrollment: **7700**
Part time: **0**

Women: **44%**

Minorities: **13%**

Dorm residents: **20%**

Library: **290,000**

Student-faculty ratio: **21:1**

Tuition: **$4622 (in-state),
$12,002 (out-of-state)**

Financial aid: **69% (32% gift)**

Apply by: **March 1, February
1 (aid)**

Disabled students: **Fully accessible. In five years, one deaf student
and one wheelchair user.**

Placement: **95% employed six months after graduation. 97% of first-
years, 97% of second-years, and 81% of third-years placed by end
of spring term. 175 employers on campus in one year; from 40
states and District of Columbia; 79% private firms, 7%
government, 5% business, 4% judicial, 4% military, 1% public
interest. Graduates took jobs in Virginia (30%), other South
Atlantic (33%), Middle Atlantic (11%), New England (5%), East
North Central (5%), Pacific (5%), East South Central (4%),
Mountain (4%), West North Central (1%), West South Central
(1%), Foreign (1%). Graduates entered private practice (57%),
judicial clerkships (21%), government (10%), military (6%),
business (4%), public interest (2%). Salary range:
$18,500–$85,000. Median salary: $38,000. Mean salary: $43,692.
Virginia bar pass rate: 93% (statewide average: 77%). Pennsylvania
bar pass rate: 94% (statewide average: 81%).**

On the outskirts of Colonial Williamsburg sits the College of William
and Mary, which offered the first law courses in America. The Marshall-Wythe School of Law has come a long way since 1779.

The school is now state-supported, so over half of the first-year
spots are awarded to Virginia residents. Nonresidents have to meet
higher admissions criteria and pay much higher tuition.

Williamsburg is a tourist town. Nearby attractions include Colonial Williamsburg, with its reconstruction of eighteenth-century
life, and Busch Gardens, a theme park. The town is small and
virtually devoid of restaurants or stores catering to the students.
But Williamsburg is only thirty minutes away from the Hamp-
ton–Newport News area, which has more in the way of twentieth-
century commercial offerings, and students find that being a mere
hour from Virginia Beach is a godsend on the warmer days of
spring and fall. Richmond, the state capital, is forty-five minutes
away.

Most students live in apartments in Williamsburg or its environs. Though off-campus housing is in good supply, it helps to look early.

Academically, Marshall-Wythe is on an upswing. Recent triumphs by moot court teams and successful graduates (including a Supreme Court clerkship) have brought the school welcome recognition. Recent surveys have recognized the law review as one of the most frequently cited in the country.

Another big reason for the improving national reputation is the law school building (completed in 1980), which features the latest in law school technology. Every student has the opportunity to use LEXIS and WESTLAW, the computerized research tools. The moot courtroom is full of electronic wizardry and video equipment to capture the best and worst in students' litigation techniques.

Despite increasingly qualified entering classes, Marshall-Wythe has managed to avoid the pressures of many law schools. Students are generally friendly, and although the work load is challenging, any reasonably organized person can find time for extracurriculars (at least after the first year).

The school is able to offer a practical perspective through several clinical programs. In addition to the organized clinicals, students can earn credit for work in private firms or prosecutors' offices. The unique two-year legal skills program requires every student to litigate several mock cases in a simulated law firm.

The Student Bar Association does a good job of presenting student complaints to the administration and working to get something done about them. Its other main role is to organize dances and parties as a break from the rigors of law school life. The Public Service Fund sponsors parties and other events to raise money to subsidize students working in public-interest jobs over the summer.

Intramural sports are *very* popular here. Marshall-Wythe students have full access to the William and Mary campus athletic facilities. The law school regularly finishes high in college-wide competition.

Marshall-Wythe is striving to become the best law school in Virginia (no mean feat) and has made some progress toward that goal. The new building and generally concerned faculty have propelled the school from mediocrity to prestige in a very short time. Should the institution's ascendancy continue along present lines, national recognition of its diplomas should continue to grow. As a note to students looking for an easy three years: Marshall-Wythe is not it. The school is looking to build a solid name by demanding competence and preparation. On the good side, all the hard work adds up to a quality education.

University of Wisconsin Law School

Address: **Madison, WI 53706**
Phone: **(608) 262-5914**
Degrees: **J.D., LL.M., S.J.D.,**
 J.D./M.B.A., J.D./M.P.A.,
 other joint degrees
Median LSAT: **40**
Median GPA: **3.36**
Applicants accepted: **26%**
Transfers: **18**
Law enrollment: **875 (853**
 J.D.)

Campus enrollment: **43,000**
Part time: **8%**
Women: **46%**
Minorities: **10%**
Dorm residents: **NA**
Library: **377,200**
Student-faculty ratio: **18:1**
Tuition: **$3479 (in-state),**
 $9499 (out-of-state)
Financial aid: **65%**
Apply by: **February 1**

Disabled students: **Moderate/full accessibility. In one year, four disabled students.**

Placement: **Approximately 85% placed by graduation; approximately 95% employed six to nine months after graduation. About 200 employers on campus in one year. Graduates took jobs in Wisconsin (60%), other East North Central (10%), West North Central (6%), Mountain (6%), Pacific (6%), South Atlantic (5%), Middle Atlantic (3%), West South Central (2%), New England (1%), East South Central (1%). Graduates entered private practice (65%), government (15%), judicial clerkships (10%), business (5%), public interest (2%), military (1%), academic (1%), unknown (1%). Salary range: $14,000–$83,000. Average salary: over $45,000.**

If your idea of what law school is like was formed by the mass media, UW Law School will be a surprise. The atmosphere is not intensely competitive, and the professors are not all stern taskmasters. If it is possible to get a degree from an excellent school and enjoy it, Wisconsin is one place where it can happen.

The law school sits on Bascom Hill in the middle of the University of Wisconsin campus, surrounded by thousands of undergraduates who deserve their reputation for partying and beer-guzzling. The large campus and the dynamic city of Madison provide a large variety of cultural activities. The lakes, many parks, and nearby rural areas put recreation within easy reach—as long as you don't mind cold weather for much of the school year. The lakeside student union is the focus of on-campus relaxation, with its theaters, social offerings, Rathskeller, and Hoofers Outing Club.

The teeming mass of undergraduates means that everything from your favorite pub to the housing market can get extremely crowded. Cheap apartments near campus are too often substandard, but the university does provide some dorm space and apartments for married students, and an above-average bus system makes living away from campus practical.

The law school takes many factors into account in the admissions process. These factors are described in detail in the law school bulletin, but summarized briefly, they include diversity in the applicants' background or experience, as well as GPA and LSAT. One result of this emphasis is that in a typical year, the majority of entering students have been out of school for more than a year since college. The search for diversity is hampered by the fact that 70 to 80 percent of each class comes from Wisconsin, and the majority of the rest are from the Midwest.

The atmosphere at the school is relaxed. In-school social life revolves around a lounge that resists civilizing influences. The lounge is equipped with the latest video games, which help pay for the fairly frequent parties hosted by the Student Bar Association. The SBA also funds law school organizations, runs the Book Mart and some counseling programs, and acts as the liaison between students and the school. Law school organizations run the gamut: There are the fraternities and associations for women, black students, Latinos, differently abled students, Asian- and Pacific-Americans, and Native Americans. Societies focusing on international, labor, business and tax, environmental, health, and public-interest law (among others) cater to students with specialized interests. Annual events include the ritual cane toss at the

Homecoming Game (if you catch yours after it goes over the goal-post, you'll win your first case) and the Law Revue variety show.

A student's first-semester classes include one small group of about 20 people, and three other classes of 80 to 100. The small groups are designed to facilitate friendship and study groups. After first year most of the mainstay classes are large, although smaller classes can be found, and there is an abundant selection of narrowly focused seminars each semester.

The school offers many clinical programs that allow credit for working in a prosecutor's office or state agency, aiding institutionalized persons, or clerking for a judge. Wisconsin has been a pioneer in interdisciplinary teaching and research and offers flexible combined degree programs. The school places special emphasis on work in the criminal justice and mental health areas.

A few professors employ a humane version of the Socratic method, and most abandon it completely after the first year. Faculty members are readily accessible and easy to get to know, at least when they are on campus. A liberal leave policy is reportedly one of the methods used by the school to offset low pay for the faculty, and that policy has resulted in complaints about sparse course offerings and the need to use practitioners as teachers. The administration also pampers the profs when it comes to grading exams, so don't expect immediate feedback. The work load varies, but, like anywhere else, it depends primarily on what you make of it.

When it comes to using your J.D., the full-time placement office claims a good success rate. Wisconsin, with its interdisciplinary approach, allows preparation for a variety of careers. The school enjoys a national reputation among employers, although it is strongest, of course, in the Midwest, with pockets of influence in New York, Washington, DC, California, Nevada, and Texas.

The education at UW is more politically liberal and more "intellectual" than you'd find at many other law schools. Wisconsin's philosophy of "law in action" means that most classes dwell on the public policy implications of cases and the impact of law on society. If that's not enough to attract you, keep this in mind: UW grads automatically become members of the Wisconsin bar. Ask people who have taken a bar exam, and they'll tell you that's a big plus.

University of Wyoming College of Law

Address: **Box 3035, Laramie, WY 82071**
Phone: **(307) 766-6416**
Degrees: **J.D., J.D./M.B.A.**
Median LSAT: **35**
Median GPA: **3.36**
Applicants accepted: **24%**
Transfers: **2**
Law enrollment: **219**
Campus enrollment: **9500**
Part time: **0**
Women: **42%**

Minorities: **6%**
Dorm residents: **NA**
Library: **167,300**
Student-faculty ratio: **15:1**
Tuition: **$1554 (in-state), $4358 (out-of-state)**
Financial aid: **70%**
Apply by: **April 1, February 15 (university financial aid), June 1 (law school financial aid)**

Disabled students: **Fully accessible. In one year, one disabled student.**

Placement: **Approximately 90% employed six to nine months after graduation. Graduates employed in Mountain (90%), East North Central (4%), South Atlantic (4%). Graduates entered private practice (42%), judicial clerkships (27%), government (18%), public interest (7%), military (4%).**

The University of Wyoming thrives in the thin air of Laramie, Wyoming. Nestled among the mountains at an elevation of over 7,000 feet, UW is sometimes known as "the highest university in America."

It is possible to live in Laramie without a car, though the walks are often long and cold. Shopping in this small town of 25,000 people is a disappointment. On the bright side, Laramie's surroundings are ideal for someone attracted to the beautiful, unspoiled outdoors—and Denver is three hours away.

Who comes to UW? People from Wyoming homes and/or Wyoming colleges, mostly. After all, this is a state school, with a three-fourths-residents de facto quota.

This school is very small. It offers the intimate atmosphere that lures so many undergraduates to private institutions, but without the accompanying stuffiness and expense. The entire first-year class of 80 takes almost all its classes together. Admittedly, the school's size precludes unlimited academic variety, and the coziness tends to reinforce the conservative attitudes and life-styles of the region. But the students' legal philosophies are shaped by a faculty diverse enough to avoid dogmatism.

UW isn't the kind of the place that attracts Harvard *summas* with mind-boggling board scores. The student body includes people with a wide range of scores and past academic accomplishments. While there is some pressure for academic excellence here, most of it is self-imposed, and it doesn't take the life-or-death form for which law school is infamous. Those who struggle academically are provided with tutors to make it through the tough times. Because most of the students plan to stay in Wyoming, everyone recognizes that they're in for the long haul together.

The first year at UW offers the basic prescription of torts, contracts, and so on. Second year, in addition to more required courses, students are allowed some choice of electives. Third-year students benefit from full curriculum choice and from optional clinical courses in defender aid, prosecution assistance, and legal services. Third-year students may also participate in legal research services; they receive pay but no academic credits.

The curriculum here stresses the fundamentals. Electives are somewhat dependent on faculty abilities. They are strongest in natural resource law and commercial law. Though the selection is definitely expanding, there will probably never be a plethora of courses on constitutional issues, unusual specialties, and interdisciplinary studies. Anyone who comes to UW expecting political-science-type courses will be sorely disappointed. Most UW students are preparing to become general practitioners. If you're intent on pursuing an atypical interest, you can go the independent study route, but no credit is given for nonlaw courses, except through the joint J.D./M.B.A. program.

Teaching styles vary according to the professor and course. Wyoming has "sons of Socrates" as well as lecture types, but even the largest classes are small enough to promote discussion and discourage anonymity. Without exception, members of the faculty and administration (one and the same) are friendly, receptive, and willing to help. It's not unusual to see a professor umpiring a law school softball game or bending an elbow with students at a local tavern. Students point to their relationship with the faculty as one of Wyoming's greatest assets.

The state capital, Cheyenne, is only forty-five minutes away. The Wyoming Supreme Court conducts at least one hearing at the law school each year, which gives students a firsthand glimpse of appellate advocacy.

Externships in Cheyenne are also offered by federal and state courts, as well as the state attorney general's office. Students frequently drive to Cheyenne one day a week, gaining academic credit and useful contacts through their externships.

The Potter Law Club is the major student organization. It sponsors academic and social events and runs a useful bookstore. The fraternities, ABA Law Student Division, Natural Resources Law Forum, and Women's Law Forum offer a variety of activities, ensuring that by the end of the first semester, everyone knows everyone else. UW has won several regional and national competitions in client counseling, moot court, and trial practice.

The school has a good reputation in the Rocky Mountain states, particularly in the natural resource field. Graduates of UW (the only law school in the state) have a big advantage when it comes to obtaining Wyoming jobs—which is exactly what most of them want to do. (UW's most famous alumnus is the nationally renowned Wyoming-based trial lawyer Gerry Spence). Though the school's reputation is much less developed outside the region, there are often a few graduates who decide to stray far from Laramie and who then succeed in finding jobs they can live with. The fact that they do is a tribute to the pioneering spirit.

Yale Law School

Address: **Box 401A Yale Station, New Haven, CT 06520**
Phone: **(203) 432-4995**
Degrees: **J.D., LL.M., J.S.D., M.S.L. (studies in law), J.D./M.A. or Ph.D. (various), J.D./M.P.P.M. (management)**
Median LSAT: **46**
Median GPA: **3.81**

Applicants accepted: **8%**
Transfers: **14**
Law enrollment: **605 (557 J.D.)**
Campus enrollment: **10,800**
Part time: **0**
Women: **42%**
Minorities: **23%**
Dorm residents: **NA**
Library: **841,800**
Student-faculty ratio: **10:1**

Tuition: **$17,610**   Apply by: **February 15**
Financial aid: **70% (30% gift)**
Disabled students: **Moderate/full accessibility. Two disabled students in one year.**
Placement: **In a previous year, 100% placed by graduation. Graduates took jobs in Middle Atlantic (26%), South Atlantic (25%), Pacific (17%), New England (10%), West South Central (6%), East North Central (4%), West North Central (3%), East South Central (3%), Mountain (3%), Foreign (3%). Graduates entered judicial clerkships (47%), private practice (38%), government (5%), public interest (3%), business (1%), academic (1%), unknown (5%). Salary range: $35,000–$85,000.**

John Osborn, the man who brought us Professor Kingsfield, spent a year at Yale getting a master's degree in law. He found the school leagues removed from the cruel world of study groups and attempted suicides he had chronicled in *The Paper Chase.*

"Yale Law School is relaxed by any objective standards—so relaxed it's almost free-form," Osborn wrote in Yale's alumni magazine. "Instead of going to class, you play Frisbee or whiffle ball in the Gothic courtyard. . . . They don't give grades, class doesn't matter, and the best instruction, like the best instruction at Oxford or Cambridge, goes on face-to-face in the professors' offices. . . ."

Osborn's admiring characterization of Yale as an "Alice-in-Wonderland anachronism" reflects the school's widespread image as a place where students ponder social justice instead of collateral estoppel. It's a reputation that every Yale student knows well from job interviews ("A Yalie, huh? Tell me, is it true that for the course in contracts you read Locke and Aristotle?"). And it may well have been what attracted him or her to Yale in the first place.

Well, those who come to Yale seeking a philosophical nirvana will be disappointed, and those worried that they may pass three years here and not learn what a tort is will be reassured. For better or worse, Yale Law School is not quite as different from other law schools as its image suggests.

Yale students do go to class, do take exams, and do receive grades (after first semester, that is). The classes include the staples of every law school curriculum, from first-term required contracts, torts, constitutional law, and civil procedure, to a full range of offerings in corporate law, criminal law, and tax. Every Yalie gets some exposure to the Socratic method. Yale students work very hard, and like their counterparts across the country, they face periods of despair, exhaustion, and crushing boredom.

But it should be stressed that, among law schools, Yale is a remarkably humane, intimate, and rewarding place. The school gives students great independence in shaping their courses of study. After first term, students are required only to take criminal law and to fulfill a writing requirement (usually two research papers). Otherwise, they're free to choose from a varied curriculum—although course offerings are fewer than at a larger school like Harvard.

Teaching quality is sometimes surprisingly uneven. Still, there are quite a few professors who are brilliant and renowned scholars, excellent teachers, and/or very nice people. The face of the faculty is likely to change throughout the 1990s as faculty members move in and out of federal government appointments.

Some students take courses for law school credit in other graduate departments at Yale or flee New Haven entirely for an "intensive semester" internship. Others gear their academic schedule around one or more of Yale's rewarding clinical activities. Students can work under faculty supervision on behalf of prisoners, indigent people, tenants, immigrants, the disabled, the environment, people with AIDS, and the homeless. Student-run programs for credit include projects devoted to battered women's issues and human rights (the latter recently litigated a case involving Haitian refugees before the Supreme Court). Students also organize moot court (mock appellate arguments) and the Barristers' Union (mock trials). Individual projects are easy to arrange.

Each matriculating class at Yale has about 170 students, less than a third of a Harvard class. Course enrollments range from 100 or more for extraordinarily popular offerings to individual tutorials; most courses have from 20 to 60 students. Every first-year student has one seminar of 16 to 18 students taught by a professor; these "small groups" combine one of the basic first-year subjects with legal research and writing instruction. Yale's smallness encourages camaraderie among students and, to a somewhat lesser degree, between students and faculty.

Another reason for Yale's congenial atmosphere is the school's